How Many Grapes Went into the Wine

THE COST BENEFIT ANALYSIS SONG

How many bricks constructed this prison
And how many grapes went into the wine
How many illusions were lost for the vision
Of how many angels advancing in line?

How many lifetimes were ended in torment
And how many people this day would resign
How many bank balances just for this moment
And how many grapes went into the wine?

How many units of human compassion
And how many grapes went into the wine
How many illusions were sacrificed wantonly
How many people have looked for a sign?

How many women are needed to fashion
The how many men who are forced to assign
How many excursions to bed were for passion
And how many grapes went into the wine?

How many men have been killed by our soldiers
And how many grapes went into the wine
How many insurgents are listed in folders
And how many children are shot through the spine?

How many truths have run through our fingers
And how many credos . . . . Believing in mine
How many have led into unthought of dangers
And how many grapes went into the wine?

Stafford Beer
Transit, 1977

How Many Grapes Went into the Wine

Stafford Beer on the Art and Science of Holistic Management

Edited by
Roger Harnden
and
Allenna Leonard

JOHN WILEY & SONS
Chichester · New York · Brisbane · Toronto · Singapore

Telephone (+44) 243 779777

Other Wiley Editorial Offices

John Wiley & Sons, Inc., 605 Third Avenue,
New York, NY 10158-0012, USA

Jacaranda Wiley Ltd, 33 Park Road, Milton,
Queensland 4064, Australia

John Wiley & Sons (Canada) Ltd, 22 Worcester Road,
Rexdale, Ontario M9W 1L1, Canada

John Wiley & Sons (SEA) Pte Ltd, 37 Jalan Pemimpin #05-04,
Block B, Union Industrial Building, Singapore 2057

Library of Congress Cataloging-in-Publication Data

How many grapes went into the wine : Stafford Beer on the art and science of holistic management / edited by Roger Harnden and Allenna Leonard.
p. cm.
Includes bibliographical references and index.
ISBN 0-471-94296-0 (cloth)
1. Operations research. 2. Cybernetics. 3. Industrial management. 4. Beer, Stafford. I. Harnden, Roger. II. Leonard, Allenna.
T57.6.H69 1994 93–37389
003—dc20 CIP

British Library Cataloguing in Publication Data

A catalogue record for this book is available from the British Library

ISBN 0-471-94296-0

Printed and bound by Antony Rowe Ltd, Eastbourne

CONTENTS

LIST OF ILLUSTRATIONS

Chapter 5

Chapter 10

Chapter 11

Chapter 12

ACKNOWLEDGEMENTS

The Editors hereby make grateful acknowledgements for permission to reprint the following materials in this book:

Chapter 1	Holism and the Frou-Frou Slander. In *Kybernetes*, **17**(1): 23–31. MCB University Press Limited (1988).
Chapter 2	A Progress Note on Research into a Cybernetic Analogue of Fabric. In *Artorga*, April 1962.
Chapter 3	A Technique for Standardizing Massed Batteries of Control Charts. In *Applied Statistics*, **2**: 160–165. Blackwell Publishers (1953).
Chapter 4	The Productivity Index in Active Service. In *Applied Statistics*, **3**: 1–14. Blackwell Publishers (1954).
Chapter 5	The Mechanical Simulation of Stochastic Flow. In *Proceedings of First International Conference on OR*. English Universities Press [Hodder & Stoughton Ltd.], London (1957).
Chapter 6	The Impact of Cybernetics on the Concept of Industrial Organization. In *Proceedings of the First International Congress on Cybernetics*, Namur (1956).
Chapter 7	The Irrelevance of Automation. In *Proceedings of the Second International Congress on Cybernetics*, Namur (1958).
Chapter 8	The World, the Flesh and the Metal. In *Nature*, **205**: 223–231 (1965). Macmillan Magazines Limited.
Chapter 9	Below the Twilight Arch—a Mythology of Systems. In *Systems Research and Design—Proceedings of the First Systems Symposium*. John Wiley (1961).
Chapter 10	Towards the Cybernetic Factory. In Von Foerster, H. and Zopf, G. (eds), *Principles of Self Organization*. Pergamon Press Limited (1962).
Chapter 11	Retrospect—American Diary. Hitherto unpublished.
Chapter 12	Cybernetics of National Development. The Zaheer Foundation Lecture, New Delhi, India (1974). Hitherto unpublished.

Chapter 13 Preface to Autopoiesis: The Organization of the Living (1973). In *Autopoiesis and Cognition: The Realization of the Living*, by Humberto R. Maturana and Francisco J. Varela. Kluwer Academic Publishers (1980).

Chapter 14 Death is Equifinal: Eighth Annual Ludwig von Bertalannfy Memorial Lecture. In *Behavioral Science*, **26**: 185–196 (1981).

Chapter 15 I Said, You are Gods. In *The Teilhard Review* (1980). The Teilhard Centre.

Transit (poetry). By permission of Mitchell Communications, Montreal, Canada.

Photograph of Stafford Beer in 1975 (page 315) by permission of Hans Blohm, Ottawa, Canada.

APPRECIATION

Stafford Beer has been, and continues to be, prolific in his intellectual output and involvement in the world of affairs. Given the heavy demands on his time, we are very grateful for his personal support. Thanks also are due for his 'retrospective' comments on the American Diary, and his permission to include hitherto unpublished materials.

In 1991, Stafford deposited his personal library and collected works with the Liverpool John Moores University, UK. The Stafford Beer Collection will remain at the University, as a permanent resource for study and research. Our own task as joint editors has been greatly assisted by access to this collection. Thanks are particularly due to Don Revill, Director of Library Services, and Denis Adams at the Business School.

On behalf of John Wiley & Sons, Diane Taylor and Claire Plimmer have shown considerable patience and encouragement to us in the course of our efforts.

Stafford Beer as Managing Director
SIGMA (Science in General Management) Ltd 1961–66

INTRODUCTION

THIS VOLUME traces the emergence and development of one man's particular vision of how we might secure more effective practical action in the world of human affairs. In doing so it gives witness to the application of a particular set of analytical tools and methods. However, our selection is intended to indicate the *contemporary* relevance of this way of thinking, rather than simply recount a *historical* tale.

There are perhaps two main principles which unify our selection:

- The notion of *variety*
- The notion of *rigour*.

These are sometimes presented as if they are opposites or in conflict, notably in respect of social affairs. 'Rigour' tends to be identified with some unitary approach, and with a remorseless trend towards the hegemony of a 'one-world' culture (usually, white, male, capitalist, middle class and Western). Conversely, 'variety' stands for that which eludes or escapes this trend.

This understanding is partly a result of how successful science is commonly held to take place by restricting the area of focus to just those variables which have bearing on the immediate matter of concern, and excluding all else. The undoubted general truth of this in describing part of the scientific process, can lead to the corollary that the key to scientific progress is to lessen or even banish variety. Rigorous methodology can come to imply a principle of exclusion. Concern with this has dogged recent Western philosophy and sociology (e.g. Herbert Marcuse's thesis as to 'one-dimensional man').

However, outside philosophy and sociology departments there has been and continues to be a rich tradition of people who are only too aware of problems to do with power, identity and individuality. In many disciplines and walks of life individuals are consciously seeking out ways and means to secure the *coexistence* of variety at the same time as they are striving to identify the minimum cohesive glue necessary to knit individuals into some group or for the purpose of some collaborative enterprise.

In 1993 we were witnessing a vindication of arguments pleading for more systemic, interdisciplinary, broad-based approaches to economies, society and nature. The dramatic events following the break-up of the former USSR, the economic dislocation in the West, the terrible contemporary problems of displaced persons and starvation in a world of plenty, the issue of pollution and the greenhouse effect—all these have focused our appreciation as to the interconnectedness of things, even if they have not offered up any once-for-all solutions.

So it is perhaps timely to remind ourselves that such types of problems were anticipated by certain groups of people many years ago, notably guided by what has come to be called a 'systems' approach. In this tradition, which loosely speaking may be said to have emerged during the Second World War although its origin was some time earlier, various tools were developed in an attempt to formulate and tackle matters of great complexity while avoiding the trap of oversimplification.

The papers in this volume, dating from the mid-1950s, tell the story of one man's conceptual journey and his contribution to the tradition of systems thinking, notably the story of a man whose principal concern was with the interaction of free human beings and the sometimes tendency of social processes, however well intended, to thwart this basic human right.

HISTORICAL BACKGROUND—OPERATIONAL RESEARCH AND CYBERNETICS

The challenge of the Second World War brought together interdisciplinary teams of mathematicians, engineers and scientists from diverse fields to mount attacks on problem situations beyond the scope of any of their single disciplines. In Britain the work began with research on how to make radar more effective, and led to the creation of an interdisciplinary problem-solving team under the Nobel Laureate in Physics, Professor Patrick (later Lord) Blackett—which was generally referred to with affection as 'Blackett's circus'. Their success quickly led to the mobilization of other interdisciplinary teams which were eventually organized under the heading of Operational Research (OR) in each of the three armed services.

Meanwhile in the United States, work exploring connections between biology and physics on the one hand, and mathematics and neurophysiology on the other, begun in the 1930s, was serving as a platform from which to investigate many complex wartime interactions between men and machines. For instance, it quickly became apparent that to build automatic tracking devices to shoot down enemy planes was not just a matter of engineering, but concerned a complex of issues, from psychology to physics. There were issues to do with human perception and ballistics that required both mathematical tools and an understanding of how human individuals experience just what they are doing.

One such group was assembled in Mexico City. In the course of their after-hours discussions, they realized that each of their disciplines was addressing similar problems of circular causality and feedback. It was Norbert Wiener's insight that such problems, whatever else they might or might not concern, had in common the processes of *control* and *communication*. His breakthrough was to realize that communication and control are not different categories—as might at first sight appear the case—but somehow have an intimate bearing on one another.

This work together with that of Warren McCulloch, Walter Pitts (in the US), Ross Ashby, Grey Walter (in the UK) and many others opened a whole new perspective on the interaction of complex systems, and human responses to them. Wiener coined the word 'cybernetics' from the Greek word for 'steersman', to describe this new science of complex processes.

After the War ended, the insight and technology that came out of the war effort were directed towards reconstruction and the return to a peacetime economy. Numerous papers and books were published (notably Wiener's *Cybernetics*, which appeared in 1948), conferences and symposia were organized and an international community of interest began to take shape. It was at this point that Stafford Beer established contact with the core group and became part of it. The regard and friendship he enjoyed led to invitations to present many papers, several of which are included in this volume (Parts One and Two).

STAFFORD BEER'S CONTRIBUTION

Born in 1926, Stafford was one of the generation whose education was disrupted by the Second World War. Studies in philosophy, psychology, and mathematics were prematurely replaced by the realities of battle. Aged 18, Stafford enlisted as a gunner in the Royal Artillery. He received his commission in the Royal Fusiliers and transferred as company commander to the Gurkha Rifles.

In the light of his later interests, concretely evidenced by the papers in this volume, one of the crucial aspects of his army life was work he carried out as a Staff Captain Intelligence in India. Leading up to the Handover in 1947, Stafford combined his knowledge of philosophy, psychology, mathematical logic and statistics to help organize forces under British command with optimal effect in the effort to contain racial strife.

On his return to England in 1947, he was appointed an Army Psychologist, and applied his interdisciplinary approach to personnel selection and researching the connection between psychopathology and illiteracy. It was during these assignments that Stafford became attached to the Human Factors Branch of Operational Research at War Office.

After his demob, Stafford pioneered the introduction of Operational Research in the dominant British Steel Company, United Steel, building, over the next dozen years, an OR staff of 70 professionals dedicated to adopting an interdisciplinary approach to problem solving. Wide-ranging experiments were the norm, leading to the development of numerous physical and mathematical models.

It is worth remembering that the bulk of this work was conducted without the aid of computers, which were in their infancy. Some of the artefacts created by Stafford at the time, notably the stochastic analogue machine with its complex series of ball-bearing interactions (see Chapter 5, 'The Mechanical Simulation of Stochastic Flow'), made a dramatic visual impact that has only recently been matched by digital computers with the emergence of multimedia and graphics.

This interest with experimentation, the physical construction of artefacts in order to establish deeper insights into such issues as computation and control and to investigate the material basis for computer hardware (once more we must remind ourselves of the date), was to lead Stafford, alone and with Gordon Pask, to investigate the self-organizing chemical and biological systems referred to in Chapter 2, 'A Progress Note on Research into a Cybernetic Analogue of Fabric' (for interested readers on these issues, see also Beer 1959 [1]).

In spite of this experimentation with the 'fabric' for computation (it was not at all certain what eventual form computers would take, nor indeed that digital machines would triumph over analogue ones), Stafford was active in the promotion and use of what we now take to be conventional computers. In 1956 he had installed one of the first computers dedicated to the management science, a Ferranti-Pegasus.

Many of the emergent issues, unanswerable because of technical limitations of the time, remain active sites for research and investigation to this day. They have not been rendered obsolete through some 'technological fix', but, if anything, their thrust and direction have become more relevant as the sophistication of technical tools has increased. These issues are of core relevance to the political debate about power and the de-humanization of social processes. Today, this debate has broadened because of the impact of automation and its effect on social forms, notably in flattening out organization structure. The problem of human identity and the rightful place of technology has never been more pressing.

For a variety of reasons, the concern with statistical control and 'quality' that permeates these papers spread over 30 years, and how these might act to enrich and emancipate human freedom rather than constrain variety, is only now being grudgingly integrated into Western management practices, notably under the flag of the Quality movement. The historical hostility to such notions is evidenced by the reception of the ideas of W. Edwards Deming, one of the founding fathers of the Quality movement. Taken up with gusto in post-war Japan, his message fell on deaf ears in his native America.

The significant distinction between Stafford Beer and the Quality movement can be traced to the key influences on his own development, notably as these emanated from contemporary findings in the brain sciences and biology. In these sciences, notably as explored by people such as Warren McCulloch, Norbert Wiener, Ross Ashby, Heinz von Foerster, Gordon Pask and Humberto Maturana, there has been a keen awareness as to the complementary relationship between matter and emergent properties that may arise through the interaction of distinct material processes. This is the case whether we consider how a tune or melody becomes appreciated (where the constituent elements are single notes), or how the phenomenon of mind emerges from biochemical and electrical processes of the nervous system.

Because of this intimate concern with *emergence* and the way in which it occurs from the *coexistence* of distinct elements, rather than by ironing out difference, Stafford's own holism has enabled the development of a coherent model to be applied across whatever the domain, whether, as one of the papers in this volume attests, in 'the world, the flesh or the metal'. In a similar vein, the reader of these papers will discover in even the most technical and 'dry', a careful consideration of implications for humanity and concern with such human phenomena as language itself. Cybernetics offers guidelines enabling a marvellous blend of the empirical and the theoretical, without ever becoming lost in one or the other.

This pioneering work of Stafford culminated in his development of the brain model of a steelworks, described in rigorous set-theoretic terms (Chapter 10, 'Towards the Cybernetic Factory'). The paper itself may be daunting for the non-mathematical, but the 'discussion' that followed its presentation is vital for an insight into the key issues being explored, and though itself difficult, is open to even the least numerate reader. We strongly recommend its perusal. It was this seminal work that was to lead to the development, over a period of years, of Stafford's best-known model, the Viable System Model, widely used and referred to in management science ([2–5]).

The flavour of these golden years of Operational Research is conveyed by the diary in which Stafford recorded his 1960 visit to the United States (Chapter 11, 'Retrospect—American Diary'). On both sides of the Atlantic, large interdisciplinary teams were tackling major projects with substantial results. The optimism current, the feeling of being at the threshold of potential, is dramatically conveyed by the Diary. However, 1960 proved to be the peak rather than threshold of these developments.

What Happened?

Operational Research, as mentioned, had primarily developed as an interdisciplinary approach to solving messy and intractable problems in the real world, notably concerned with the life and death of war. As such, it was remarkably free of codification and prescribed rules, although techniques were shared across the board as they emerged and proved their worth.

It was its very success that led to its admission as a subject to universities, on academic terms. There was an intrinsic tension in this, as it had now to become a concrete 'discipline'. Its knowledge was required to be taught in lectures, and structured around formal programmes so that student progress could be reliably assessed and examined. The difficulty in this is that messy problems do not lend themselves to standard academic practice. In point of fact what happened was that focus upon problem solving gradually gave way to tasks to master the various techniques of applied mathematics and statistics. Rigour indeed advanced, but at the expense of variety.

On the industrial side, Operational Research had achieved major success in raising production and lowering costs. However, as practitioners turned their sights to the human side of production they began to be seen as challenging some of the prerogatives and privileges of management. Traditionally, scientists and other technical experts had been seen as distinct and separate from the management process, part of operations 'out there', rather than part of the decision-making process 'in here'. The more conservative and entrenched establishment did not welcome activities that trespassed on their own territory.

Enthusiasm for supporting such work, whose 'messy' subject matter appeared to include management practice itself (as indeed, was the case), rapidly faded. The intrusion into management strategy was resented and mistrusted. At this dawn of what has since become known as the 'information age', the notion that control itself might be to do with information and not just power or status, was not at all welcome.

A further important point is that around this time large-scale computerization had begun, with major demands on both money and scientific talent. A consequence of this, which we are still recovering from, was that computers and associated 'hard', product-oriented technologies, appeared a more attractive avenue for change than attempts to come to terms with complexity itself. At first sight, an understanding not contradicted by the salesmen of the day, the technological 'fix' appeared to make existing systems run more efficiently, warts and all. The point about such a reassuring fix was that it did not at all question dominant systems themselves.

It is as well to once more point out that this period corresponds to the widespread influence in the social sciences of the Frankfurt School and Critical Theory, with their deep suspicion of claimed automatic emancipatory potential of technological advance. As pointed out by many thinkers who emerged from this tradition, what was at stake was the one-dimensionality of any particular rationality that claimed to speak for the variety of human affairs and different cultures. The important point, one amply evidenced in this volume, but also in the writings of such people as Jacob Bronowski and Eric Jantsch, is that this polarization of the 'Two Cultures' (C.P. Snow) was not the inevitable outcome of some fundamental opposition between science/technology and arts/human affairs. Both science and art give rise to artefacts of human understanding and talent. Both are human constructs.

During this same period in the United States, much of the work in the field of Systems was supported by Defense Department research grants. In the 1960s, Senator Mike Mansfield of Montana sponsored an amendment requiring that all Defense Department grants be related directly to military applications, and not allowed to be spent doing 'basic' research. Although the restriction was of short duration, it was long enough for research teams, dependent as they were on short-term grants and contracts, to be disbanded and dispersed. Unlike NASA's space programme, work in both Operational Research and cybernetics had neither a public profile nor a unitary goal. The Vietnam conflict exacerbated this situation, as it further drained resources.

Thus it was that Stafford returned from his American tour, a tour, as recorded in the diary, so marked by optimism and a sense of the future, only to find that in the steel industry, the window for his sort of innovative practices was closing. This more problematical mood of the times, and a deepening questioning of the role and scope of OR, corresponds to Part Two of the current volume. In his own life, under the sponsorship of a forward-looking French organization, Stafford decided to leave steel and moved into general consultancy, building up a team under the title of SIGMA (Science in General Management).

Five years later, upon successfully establishing SIGMA on the international stage, Stafford became Development Director with the International Publishing Corporation. This period, around the mid-1960s, corresponds with the publication of his prize-winning book, *Decision and Control* [6]. It may be characterized as a shift in focus to the larger social and human context of the entailed interdisciplinary ideas.

Since 1970, roughly corresponding to Part Three of our book, Stafford has worked independently, consulting both to industry and government, writing and maintaining his several visiting professorships. The flavour of this period and the range of areas of concern are richly conveyed in the volume *Platform for Change* [7].

Perhaps his best-known assignment early in the 1970s, was in response to President Allende of Chile. Working closely with Fernando Flores, then Chilean Minister of Economics, Stafford was contracted to design a nation-wide, real-time system to manage the national economy (see Chapter 12, 'Cybernetics of National Development'; see also *Brain of the Firm* [3]). Flores is perhaps better known for his recent collaboration with Terry Winograd to consider the implications of language as action in the design of computer and office systems [8]. The selections from this period reflect Stafford's continuing interest in and exploration of the philosophical roots of actions taken in the world, and their human implications.

That the world is in a mess today is open to little doubt. Why this is so may not be obviously clear, but many lessons can be drawn from the papers in this volume. However attractive at first sight, and however seductive in terms of short-term accounting, simple solutions and technical fixes are rarely effective except in clearly defined and controlled situations, seldom found in the human social domain. The lesson of these papers together with current emphasis on Quality and the Learning Organization, is that our tools and our mindsets must reach out to understand and grapple with the requisite variety of any real-world situation, rather than attempting to fit that reality neatly into a closed box whose boundaries are marked by our own preferred variety.

STRUCTURE OF THE BOOK

The papers in this book span 35 years, and for the most part our structure traces a chronological progression. However, there are exceptions, and we need to convey our criteria for selection and grouping.

We have included particular poems by Stafford, for the most part published as *Transit* [9]. Their place in the text is by reason variously of interest, relevance, and occasionally, light relief. So too with the cartoons. A more serious function is to indicate the range of interests of the author, for whom poetry and painting are as significant as any strictly professional activity.

With two exceptions, we have grouped the papers in three parts. The exceptions are 'Holism and the Frou-Frou Slander', an address given in 1987;

and the 'Progress Note on Research into a Cybernetic Analogue of Fabric', which was published by the journal *Artorga* in 1962. We want to suggest that for ourselves this pair set the theme for the book, and whatever order the reader browses the other papers, he or she might benefit from looking at these first.

'Holism and the Frou-Frou Slander' (Chapter 1) discusses holism. This is the underlying philosophy of Stafford Beer, not in an esoteric sense, but as a guideline for the practical actions required by a 'mechanical philosopher'—a phrase used by Gordon Pask to describe his own professional status, but as apt in reference to Stafford. The point is that for these men philosophy was not something to ponder in an ivory tower, but something with which to engage reality.

The 'Progress Note' (Chapter 2) is very different. It is a hasty memorandum describing the ongoing activities of a busy man at the height of his powers, investigating and pursuing a range of activities. Its inclusion at the opening of this volume is because of its eloquent demonstration of the advanced nature of the work being carried out all those years ago, by people such as Gordon Pask and Stafford Beer. Reading this paper collapses our sense of history, and places in perspective the claims and counter claims for 'Artificial Intelligence', and the current renewed interest in parallel or distributed processing and in neural nets.

These two papers, though distanced by subject and history, yet capture and indicate the underlying richness and relevance of cybernetic ideas and methodology.

Part One gives an idea of just why an interdisciplinary approach to industrial and production processes offered such exciting promise. This part concludes with the more ambitious insight into how the whole industrial organization might benefit from concrete insights emerging from cybernetics and systems thinking, an insight to be developed further throughout the papers in Part Two.

As the heading for Part Two implies, Stafford was developing the tools to formalize a 'new world view', one which would later be encapsulated in the Viable System Model.

In Part Three the theme is once more 'application'. However, now, from the early 1970s onwards, the focus is explicitly on the more indeterminate or 'messy' human processes which constitute society. Although they emerged from his own OR background, and incorporated many lessons from his empirical work and practical experience, these papers adopt a wider vantage than concrete and 'hard' issues of industrial production. Instead, attention is turned to the more general issues which, if allowed to remain a blindspot, are likely to undermine even the best intentioned moves towards more effective social interaction and more efficient production processes, whether automated or human.

The final chapters, 14 and 15, form a pair in a special sense. They were written concurrently throughout the year 1980, and were delivered on opposite sides of the Atlantic within weeks of each other as the year turned. They were intended as complementary, and deliberately converge on the same conclusion expressed in identical words.

CONCLUSION

Stafford has been a prolific writer, and in compiling this book we were forced to omit a great many equally powerful and original papers. This selection should not be taken to be *the* definitive Stafford Beer. Nothing could be further from the truth, and we encourage the interested reader to follow up references and explore the many paths suggested by these papers.

Although for the most part published in various forms over the years, many of the included works are difficult to get hold of. The 'American Diary' and the Zaheer Lecture ('Cybernetics of National Development') are hitherto unpublished, while others (e.g. the *Artorga* reprint) are virtually unobtainable. For these reasons, this volume provides a valuable historical and intellectual context for Stafford's published books.

For those readers who have only associated Stafford's name with management cybernetics, these papers will give insight into the intellectual foundations out of which his models and understanding emerged. Other readers, hitherto unfamiliar with the name Stafford Beer, will be inspired by evidence of one man's successful battle against unreason and the divisive trend of simplistic and reductionist thinking so prevalent in our contemporary world.

Lastly, there will be many people, whether or not familiar with systems ideas and thinking, who are passionately interested in new ways of approaching the complex problems which so dominate contemporary debate. Their area of concern might be politics, sociology, education, health care, the environment, pollution, AIDS, or human society in general with its never-ending challenges and sometimes terrible faults. What will unite such people in appreciating the issues explored in this volume, is their own seriousness in attempting to secure a way of effectively addressing matters of great complexity, whether in their thinking or in their professional domain of actions. For such people, this volume, however difficult in places, should prove that it is possible to address complex issues without platitudes, prevarication or deceit. There *are* coherent actions and methods that encourage social responsibility without diminishing a sense of humanity. With due thought and determination, inspired by an overall optimism and care, there *are* ways to help safeguard the coexistence of variety that signifies the peculiarly Human in the natural World. As editors, our modest hope is that this volume gives evidence of some such ways, helping the thoughtful reader establish his or her own path of effective action.

REFERENCES

1. Beer, S., *Cybernetics and Management*. English Universities Press, London, 1959.
2. Beer, S., *The Heart of Enterprise*. John Wiley & Sons, New York, 1979.
3. Beer, S., *Brain of the Firm*, 2nd edn. John Wiley & Sons, Chichester, 1981.
4. Beer, S., *Diagnosing the System for Organizations*, John Wiley & Sons, Chichester, 1985.
5. Espejo, R. and Harnden, R. (eds), *The Viable System Model: Interpretations and Applications of Stafford Beer's VSM*. John Wiley & Sons, Chichester, 1989.
6. Beer, S., *Decision and Control: The Meaning of Operational Research and Management Cybernetics*. John Wiley & Sons, Chichester, 1966.
7. Beer, S., *Platform for Change*. John Wiley & Sons, Chichester, 1975.
8. Flores, F. and Winograd, T. *Understanding Computers and Cognition: A New Foundation for Design*. Ablex, Norwood, 1986.
9. Beer, S., *Transit* (poetry). Mitchell Communications, Canada, 1983.

Other Relevant Books on or by Stafford Beer

Beer, S., *Designing Freedom*. Canadian Broadcasting Association, 1974.

Clemson, B., *Cybernetics—a New Management Tool*. Abacus Press, Tunbridge Wells, 1984.

Espejo, R. and Schwaninger, M. (eds), *Organizational Fitness: Corporate Effectiveness through Management Cybernetics*. Campus Verlag, Frankfurt, 1993.

1 HOLISM AND THE FROU-FROU SLANDER

Opening Presidential Address at the Seventh Triennial International Congress of Cybernetics and Systems, Imperial College, London, UK, 7-11 September 1987

STAFFORD BEER
President, World Organization of General Systems and Cybernetics

DEAR COLLEAGUES and Friends—and especially those organizers and presenters from 35 different countries whose presence dignifies this occasion—WELCOME.

Rather than consume time with fulsome but contentless greetings to all and sundry, I should like to use my opportunity to address you in a personal and probably controversial way.

It is my privilege to speak here as President of this world organization: not *for* you but *to* you, not on behalf of our very own Establishment, but for myself. All times are difficult, and not least these times, when [Shakespeare says] that we should: 'speak what we feel, not what we ought to say' [1].

What I feel above all is that our science is essentially holistic, but is in danger of decomposition. I shall later indicate how this possible betrayal of philosophic principle may be robbing humankind of solutions to many dire systemic problems ...

Warren McCulloch, my friend and mentor, was one of the founders of our subject. In 1969 he wrote his last paper [2]. Having pointed out that cybernetics was by then already a quarter of a century old, he said in his last published paragraph:

First published by MCB University Press, Bradford, UK.

> it is ready to officiate at the expiration of philosophical Dualism and Reductionism, . . . the 'Nothing-buttery' of Mentalism and of Materialism. Our world is one again, and so are we.

Here was the signal that holism had a new basis in science: cybernetics as the science of the regulation of large, complex, probabilistic systems that are cohesive—and must be looked at whole.

The word 'holism' was invented in the year I was born by Jan Christiaan Smuts—in his little-known capacity as a philosopher. He spelled the word with an 'h' on good linguistic grounds: the English 'wh' was an intrusion dating only from the fifteenth century. Let me quote him:

> Instead of the animistic, or the mechanistic, or the mathematical universe, we see the genetic, organic, holistic universe [3].

As for me, that sums up my own outlook since I was a schoolboy. As a student of philosophy, at the age of 17, I wrote a dissertation called *Omnis*. Later, with an eye on a doctoral thesis, I wrote a huge tome in three volumes which no one has seen to this day. I swapped the Latin for Greek, and invented the title *Panencleisis* to mean 'all-inclusive'. This was not a claim to universal knowledge. It was a contention about the inter-relatedness of all things, which was worked out from metaphysical, logical and mathematical perspectives.

All this was 40 years ago. Consider how much, even then, supported the holistic outlook. Sir Arthur Eddington [4] one of our greatest physicists, believed that the universe can be deduced from considering fundamentals, and did not have to be induced from experiment. Western philosophy had Hegel and his Axiom of Internal Relations, it had subjective idealism, it had above all that so-little-understood work the *Monodology* of Leibniz. It had the tradition of Christian mysticism and it had the Jewish Kabbala.

There is nothing exhaustive in these casual lists. But I am anxious to remind you that holism has a strong and profoundly intellectual background. It was not the invention of Smuts who invented the word, and still less of people such as those who (very sensibly) want to eat clean food and refrain from destroying this planet, as many seem to suppose.

The end of the Second World War found me in India, where I continued to serve until the end of the Raj in 1947. The study of Vedantic philosophy, so close to hand, launched my 40-year involvement in Eastern philosophy—which continues. There you may find in all its richness the holistic insight that the universe is one, and so we are, and so moreover is all of that.

I dare not embark on even an embryonic list of teachings that go back 7000 years, and were highly mature by the time of Christ. The later development of Zen was fully articulated a thousand years ago. These were spiritual insights, certainly, but they were and remain massive contributions to other topics of concern. Most notably, these teachings comprise an epistemology founded in human physiology and in what the West calls 'Nature'. If you study that epistemology, you begin to see what is lacking in the Western treatment of large complex, probabilistic systems. We cannot even *recognize* them, as I shall try to show in a few minutes' time.

In my own days, epistemology was about the 'Problem of universals': is 'red' a property of things, or is there something called 'redness'? Cybernetics, but only cybernetics, has made some great epistemological advances in these recent years; but it has yet to build its intellectual bridges with Eastern teaching, and is far, far away from explaining anything of the kind to managers and ministers.

You now have some idea where I was standing, a convinced holist, at the crossroads between Western and Eastern philosophy (and science and aesthetics), when I read Wiener's book [5] announcing cybernetics in 1950. Within the decade I knew and was befriended by the first generation of cyberneticians: in particular, Warren McCulloch, Norbert Wiener, Heinz von Foerster in the States, Ross Ashby and Grey Walter in this country. They helped me to publish both my industrial work, and that on epistemology and neurocybernetics. In 1959 I launched managerial cybernetics with a book of my own [6].

The five men I have mentioned had two things in common. All were world authorities in established fields of science. Secondly, none of them minded that they had such an awesome title: they were all too interested in being holistic cyberneticians. Margaret Mead had these two qualifications when I met her later on. And so it has gone on. Soon I hope to meet Ilya Prigogine—who must have them too: I hope you know that this renowned physicist is the President Elect of the Society for General Systems Research.

Before turning to the examples that I promised, I want to explain why I have made this type of introduction. Remember McCulloch: the world is one and so are we. Remember the expiration of Dualism and Reductionism, of the 'Nothing-buttery' of Mentalism and of Materialism. But the world has not become one, and we—its systems thinkers—are not one either. Our confraternity is schizophrenic in the extreme. The dualism and reductionism are as rife with us as with any other part of science. I recall with affectionate ruefulness that even in the early days of promise, the first international conference on cybernetics held at Namur in 1956 was so divided into orthodox sections that I had to give three separate addresses to expound one outlook.

Reductionism is the rock on which Western science is founded; and it is the self-same rock on which society has foundered.

We are the people who have the intellectual mandate to regard and to treat systems as wholes, and not as mere collections of bits and pieces. But something called 'professionalism' intrudes. Pieces of territory are carved out by experts who are buttressed in their castles by their own idiosyncratic technologies.

No one can deny that these kinds of systems people know what they are doing. I do not question that. But if we question what they are doing in relation to a larger system within which their work seems to lose relevance, or even to be counter-productive, they become like historians for whom a question is 'not my period'. And if an appeal is made to holism, to the very genesis of cybernetics, the answer is dismissive. The expression 'Frou-frou dust' has been used to label objections that are principled rather than analytic, that are epistemological rather than technological.

So this is why I have referred to the profundity and historicity of systems thinking, and to the eminence in their fields of our cybernetic founders. They were not dispensers of frou-frou dust. Read their works and see—before the vision is lost.

I turn to examples. My purpose is to show (as I said) that the authorities *do not even recognize* the holistic systemic characteristics with which they deal. Our approach is able to recognize them, and to make initial diagnoses that can lead to solutions. You will not expect solutions in a short address: my sketches are vignettes intended to show the point and no more.

The issue of social violence preoccupies this country, among others. Harmony in the community is modelled in our terms as polystable homeostasis. This is because society is a very complex system, and Ashby's Law of Requisite Variety requires that subsections of the community absorb each other's variety. Family relationships, church groups, sports groups, arts groups, and above all peer groups are *intrinsic controllers* in the community.

Consider an extreme alternative, in which peace is maintained by the police. A first application of Ashby's Law suggests that half the population must be policemen: every second person must both invigilate and protect every first person. But this is impracticable. In 1970 the ratio of policemen to non-policemen was 1 in 500, though it is doubtless higher now. How then has the Law of Requisite Variety been met?—by amplification of course. Fast cars, close communications, forensic science, and in the limit guns, generate on the average more variety than a criminal subset can absorb. It works.

That is, it works until disharmony gets out of hand in football hooliganism, the disintegration of a carnival, or rioting triggered by seemingly trivial incidents.

The official solution to this is to build up the police-to-public ratio until the police have the upper hand. There are many ways of doing this and long are they discussed by the authorities—who talk about the risks of antagonizing and incensing the crowd. But the two key cybernetic points are not even recognized.

The first is this. Since community harmony depends on polystable homeostasis, then the escalation of police intervention will reach a threshold where that machinery breaks down. It is not just that community leaders may be arrested or beaten to the ground. The entire community network, the domain of the social 'conversation' in second-order cybernetic terms, is disrupted. Community leaders in Toxteth (Liverpool), Moss Side (Manchester) and Mantua (Philadelphia), to quote the ones I happen to know, and certainly in Notting Hill (London) understand this. A lot of my confidence in cybernetic science derives from the fact that practical people on the spot always come up with cybernetically valid answers—because they are *living* a cybernetic reality.

This is more than you can say for the authorities. For them, the intervention of the police *defines* a criminal act. For the holistic observer to note all the many indicators of societary breakdown, such as unemployment, inner-city decay, and all the rest, suddenly becomes the scattering of frou-frou dust. Indeed, when these indications were noted after the Handsworth (Birmingham) riots in 1986, both the Prime Minister and the Home Secretary were constrained to announce that the acts concerned were 'merely criminal'. I say 'constrained' advisedly. This is the only conclusion that could validate the authorities' model.

Parallel to the simplistic model of polystable homeostasis, or perhaps deriving from it, is the simplistic model of causation. 'There is no causal connection between massive unemployment and rioting' it was announced last year. 'No causal connexion has been proven', have declared both Britain and the United States, as to the devastation of other people's forests by acid rain. Scandinavia and Canada respectively but not respectfully disagree. It is now generally agreed that it is not a good idea to smoke tobacco, although for 30 years people have not *proved* a causal connection, and although for all that time thousands of experimental mice have been chain-smoking cigarettes without producing a lung carcinoma between them.

It is 200 years since Hume devastated the simplistic notion of cause on which all our affairs seem still to be run. All of contemporary science, and not just cybernetics, self-consciously studies complex systems in which this kind of causation is quite meaningless. Without delving into abstruse physics (where the point is best made) we have only to think of biological systems that are more immediate. How can you invoke 'cause' in the political sense to describe food webs or the endocrine system?

The epitome of the holistic system that is not amenable to causal analysis in the simplistic political sense is the planet—Gaia herself. It is amazing to me that James Lovelock's brilliant presentation [7] of the cybernetic regulatory system that sponsors life itself has not become the cynosure by which planetary trends away from survival are judged. But of course a change of paradigm is involved. The image of life crawling around in its multiplicity of species, looking for a 'biological niche' to which it can somehow adapt, is replaced by the creation of an environment that implies such life. It is an environment in which tiny changes in the salinity of the oceans, the composition of the atmosphere, and indeed all other major variables make life impossible.

Without insight into that holistic description, it is small wonder that human mismanagement of the environment causes cataclysms to which we are almost inured. And here perhaps I am entitled to say 'causes'—because we must be using the wrong model, wrong in the sense of low variety. The Conant–Ashby Theorem points out that the effectiveness of a regulator is determined by the model it contains [8]. Evidently, in fact, a low-variety regulation cannot distinguish all the states of a high-variety system. So much for the 'cause' of riots; and so much for our absolute inability to deal with world hunger, which as you know is not due to a shortage of food but to our inability to create a holistic, cybernetic regulatory system.

So it is (and surely these figures cannot be too often acknowledged) that at least 700 million people suffer from chronic malnutrition, and 40 000 children a day starve to death [9]. Two billion people do not have a clean water supply, so that 80 per cent of disease in the Third World is water-borne. The crisp analysis of the situation as to hunger made by the Food and Agriculture Program of the International Institute for Applied Systems Analysis (of which Britain is significantly no longer a member), shows clearly that the world *already* grows enough food to feed the entire population of the earth. What is wrong? FAP says: 'The system is full of distortions' and 'even if these were corrected the hungry would not necessarily benefit'. That means that the regulatory model is at fault. Then we should next ask the further cybernetic question: why do not the bodies designated by the United Nations and the European Economic Community (for example) change it? Let us look for cybernetic clues as to that.

According to Maturana and Varela [10] a substantial regulatory effort has to be made by a living organism in order to 'make itself', which is to say to keep in good repair the relationships by which replaceable elements, such as body cells, define the system to be what it is. They call this phenomenon *autopoiesis*. Because I believe that holistic social systems are organic, I have extended their concept to institutional organisms. Many people consider this development to be purely analogical. I do not, and have defended my thesis elsewhere [11]. But I am careful not to implicate those authors in what I shall now say.

Please allow, if only for purposes of discussion, that a hospital may retain a character and a reputation in a particular branch of medicine that outlasts all its elements—medical staff and patients alike. The same is true of a distinctive university, which may be 1000 years old. These institutions will make a big investment in their own autopoiesis. We know the mechanisms involved: careful definition of roles, committee structures, commitments to excellence in special areas; these are only some of the respectable activities we may note. Now suppose, which God forbid, that the staff slides into the error of paying more and more attention to those matters that explicate relationships than to healing or to teaching—so that in the end a cured patient or an educated student were only the product of self-help and good luck. Then I should describe this institution, long before the *reductio ad absurdum*, as *pathologically* autopoietic.

Well, I have worked in 17 countries at the government level, and I have seen a great deal of the way in which international and well-meaning institutions interpenetrate the local culture. Not to mince words, they are all pathologically autopoietic. The short FAP report from which I was quoting makes it quite clear that the system perpetuates the hunger it is meant to ameliorate. If anything is to be done, however, the cybernetic pathologies must be identified and extirpated. Obviously this is a monumental task. But it does not help at all for the powers-that-be not to recognize the holistic lineaments of the systems over which they have charge, not to know the cybernetic pathologies of viable systems, and therefore of course not to have any idea how to find solutions.

Meanwhile we are faced with the bizarre fact of so much death, disease and suffering on the one hand, and accusations about alarmism, pessimism, and frou-frou dust on the other.

On the 24 March this year I watched parliamentary question time on Canadian television. The minister replying made (I suppose) a slip of the tongue. But it stuck in my mind as reflecting the bizarre clash of fact and reaction—although it was in another context. Mr Clark said: 'The Honourable Member should not raise false alarms too early'. Such is our fate: our alarms are not false, and cannot be too early.

Just now I mentioned viable systems, those capable of independent survival, to the study of which I have devoted much of my professional effort over 40 years. There is one feature of viability that I see as so important that I even took the liberty of constituting it as a 'law'. It is the *Law of Cohesion for Multiple Recursions of the Viable System* [11]. This law, in its full development, governs the vexed question of autonomy. Centralized systems do not work and decentralized systems do not work. In struggling to find the right balance, the institutions I have criticized, and indeed large companies, and indeed whole governments, set up machinery to help and even to adjudicate. They soon find that they suffer from a huge bureaucracy, the purpose of which turns out to be that it sustains itself. It is as tenacious as a cancer; it is galloping pathological autopoiesis. So the pointer I offer to solutions here, which in truth is more than a pointer but a solution that would take a week to expound, is to *design* autonomy according to cybernetic principles. This I go around attempting to do. But empires are difficult to undermine; I know only two things about emperors: one, they have no clothes; two, to conceal their nakedness they wallow in power.

The most egregiously awful (in both senses) example I can offer you is one that might at first seem surprising—because people think of it as 'a thing in itself' and not as a pathology at all. I refer to what Eisenhower called 'the military–industrial complex'. Consider: this strange institution is ostensibly in existence as a *service* to society. Instead it *drives* society, and by now that society is the planetary society: everyone, everywhere is implicated. There's another fact to remember in face of death and deprivation: a world expenditure on armaments of *one trillion dollars* a year. Everyone agrees that this is madness. As to solutions, though, you cannot get inside the monster, which serves too many vested interests to be assailable at all.

The only pointer I can offer here derives again from Ashby's Law. The international military–industrial complex cannot operate without scientists. We know that the overwhelming majority of scientists—decent family women and men for the most part—depend, directly or indirectly, on the complex. I think they see themselves as having no choice. It follows that if we can find the route to completely peaceful science, we provide such people with Requisite Variety—that is, with choice. Since funding is wholly in the hands of the system we seek to circumvent, new methods of support must be invented. The beginnings are there—in co-operatives, and in systems of barter which (thanks to computers) are now quite richly interconnected. The credits in these systems (called 'green money' in Canada) bear no interest, and cannot be redeemed, only transferred. But they seem to work. In truth, scientists choosing to work like this will not become 'yuppies'; but they may be able to look their children in the eye.

Along with this would go an equivalent Hippocratic oath. Two versions are being canvassed by the Institute for Social Inventions, and I read to you the one to which I subscribe (see page 23). Is it possible to make so minimal a statement in today's world—if you want to survive professionally? Surely we should strive to make it possible—and ignore the slander of the frou-frou dust.

Here is my final discussion exemplifying cybernetic holism. It concerns the government of Gaia.

The Constitution of UNESCO declares:

> Since wars begin in the minds of men, it is in the minds of men that the defence of peace must be constructed.

Surely this is so. And surely the ordinary member of the human race does not turn his, and less still her, mind to war until incited so to do. But the incitement comes from a minority, whether they be soccer hooligans, racists, religious fanatics, manipulators of the military–industrial complex, or simply insane leaders of nation states. These minorities take on power because they have access to the appurtenances of power. The actual machinery is often fire-power; but it may be no more than access to television—as we see when a minority manages to have itself labelled 'the moral majority' by intensive televisual brain-washing in a free society.

It seems that the process of wresting power from those who misuse it is usually undertaken by an alternative power-crazy minority, so that ordinary folk survive (if they do) to suffer in any case. Then the issue of war comes down to constructing a means of empowering humankind as such to be itself.

It is straightforwardly a systems viewpoint which has to say: in that case, the edifice that has been built around the nation states must be systematically counter-productive. This is because none can be expected to yield an iota of power in an internationally *competitive* environment. What then of those international projects that we occasionally see? Our answer must be that they are metasystemic to the domain of competition. They are co-operative not because the conflicting aims of nation states have been resolved, but because they have been transcended. The synergistic domain is one in which a non-zero-sum game is made possible, and that would count as the empowerment of ordinary people.

We cyberneticians know how to design such a system, but only individuals can empower it. Meanwhile:

> the living nations wait
> Each sequestered in its hate [12]

because that is what their leaders ordain. And the only way to take the official diplomacy that is supposed to mediate all this seriously is in fact to take it satirically. It is many years (and things have not improved) since Ustinov [13] wrote:

> A diplomat these days is nothing but a head waiter who's allowed to sit down occasionally.

Then what would count as a move towards holistic world government if the existing game is zero-sum, its structures are impotent, and its bureaucracies are pathologically autopoietic?

I can at least exemplify an answer. Here in my hand is my World Passport. It is issued by the World Service Authority, an extraordinary institution which, for 40 years, has been the unremitting work of just one man. He is the extraordinary Garry Davis. You will not I think be able to guess the number of sets of documents that he has issued. The answer is a quarter of a million. Most of these have gone to people who were stateless, who had no documents. They have *empowered themselves*, with Davis's help, and their documents have been duly noted in all parts of the world.

What can good systems people do about that? My answer is 'see the point' and then 'give a lead'. I shall ensure that the address is available outside [14]. Such efforts deserve support, if humankind is ever to break its organizational deadlocks. Little will be heard of this important conference outside our confraternity, if past experience is anything to go on. But 'Systems Thinkers Support New Vision of World Government *en masse*' might cause someone to think: even our goodselves.

I said that I would be controversial, and I hope that I have lived up to that. It seems to me that the systems approach has not yet demonstrated a fraction of its potency, because we have all been too timid. For example, in my last and necessarily brief reference to world government, how many of us thought: 'I am not getting mixed up in politics'? Being starved, being tortured, and being volatilized is getting mixed up in politics for sure: how far removed from those realities can any of us claim to be? Then we must consider our responsibilities.

Here is my final thought. Most of us are secure in respected Establishment jobs—in universities, in government. As we get older, we who had the new ideas are constrained to pooh-pooh, to ridicule, newer ideas—or even the consequential ideas that followed ours ...

Well, there exists a picture of a roomful of famous Victorians. One of the chairs is occupied by the great scientist Lord Kelvin, after whom a number of discoveries was named. I have occasion to use that room, and to sit in Lord Kelvin's chair. And I reflect how that President of the Royal Society at the turn of the century, declared that heavier-than-air flying machines were impossible, and that X-rays would prove to be a hoax [15].

Cybernetically designed viability is, I tell you, not impossible. People-empowered world government is not a hoax.

REFERENCES

1. Shakespeare, W., *King Lear* (concluding speech).
2. McCulloch, W. S., 'Recollections of the Many Sources of Cybernetics', *Forum*, **6**(2), The American Society for Cybernetics, Summer 1974.
3. Smuts, J. C., quoted in the supplement to the *Oxford English Dictionary*, 1971.
4. Eddington, A. S., *Fundamental Theory*. Cambridge University Press, Cambridge, 1948.
5. Wiener, N., *Cybernetics: Control and Communication in the Animal and the Machine*. John Wiley, New York, 1948.
6. Beer, S., *Cybernetics and Management*. English Universities Press, 1959.
7. Lovelock, J., *Gaia*.
8. Conant, R. C. and Ross Ashby, W., 'Every Good Regulator of a System Must Be a Model of That System', *International Journal of Systems Science*, **1**(2), 1970, pp. 89–97.

9. *Options* (ISSN 0252 9572) IIASA 1–2 (1987).
10. Maturana, H. R. and Varela, F. J., *Autopoiesis and Cognition*. Reidel Publishing Co., Holland, 1980.
11. Beer, S., *The Heart of Enterprise*. John Wiley, New York, 1979.
12. Auden, W. H., 'In Memory of W. B. Yeats', *Collected Shorter Poems 1930–1944*. Faber & Faber, London, 1950.
13. Ustinov, P., *Romanoff and Juliet* (play).
14. World Service Authority, 1012 14th Street N.W., Washington DC, 20005, USA.
15. Morgan, C. and Langford, D., *Facts and Fallacies*. Exeter, 1981.

HIPPOCRATIC OATH FOR SCIENTISTS, ENGINEERS AND TECHNOLOGISTS

I vow to practise my profession with conscience and dignity;

I will strive to apply my skills only with the utmost respect for the well-being of humanity, the earth and all its species;

I will not permit considerations of nationality, politics, prejudice or material advancement to intervene between my work and this duty to present and future generations;

I make this Oath solemnly, freely and upon my honour.

Signed ...Stafford Beer... Date ....

Modelled on the Hippocratic Oath for doctors from probably the 5th Century BC, modified in the *World Medical Association's Declaration of Geneva*.

Published 22/7/87 by the *Institute for Social Interventions*, 24 Abercorn Place, London NW8 9XP.

ARTORGA

We are happy to have persuaded Stafford Beer, a member of the Artorga Committee, to have written this paper [Chapter 2] as Artorga Communication 40. There is an obvious reluctance to summarize experiments that have not been conclusive. However, in the difficult and untried field of constructing or identifying 'Artificial Organisms' the credit must go to those who have the courage actually to attempt such construction and identification, knowing they will be unsuccessful, rather than merely discussing the theory of such attempts.

We thank Mr Beer, and think his paper will be read with intense interest by many Artorga members.

Artorga,
Beaulieu,
Brockenhurst,
Hampshire

April 1962

Operational Research man, ex-Indian Army, Thinking

1951

2 A PROGRESS NOTE ON RESEARCH INTO A CYBERNETIC ANALOGUE OF FABRIC

STAFFORD BEER

In view of requests from several quarters for information about this problem, I compile the following notes. These are written for professionals in the field; that is, they assume familiarity with basic cybernetics. There is nothing at all definite to report: nothing, that is, that has been explored with sufficient thoroughness to warrant publication. Everything that follows is very much a spare time activity for me, although I am doing my best to keep the work alive—for I have a conviction that it will ultimately pay off. Ideally, an endowed project is required to finance my company's Cybernetic Research Unit in this fundamental work.

The starting point for this thinking is to be found in chapter XVII of *Cybernetics and Management* (English Universities Press, 1959, John Wiley & Sons Ltd, 1960). It is argued there that a self-organizing system need not have its circuitry designed in detail—otherwise what virtue is there in the self-organizing capability? Furthermore, if systems of this kind are to be used for amplifyng intelligence, or for 'breeding' other systems more highly developed than they are themselves, a fixed circuitry is a liability. Instead, we seek a fabric that is *inherently* self-organizing, on which to superimpose (as a signal on a carrier wave) the particular cybernetic functions that we seek to model. Or, to take another image, we seek to *constrain* a high-variety fabric rather than to fabricate one by blueprint.

THE REQUIREMENT

The basic mechanism for which we seek an appropriate fabric is undoubtedly that of the homeostat described by Ashby. This system offers a control

First published by *Artorga*, Hampshire, UK.

mechanism that is ultrastable: a necessary feature of any control which is to deal with environmental disturbances of a kind not envisaged by the designer.

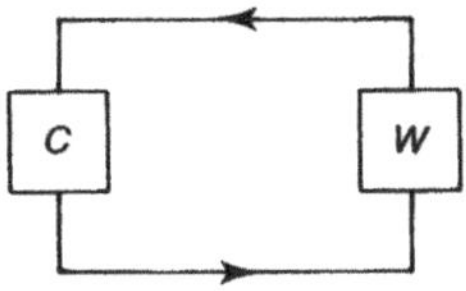

Figure 1 Basic homeostat connecting a control system (C) to a world situation (W)

The essence of this control theory is that the outputs of a world situation are fed as inputs into a control mechanism, which in turn feeds its output into the world situation. This is to say that we set up a homeostatic relationship between the controller and the world (Figure 1). There seem to me to be just four basic requirements for a system of this kind.

(a) That the variety of C $\geqslant$ the relevant variety of W.
(b) That the behaviour of each system can be transduced into the other (although not necessarily by linear transformation, nor indeed by any known transformation).
(c) That the richness of interaction between C and W is high.
(d) That the control system itself should be a homeostat.

The reason for the first requirement is given by the law of requisite variety. The reason for the second is obvious, in that the systems must be coupled; the only point is whether much needs to be known about the actual parameters employed or the transformations involved. In view of the fact that each system is richly interactive internally, I cannot see that either matters very much: the overall system can be given the facility to learn how to weight its own ouptut to achieve stable states more speedily if algedonic feedback provides a reward mechanism. The third point reflects the information–theoretic conditions governing channel capacity. The fourth requirement comes about because system C must be viable in its own right: it must keep its variety 'on the boil', ready to trap and deal with the disturbances reaching it.

Thus the problem with which we are first concerned is to construct system C, defined as a homeostat of high variety, which will simply go on operating —that is, will ceaselessly reach stable states and then disturb itself from them again. Such a system is in permanent oscillation, but is tending all the time towards stabilization.

A REVIEW OF POSSIBLE FABRICS

At the start of this work (in about 1954) I considered that electrical and electronic mechanisms should be discarded. They, it seemed, had to be designed in detail; and what kind of viable fabrics are glass and wire? However, in more recent years it has become clear that developments in solid-state physics may overcome this objection. For if it is possible to operate on the molecules of a germanium crystal, then we have a high-variety fabric which can be continuously constrained. Even so, the thinking that has been done about other kinds of fabrics should be recorded.

Chemical Systems

These are the machines I have labelled 'fungoid'. My own experiments with them have not been very satisfactory: these have involved modifications of ideas developed by three other workers.

Firstly, there are Pask's thread structures—depositions of metallic iron inside colloidal cells. Secondly, there is Chapman's use of cotton threads soaked in sodium hydrochloride (which have the property of increasing their electrical resistance as they dry out with the repeated passage of electric current—and thereby model conditional probability learning devices).

Having collaborated with Pask in some of his work, I tried to simulate the undifferentiated networks of the reticular formation of the brain stem with his threads in three-dimensional spaces. I have not even met Chapman, but have tried to do the same with his cottons. Probably such a development as the latter requires close humidity control: at any rate, I got nowhere.

Thirdly, there is the attractive idea (suggested by George) that lipids might be used to create interfaces between cells. Semi-permeable membranes offer obvious advantages in any progress requiring selection and segregation. The need for them had been felt as the result of bifurcating Paskian colloidal cells with impermeable membranes. Fungoid machines, it was found, grew branches over plastic dividers—a gross sort of artefact of osmosis. But if (for example) lecithin sols could be used, they would form suitable membranes between any two aqueous liquids. The stability of such membranes, their viscosity, and their permeability to electrolytes, are dependent on many variables (such as temperature); in particular, the state of the cell itself (pH value) alters the characteristics of the membrane. Thus thresholds could in principle be modified by feedback from the amount of intracellular activity—a conditional probability learning trick.

The biological controls needed to handle lecithin aseptically were beyond the capability of my laboratory, and collaborators thought that it would be unnecessary to use organic material at all. Even so, it is worth recording the idea: simplicity and smallness are important in this kind of engineering (because of the enormous numbers of components involved), and interfaces that are themselves both structural components and system variables are appealing.

Human Beings

In 1956 I devised a game for solving simultaneous linear equations in two variables. The theory used the properties of groups to simplify the arithmetic: the game worked in homomorphic transformations modulo 5. It was played by unsophisticated persons, such as children, who could not be expected to know everything about simultaneous equations. They competed with each other to make correct selections from sets of five, and then to synthesize the selections and select therefrom, by means of a simple machine. This simulated algedonic feedback by means of coloured lights which announced that 'pleasure' or 'pain' was being experienced.

The idea of this was to demonstrate the possibility of intelligence amplification. Intelligence, in the sense of an ability to steer one's way from pain to pleasure within a simple game language, was certainly amplified in that (unknown to the competitors) the equations were actually solved. Was any particular solution implicit in the game language? I think not; because the game could and did handle actual equations which had not been previously studied by the inventor. This series of experiments was entirely successful; unfortunately the opportunity to write them up for publication has now been lost.

The extension of this work was intended to be as follows. By using human beings, one reduces the technical problems of communication—the experimenter and the system could talk to each other. But in so far as all this worked, it seemed in principle possible to use any other kind of animal for the purpose. Some effort was made to devise a 'mouse' language which would enable mice to play this game—with cheese as a reward function. The advantages of using animals are clear: in addition to any language imposed upon them by the scientist, they presumably have their own mouse language. That is, they live in communities and communicate. Such a community obviously constitutes a high-variety self-organizing fabric from the 'systems' point of view.

Vertebrates

In this way I was led to consider various kinds of animal, and various sorts of language (by which I mean intercommunicating boxes, ladders, see-saws, cages connected by pulleys and so forth). Rats and pigeons have both been closely studied for their learning attributes, both as individuals and as groups, by many workers; they seemed possible components for a system. The Machina Speculatrix of Grey Walter might also be considered (with apologies to the organic molecule) as a vertebrate for such purposes.

Consider, for example, an animated nomograph. This would be driven by two animals, intercommunicating in the sense that each is aware of the activities of the other at the opposite end of the cursor. A coupled arrangement of two such nomographs was designed to play the simultaneous equations game. However, no actual machines were built.

Social Insects

By the same token, bees, ants, termites, have all been systematically considered as components of self-organizing systems, and various 'brain-storming' machines have been designed by both Pask and myself. But again none has been made.

Animalcules

One of Pask's designs used *Aedes Aegypti*, the larva of the yellow fever mosquito; and I designed another incorporating *Daphnia*, the freshwater crustacean.

Many experiments were made with the latter machine. Iron filings were included with dead leaves in the tank of *Daphnia*, which ingested sufficient of the former to respond to a magnetic field. Attempts were made to feed inputs to the colony of *Daphnia* by transducing environmental variables into electromagnets, while the outputs were the consequential changes in the electrical characteristics of the phase space produced by the adaptive behaviour of the colony.

Be it noted that a system of this kind retains stochastic freedom within the pattern generally imposed—a necessary condition in this kind of evolving machine; it is also self-perpetuating, and self-repairing, as a good fabric should be. However, there were many experimental problems. The most serious of these was the collapse of any incipient organization—apparently due to the steadily increasing suspension of tiny permanent magnets in the water.

'Gas Particles'

Next were considered the very small organisms which because of their great numbers can be regarded as a 'biological gas', and are interactive but independent entities. Amoebae and others have been considered. The protozoon *Euglena* seemed to have special attractions.

This is a photosynthetic free-swimming protozoon, which in culture offers an unconstrained fabric of high variety, having the capacity to respond (in a well-documented way) to a variety of stimuli with detectable behaviour. When we started this work, we thought *Euglena* was relatively easy to culture in an inorganic solution (plus traces of organic factors).

Euglena is sensitive to light: the tropism reverses after illumination has reached a critical value. It is also sensitive to heat, chemicals and mechanical shock. As its metabolism depends on light, the normal positive response to light would be reinforced by reproduction (binary fission—reproduction by fusion unknown). In the prolonged absence of light, the beast loses its chlorophyll and tries to make a living on the organic matter in the medium.

As to interaction, several *Euglena* in a culture will affect each other in a number of ways:

(a) By reducing the nutrient concentration of the medium.
(b) By blocking light paths, which will interfere with the phototropic and photosynthetic activities of those to leeward.
(c) By their waste products.

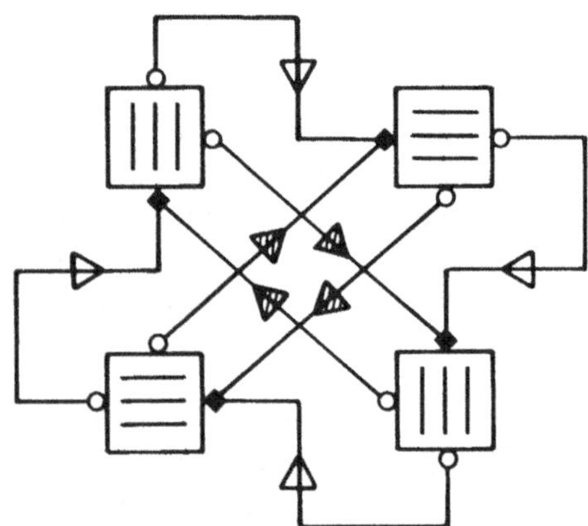

Figure 2 Effects of *Euglena* upon each other. ☰, *Euglena* culture, with tropism displayed as shown; ◆, stimulus; ○, sensory receptor; ▲, inhibiting and △, stimulating influence of a's sensation on b's stimulus

The design shown in Figure 2 was made for this system. It is evident from this design that the two sensory receptors are logical contraries. In fact, there is of course no need for more than one actual cell, which would relay a stimulating impulse to one of its target cultures and an inhibiting impulse to the other.

It seems that this system should tend to an equilibrial state, but that chance variables are likely to procure step functions in the system, thereby meeting the 'on the boil' criterion.

It was found possible to read in and out of the cultures, using a point source of light as the stimulus, and a photocell as the sensory receptor. However, the culturing difficulties proved enormous. *Euglena* showed a distressing tendency to lie doggo, and attempts to isolate a more motile strain failed.

Working with *Euglena* brought home the factors already mentioned as relative to this problem. Each small tank of greenish liquid contained several million independent creatures behaving in complex ways, photosynthesizing and reproducing interminably: a staggering source of high variety. The reinforcement given by the loop 'more light → more photosynthesis → more *Euglena* → more light' could be viewed as an algedonic control: it is essentially a reward mechanism.

Ponds

So pure cultures were difficult to handle. Moreover, they are not, perhaps, ecologically stable systems. Dr Gilbert, who had been trying to improve the *Euglena* cultures, suggested a potent thought. Why not use an entire ecological system, such as a pond? The theory on which all this thinking is based does not require a knowledge of the black box employed.

Accordingly, over the past year, I have been conducting experiments with a large tank or pond. The contents of the tank were randomly sampled from ponds in Derbyshire and Surrey. Currently there are a few of the usual creatures visible to the naked eye (*Hydra*, *Cyclops*, *Daphnia*, and a leech); microscopically there is the expected multitude of micro-organisms. In this tank are suspended four lights, the intensities of which can be varied to fine limits. At other points are suspended photocells with amplifying circuits which give them very high sensitivity. Roughly, I am trying to treat this system in the way designed for *Euglena*, superimposing the four tanks of Figure 2 on to each other in the one tank. There is an ecological guarantee that this system stabilizes itself, and is indeed ultra-stable. But, of course, the problem of making it act as a control system is very difficult indeed.

I regard the machine as a tending-to-be-stable-but-not-quite homeostat, like the box labelled C in Figure 1. Events in the world (W) have to be transduced into the control machine, thus providing an independent modification of the light sources. The stochastic variety of the control machine *must* then absorb the world variety and demonstrate the phenomena we are anxious to display. But the channel capacity of the photoelectric feedback to the world situation is insufficient to resolve the ambiguity of the signals in the tank. In other words, at present there seems no way of meeting the requirements of Shannon's Tenth Theorem. Also, there ought to be some way of nominating a threshold below which the rate of change in the homeostat of this not-quite-stable system would be deemed to represent stability. I do not know how to measure this.

The state of this research at the moment is that I tinker with this tank from time to time in the middle of the night. My main obsession at the moment is at the level of the philosophy of science. All this thinking is, perhaps, some kind of breakthrough; but what about an equivalent breakthrough in experimental method? Do we really know how to experiment with black boxes of abnormally high varieties?

Our scientific training, modified as it may be by years of experience in cybernetics, pushes us always towards attempts at analysis. I tell myself repeatedly that this thing is a black box in whose transfer functions I am not interested. Yet I repeatedly try to isolate experimental effects: to discover light intensities at which attraction flip-flops to repulsion for the creatures operating in the zone between a light and a photoreceptor, for instance. I do not want to do this, but I do it. The reason is, of course, that although one can see experimental techniques for handling the total system and measuring its behaviour, the results defy the kinds of interpretation at our disposal.

Perhaps the next step is to think of a small, readily examined, uncontrolled system to represent 'the world'. It might then be possible to couple it to the tank and measure the extent of control. Has anyone any ideas? At the least, a reader unconventional enough in his scientific outlook to have read these notes to this point selects himself as having a sufficiently bizarre mind to help!

PART ONE Beginnings: Interdisciplinary Application of Operational Research to Tangible Problems

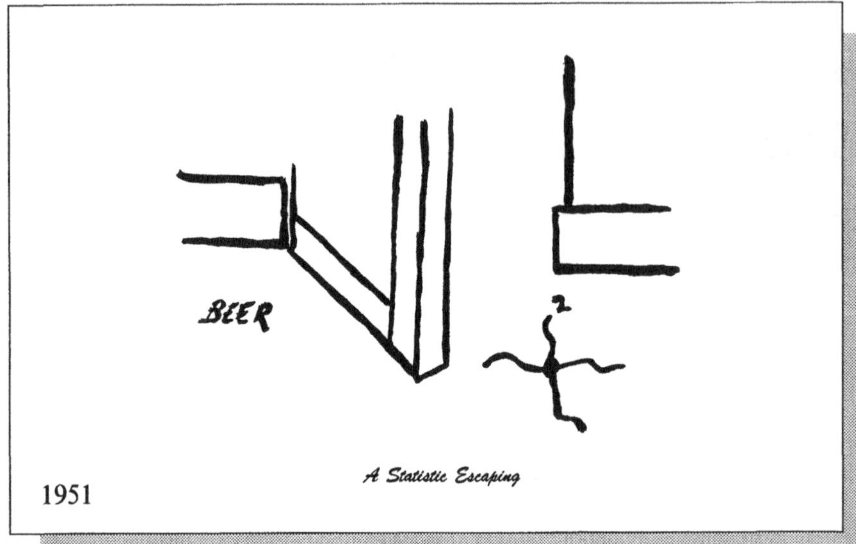

A Statistic Escaping

1951

3 A TECHNIQUE FOR STANDARDIZING MASSED BATTERIES OF CONTROL CHARTS

STAFFORD BEER

Mr Beer describes a simple apparatus and a method of standardizing control charts, with the aid of which a large number of charts can readily be kept under surveillance. He describes an application to production control in a factory.

INTRODUCTION

When control chart procedures have been adopted to provide statistical surveillance of some wide scheme of control, the user is confronted with a number of operational difficulties. Suppose that his control scheme covers 50 measured quantities, each with its underlying frequency distribution and each distribution having parameters peculiar to itself. According to orthodox methods, there will be two charts for each distribution: one of sample averages and one of sample ranges. Since the positions of limit lines depend on the standard deviations, there will be 50 pairs of graphs, mostly with different limits.

Attempts to plot these graphs adjacently on a large sheet of paper are foredoomed to failure. Not only does the variation in spread give the chart a chaotic appearance, but it continually needs alteration. A change in the facts of the situation being controlled can easily mean a change in the mean and variability of a distribution. The limit lines on two graphs must then be redrawn. At best, this will make the sheet of graphs look increasingly muddled; at worst, the graphs may begin to overlap.

Some technique is thus required which will overcome these difficulties and produce an intelligible massed battery of charts. A simple solution is here put forward, with a description of the situation in which it has already been applied.

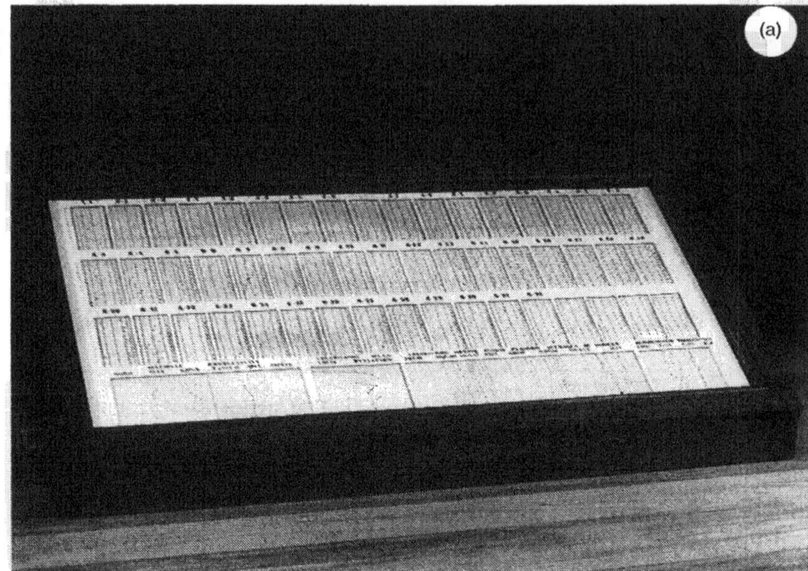

Figure 1 (a) and (b) Apparatus for displaying massed control charts

APPARATUS

Figures 1(a) and (b) show the apparatus which was devised to house a massed battery of standardized control charts. This is simple both to use and to consult. Here 51 similar control charts are identified by numbers (e.g. 6.30); the lowermost line of charts carries additional information about the control system.

Each line of charts is drawn on a continuous roll of millimetre graph paper (70 cm wide) and is attached to rollers operated by T-shaped handles protruding on both sides of the device at its base. Thus the control charts are continuous for a number of years, and move below the fixed mask on which the designations of the graphs are written. This introduces an unfamiliar feature: the time scale runs vertically instead of horizontally.

The single graph which is reproduced in Figure 2 demonstrates how this works (the numbers on the right should be ignored for the moment).

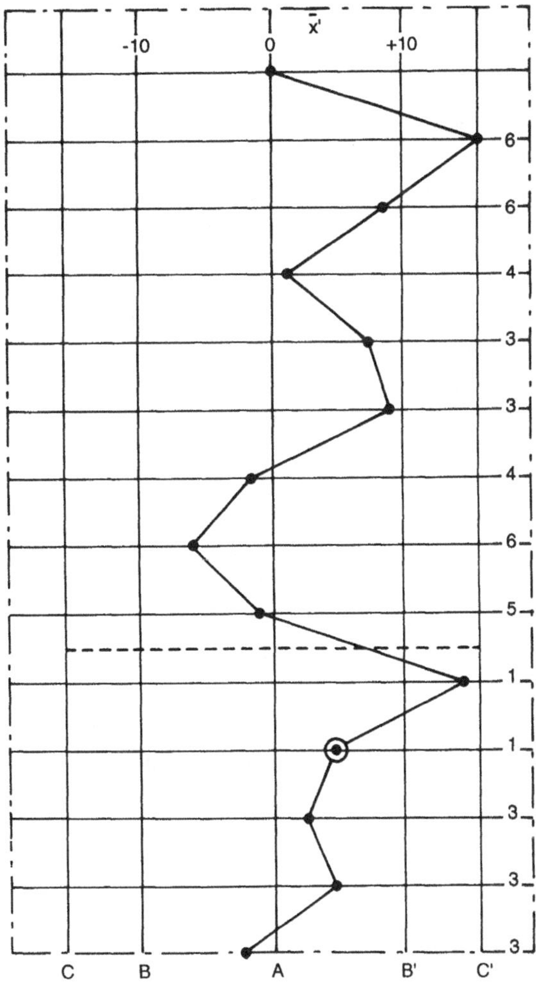

Figure 2 Statistical control chart for group 6.27. The limits of this standardized chart do not change with changes in the parameters of the controlled distribution

The mean of the group (the quantity measured is productivity) is represented by the central line A; the lines B and B′ represent 1 in 40 limits, C and C′ represent 1 in 1000 limits. Each point on this graph is the mean productivity for a sample period, and a horizontal line denotes the year end. The 'window' in the mask through which any chart is seen is cut to make visible a year's record of the chart, which is rolled up every time a fresh point is added.

The chief convenience of the charts lies in the fact that they are all drawn on the same scale, with the limit lines at the same distance from the 'mean' line for each chart. The next section shows how this is achieved.

CONTROL OF SAMPLE AVERAGES

In the usual control chart for sample averages, the sample average, $\bar{x}$, is usually drawn on a chart with the control level drawn to represent m, the estimated population mean, and control limits drawn at distances $t_{\sigma}/\sqrt{n}$ above and below m, where σ is the estimated standard deviation of the individual items in the population, n is the number in the sample, and t depends on the probability corresponding to the limits, being 1.96 for the 1 in 40 limits and 3.09 for the 1 in 1000 limits. For different charts the levels and limits will be at different positions according to the values of m, σ, and n.

In our scheme the sample averages are standardized by calculating for each value:

$$\bar{x}' = \frac{10}{1.96} \times \frac{\bar{x}-m}{\sigma/\sqrt{n}}$$

$$= 11.4\frac{\bar{x}-m}{\sigma} \text{ for samples of 5}$$

Then the control charts for $\bar{x}'$ have the control level at zero, the 1 in 40 limits are 10 graphical units away from the control level, and the 1 in 1000 limits are 5.75 graphical units further away, whatever the values of m and σ. A change in either m or σ changes the calculation of $\bar{x}'$; it does not alter the chart. When the sample averages are a computed ratio such as productivity, the transformation to the standardized form may readily be incorporated in the computation schedule.

This method involves sacrificing the representation on the chart of any change in the population mean or standard deviation. This can be remedied to a large extent by annotation, and the individual statistician has to decide whether the whole procedure presents enough information.

CONTROL OF SAMPLE RANGES

The next question to be discussed is that of sample ranges, and here it is hoped to justify a more radical reduction in the customarily presented information. Orthodox range charts can conceivably be treated in the same way as the charts for sample averages by plotting the range on a standardized chart such as that already discussed, by using a statistical transformation. This would, however, be a more complicated method than the situation usually warrants, and a simple substitute of the kind described below is often sufficient.

I take the general point of view that the curtailing of orthodox statistical procedures is permissible when strictly limited aims have been defined. Cases are sometimes noted where statistical effort is disproportionate to the accuracy of available data on the one hand, and to the nicety with which subsequent action can be graded on the other. Orthodox charts of sample ranges seem frequently to fall into this second category. In the present context, certainly, an exact estimate of the probabilities attaching to sample ranges is totally unnecessary.

If the line for averages should jump outside its control limits the range chart is usually consulted to judge whether the displacement is a uniform change and therefore serious or the result of wildly erratic behaviour in perhaps one individual in the sample. Conversely, if the average chart is quite steady the range chart is consulted to ensure that this appearance is not illusory and merely due to the cancelling of extreme values of individuals within the sample. Thus it is submitted that, at least for the routine use of a massed battery, the statistician is only interested in *zones* of the range chart, such as the following.

In an ordinary control chart for ranges we may use five limit lines: one representing the mean range, which runs between two pairs of asymmetrical limits. These five lines embrace four 'zones of probability'. A fifth zone will lie between the lower outer limit and the base line of zero range, and a sixth zone will exist above the upper outer limit. If it be conceded that a range value can, in exceptional circumstances, be so high as to be absurd,

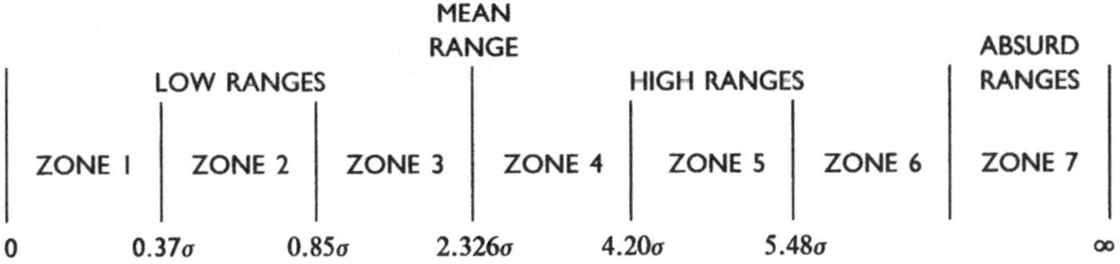

Figure 3 Zones and boundaries for range chart in samples of five. The boundary between zones 6 and 7 is chosen arbitrarily at some high value

a seventh zone will also arise. For use in massed batteries these zones may be coded as in Figure 3 and the zone numbers may be written against the points plotted to represent sample averages. This will indicate each point's significance in relation to the sample range. The 'absurdity' value has been found useful as indicative of invalidity in the sample, perhaps due to a clerical error, rather than of lost process control.

A PRACTICAL APPLICATION OF THE MASSED BATTERY OF CHARTS

A scheme of production control had been installed in a works department producing a great variety of products on varied machinery. The essence of this scheme lay in its ability to forecast production times in circumstances predictable only in terms of statistical chance.

It was certainly possible to compute, in any given case, what the theoretical production time should be, and a multi-stage nomograph was designed to do this. But the contingency factors of variable efficiency in mechanical performance and materials handling, of arbitrary hold-ups and breakdowns, and of inhibited levels of activity, could not be accounted for in this way. A productivity index was therefore calculated to measure the effect of these losses, which consisted of the percentage ratio between theoretical and actual times for a given job.

This index was computed for every production job done over a very long period and the distribution of the indices was examined. With the aid of machine methods to sort punched cards bearing these data, various statistical analyses were carried out and causes of variation in productivity were identified. Thus it became possible to divide production into 45 significantly different groups. Each group was verbally defined in terms of machines and processes and was associated with a definite frequently distribution of productivity indices, estimates of the parameters of which had been calculated.

A final stage could now be added to the nomograph. This multiplied the theoretical time for a job by the reciprocal of the mean productivity appropriate to the group to which the job belonged. Thus a dependable forecast of actual time became obtainable from the nomograph in a few seconds' work. Forecasts predicted in this way have been used for all purposes of production control for a year, and have proved very accurate.

It is, however, evident that this system can only operate in this rigid form while productivity remains substantially constant. If the factors affecting productivity change the nomograph ceases to be appropriate. Hence it is essential that the mean level of productivity for each group should be constantly watched, and this is done by routine sampling from each group coupled with the use of control charts. When it becomes clear from the chart that a significant change in mean productivity is occurring a special analysis is made of the group affected. Should a new mean be established the movable final scale on the nomograph is altered. In this way all forecasts made take into account the very latest information about changes in productivity on the shop floor.

The working of an actual chart can be illustrated from Figure 2. The figures on the right indicate the zone of range probability associated with the sample average plotted. (This is an actual example: it figures in the apparatus as group 6.27.) In more than half the cases the zone is either 3 or 4, which is to be expected if control is good. The three cases of zone 6, however, certainly indicate the need for investigation into process variability.

In two instances alone did the sample average point give rise to doubts. On the first occasion the range zone was 6. This indicated that the process variability had gone out of control; hence the limits for the sample average had become temporarily inappropriate and its significance was therefore doubtful. A check sample gave a similar result. Enquiry in the works revealed that the process was undergoing experimental modification in an attempt to improve performance without any definite result. No action was taken. The next sample showed the same process variability, zone 6, with a return to normality in the average. The attempt to improve productivity in this way was, in fact, proving abortive and was abandoned. Subsequently the range came back into control, as can be seen from the chart.

When next the inner limit for the average was exceeded, however, the range was in zone 1 and thus significantly low. This indicated that the upward change in mean productivity, highly significant in its extent as the chart shows, had been achieved with remarkable uniformity. A full-scale experiment was therefore instituted immediately and a new and significantly different estimate of mean productivity was obtained. This new value was then fed into the production control system; the nomograph was adjusted to give improved forecasts, and the new mean was substituted in the control chart procedure. Thus the next sample average point was ringed to show that the group was now working on a new level of productivity. The ringed point, and those points following, had in fact been calculated from the new figure.

CONCLUSION

If, as is to be hoped, the use of statistical control is becoming more extensive, it seems likely that large-scale schemes of control may become less rare.

In the present case the scheme quoted was part of a pilot system of production control installed in one department. Its success is to lead to a much more general application. The implied problem of statistical control is vast, as the use of several hundreds of control charts must be envisaged. Anyone responsible for such a scheme who tries to keep a personal check on graphical progress will be confronted by a serious problem in terms of time and convenience. The present technique of massed batteries is seen as a first step towards the solution of this problem.

Thanks are expressed to David A. Hopkins, who collaborated, and to the management of Messrs Samuel Fox & Company Ltd for permission to publish this account.

CATTEREL

I don't like cats I am afraid—
They are my pet aversions.
I will not toast a marmalade,
I've had my mede of persians.

The messy brutes come home at dawn—
They look morose and baleful.
They're making hay, not earning corn;
They drink milk by the pailful.

The vet came round and fixed our cat—
But he remains exultant.
With glasses, brief-case, bowler hat
He's now a top consultant.

Stafford Beer
1962

4 THE PRODUCTIVITY INDEX IN ACTIVE SERVICE*

STAFFORD BEER
Samuel Fox and Co. Ltd

Mr Beer describes a productivity index that has been used in a steel works in production planning and control. He deals with the technical and administrative as well as with the statistical aspects of his subject and discusses additional management uses of the index. The subject is treated from the point of view of a works with a large number of varied and changing products.

WHAT IS THE PRODUCTIVITY INDEX?

THERE ARE many ways of measuring productivity, some more effective than others. 'Output per man-hour', for instance, is not a very satisfactory measure because it takes no account of input factors other than time and labour. A rather different approach, recommended by the Anglo-American Council on Productivity [1], compares the *objective* time for a process (the time it really should take when everyone is working hard and the process has been brought to its ultimate level of technical efficiency) with the *actual* time for that process (the time it really did take). Thus:

$$\text{Productivity Index (PI)} = \frac{\text{Objective time}}{\text{Actual time}} \times 100$$

The advantage of this form of index lies in its comprehensiveness; it takes everything into account, and provides a common measure of productivity for any mixture of machines, processes and products.

The main difficulty in producing such an index lies in obtaining a good estimate for the numerator. The best basis is a mathematical formula of

*This article is based on a paper given at a conference of the Industrial Applications Section of the Royal Statistical Society held at Cranfield in September 1953.

First published by Blackwell Publishers, Oxford.

the process concerned. If such a formula can be constructed it is a simple matter to apply any set of variables to it, and to read off the objective time for the job to which the variables relate.

Here is a simple formula for a cold rolling mill in the steel industry. We have a number c of coils of steel strip, b inches in breadth, to be rolled to g inches in thickness, and weighing w pounds in all. The steel has a density of d pounds per cubic inch, and the average speed of the mill is v feet a minute. It takes H minutes handling time to mount and take off each coil; and h minutes handling time is further consumed each time the strip is passed through the mill, which happens p times. Then the objective time will be given by:

$$t = p\left(\frac{w}{12dbgv}\right) + chp + cH$$

This formula will be correct whatever the actual numbers, and so we can feed into it the numerical details for any job. It simply calculates the theoretical length of the strip, which is then divided by the theoretical speed to give a total 'run through' time. This has to be multiplied by p, which may be either an empirical estimate or a theoretical calculation. The allowances h and H are best obtained by time study. Dividing 100 times the result by the time the job actually took will give a percentage measure of productivity. This is the index for that job.

ANALYSIS OUTPUT IN TERMS OF THE INDEX

If we now take a record of production and calculate the productivity index of every job contained in that record, a set of results will be obtained to give an extremely good picture of what is happening on the shop floor. Remember that these results can be compared with each other, whatever the product of process may be, because objective times have all been calculated in relation to an ultimate standard of attainment.

There are, however, some dangerous pitfalls in choosing a statistical sample of production for this purpose. In collecting data from a whole department, the temptation to tabulate them as a matter of course in groups with which everyone is already familiar should be resisted. Products which are associated in everyone's minds for marketing reasons cannot necessarily be grouped together as having commensurable levels of productivity. Equally, machines with similar levels of *production* may operate at quite different productivities. For this sort of reason there may be no genuine basis for regarding a specially chosen sample of work as typical of production: it may merely be typical of the chooser's prejudice. Random sampling is also unwise at this stage because it would have to assume a framework within which to operate. For example, since the precise weighting over an unknown period or unrecognized cycle of any one unknown factor may be of crucial importance, random sampling may not yield sufficient information. Unfortunately, the use of balanced designs is nearly always impracticable in plants working under the pressure of full production; there may be unacceptable delays in obtaining the necessary combinations of factors, and replication may be literally impossible. In short, any sort of experimentation is difficult; we must use data relating to the situation as it already happens to be.

The only practicable procedure in making the primary analysis seems to be to lift the whole body of production records on to statistical data sheets, covering as long a period as seems needed to take into account any cyclical variation which may exist. Fixing this period means making an assumption, and it is well to test the proposal beforehand. In one department a six-week period proved adequate; in another, it was more than six months.

When a mass of data has been collected in this way, and operating schedules have been built up to supply the values of variables required to work out the formula for objective time, it can be collected ready for the calculation of indices. This is accomplished on desk-calculating machines which work out the formula according to a set routine which the operator quickly learns. Thousands of commensurable indices then become available for examination. They probably range from zero (a measure of complete breakdown) to over 100 (a measure of the exceeding of allegedly maximum performance). In a big department these data will need to be handled on punched cards; even so, a full-scale multifactor analysis of variance would be a virtually impracticable task.

The means adopted to introduce order into this chaos vary and are difficult to describe in detail. Firstly, however, we break up the data into 'atomic' sub-groups. This means separating products, process and machines, and gradually increasing the number of divisions until the whole situation has been factorized. The stage of atomic factorization is recognized both by the logic of the situation, and by the statistical factor of productive homogeneity within each group as determined by significance testing. That is, each little group of indices has a homogeneous frequency distribution with a single mode, which represents a distinct 'parcel' of output.

The second stage is to synthesize the 'atoms' into 'molecules'. By this I mean that similar atomic sub-groups may be coalesced to form 'molecular' groups, use being made of the orthodox techniques of significance testing. When a molecular group is completed (that is, when no further atomic parts can be merged into it), the effective cause of its significant difference from other groups can be determined as the common factor of its constituent atoms. This analogy from chemistry is useful, because it indicates the sort of grouping that is valid. Only those atomic groups which there is logical reason to suppose really hang together should be tested against each other.

To elaborate this point a little, let us consider what might happen in practice. Product A and product B are manufactured on the same machine by the same operators. A and B themselves are almost the same: they differ only, say, in that B is half an inch wider than A. These are atomic groups already isolated by the primary analysis, and it is reasonable to ask whether these atoms belong to the same molecule. Unless some critical limit exists in that half-inch of width, there seems no good reason why they should not be classified together. We therefore compare the parameters of each atom, A and B, by *t*- and *F*-tests and find no significant difference between them. The molecular group (A + B) is then established. If, on the other hand, there were a significant difference, we should be driven to the conclusion that for some reason—possibly the existence of a critical width, possibly of another and unrecognized factor—the two atomic groups must be kept separate as belonging to different molecules. The attempt to merge two atoms into a single molecule may even be justified when A and B refer to different machines if there is some strong link between them. For instance, the two machines may both operate within the same scheme of wage incentives. If they have been rated for this purpose in a way calculated to tie comparable rewards to comparable effects, it will not be surprising if the productivity distributions are also tied together.

We must not, however, be misled by a coincidental similarity in statistical parameters to merge atoms which clearly cannot belong to the same molecule. Consider two products X and Y, which have nearly the same mean productivity and variance. Product X is a coil of wire resulting from a drawing process; product Y is a small forging produced in a press. Significance tests will indicate that X and Y belong to the same population, whereas they quite obviously do not. This pitfall is particularly important in this type of work but it is not unfamiliar in statistics generally. In fact it is a sort of 'nonsense correlation' and merely indicates that methods of statistical inference are not independent of other forms of logic. The building of a realistic statistical framework on which data can be hung always calls for insight and diligence.

Summing up, we may say that the output of a whole department can be subjected to this analysis. As a result, that output will be split into a number of 'productivity groups', each of which will be defined in two ways. Firstly, it refers to certain products undergoing certain processes on certain machinery. Secondly, it is most important statistical parameters are known: there is a mean productivity with a known variance. Our insight into the department is almost complete, and is expressed in a statistical form convenient to handle.

A NECESSARY TRANSFORMATION

Before we can follow the development of this productivity system into any sort of action, a statistical problem must be faced. The statistical parameters mentioned are not sufficient unless the distribution of productivities within each group is also stated or is normal. If, as has been so far assumed, the analysis is carried out on the raw indices themselves there is a strong tendency for a distribution skewed to the left. The reason for this is easy to see.

Suppose that the mean PI is 90 with a standard deviation of 10. If, for the moment, we assume the distribution to be normal, 31.73 per cent of the total area will fall outside the one-sigma limits of 90 ± 10. Hence nearly 16 per cent of occurrences will fall beyond the 100 value. But the index is so constructed that a PI of 100 cannot be exceeded. The result is that productivity rising above the mean of 90 will tend asymptotically to the 100 maximum and the 16 per cent of occurrences which would in normal circumstances spread beyond the 100 mark will agglomerate between the mean and 100, together with the 34 per cent of occurrences contained in that 99–100 area as of right. This 'agglomeration effect' is inherent in the nature of the index; if it is not present, it will tend to become present as efficiency increases. Even when the mean PI is so low that the spread is in no danger of agglomerating against the 100 limit, the resistance of that ultimate inhibition may be felt and may produce an asymmetrical distribution. I have found these productivity distributions particularly susceptible to this form of skewness, which can easily give rise to a 'precipice' effect.

The PI distribution is similar in appearance to the binomial distribution, and the transformation that would be used for the latter, that is the inverse sine transformation, eliminates the objectionable agglomeration effect, as may be seen in Figure 1, and makes the distribution substantially normal.

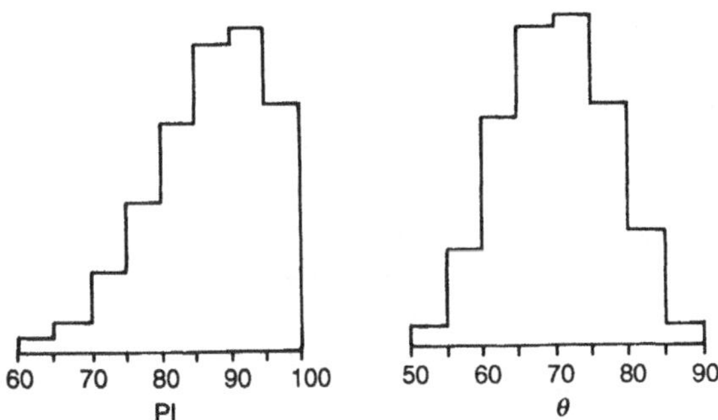

Figure 1 Distributions illustrating how the 'agglomeration effect' of indices against an ultimate limit is dispersed by the inverse sine transformation which makes the distribution approximately normal

Accordingly, every productivity index is transformed to the angle θ, according to the expression:

$$\theta = \sin^{-1}\sqrt{(x/X)}$$

where x is the PI and X is the inhibiting limit, which in this case is 100. Tables are available [2] from which θ may be read directly for the ratio x/X $(-x/100)$.

The mathematical account of this [3] and of another, similar [4], transformation is interesting; but the practical conclusion is that all indices should be transformed from the start, when they will become more amenable to treatment as members of normal distributions.

HOW TO KEEP THE GROUPS RUNNING

The picture so far is a static one, correct at the time of primary analysis. But what of the future? If the analysis has been properly done, the analyst expects that the productivity groups will not promptly disintegrate. But productivity does change; so it is likely that the groups will change in mean value as time goes by. Hence, to make the picture dynamic it will be necessary to *control* the parameters of the groups as a matter of routine.

This may be done by means of control charts, one of which is drawn up for each productivity group. The data are obtained from a sampling programme according to which every shift in a four-weekly period is numbered. At the end of each period, a group of these code numbers is randomly selected and sent to the recording section of the production department, where the output details of the shifts thereby identified are entered on a form. The data constitute a random sample of each group; but the adequacy of the sample sizes is difficult to forecast because the amount of production time spent under each group heading varies from period to period. In order to ensure that the sample size cannot possibly fall below 5 per cent of the output, it has been necessary to fix the number of shifts drawn in each group independently and at a level which in practice results in an average sample size for the whole department of 12 per cent.

The data sheets on which the periodic samples are compiled are then subjected to the computation schedule mentioned earlier. This calculates the index for each shift, and its 'inverse sine', and finally produces the sample means and ranges in terms of θ. The charts on which these figures are plotted are based on parameters of the original but transformed indexical groups, with inner limits at $1.96\sigma/\sqrt{n}$ and outer limits at $3.09\sigma/\sqrt{n}$. Thus they are orthodox charts from the point of view of theory, although a novel graphical method of plotting them has been devised. This technique [5] enables the charts to be massed in batteries of uniform ranks, thereby facilitating their handling in large numbers.

By operating these statistical controls in the usual way, we can keep the picture of productivity permanently up-to-date, altering the controlled parameters (after special analysis) whenever they go out of control. In practice, of course, the statistician in charge of the charts will normally notice a tendency towards significant change. Except in unusual cases, which are probably heralded, such changes do not happen overnight. When the periodic sample regularly gives a value outside the inner limits, the statistician will take some measure to reach an early decision; he will at least ask for intermediate samples so that the incipient change may be watched.

As far as trends are concerned, various techniques of recognition are particularly appropriate and deserve mention. Firstly, there is the chi-squared testing of the frequencies attached to plus and minus values of samples about the control mean. Secondly, there is the ratio test developed by von Neumann which recognizes sequences, a form of which (complete with significance tables) has been evolved by Baines [6]. The application of this is well treated in a useful American publication [7]. Again, there is the expedient of hastening decisions on control charts by contracting the outer limits. This may be done, without waste, by increasing the sample to what is by definition [8] its most economical size.

So far, we have been considering the control of established groups; this leaves the question of new groups, which may be constructed from data relating to new machines or new processes. Assuming that a new group has been identified, and validated in the way earlier described, it can either be regarded as a new discrete entity, or (if the proper conditions are fulfilled) it can be coalesced with an existing group. In an established and comprehensive system, it is likely that the new group will correspond markedly with one or two existing groups.

The decision as to whether two groups can be coalesced will be based as before on the logic of the situation; statistically, it will require the acceptance or rejection of the null hypothesis as to the identity of their two means. Further, it is desirable that a significance test aimed at making this decision should pronounce on the question with all speed, and this suggests the use of a sequential test. Such a test [9], derived from Wald's theory of sequential analysis, has been used. It does, however, present difficulties in this particular context and a simple sequential version of the u-test may be preferable. This tests undistributed samples into an existing group variance according to the statistic $u=(\bar{x}-\mu)\sqrt{n}/\sigma$. All that is required is to accumulate the results of the new product as time goes by, plotting Σx against n for a chosen significance of u. This procedure is extremely economical in sample sizes.

A VALUABLE MODIFICATION

The general Productivity Index so far described is a ratio between the *objective* and the *actual* time. Its movements indicate changes, the nature of which it is impossible to assess without further information. A refinement may be introduced by creating a third time concept called the *standard* time. This will normally fall between the other two times. It is arranged to modify the full objective time, which represents all factors as operating at maximum efficiency, by relaxing the stringency of each of those factors. The criterion for this procedure is the extent to which it is technically difficult to achieve the objective levels. For example, the speed of the process may have to be scaled down to accord with current limitations in lubrication or temperature control; ratings for handling may be lowered to allow for imperfections in the handling techniques; and, most of all, an allowance will have to be added to allow for the current level of technical stoppage to the plant.

This standard time, like the objective time, is worked out from a modified form of the original formula. The point is that the difference between objective and standard is a measure of current technical shortcomings. The ratio of the two times provides a new index thus:

$$\text{Current Technical Index (CTI)} = \frac{\text{Objective time}}{\text{Standard time}} \times 100$$

Movements in this index provide a measure of change in *technical* efficiency.

Since, moreover, the technical influences on the general Productivity Index have been isolated in this way, it follows that the element of change still unaccounted for must be due to non-technical operating factors. This element is the difference between the standard and actual times and is a measure of labour utilization. This yields the index:

$$\text{Labour Utilization Index (LUI)} = \frac{\text{Standard time}}{\text{Actual time}} \times 100$$

Movements in this index provide a measure of change in *labour* efficiency.

If these two subsidiary indices are multiplied together and divided by 100 the general Productivity Index is the result. Hence, by keeping records of these indices as well, we provide ourselves with an insight into the nature of productivity changes as well as a measure of their movements. This procedure is recommended by the originators of this productivity measure [1].

FORECASTING PRODUCTION TIMES

Once the whole output of a production department has been analysed in terms of the triple index of productivity, organized into statistical groups, and subjected to routine statistical control, real action can begin. The fundamental notion behind all the uses to which this set-up has been put is the notion of a production forecast. However complicated the job, and even if it is a hitherto untried manufacture, this forecast is now quite easy to make.

The specification of the job, together with the appropriate scheduled factors, are fed into the mathematical formulae for the objective time. The objective time is a useful limiting concept in that we have a target and a measure of ultimate capacity, but is unrealistic as a forecast. Suppose that, postulating ultimate labour efficiency of 100 per cent, it is desired to know the standard time; then it is only necessary to multiply the objective time by the reciprocal of the Current Technical Index. To find the realistic production forecast, duly weighted for both technical and labour factors, we multiply the objective time by the reciprocal of the Productivity Index itself. The PI figure used is the mean value of the productivity group to which the job belongs. Its current validity is guaranteed by the statistical control.

In what way is this technique of forecasting preferable to the more primitive method of taking actual average times and making corrections to suit changed circumstances? Firstly, in jobbing production it might be necessary to hold a library of perhaps 4000 such actual averages, which can now be replaced by about 70 PI control groups. Secondly, the keeping of control charts for the separate jobs would be a superhuman task; experience shows that these historical standards rapidly become out of date and cannot be kept up-to-date by a staff of reasonable size. Thirdly, a considerable proportion of jobs may be new work, previously unattempted. Someone then has to guess which standard to use. By the new method, a new job can be fitted into its proper PI group on sight, because the catalogue of groups collectively exhausts the possibilities of production. An experiment carried out on the ability of historical standards to forecast the actual times of jobbing work on samples of five shifts gave an error of 70 per cent. This was partly due to the standards being out of date, and partly due to wrong judgements as to which would be the nearest standard to use. The error incurred on similar samples when the new technique was used was less than 3 per cent.

The accuracy of these forecasts is extremely high and it is worth considering the main reason why this should be so, for, one might argue, the whole calculation is based on a rather arbitrary estimate of objective time. Suppose, for instance, the handling allowances made at that stage were quite unrealistic? The answer is that this simply does not matter. If the primary analysis has incorporated an error of this sort in the objective, the index will also incorporate the error. When the forecast is made, the same mistake is made in the objective, and is cancelled out when the index is applied as a weight. To demonstrate:

$$\begin{aligned}\text{Forecast time} &= \text{Objective} \times 1/\text{PI}\\ &= \text{Objective} \times \text{Actual}/\text{Objective}\\ &= \text{Actual}\end{aligned}$$

Any constant added to or subtracted from the objective in error or by misjudgement will not affect this forecast.

This formulae in Figure 2 gather together all the threads of this discussion to this point, and consider them from the standpoint of their main function—forecasting. This is an actual example, which extends to its full state the system as applied to steel strip manufacture. The model is applicable to all continuous processes and not merely to rolling as described in the introductory section.

PRODUCTION CONTROL

I have shown how heterogeneous output may be measured in terms of a triple index of productivity, how the work of a factor may be classified in terms of this measure, and how this measure may be used to convert theoretical expectations of production into dependable long-term forecasts. I have also described a means of controlling this system, once installed, with the object of ensuring that the forecasts made are consistent with latest developments on the shop floor. There are refinements, not mentioned, but I have described the general structure of a scheme which has been found to be practicable. A tool of some power has been forged, which, for the reasons given two paragraphs ago, is independent of the uncertainties of time study, and which has many applications remote from its immediate provision of forecasts.

It was, indeed, to facilitate production control that the scheme was actually devised. Thorough control of planning requires a thorough understanding of production. It is this which is so hard to obtain in a diversified works, and this which once obtained is so hard to formulate exactly. The technique achieves both these objectives. It remains to settle the mechanics of programming on this basis, which resolves into a question of how to compute these scientific forecasts in an ordinary clerical office.

Where $T = 100t_o/P$

$$P = 100\frac{t_o}{t_s}\cdot\frac{t_s}{t_a}\ (t_o \leqslant t_s \leqslant t_a)$$

$$t_o = p\left(\frac{w}{12dbgv}\right) + chp + cH$$

$$t_s = p\left(\frac{w}{12dbgv'}\right) + ch'p + cH' + zc + Zc$$

and

$$t_a = re/i$$

θ is normally distributed for:

$$\theta = \sin^{-1}\sqrt{(P/100)}$$

Key:

T = forecast time, P = productivity index

Inferred quantities
t_o = objective time
t_s = standard time
t_a = actual time

Given quantities
i = time involved
e = time expected to work
r = time recorded as worked

Variables
p = number of passes
w = weight in lb.
b = breadth of strip
g = thickness of strip
c = number of coils

Constants for any given job
d = density in lb per cu. inch
v = objective, v' = standard } process speed
h = objective, h' = standard } handling time per pass
H = objective, H' = standard } handling time per coil
z = regular, Z = irregular } technical stops estimated per coil

Note Slight adjustments are also made in practice to compensate for time losses due to acceleration and deceleration.

Figure 2 A display of the quantities and formulae used in developing the productivity index and forecast of the time to pass a batch of coils of steel strip through a given process on a given machine

That problem of the day-to-day calculation of forecasts was overcome by a multi-stage nomograph. This was designed and built specifically to calculate, from an order for strip, a forecast of production time required. The particular chart is 6 feet long and consists of 11 interlocking nomographic cycles, but other charts have been produced to solve different formulae. All are covered with sixteenth-inch transparent plastic, and transparent rules with sharply pointed ends are used to move across them; this, it is found, gives an error of the order of only 1 per cent. Constants are built in, and the operator has merely to impart the information on the order form, and the value of the variables contained in his schedules. The nomograph then solves the equation for objective time, and adjusts it by the appropriate productivity constants. Thus the objective, the standard and the actual times may all be forecast for a given job in something under a minute.

These three times are the raw material for whatever answers may be required from a production control scheme. Budgets and forecasts based on a variety of assumptions can be composed from them and the differences between them can be interpreted in research, labour, financial, or commercial contexts as required.

The production control scheme within a works department is thus able to operate as an independent entity, except for the functional control of its statistical mechanism. This requires simply that significant changes detected on the centralized control charts are immediately 'fed back' to the nomographic scales dealing with productivity weights. By this means, departmental forecasts are always realistic, being based on the very latest evidence from the shop floor. A diagrammatic representation of the central process by which a departmental scheme is functionally controlled is provided in Figure 3.

DETAILED PRODUCTION STUDIES

It sometimes happens that more detailed insight into production is required than the triple index provides. For instance, it may be necessary to isolate certain factors in order to examine where losses in productivity are occurring. In both types of enquiry, those immediately concerned are tendentiously inclined to use one of the spurious measures (say cost or weight) readily to hand, for one can usually be found to lend verisimilitude to any case. The index, however, is a most useful comprehensive measure from which to start, and by various devices we have been able to elaborate the information contained in the triple index to the point where an answer is forthcoming to both these questions.

When the productivity is already known, and the losses are moreover already allocated (as they are) between technical and labour factors, it merely remains to fill in this framework. The problems of method involved are then more readily solved than by traditional work study investigation. Statistical methods are admirable in this context; those suggested by Abruzzi [7], and the Tippett 'snap-reading' technique [10] have proved especially useful.

ROUTINE REPORTS TO MANAGEMENT

The form in which statistical conclusions can best be presented to management has properly received much attention. For a scheme of this sort,

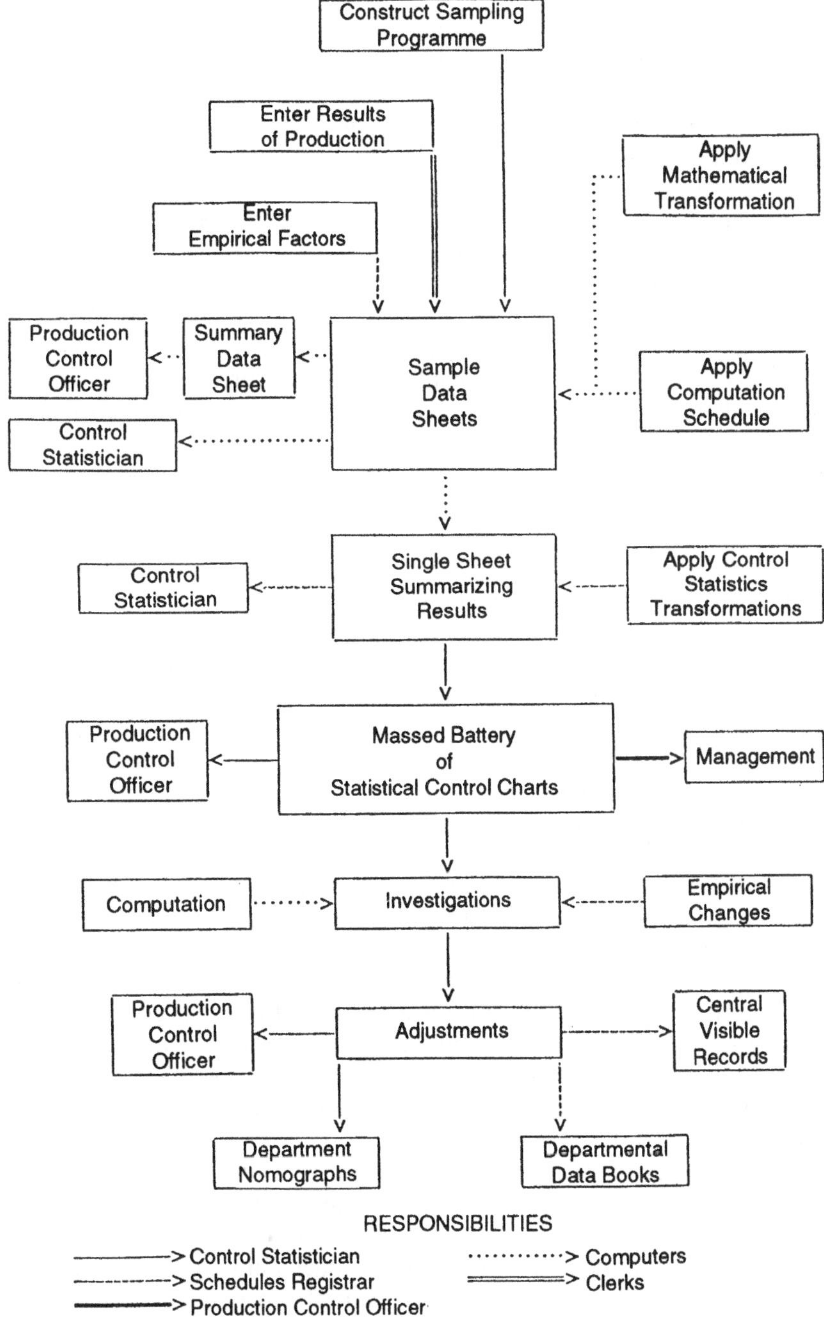

Figure 3 A departmental scheme of production control

the reporting is done in two parts. First, an indexed book is provided as a permanent 'dictionary of productivity', which is kept up-to-date by amendments issued whenever a controlled mean is adjusted. Reference to this book provides management with the history of productivity for any job together with its present level. Second, a report is issued each time a routine sample is drawn, on which are recorded those groups which have departed from the controlled mean to the extent of $1.96\sigma/\sqrt{n}$ or more. The probability level associated with such a sample average is designated on a 'scale of importance' which reaches 10 at the 1-in-40 level and somewhat over-runs the 1-in-100 level at a reading of 16. In addition to this scale, a second or 'variability scale' is quoted which derives [5] from the sample ranges. Each of these scales is calibrated to interpret significance levels to management in ordinary English, using language calculated to inspire action.

COST ACCOUNTING

Without entering into technical details [11] which would not be germane to this article, it will be clear that actual times inferred from this forecasting system can be used in the establishment of accounting standards. The experiment has, in fact, been tried, when the processes described in this paper alone were used to generate (on desk calculators) 120 000 machine/job standards. In the outcome, the discrepancy between the standard cost thus computed and the actual cost of production in the very first month's application was less than 1 per cent.

Apart from its application to standard costing, the productivity index system can offer assistance in analysing the cost of flexibility: a desirable factory 'commodity' which has nevertheless to be bought. The price of flexibility is an 'opportunity cost' of a profound sort, and one which present-day cost accounting practice is probably not in a position to assess at all accurately. I say this because to cost an opportunity forgone requires the costing of an ideal situation; but the ideal situation cannot be identified until *after* it has been costed. This is because the raw measures of output used by accountants are themselves immiscible, and are often put into arbitrary groups.

Triple indices of productivity, however, that are properly understood, systematically ordered, and statistically controlled, can be used very easily to construct an estimate of this opportunity cost in terms of output capacity. They can also apportion this abandoned capacity among the various reasons for which flexibility is demanded; for example, in achieving especially high quality, in implementing a liberal personnel policy, or in meeting special and sudden demands from important customers. Such decisions are matters of company policy. But a statistical control scheme is surely uniquely situated to provide evidence towards the formation of that policy.

THE FUTURE OUTLOOK

A few thoughts on what these statistical applications of productivity indices have led me to think lies ahead may not be out of place. Possibilities for the extension of this type of work appear to be extremely great; and the more traditionally intractable the industry, the more stimulating does the prospect become. Models of the problems undertaken by production control are envisaged which would embrace the whole complex manufacturing structure of, say, an integrated steelworks. The type of model discussed here might, through the theory of queues, be extended to deal with the flow problems of hot metal. Steel making itself will perhaps be amenable to inclusion in models as a stochastic process.

More importantly, comprehensive models of the Leontief type might be constructed, and matrices can be visualized incorporating even the huge number of factors involved in a steelworks economy. Thanks to the theories of games and of linear programming, such static models can now be made dynamic. If electronic calculating machines are ultimately to become available at combine and even company level, as seems likely, the routine handling of such matrices will become possible.

Most major works' control problems are problems of balancing factors to maximize profitability. Some form of linear programme using the productivity index as a common measure of effectiveness might provide a means of solving such problems for industries of the most complex type. The possibilities emerge clearly from the Carnegie Institute discussion [12] of their 'nut-mix' problem. The imposing anthology [13] of work done in America on activity analysis also provides many pointers to the future.

Advances in the increasingly discussed subject of cybernetics, allied with the complex models mentioned, might result in a fully mechanized form of control based on the technique described here. An electronic machine might be fed with punched-card orders, which would promptly be translated into objective times, weighted by a productivity index, and tabulated as production schedules from a linear programming calculation. If the results of production were returned to the machine, fresh productivities could be assessed, as also the statistical probability of the significance of the latest deviation from any given productivity mean. This probability could then be used automatically to adjust the weighting factor by a feedback device.

Such conjectures as these seem to be far-fetched at present, although various experiments are actually in hand along these lines. But if, as I believe, the 'technology of control' has been absurdly outstripped by the technology of the controlled situation, they may serve to encourage the development of the relatively elementary sort of control scheme proposed in this paper.

ACKNOWLEDGEMENTS

I wish to thank Mr David A. Hopkins and my other assistants for their help, and the management of Samuel Fox and Company Limited, Stocksbridge Works, Sheffield, for permission to make public this material.

REFERENCES

1. Anglo-American Council on Productivity, 'Assessing progress by indexes', *Productivity Measurement in British Industry*, 1950.
2. Fisher, R. A. and Yates, F., *Statistical Tables*, 1950. 4th edn, Table XII. Oliver and Boyd, London and Edinburgh, 1953.
3. Eisenhart, C., *Selected Techniques of Statistical Analysis*, Chapter 16. McGraw-Hill Book Co., New York, for Columbia University, 1947.
4. Stevens, W. L., 'Tables of the angular transformation', *Biometrika*, **40**, 70, 1953.
5. Beer, S., 'A technique for standardising massed batteries of control charts', *Applied Statistics*, **2**, 160, 1953.
6. Baines, A. H. J., 'Methods of detecting non-randomness in a given series of observations', Report R/12. Ministry of Supply, Advisory Service on Quality Control, London, 1942.
7. Abruzzi, A., *Work Measurement*, p. 43 *et seq.* Columbia University Press, New York, 1952.
8. Weiler, H., 'On the most economical sample size for controlling the mean of a population', *Ann. Math. Statist.*, **23**, 247, 1952.
9. Columbia University Statistical Research Group, 'Differentiation of measured lot from standard (first method)', Report 255 (revised), Section 5, 1945.
10. Tippett, L. H. C., 'A snap-reading method of making time studies of machines and operatives in factory surveys', *J. Text. Inst.*, **26**, T51, 1935.
11. Beer, S., 'Operational research and accounting', *Operat. Res. Quart.*, **5**, 1, 1954.
12. Charnes, A., Cooper, W. W., and Henderson, A., *An Introduction to Linear Programming*. John Wiley, New York, and Chapman and Hall, London, 1953.
13. Koopmans, T. C. (ed.) *Activity Analysis of Production and Allocation.* Cowles Commission Monograph No. 13. John Wiley, New York, and Chapman and Hall, London, 1951.

COMPUTERS: THE IRISH SEA

That green computer sea
with all its molecular logic
to the system's square inch,
a bigger brain than mine,
writes out foamy equations from the bow
across the bland blackboard water.

Accounting for variables
which navigators cannot even list,
a bigger sum than theirs,
getting the answer continuously right
without fail and without anguish
integrals white on green.

Cursively writes recursively computes
that green computer sea
on a scale so shocking
that all the people sit dumbfounded
throwing indigestible peel at seagulls
not uttering an equation between them.

All this liquid diophantine stuff
of order umpteen million
is its own analogue. Take a turn
around the deck and understand
the mystery by which what happens
writes out its explanation as it goes.

Stafford Beer
Transit, 1977

5 THE MECHANICAL SIMULATION OF STOCHASTIC FLOW

STAFFORD BEER
United Steel Companies Ltd, Sheffield, England

This paper describes the development of a simulation device intended to solve complex queueing problems by the Monte Carlo method.

The basic component of this stochastic analogue machine (SAM) is called a synthetic data generator (SDG). One SDG will simulate any desired probability distribution of process or delay times mechanically. It has an output of ball-bearings such that any one time interval separating one ball from its successor: (a) is directly proportional to a time occurring in the distribution being simulated; (b) occurs with the probability allocated to it by that distribution; (c) is otherwise unpredictable.

SAM itself consists (arbitrarily) of 10 SDGs, which can be connected at will so that the output of any one is the input of any other. A complex interacting situation can thus be set up and run at a fast speed. The machine is intended primarily for the study of steelworks' flow problems, the fluctuations in process stocks being studied in the store of ball-bearings between any pair of SDGs. SAM is, however, a fully versatile OR tool, and has the advantage over electronic computer Monte Carlo methods that its operations can be watched and discussed by management.

IT WOULD be generally agreed that a high percentage of operational research jobs concern stochastic processes in one form or another. In the case, for example, of some queueing problems a rigorous mathematical solution can be obtained. But again there will be general agreement that the mathematical theory is not yet sufficiently developed to undertake many of the problems encountered in practice, and for two main reasons. In even the simplest problem we are as yet limited by the classes of probability function that can be handled; and secondly, many problems are in any case far from simple: they involve a network of interacting input–output

First published by English Universities Press, London.

processes. It is in these circumstances that operational research normally turns to Monte Carlo techniques.

Suppose that an isomorphic model of a complicated stochastic network has been constructed. For example, in a works one production lot passes through a large number of 'episodes' in the course of manufacture. Some of these are processing episodes, some transportation episodes, some stockholding episodes, and so on. The plant is diversified, and there are many different production lots following different routes through the plant. The result is that a large number of episodes, each covering a large number of different types of product, can be catalogued, which between them exhaustively define the whole operation of the plant. If each episode is studied as a population of time variables, and if a satisfactory statistical account can be given of each population (allowing that each episode may divide into a number of significantly different homogeneous groups by virtue of some distinguishing characteristic in products or plant operation), then an isomorphic model has been derived.

A model of this kind is static, lacking the organic thread which traces a particular production lot where it appears in a number of episodes. But if we can generate production lots *through* the system, the model begins to operate. Assuming that successive episodes are not correlated (and this can often be justified in practice by defining episodes so that they are independent with respect to time), the model can be made dynamic by generating a specimen production plan. Each order is started at its first episode, and each episode distribution is randomly sampled in turn until the order has 'left the works'. If this is done for all orders in the production plan, and the results plotted on a time chart representing all episodes, the operation of the works has been simulated.

This has doubtless been done in many places and in many different contexts. When it is done in a steelworks, for example, useful results can be obtained about the balance of plant, the need for stockholding, the utilization of ancillary processes, the accuracy of delivery promises, and the possibility and relative probability of alternative methods of scheduling. All this is most useful. The trouble is that this type of Monte Carlo solution is appallingly tedious and expensive in time; in fact it may be quicker to observe the works than to study the model.

THE APPROACH TO THE MONTE CARLO

What are the possible approaches to the mechanical simulation of stochastic flow? The first and most obvious technique is to set up a Monte Carlo on an ordinary electronic computer. This solution offers the problem of feeding so determinate a machine with a source of random variation. Several methods suggest themselves, from a punched tape version of a table of random numbers to the capture and coding of alpha-particles from radioactive emission. No doubt a satisfactory solution can be found, although one ought perhaps to entertain philosophic doubts about any determinate computer-like technique. It is difficult to offer a convincing artefact of a process like randomness, the real meaning of which is doubtful. But the major objection to the computer technique is undoubtedly cost.* If one wished to study a really complicated production situation through most of the major combinations of its episodes, one could easily engage a computer's whole capacity for many weeks.

Once an *ad hoc* machine is considered, a major decision has to be taken. This concerns the *selling power* of the machine. Is it enough to build a large box which points out the results required? The answer is: probably not; and this is an argument which also applies to the standard electronic computer when used on this work.

Consider a typical stochastic flow problem; for example, one where the object is to investigate optimal levels of buffer production stocks. The mathematical problem is well understood; the operational research problem as a whole, however, must be taken as something more than a mathematical exercise. Stock levels, once calculated, have to be accepted by management. Now stocks are in insurance against 'the evil day', against mischance. Managers generally are chary about reducing stocks and are not likely to do so with a good grace merely because a box of electronics tells them that such a course is safe.

Please note that this psychological problem arises here because of the subject being considered. Managers do accept computer results on accounting calculations and on the solution of research problems involving, say, the evaluation of partial differentials. But we have not yet convinced managers generally that it is even possible to calculate an optimal stock level incorporating a given risk. Men are inclined to regard advance statistics of this kind with suspicion, and, after all the talking has been done, to claim that their experience cannot by any means (especially by what they may regard as pseudo-scientific means) be gainsaid.

Thus of all the possible machines which could be built to simulate a stochastic process, it is necessary to choose one which *demonstrably* produces the solution. We assume that managers are, or can be made, familiar with the histogram generated by a probability function. They can be persuaded that results (safe stock levels) depend upon the random selection of episodic time variables from such a 'population of risks'. If they can see a process of sampling deriving the required results, we are able to obtain their co-operation.

**Editors' Note* A timely reminder of the historical context, and the computational limits faced.

Figure 1 shows the way in which this argument is presented. It is seen that, if the two distributions are independent, a pair of events selected randomly, one from each distribution, may result in one of three situations. If the two times are identical, then theoretically no stock is created between the machines. If the second machine takes 10 hours while the first machine takes only 6 hours, the piece produced in the first machine waits 4 hours in a queue, and forms a positive stock. In the reverse situation, the second machine is idle (if there is nothing waiting) and a production vacuum, or 'negative stock', is created. Obviously, the manager agrees, the size of a safe buffer stock will depend on the way in which these random occurrences happen to work out. Emphasis on this adventitious feature of the problem appeals to the manager: it accords with his experience and understanding of the unpredictability of works' events.

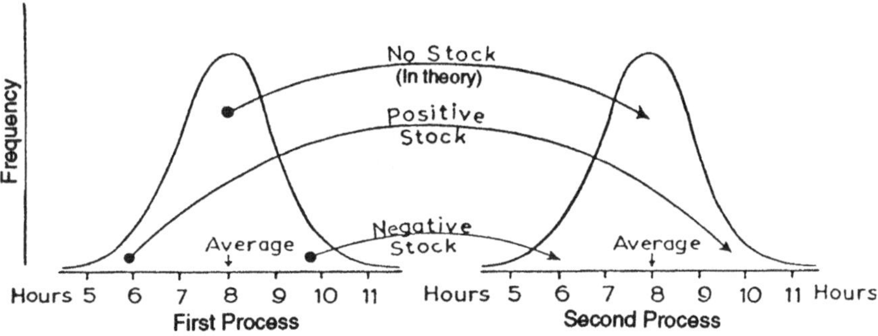

Figure 1 Presentation of queuing process in probability distribution of process times

The answer to this operational research problem of stochastic flow plus solution selling has been to construct a pair of synthetic data generators, which function together as a stochastic analogue machine. SAM will produce answers for a pair of successive episodes in a visible, saleable, way. We are producing a greatly enlarged version of the prototype SAM, capable of handling at least 10 probability functions. Whether this can be a mere 'box of tricks', relying for selling power on the original two-stage visible artefact, or whether the whole 10-stage version must also be visible, is a difficult question. (It is emphasized that this problem is solely a psychological one.) It is possible that the final machine may be entirely visible, but less cumbersome than the prototype version here described.

LOGICAL SPECIFICATION OF THE STOCHASTIC ANALOGUE MACHINE

A stochastic analogue machine measures the probability interaction of a number of temporal functions representing a network of episodes in a model of stochastic flow. It is designed for the general case of a Monte Carlo experiment and can be turned into the visible artefact of any stochastic situation.

These are its main features:

1. It must consist of a number of synthetic data generators, where an SDG is defined as a machine having an output of times, uniformly proportional to clock times, which conform in the long run to a given probability distribution, but in which any particular event is unpredictable.
2. Each SDG must deal with any kind of probability function (and not just those of Poissonian type), even to the point of simulating pragmatic distributions which are insusceptible to description by mathematical statistics.
3. The SDGs must be interconnected, in any desired fashion, so that the output of one is the input of another. Each defines an episode in the model, and the episodes conjointly exhaust the model.
4. Normally, the nth episode SDG is directly connected to the nth + 1 episode SDG. But it must be possible for any SDG to feed, or be fed by, two or more SDGs. This multiple input/output may be arranged according to either a determinate rule (e.g. alternate outputs to SDG (m) and SDG (n)) or a statistical rule (e.g. proportions of output to m and n).
5. The output of any SDG must be a constant function of its input but is not necessary a one–one correlate. For it is possible that the units whose separation measures the episodic time variable will not maintain their identity. For example, Episode 1 may have an output of ingots which form the input to Episode 2. But whereas Episode 1 stands for a process which handles ingots as separate entities, Episode 2 may refer to a process which handles ingots in lots of 10. Conversely, a bogey of 10 ingots in Episode 2 may disintegrate into five pairs of two ingots in Episode 3.

This specification excludes two aspects of the general case of a Monte Carlo simulation. Both derive from the fact that we have assumed the stochastic process involved to be fundamentally Markovian. In practice, the Markov property may be modified either by autocorrelation in the time-series of episodes, or by specific feedback from a finishing episode to its forerunners.

There seem to be three possible approaches towards evading this limitation. The definition of episodes is arbitrary, and (as mentioned earlier) ingenuity may sometimes succeed in adopting a system of groups which are definitively independent. Secondly, it may be possible to feed non-Markovian interference, or specific feedback, into the system using an SDG as an artefact of this kind of noise. Thirdly, for certain kinds of feedback, it may be possible to interfere with either SDG input rates or their 'constant delay' mechanisms by *ad hoc* electrical connections. Depending on how these possibilities work out, it may be decided to adopt the present design. Alternatively, this argument may prove to be the final justification for abandoning visible operation in the big machine.

PHYSICAL SPECIFICATION OF THE SAM

Many possible SDGs could be designed, and quite a number have been. The Mark 2 and Mark 3 versions are discussed here, with reference to Figure 2.

In each case, the unit of product is represented by a ball-bearing: this is the physical input and output of the SDG, although the logical input and output is the lapse of time between the ball-bearings. Ball-bearings in the neutral and return reservoirs have no analogue significance. We will now consider the operation of an SDG representing Episode 2 of a series of Episodes 1, 2 and 3.

The output of SDG 1 activates the artefact input gate of SDG 2. This has the effect of inserting a unit of product in the analogue store which measures the queue of products in front of Episode 2. The output of SDG 2 activates the gate leading out of the analogue store and withdraws a product unit from this queue. This ball, which now has product significance, falls through the three-stage equiprobability statistical randomizer. This is an empirical device for admitting the ball into one of 100 compartments, so that it has the same probability of arriving in each. These 100 compartments are randomly connected to 20 other compartments in the frequency distribution artefact. The number of connections to each of the 20 compartments is preset according to the probability function it is desired to generate.

Thus any probability distribution, whether mathematically defined or not, is set down as a histogram compounded of 100 equal squares. If there are 20 squares in the modal column, 20 of the equiprobable compartments (randomly selected) are fed to one compartment in the artefact. If there are two squares in the minus-two-sigma column of the histogram, two compartments are fed to another compartment of the artefact. In this way the artefact is set to produce exactly correct proportions of balls in each column of its histographic paradigm. But the prediction of arrival order is impossible, because of the randomizer.

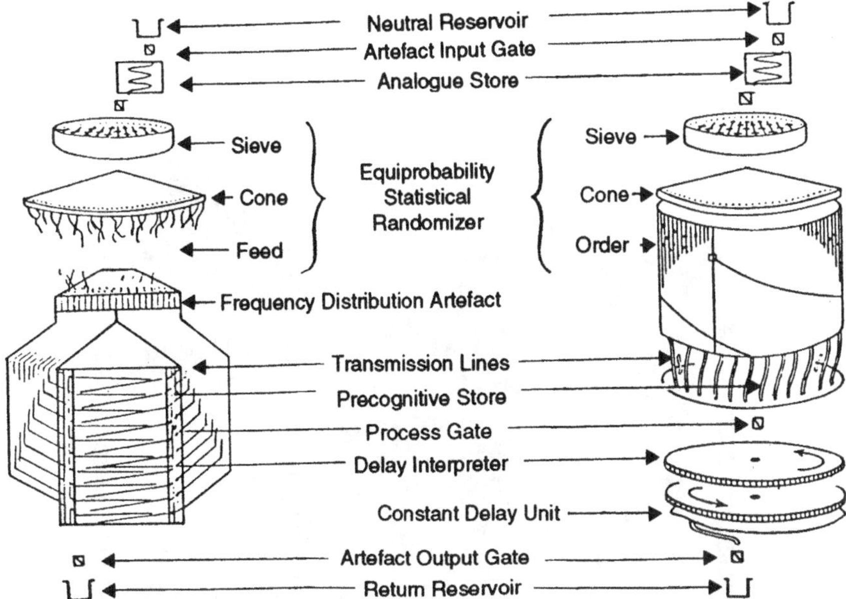

Figure 2 A stochastic analogue machine, incorporating two synthetic data generators. *Left*, SDG Mark II; *right*, SDG Mark III

The three stages of the randomizer can now be enumerated. Firstly, the ball falls through a revolving sieve, whence it falls on to a machined cone. Secondly, it runs down the cone, into one of 100 holes around its periphery. Thirdly, the feed to the artefact compartments, although predetermined as to proportions by the histogram, is set up by random selection. Each of these three stages *separately* produces the required rectangular distribution over the range of 100 holes as tested by various statistical methods.

Once a ball has been channelled through the artefact, it automatically follows a transmission line and arrives in the precognitive store. At this point its time value in the process has been determined; it is merely stored to be ready for use in the actual Monte Carlo. A ball is already being delayed in the delay interpreter. When it emerges, it operates (on its way to the return reservoir) the artefact output gate of the SDG—which is No. 2. This automatically: (i) opens the SDG 2 process gate, allowing a delay to be imparted to the ball we left in the precognitive store; (ii) opens the analogue store gate in SDG 2, sending a new ball through the artefact to be made ready for 'processing'; (iii) opens the artefact *input* gate in SDG 3, thereby sending the 'product' of Episode 2 to join the queue of products in front of Episode 3.

In this way data for Episode 2 are synthetically generated. Similarly, in SDG 3, data for Episode 3 are synthetically generated. The stochastic variation in the queue for Episode 3 is given in the analogue store of SDG 3.

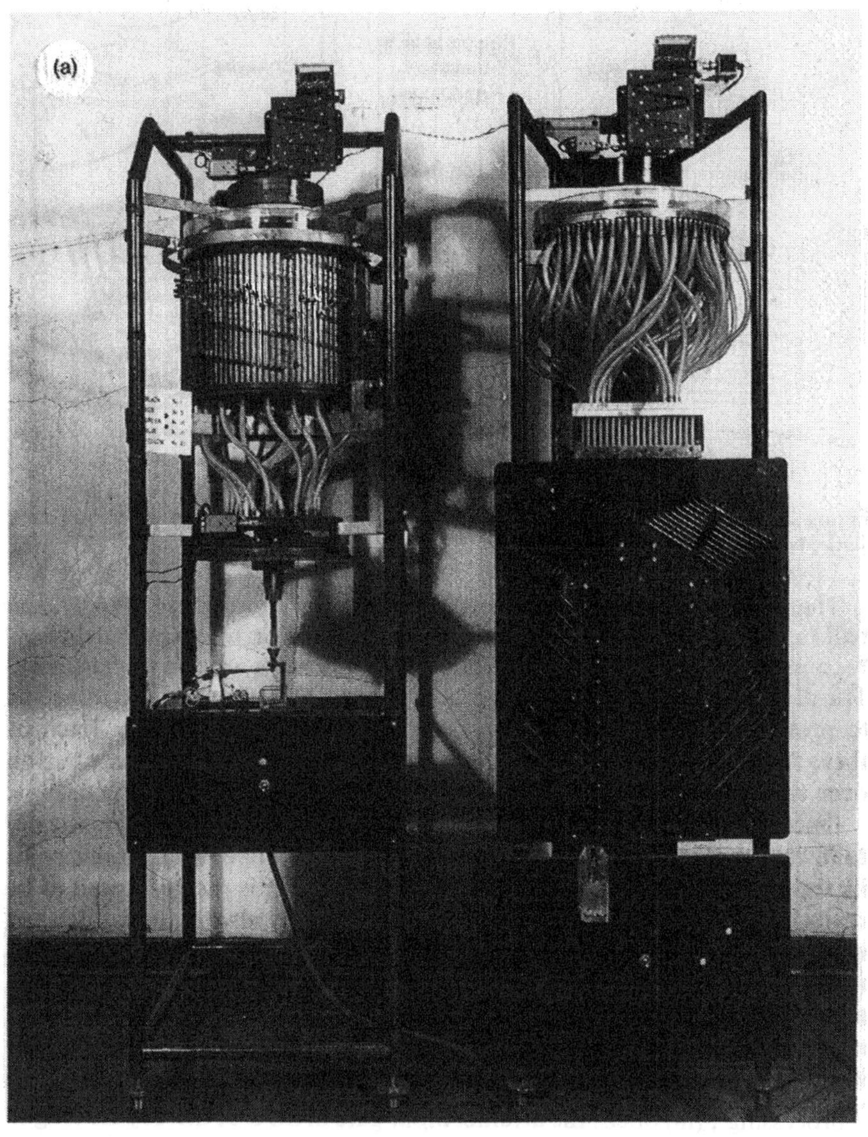

Figure 3 (a) A stochastic analogue machine. *Left*, Mark II; *right*, Mark III. (b)–(d) Detailed pictures of the machine constructed by the author

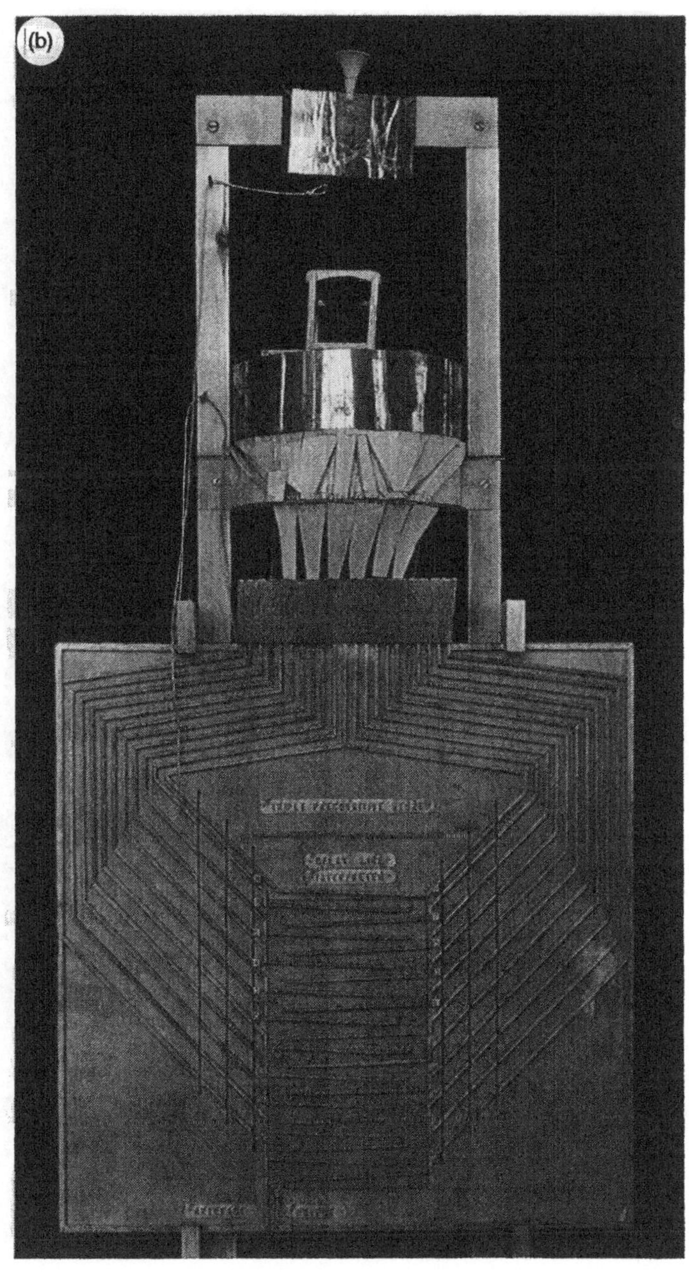

Figure 3 (b)

Figure 3 (c)

Figure 3 (d)

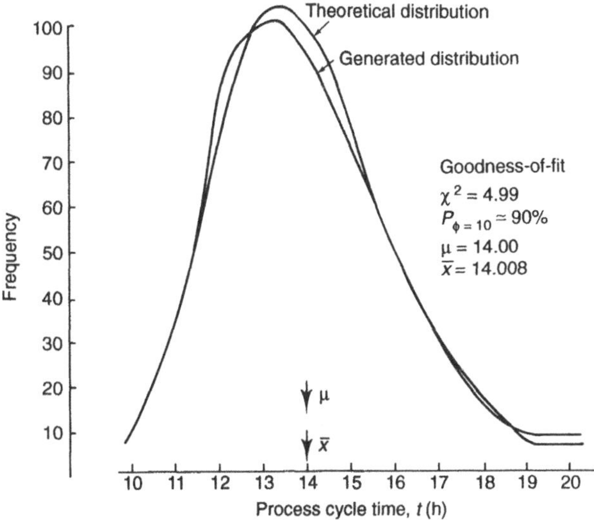

Figure 4 Synthetic data generator (Mark I)

This being increased continually by the output of SDG 2, and diminished continually by the output of SDG 3. Here, then, is the interaction it is required to observe.

This is the simple two-stage situation, and photographs of a SAM for this simulation appear at Figure 3. The means whereby the system may be modified to meet the specification given in point 3, page 65 above, are sufficiently obvious. The constant delay unit incorporated in Mark 3 of the synthetic data generator adds a constant time delay, if required, to move the whole distribution being generated along the time scale. This is sometimes required to make the data between two episodes commensurable.

In Figure 4, as a matter of interest, is given the result of a test (actually on a Mark 1 SDG) in which one generator was tested as a simulator. The simulated distribution was of the Pearson Type III variety. Results, which should be drawn as histograms, are shown as curves for visual effect. The synthetic generator (Mark I) generates:

$$dF(\tau) = \frac{\lambda^{p+1}}{\Gamma(p+1)} e^{\lambda}(\tau - 1)^{p} e^{-\lambda\tau} d\tau$$

$$\lambda = 12 \quad p = 15 \quad t = 6\tau \quad \mu = 6\left(1 + \frac{p+1}{\lambda}\right) = 14$$

It will be noted that the mean, 14 hours in the model, was simulated as 14.008 hours after 500 runs, and that the goodness-of-fit of the whole curve was 90 per cent by a chi-squared test on the histograms.

THOUGHTS ON THE NIGHT BEFORE OPENING A SCIENTIFIC CONFERENCE

Here we are then
in the university hall of residence
where we have the privilege
of putting you up for the night.
And god help you
if you are not up by seven.
Breakfast is served
(collect your knife, fork, spoon)
at eight onwards until eight fifteen
on the far side of those buildings.
And you will not be called,
nor will you be given morning tea,
and you will not even survive
unless you are mighty clever.

You will address three hundred delegates
or so at nine thirty ack emma
having caught the bus
which leaves the gates at nine
for the university proper.
We cannot tell you about blackboards
which you should have asked about earlier.
You will be very comfortable
as our most welcome guest,
and god help you
give a superb keynote address
with or without breakfast
whether you wake up or not.
Goodnight, and that's your lot.

You have some kind of reputation
or you would not have been asked at all
and you will lose such reputation overnight
if you are not brilliant
bloody well brilliant
at nine thirty in the morning.

continued

There is no ashtray
but there is a glass,
moreover a wardrobe—
which is full of Effects
unlocked-away for next term.
Make no mistake
this is not *your* room my friend:
it belongs to a boy worth more than you
he has potential.

Room C11 it is
and there is no bedside light
(students must not be pampered)
and there is no left-over lady
in the chest of drawers.
If you want a drink or a sandwich
please don't ring—because there is no bell
and no staff, and no food
anyway

just be there tomorrow like a good chap
and do your stuff brilliantly
for god's sake, and go.
There is no car—and sorry
the taxis may be called but don't come.
So just go
go on the wings of the morning
and don't come back.
But we will give you lunch
if you request it
without any charge
which is four-and-sixpence—
not that you should feel uncomfortable
about that.

Stafford Beer
Transit, 1977

6 THE IMPACT OF CYBERNETICS ON THE CONCEPT OF INDUSTRIAL ORGANIZATION

First International Congress on Cybernetics

STAFFORD BEER
Head of Department of Operational Research and Cybernetics, United Steel Companies, UK

INTRODUCTION

Survey

THE STUDY of the way in which industry behaves, at all levels of its organization, has made slow but commanding progress over the first half of the twentieth century. The history of this study is a testimonial to the analytical method.

Companies have been studied in their economic context, in their sociological context, and in their political context. They have been studied in vertical strata by functions, in horizontal strata by levels of responsibility, and in terms of their centralization or autonomy. In all this work, which is largely descriptive, the sort of model adopted is typified by the 'organization chart', which tries to give a picture of the anatomy of organization. But although we have developed from these studies a rationale of company structure in the macrocosm, most issues are blurred and contentious: and the blame lies with our science. The models are not dynamic; the structures of theory are not viable; the organization chart is dead.

In the microcosm, the analytical method of study has been pursued to even greater lengths. The performancc of machines has been closely observed: their settings, speeds, stoppages and accuracy have been measured and charted and controlled. The behaviour of the operators has been illuminated and photographed, scrutinized and itemized. By these means methods of improvement have been recognized, and great advances in industrial productivity have been brought about. But sometimes these very methods

First published by Imprimerie Gauthier-Villars, Paris.

have defeated their own object. Incentive payment scales must contain step functions, and these become artificial barriers to greater effort. Differential payments between different classes of work cannot be an exact reflection of the differences in effort which the operator recognizes intuitively: imbalance in production flow results. The fault, again, lies in our science: analysis leads us to measure and to alter small areas of complex behaviour patterns, the total reactions of which those methods are powerless to predict.

The difficulties we have been meeting in understanding the concept of industrial organization arise, I suggest, from this dissection. Industry is alive: it behaves as an organic whole. Notoriously, vivisection is painful and damaging to the subject; he is never quite himself again. The cybernetic analogue suggests the machine and the animal, both organic wholes, as models of industrial organization. If this analogy is sound, and the models can be made to work, it should be possible to develop an understanding which is not open to any of the serious criticisms implied above.

The Cybernetic Analogue of Organization

In a model of industrial behaviour, the feature that is perhaps most difficult to visualize is what we call 'the human element'. This is by definition unpredictable: a large element of randomness enters into all human intercourse. The point is, however, that many indeterminate actions have a unified and predictable end. Thus causes and effects make a coherent study, amenable to treatment as probability patterns, by the methods of mathematics and statistics.

This is the link we require: the notion of transition probability, rather than that of mechanical connection. When the management of a company issues an instruction, it expects to obtain a given effect; and there are many causatory chains in the organization by which this effect could be achieved. The exact route that the instruction takes, the precise number of people involved, and their identity, the various institutional services brought into play—all these cannot be programmed by the management as one programs a computer. In even the most efficient and carefully constructed organization, chance must dictate which of a finite but very large number of routes is actually taken.

In cybernetics we have a sure analogue of this situation. We have a 'black box': that hidden and unknown mechanism which is defined in terms of the probabilistic connection between its observed input and output. Consider now the human body. As a mechanical entity, this is a tall thin structure in unstable equilibrium. If a heavy weight is suddenly placed in one of its hands, it will (as a mechanical system of levers) topple over. The human body, however, does not fall: it makes appropriate adjustments to the change.

The imbalance is detected, measured and counter-balanced by an almost unconscious reflex mechanism. No one can predict the precise movements of hand and arm, the shift of weight from one foot to the other, or the adjustment of muscle tonality. What can be predicted, and all that we need to predict, is that somehow the body adjusts itself to this environment change. In a similar way, the influence of many types of external change may be forecast.

Further, internal changes may also be assessed in their effects. To this class of change belongs the whole gamut of homeostasis. Again we may safely predict that the body will regulate its temperature, its oxygen content, and other biochemical homeostats, and contain these conditions within fairly narrow physiological limits. And yet all these regulators are 'black boxes': in so far as we are both largely ignorant of their mechanism, and aware that the succession of their internal states is randomly determined.

This system of the human body, with its randomness and its reflexes (its black boxes and its servomechanisms), constitutes my basic cybernetic analogy. It seems to me that an organization of people, brought together in certain relationships to undertake certain tasks, is amenable to much the same description. We do not need to ask about the detail of their behaviour, which it is agreed will be unpredictable. What we shall need to ask, is whether an organization can react quickly enough and reasonably enough to any given situation, and with what outcome. Such a model, once established, would lend itself to experiments which I feel sure would alter our concept of industrial organization.

THE APPROACH TO A NORMATIVE THEORY

The Quantitative Description of Organizational Pattern

In order to discuss the pattern of organization in scientific terms, we need some clearly defined concepts susceptible to measurement. Without describing again the experimental work [1], [2] which led to their definition, I propose to make use of three such concepts which are due to Bavelas. To illustrate these definitions, I will use the example of an organization of three men. This trio might be organized in one of two ways: either each man can communicate with each of the other two (forming a Ring Net), or two of the men cannot communicate except through the third who is in touch with each (forming a Line Net).

The first organizational concept is called the Dispersion of the Group. To calculate this statistic we first consider group member A. We count the minimum number of steps in which he can communicate with member B, then the minimum number of steps in which he can communicate with member C, and so on; then we sum these results. This is the minimum connectivity of A with the group as a whole. Having made this calculation for each member, we sum their minimum connectivities: this is the Group Dispersion. Using our illustration, we see that the Ring Net organization of three men has a Dispersion of 6, whereas the Line Net has a Dispersion of 8.

The next quantitative concept is that of Relative Centrality. Whereas Dispersion is defined for the group as a whole, each man has his own Relative Centrality: this is defined as the Group Dispersion divided by the minimum connectivity of the individual concerned. In the Ring Net, the minimum connectivity of any member is 2: therefore his Relative Centrality is $6 \div 2 = 3$. The central member of the Line Net has a Relative Centrality of 4, but each of his colleagues has a rating of $2\frac{2}{3}$.

Thirdly, there is the measure for the Peripherality of any man in a group. This is found by subtracting his Relative Centrality from the Relative Centrality of the most central member of the group. The Peripherality of a Ring Net is uniform, and the value of this measure is zero for each member. In the Line Net, the Peripherality of each out-station is $4 - 2\frac{2}{3} = 1\frac{1}{3}$.

These are objective and quantitative measures which can be used to describe any organization in terms of its ability to communicate within itself. Any available measure of the success of an organization in performing its task (whether based on some objective measure, or using the subjective ranking of a superior) can be correlated statistically with the organization's pattern by using these three measures. More advanced quantitative descriptions may yet be created: this is, however, the sort of basis which a normative theory of organization in cybernetic terms would require.

The Emotive Tone of the Organizational Organism

An industrial organization is very much concerned about the morale of its members. Managers know that low morale in a section of a factory means depressed outputs and labour unrest. Usually, problems of this kind are given *ad hoc* consideration, and involve a discussion of personalities: is a particular foreman failing in leadership? Is a particular chargehand disliked? Is a particular member of the team disaffected? The cybernetic notion of the organization as an organic whole permits the consideration of industrial morale in a new way, and one which is especially realistic because it does not separate questions of morale from those of efficiency.

Industrial organization has tended strongly away from autocracy: full consultation at all levels is widely advocated and practised. This means that we are trying to decrease Peripherality.

So far we are in accord with experimental conclusions. It seems that those who are organizationally deployed on the periphery of a network, really do not understand what is happening within the organization, and therefore become disaffected. Furthermore, this ignorance and their low morale combine to make it very difficult to convey any real information to them at all. Indeed, it has been suggested in America that works' bulletins (distributed to the workers in their pay packets, and intended to acquaint them with higher management policy) may be ineffectual because of this difficulty. They are perhaps messages 'written by the boss to himself'. In organic terms, we might say that the synaptic chain to the periphery is so long that at the best communication itself is inefficient. With the inevitable relative disuse of peripheral reflexes, the defective function of synapses is given in the neurophysiological model. Certainly the same effect is apparent in human organizations.

This organic approach, then, like the practical approach of modern industry, seeks to remedy the isolation of the individual at the periphery. However, if this is done by putting in more communication links to the isolated member, his Relative Centrality is raised. Now it is apparently the experience of the experimenters that there is no very high correlation between morale and Relative Centrality. In other words, the obvious means of remedying the situation are not the best. Perhaps this is because the introduction of new communication links lowers the Dispersion of the group, and therefore the Relative Centrality of the controlling members; thus the efficiency of management is likely to decrease. This possibility is strengthened by some field investigations undertaken by Revans [3], in which morale (as measured by accident rate) in coal mines and quarries was found to be related to the logarithm of their size. Cybernetic light is thrown on this by a theoretical result derived from Information Theory. According to this, if in a given network at a given moment each member of the organization sends the best possible message to the most appropriate person, then the amount of information in the net at that given moment is directly proportional to the logarithm of the number of nodes in the network.

The feelings of industry about consultation are certainly correct: experimental workers have found that morale is good in Ring Nets, and decreases rapidly as the net becomes more peripheral. The trouble is, that efficiency decreases with the dispersion. So definite is this tendency, indeed, that if conditions of 'full democracy' are set up, that is to say, if we connect every station with every other station, then frustration and chaos supervene. The reason for this seems to be that no leader can emerge unless his centrality is relatively high—and this condition implies low Relative Centrality for others.

A paradox has emerged. If we pursue the current trend of improving morale by abolishing peripheral isolation within the organization, we must lose efficiency and inhibit the emergence of leadership. Within the definitions we have created, an attempted solution leads to a contradiction. Thus I am led to suggest that organizational adjustments of Relative Centrality cannot provide an answer to our industrial problems of morale, and that we must look for our solutions in *absolute* terms. The cybernetic model should now be used to examine the optimum size of the organization: for I conclude that there is a physiological limit to the complexity of the organism. There are ecological analogues of this in the history of animal evolution.

This thinking has perhaps been paralleled by industrial moves towards decentralization. If the thinking were quite rigorous, however, one would conclude that absolute autonomy of the decentralized units may prove necessary. The cybernetic analogy provides us with clear insight into the radical difference between a part of an organism, however decentralized, and a creature with independent life of its own. We might turn to genetics for an elaboration of this theme.

A new dimension remains to be introduced into this discussion of pattern: that is the question of institutional authority considered independently of organizational centrality. I feel that the connectivity of the organization ought to be arranged to guarantee the natural emergence as leader of the man institutionally appointed to lead. But we cannot neglect the hierarchical structure of the organization, which might not correlate as well as it should with the connectivity. Revans discovered in his work on mines that there was a definite dilution of management as the mines become larger. That is, the ratio of men to supervisory grades steadily increased. (Many factors which are inextricably connected with the size of mine were excluded from the investigation by the statistical technique of partial correlation, so that size itself was indicated as a causal factor.)

Bringing this management dimension into the picture, Revans created a concept which he called 'management opacity'. This excellent term is fully descriptive of the difficulty with which information (and therefore high morale) is disseminated: it relates both to management structure (and particularly the ratio of men to supervisors) and also to communication structure at each level (and particularly to the peripherality of individual men). The measureable concepts of dispersion, relative centrality, peripherality and management opacity do appear to furnish a basis for a discussion of efficiency and morale. If we were used to exploit the cybernetic analogue, we should acquire a deeper understanding of emotive tone in the organism that is industrial organization.

The Model of Organization from Neurophysiology

Although the previous section has been devoted largely to the discussion of morale itself, the notion of the organization as a living organism has been implanted. This is I think its most important aspect. In particular, I think the analogy from neurophysiology ought to be exploited. We have spoken briefly of synaptic transmission: the whole stimulus–response mechanism within an organization could perhaps be treated as an analogue of synaptic reflexes.

Considering the propagation through a monosynaptic reflex system of an orthodromic volley, there is a direct excitatory action which encounters thresholds of response. This is the very nature of the propagation of instructions through an organization, and their repetition in various ways parallels the building up of post-synaptic potential. There is direct inhibition in antagonist muscles of motoneurone impulses. Organizationally: verbal inhibitors, which react on departments of the organization which normally perform the valuable function of restraining the addressed department, are included in the signals (probably implicitly). This form of inhibition is required in industry and in physiology for the same reason: the steady state might otherwise become a functional paralysis.

In a simple monosynaptic situation, according to Eccles [4], the decay rates of the synaptic excitatory and inhibitory processes are similar and exponential; but in more complex connections the inhibitory curve deviates widely from this natural death process for reasons which he discusses. And so in the industrial organization. I have found by measurement that the inhibition of synaptic transmission, for instance the delay imposed on the passage of written messages at a distribution point, decays exponentially for a secretary dispatching her executive's correspondence. For polysynaptic paths, however, where there are interneurones in the form of pneumatic tubes, the death-curve is initially more rapid and eventually more persistent than the exponential law expects. The relevance of each of these neurophysiological points to industry's experience of evoking response is so startling as to merit close study.

Turning, furthermore, to indirect inhibition (and the same authority) we find reasons for the prolonged inhibition of extensor motoneurones in the hyperpolarization process resulting from a cutaneous afferent volley. Firstly, there is delay of inhibitory influences by passage through polysynaptic paths. As our industrial synapses grow more complicated with consultative sanctions, the axons of management transmit a stimulus to more and more neurones, whose dendrites are receptive to more and other axon potentials. Secondly, there are afferent fibres of high threshold which have long conduction times. Some industrial interneurones, too, have thresholds as high as their 'in-trays', and importunity alone is likely to depolarize these executives to the point of reflex discharge. Thirdly, an inhibitory transmitter substance appears to accumulate, which in some cases is probably acetylcholine. In the reflexes of industrial organizations, the inhibitory transmitter substance is probably *paper*.

Finally, we do at least know that excitatory impulses procure a reflex discharge by depolarizing the motoneurone, and that inhibitory impulses delay the discharge by hyperpolarization. The histological basis of this fact is apparently unknown: the psychological basis of hypersensitivity in members of an organization is more evident.

At any rate, the development of this cybernetic analogue from neurophysiology might be fruitful. Very little is known of the way in which institutional communication systems actually operate, or of the extent to which they really meet the needs of the organization; and their importance is usually underestimated. I realize the appropriateness of Communication Theory to these problems, and am aware of some work that has been done on the signal-to-noise ratio within human organizations. That approach is certainly cybernetic in character; but surely the full-scale neurophysiological model deserves its application too. Apart from synaptic transmission, which has been mentioned here, there are many other possible applications. For example, there is certainly an organizational analogue of the conditioned reflex and of the storage of information in this connection by synaptic plasticity. There is also a comparison to be made between the different levels of organization from the autonomous reflex to the higher functions of the brain, and the different industrial levels from the mechanical relay to the directorate. Besides, a normative analogue would be of immense help to the discussion of Abnormal Theory, including such questions as the organizational counterpart of the various forms of ataxy.

The argument now passes to its electromechanical phase, and readily so. For the neurophysiological system just considered is a servomechanism for the regulation of movement. The feedback controls are maintained at the segmental level of the spinal chord, and 'the special function of the cerebellum appears to be servo-control' [4].

The Model of Organization from Servomechanism Theory

There is endless scope for the construction of analogies between servomechanisms and the reflex controls built into industrial organization. Most progressive action in industry is driven forward by the organization using the positive feedbacks of formal sanctions and informal encouragement. Most catastrophes in the field of industrial development, as well as in the sphere of routine production, are averted by the organization using the negative feedbacks of criticism and inspection respectively. A study could, and probably should, be made of these organizational servomechanisms in mathematical terms.

For the present, however, I wish to comment on only one aspect of this analogue: the steady state. It is very difficult indeed to alter permanently the natural behaviour of a man–machine system. The steady state is very stable: the connections of the system with its various sources of motivation and conditioning (mainly economic and psychological) seem to constitute a major servo-system loop, enclosing a variety of subsidiary loops and monitoring feedback links. Consider such a system which comprises a piece of plant, its operatives, and most importantly some of the external factors which influence it: the supply of material, fortuitous breakdown, and the planned readjustment of settings. The cybernetic model of this production organization is a major servo-system. To understand its performance, we must study its transient behaviour. That is, we must know its response to a unit step function of displacement.

Now consider the orthodox attitude to the raising of productivity. An incentive scheme can be instituted, and this will be based on studies of present operations. The effort applied by the man will be 'rated', and utilization of the machine will be evaluated in work-units to take account of the external factors of inherent difficulty, supplies, breakdowns, and resettings. This gives answers which conform to facts; the technique is really a categorization of component influences, and the summation of their weighted averages. But this model is static; it takes no account of the *organization* of the system into a dynamic organism. It can be used to *describe*, but not to *control*. This is, I consider, why some incentive schemes 'freeze' while others 'run away'. These problems could be handled through the insight mentioned above into the transient behaviour of the servo-system.

This point is illustrated from experience. If a job is running on a machine, the total time consumed is T. The objective time for this same job, that is the absolute minimum, is M. By measuring the technical difficulties which affected this job (supplies, breakdowns and the rest) as consuming D, a third measure is obtained $(T-D)$ which is the actual time taken independently of technical difficulties; call this N. Using these measures, we say that the productivity of this job was M/T. This ratio is the product of the two subsidiary ratios M/T and N/T, and the first of these measures the element of technical disturbance encountered by the system. Hence the second ratio, N/T, measures the non-technical element: that is, the component of labour effort. If these three ratios are plotted as a time series for a succession of jobs on the machine, the influence of the servomechanism becomes apparent. In appropriate conditions we have always found that the technical index is damped; that is, there is negative correlation between M/T and N/T; that is, again, the steady state M/T tends to be more stable than observers of component variability expect.

This is borne out, and use is made of the fact, in considering statistically the population of jobs on a given machine. When a large sample of M/T ratios has been obtained (and when, for statistical reasons connected with the limiting nature of M, the ratio is transformed to the inverse sine of its root) the population is treated as a statistical distribution. On a single machine in the simplest case we find a homogeneous set of ratios, conforming to a Gaussian curve, and having a variance (σ^2) very much less than would be expected if the orthodox work study operated on a good model, and the variances of its components could be summed. Statistically, this is not surprising because the component variables of the work study are obviously not independent. But we are saying much more than this; the interdependence of the variables cannot be controlled statistically at all, because the model is bad. The servomechanism model is needed, and becomes still more necessary in more complex cases where the distribution of M/T ratios is multimodal. Homogeneous Gaussian groups can always (in my experience) be deduced from such a complex, conforming to definable sets of jobs; but these groups are not independent of each other either, their structure being reflected in connected serve loops.

Considering the steady state of the production organization as measured by the M/T ratio, we can find its response to a unit step function of displacement. When management requires to raise productivity, that is to change the mean M/T significantly in relation to its statistical variance, a new steady state is required. Once the transient behaviour of the organization as a servomechanism is understood, it should be possible to design a sound incentive scheme which neither confirms inefficiency in setting up a barrier to the change of state, nor causes production to increase in an uncontrolled way. The dangers of this latter risk, by the way, are apparent from the cybernetic model. It is not just that the management is faced with an impossible wage situation; the servo-controls are thrown out of balance, and the monitoring feedbacks which guarantee quality, safety, and so on, may cease to function.

The Model of Organization from Mathematics and Logic

Let us now return to the network concept of organization; and to the question of efficiency as it resides in the intrinsic structure, rather than in the nodal individuals. The work to which I shall now briefly refer is an attempt to investigate by formal mathematical analysis the efficiency of a specific network in terms of the facility with which messages, instructions or even actual things can be passed around it.

The most obvious mathematical approach to the study of behaviour in such a network as we considered on pages 77 to 80 is perhaps through the combinations into which members of the network may group themselves, and the permutations of order within them. I think that this approach is barren in terms of the measurement of efficiency, but it certainly leads to an understanding of the magnitude of the problem which such an investigation sets. If N people are engaged in a network, and the passage of some form of message involves any unspecified number of them, then the number of ways in which the group could behave is approximately $eN!$ Working this out for a network containing only 10 people, we find that the number of arrangements reaches nearly 10 million. Clearly, we require a technique which will take account of this total set of possibilities in a probabilistic way: that is, the technique should select from this total (as does real life) according to some principle of randomized behaviour. This requirement is met in the branch of mathematics known as 'random walks'. The simplest case of a random walk is given by the mathematical construction known as a Markov Chain.

The individuals in the organization are set up in a matrix, so that the horizontal plane indicates 'level' or status, while the vertical plane separates each man from his neighbour on the same level. To each small square in the matrix is assigned the probability that the individual designated there will transmit a message received to some other specified individual. This provides a matrix of transition probabilities, which is used as a model of the organization studied. Where there is a pyramidal structure, the probabilities (which must sum to unity across the line and cannot be negative) are concentrated exclusively on the individuals present: that is, a square unoccupied by an individual has a probability of zero.

Mathematically:

$$P = \begin{bmatrix} P_{11} & P_{12} & P_{13} & \dots \\ P_{21} & P_{22} & P_{23} & \dots \\ P_{31} & P_{32} & P_{33} & \dots \\ \dots & \dots & \dots & \dots \end{bmatrix}$$

$$Pj_1 = Pj_2 + Pj_3 + \dots = 1, \quad Pj_k \geqslant 0$$

This stochastic matrix defines the probability of a transition from any one state to any other, the states being represented by the suffixes. The Markov Chain we intend to generate is then completely defined: for there is a stochastic matrix, and a probability distribution of states.

It is now possible to inject the required cybernetic mark of randomness into this theoretical study. For, using a Monte Carlo technique, the passage of model messages may be observed. Still better, the behaviour of this organization can be investigated by formal mathematics (some unpublished work on these lines has been done by my colleague M. A. Aczel).

There are two points that I should like to note. Firstly, this model will be unrealistic as representative of even the simplest organization, if there is no means of stopping the message from travelling for ever round the system. As a simple means of stopping the chain from perpetual self-propagation, a 'dead man' was introduced into the organization. The model was so arranged mathematically that a chain which encountered the 'dead man' would cease to propagate. This was used as an elementary analogue of the real-life situation in which some person (although, it is to be hoped, not actually dead) fails to pass on the information he has received. Secondly, the process which I have described is only a special case of the class of 'random walks'. Random walks permit the probabilistic study of any message-propagating system, for whatever type of constraint we wish to prescribe. For example, just as in the Markov process the chief characteristic of the walk is that each new state is determined by its predecessor, so in other types of stochastic process other major characteristics emerge. A case in point is the so-called 'self-avoiding walk', in which it is a predetermined condition that the path cannot cross its own track. One can visualize certain types of organizational study in which realism would be served by adopting this particular constraint.

Once this mathematical approach is made, and whether it is solved by mathematical or empirical means, quantitative measures of efficiency (in whatever form) become possible. For example, efficiency might be defined as the ratio of the number of people involved in a given walk to the number of moves made in generating a Markov chain. For a self-avoiding walk, this ratio would by definition have the value of unity in any circumstances. Depending on the type of 'dead man' technique employed to simulate the cessation of the process (and this can itself be considered separately as having its own independent probability generating function), efficiency might be defined as the percentage dissemination of a message achieved before the conclusion of a given walk.

This section has given the briefest possible introduction to the potential use of stochastic matrices in this work. Since there is a more or less infinite number of possible matrix models, it has already become clear to us that little purpose is served by a mathematician endlessly setting up possible organizations operating under possible constraints and then solving them. What is required is that a team of cyberneticians should use their mathematical ability to operate this suggested model to study a particular organization, in conjunction with other approaches suggested in this paper.

Incidentally, the consideration of a conflict of instructions within the matrix model is interesting. This has been investigated cursorily by two methods. Firstly, as above, Markov chains were generated simultaneously by Monte Carlo means, and assumed to be carrying conflicting instructions. The chances of survival of the one designated 'right' (which issued from the higher level) were examined for different organizations. Secondly, symbolic logic was used: Markov chains, being fully determined, can be stated in Boolean algebra. The conflicting logical propositions were tested for consistency with various hypotheses (the forms of organization) either by setting up truthtables, or by algebraic truth-value analysis. For the same reasons as those given in the last paragraph, I have not carried these investigations sufficiently far to give quantitative results: the general problem is too amorphous, and specific ones should be attacked instead. But I will make this comment, while it must be clear to anyone that organizational structure has a vital bearing on efficiency, I doubt whether it is understood that there are very wide differences in efficiency between organizations which are not markedly different. If this conclusion is even probably correct (for I cannot call it proved) it forms a strong argument for the cybernetic investigation of organization, and against the belief that effective *ad hoc* organizations can be constructed at will by suitable people.

Finally, I must mention that there is a well-established mathematical technique, already used by operational research workers to study problems of organization where supply and demand are the key factors. This is the Theory of Queues, by which the number of people supplying a service can be calculated at an economic minimum consistent with a known small risk of not coping with the demand.

The Model of Organization from Entropy

In concluding this discussion of possible models for a Normative Theory, I turn firstly to thermodynamics and the concept of entropy. Now the connection between this entropy in its classical context, and the entropy of Information Theory which derives from Gibbsian statistical mechanics, is of vital cybernetic interest. The founder of Cybernetics himself points this out in his stimulating discussion of ergodic theory [5]. However, Wiener is compelled to warn us against using classical thermodynamics as applied to heat engines as an analogue for a 'thermal' treatment of living matter. Because of the fineness of structure of protein tissue, it is impossible to conceive of temperatures except as gross averages: the thermodynamic notions become meaningless.

But if someone were to develop the measure of entropy as a model of industrial organization, I suggest that this danger could be avoided. There should be enough organizational homogeneity within local regions to make the model appropriate, and then three-dimensional ergodic theory would be applied to the organizational analogue (which is spatial) of temporal equilibrium.

Considering, firstly, the entropy of thermodynamics itself is applied to organizations, we remember the need for centrality. In the fully connected organizational network, Relative Centralities tend to equality: the entropy rises, and less energy is available to work the system. This agrees with our earlier conclusions. It is amusing to note, also, that entropy increases with friction within the system (independently of outside influences). Further, as a consequence of the Second Law, there is a *natural* tendency for the entropy of the system to increase; and this seems to be paralleled by the steady social (and even political) pressure from within industry to lower Dispersion to a minimum, i.e. to $n(n-1)$. Small wonder, then, that Maxwell demons should be seen operating in industrial organizations. They refrain from sending copies of correspondence to others; they veto proposals to install yet another telephone; they send fellow-workers to Coventry. All this decreases the entropy: it raises the Peripherality of the outstations in the network. The Maxwell demons I have nominated are generally regarded as scourges: perhaps they are in fact essential to the working of the organization, which might collapse into inactivity without them.

The analogy gains force and interest, however, when we exploit other insights into the nature of entropy. Leaving the heat equations of the classicists, we consider entropy as proportional to the logarithm of the statistical probability of the universe—or of a given phase space. And here we meet the connection with Information Theory discussed by Wiener, who beautifully demonstrates that an amount of information is the negative logarithm of a probability, and goes on to show that it has the properties of an entropy. It follows that losing information and gaining entropy are analogous processes, and that to lose entropy is to gain information.

Hence we meet again the conclusion that to acquire energy available for useful work in the organization, we must centralize our networks, increasing centrality, and encountering the loss of morale associated with peripheral ignorance. Again we must ask whether decentralization to the point of autonomy is required. Perhaps this model can tell.

The second point I wish to make, quite briefly, under this heading concerns again the living organism. Without considering thermodynamics in regions only penetrated by the electron microscope (against which Wiener warned us) we might entertain a few biochemical thoughts. Consider that chemical change involves the loss of free energy; but it will not take place at all unless the molecules are in a reactive state. In a biochemical system, the hydrolysis of a neutral aqueous solution of sucrose is thermodynamically possible. But it does not occur without the aid of a catalyst. Has an organization latent metabolism of this kind, and if so what catalysts evoke the change of entropy? If the biochemical model were developed, the analogue of anabolism might be found, drawing free energy not only from catabolism within the system (which we know to happen organizationally when, for example, a top executive releases stimulating ideas in the region of a junior who absorbs them, and both men 'change their state'), but also from outside the system. So far we have considered an industrial organization as a closed system; possibly this is a mistake which this model would reveal. Ecological questions would then be raised, and the social sciences could at last be mobilized to help this study.

Finally, I recall Wiener's remark that enzymes might be regarded as metastable Maxwell demons, with some special biochemical mechanism for decreasing entropy. And, having said so much about steady states and maximum entropies, it is worth pondering his following sentence. 'The enzyme and the living organism are alike metastable: the stable state of an enzyme is to be deconditioned, and the stable state of a living organism is to be dead.' Perhaps the Second Law of thermodynamics will overtake all industrial organizations in the long run, as it seems to overtake socio-political organizations too. Meanwhile, the management task is to keep the entropy low.

THE APPROACH TO AN ABNORMAL THEORY

Subnormal Structures

Once a normative theory, aimed at establishing the conditions in which an organization will tend to behave in a normal and satisfactory manner, has been established, the next step will be to discuss its abnormal behaviour also in a generalized way. The simplest case of abnormal behaviour is subnormality itself. This is the condition of intrinsic inadequacy: the organization is simply not able to cope with the task for which it was designed, because of innate, fundamental characteristics. It follows that when this organization is studied by any of the methods already proposed for normal behaviour, it will either produce the wrong answers, or take an inordinate time to produce any answer, or else it will break down entirely before any answer is produced at all. What advantage is to be gained by studying such an ineffectual arrangement? I think it will achieve three main things.

Firstly, we should be able to discover in what regard (whether as to numbers, or communication links, or actual structure) a normal and adequate organization is most prone to collapse, and therefore most likely to benefit by reinforcement. Secondly, it should be possible to discover what are the warning signs of incipient breakdown. Thirdly, it should be possible to compare the economic gain in sponsoring a subnormal organization (which would presumably be less complex in some way and therefore cheaper than a normal one) with the economic loss deriving from the lowered efficiency of the subnormal group in ordinary operation, together with the risk of definite catastrophe.

The method which could appropriately be used to study subnormal structures is to set up the analogue of inadequacy. This would require that a balanced and adequate organization, as prescribed by the normative theory, should be systematically examined and deprived, seriatim, of its essential characteristics. Thus, for example, if a Ring Net had been proved ideal for the solution of a certain problem, then we might deprive it of a link, and then observe empirically in what ways it failed to perform the allotted task. Or, in a Queue Theory study, having established what the correct number of servers should be in a given situation, we might use the Monte Carlo method to find out in what ways the service is in practice impaired if one less server than the optimum number is employed. And so on: there is no real difficulty in imagining how subnormal structures can be set up and examined scientifically in a controlled experiment. The main point to note is that we are, in this section, postulating shortcomings which amount to no more than inadequacy; we are discussing deficiencies and not certifiable behaviour.

The Psychopathology of Organization

Once the deficient organization has been adequately studied in terms of a normal and healthy organization in a state of deprivation, we may turn to the study of full-scale abnormality. This whole concept depends upon the cybernetic analogy between an organization and a living body. For I think we ought to discuss the organization which is going wrong in terms of the human body which is going wrong: the fault may lie anywhere, in the nervous system (communications), in the brain (co-ordination), in the limbs themselves (paralysis or atrophy of outstations), or indeed in any other aspect. In the following examples, I consider four analogies drawn on these lines: these are chosen simply as examples of the way in which a 'psychopathology' of organization might be developed.

Overwork

The strain of the situation given by consistent overwork in the human being can result in a number of symptomatic small-scale failures, followed by a general nervous breakdown. What happens in the organization analogue may readily be discovered, by setting up a system shown by normative theory to be adequate, and then over-straining its capacity. Consider, for example, the Queuing type of problem. If too much work is thrust upon this system, a point is reached where the average servicing time is longer than the average interval between arrivals, and then an infinite queue develops. In communication systems, overload invariably has the effect of generating so much 'noise' in the system that the proportion of information which can be passed constantly sinks, and the final state consists in the jamming of exchanges. In an empirical experiment with human subjects described by Bavelas, it is fairly clear that overload could be responsible for the final revolt of the subjects being tested and the abandonment of the whole experiment—a precise analogue of nervous breakdown. There is little difficulty in envisaging how the methods already advocated can be adapted to simulate overwork. This surge in the level of performance required of the organization is a natural antithesis of a normal level of work which has to be undertaken by a subnormal organization, and no doubt this could be excellently treated by servomechanism theory also.

Shock

No particular difficulty will be encountered in administering shocks to any of the model systems with which we have been dealing. Shocks may vary from the introduction of semantic noise, through quite serious disturbances, and on to the analogue of virtual catastrophe, by injecting random elements into the system. For example, in a study using the approach of mathematical programming, an artificial vector might be introduced into the matrix: its variables would be fixed by a stochastic process independent of the processes being studied. Similarly, if a solution is being obtained by the Monte Carlo method, a new series of random numbers can be used to disturb the even pattern of the results. In the case of a mechanical analogue machine, the random element would be introduced by cams, levers, or electronic pulses actuated from outside the general mechanism. In short, we may picture the sort of influence we propose to have on any system to which a shock is to be introduced, as the unpredicted arrival from outer space of a comet into a solar system whose behaviour is understood.

An interesting example of shock administered in the form of semantic noise is recorded by Bavelas [1] in his empirical experiments.

Trauma

Little need be said about the simulation of a trauma in an organizational system, because its genesis will closely resemble that of shock. Whereas, however, in the case of shock the system is permitted to rehabilitate itself; in the case of trauma we shall regard some part of the system as paralysed or destroyed. In terms of analogue, this is easy to achieve; all that is required is that an aspect of the system (for example, one of the people, or one of the communication links, within it) should cease to function. This can be accomplished readily for any type of model.

In this type of study, we wish to find out how the organization will react to traumatic conditions. These arise (by analogy) in real life when some individual member of the organization suddenly dies, or when a unit of plant or of the communication system goes out of action. When this type of reaction is fully understood, the object of the research will be to discover the cheapest and most convenient means of insurance against such an eventuality, by building alternative modes of functioning into the system.

Neurosis

We might also suggest the extension of our psychopathological analogy to the point where an organization is described as suffering from neurosis. To justify this extension, it will be necessary to examine briefly the conditions under which individuals do in fact become neurotic.

The individual lives in a world in which he has defined himself as existing. He inherently belongs to the environment in which he partakes; his behaviour cannot be considered independently from that environment. The man is not confronted with an external situation from which he is at liberty to divorce himself; he interprets his environment through his own reaction to it. An event within his comprehension only means something to him because it is defined within the general terminology of the interpretation that he personally puts on the universe. Consequently the individual's world is not made up of external, objective and meaningless things; rather, the environment exists for him because it is a part of his own consciousness. Here are only things and relations that are meaningful: each of them is designated by a personal symbol. A variety of possible causes may lead this system of description into confusion. The symbol and its meaning may become disjointed or out of proper proportion. When this happens the individual becomes recognizable as neurotic.

In a machine a form of neurosis may be recognized. It might indeed sound strange to speak of a 'neurotic machine', but this is a perfectly appropriate description of some forms of mechanical defect. For example, in a feedback mechanism, the machine is measuring its own propensity to error and is then making a correction for it. If the symbol of error (that is, the machine's measurement of its own maladjustment) and its meaning (that is, the interpretation of that symbol as revealed in the process of adjustment) become slightly out of proportion, the machine will begin a continuous process of over-correction. That is to say, the feedback circuit will begin to reverberate. (This is the phenomenon familiar to engineers under the name of 'hunting'.) In human action, this behaviour may occur without structural defect:

as when two people try to pass each other, and are eventually brought face to face after an erratic course of rapid corrections. Alternatively, there may be a definite defect, as in ataxy: for instance, in the so-called 'purpose tremor'—which is not a neurosis.

Applying these ideas to an organization, its description as neurotic will certainly be appropriate if some circuit within its system of communication and control begins to reverberate. I think that such behaviour is fairly familiar to most people in the way in which tension builds up between groups of individuals in an organization. Many people have noticed that squabbles develop between individuals and reach 'storm in a teacup' dimensions, when the discussion that generates the row has taken place by correspondence rather than verbally. This is, in my opinion, because the fine adjustments of nuance (which are very largely a function of tone of voice and manner) have been lost: the written word institutes a gap between symbol and meaning which is very largely implied in the mind of the reader, and a process of over-correction begins.

Similarly, in the passage of a message or of instructions through a system, the information may well become distorted. While this remains a simple process of gradual distortion, it is most aptly described as 'noise' in the communication system. But in a real organization particular individuals tend to embellish or correct messages in a way characteristic of their own personality. Thus, as the information passes backwards and forwards through the system, a reverberatory process may well begin. The symbol and the meaning become separated into separate interpretations in the minds of two individuals, their disproportion begins to affect the behaviour of the whole system, and the organization thereby becomes neurotic. Other examples of neurosis could be given: the point to recognize is that by describing an organizational malady in this way (that is by a definitely psychopathological analogy) we make sure that the situation is recognized as akin to a *disease*, and is not mistaken for mere inadequacy or malformation.

What is the cure for this disease likely to be? For the individual, psychotherapy prescribes a 'proportioning treatment'. There must be a redefinition of the symbols and meanings that make up the environment, in which the manias and phobias which confirm and ingrain the neurosis are eliminated. In other words, we should seek to cut away the vicious reverberatory feedback circuits. Organizationally, an analogous process would have to be attempted. It would probably amount to a redisposition of individuals, and a redefinition of functions and responsibilities.

CONCLUSION

Aristotle began his *Metaphysica* with the words: 'All men by their nature desire to know'. From his day and for 2000 years a few men, mostly philosophers like Leibniz, have persisted in holding the grand concept of knowledge as an ultimate good and a unity. This idea of knowledge as an indivisible whole has fought a losing battle with the idea of scholarly specialization. Today, we see the fragmentation of knowledge into parts of areas of fields of subjects. The result is pitiful: we have apotheosized topics and castrated intellect.

If the discipline called Cybernetics has something to offer beyond the solution of some of the most recondite problems of automation, it is surely this: for the first time in centuries there is a rallying point around which thinkers may unite without regard to intellectual trespass. And yet, already—within 10 years—we find interpretations of our subject which (without regard to its foundations, or to the world leadership of the 10 brilliant annual symposia held yearly in America until 1953) seek to subsume the whole in some small part.

The subject to which this paper is addressed—human organization—is fundamental to society. Particularly, it is the vital framework of our industrial life on which the future of society depends. And yet, although 'all men desire to know', our understanding of it is rudimentary. There happens to have developed no particular 'science of organization'. We are conditioned by our academic framework: no one seems surprised that there is almost nothing scientific to be said upon so great an issue. And so our fragments of learning have been casually applied, now here, now there, with results criticized in my Introduction.

This paper, too, is necessarily fragmentary: a collection of occasional thoughts. What I have tried to show is only this: we are dealing with something organic, something susceptible to study as a unity, something which once properly understood could be manipulated with important social consequences. Automation is stirring its new-born limbs; managements and workers, governments and unions, kings and clerks, are anxious and afraid. Now is the time to master the nature of the one thing, organization, which will control the new industrial outlook or abdicate in its path. Cybernetics is the one tool, the one integrated science, which—so I believe—could develop that mastery.

REFERENCES

1. Bavelas, A., 'Communication Patterns in Problem-Solving Groups', *Cybernetics, Transactions of the Eighth Conference, 1951*, Josiah Macey Jr. Foundation, New York, 1952.

2. Christie, Lee S., 'Organization and Information Handling in Task Groups', *J. Operations Research Soc. Amer.*, **2**(2), 1954.
3. Revans, R. W., 'Scale Factors in the Management of Coal Mines', *Operational Research Quarterly*, **6**(3), 1955.
4. Eccles, J. C., *The Neurophysiological Basis of Mind*. Oxford, 1953.
5. Wiener, Norbert, *Cybernetics*. John Wiley, New York, 1948.

Stafford Beer addressing a plenary session of the First International Congress on Cybernetics, Namur, Belgium, 1959

PART TWO

Cybernetics: A New World View

x̄
BEER
1953
. . . on computers we work with binary digits

7 THE IRRELEVANCE OF AUTOMATION

Second International Congress on Cybernetics

STAFFORD BEER
Head of Department of
Operational Research and Cybernetics,
United Steel Companies, UK

THE 'SECOND INDUSTRIAL REVOLUTION'

EVERYONE CAN visualize the picture which factories presented late in the eighteenth century. In those parts of the world which were by then industrialized, men, women and children laboured in appalling conditions to make the products on which their society depended. Into this scene of squalor and back-breaking toil was flung the machine. Its advent was sufficiently sudden and its impact sufficiently dramatic that historians have since called the event revolutionary. The short period of years into which were compressed the early achievements of production engineering and a simultaneous social upheaval have become known as the Industrial Revolution.

Today we think that we detect a comparable event. A century-and-a-half of increasing mechanization has led us to an era which most observers refuse to regard as merely an extension of those early developments. They feel that a new step has been taken. Automation has arrived. And so a new phrase has become fashionable, the phrase 'the Second Industrial Revolution'. Now it is very difficult to recognize any revolution from a contemporary standpoint, and still more difficult to define its scope. Why indeed do we speak of a second revolution at all? It is less, I suggest, because of the novelty of automation as because it has provoked another social upheaval. A threat of large-scale redundancy of labour has been created, a threat visible to anyone who applies his imagination to a future dominated by automatic machinery. Whether this threat is illusory or not is an interesting but mainly irrelevant question. The fact remains that a fear of what might very well happen in the future has focused the attention of industrial society on its own security. And I believe that comment applies as strongly to managers as to the labour force.

This climate of insecurity in the industrial society is having, it seems to me, a very extensive and also intensive effect on the progress of automation. People have a deep and probably unrealized motive for deciding that a given works process should not be made automatic, that a given clerical routine should not be entrusted to a computer, or that no attempt ought to be made to augment the managerial function of human judgement by machinery capable of taking a decision. Let us consider for a moment an argument that has very frequently been advanced. 'Automatic machinery', runs the assertion, 'cannot be expected to take into account all the many factors which affect this process, this routine, this judgement. There are too many variables to consider.' This is a plausible story: we like to flatter ourselves by thinking that our brains are capable of juggling with dozens of variables. And yet it would be difficult to find more absurd grounds than these for contesting automation. For the brain, which does many things superbly well, is notoriously inadequate when it comes to handling more than a few variables. With how many unknowns can we deal? Three? Consider:

$$\begin{aligned} 2x+5y-3z&=7\\ 8x-6y+2z&=6\\ 7x+9y-8z&=9 \end{aligned}$$

Here are these unknowns, and enough information to determine them. None of the numbers shown contains more than one digit. Can we solve even this trivial set of simultaneous linear equations mentally, with the unaided brain? The computing machinery which backs automation, on the other hand, can deal with matrices of indefinitely high order; that is, it can solve problems involving hundreds of variables. What becomes of the plausible argument and of what malaise is that argument a symptom?

In the few minutes for which I have so far spoken, I have tried to create a sketch of the present scene in advanced industry. This sketch does not dwell lovingly on the colossal achievements of engineering, on the lines of transfer machines, on the huge electronic information-handling systems. Perhaps we have congratulated ourselves enough on these advances already. The sketch is drawn at a deeper level. It is a picture of an industrial society undergoing a second industrial revolution, a society which has focused its attention on a particular and narrow manifestation of its own inventive ability in the belief that this manifestation, automation, constitutes the revolution.

This is a society with a sense of unease, sometimes amounting to guilt, about its own future—because it is creating for itself problems which it cannot honestly say it knows how to handle, problems which have a significance deeper than engineering or economics can bestow.

The case I submit to this Conference is now building up to its first major point, and it is most important that the sense in which I am speaking should not be misunderstood. I am not attacking automation. I am attacking the apotheosis of automation. It seems to me that we who are mounting the second industrial revolution have seized the wrong point. A vision is being created which is a false vision, and the direction in which we may be trying to move is one which we instinctively recognize as based on false values. Let me say plainly what I mean, on the understanding that what is said refers not to the conquests of production problems which began perhaps with Sargrove and have become a legend with Diebold, but to some more ultimate concept of automation, buried in our dreams, half glimpsed and only partly understood.

Consider 'the automatic factory' as it figures in this scene as a supposed target, as an archetype of the new industry. If it is to be economic in terms of the investment it represents, it demands an automatic market; for it has little flexibility to respond to change, and cannot afford to slow down. It demands an automatic influx of capital: to stock it, to maintain it, to keep it running come what may. It demands also the subservience of its manpower. For managers must initially take a vast set of almost irrevocable decisions which are built into the plant, and to the extent that they have once taken them they must then abdicate. And the labour force has to accept a steady downgrading, as men are shifted from jobs which disappear into jobs too trivial to abolish by machines. Above all, and permeating all, this technological marvel demands the abandonment of the accepted criteria for running an industrial society; for the fact of its existence commits its capital, its market, its stocks, its spares, its managers and its men to a policy of 'no return'. That it is possible to build this automatic factory is the obsessional justification for its being built: 'the world owes it a living'. It is for this reason that I make bold to call ethical matters in question. The old ethical dictum (which is to be found in Kant) that obligation implies possibility, has been reversed. Instead of 'must' implies 'can', we have 'can' implies 'must'.

Clearly, this will not do. Now I believe that this vision has come to underlie the second industrial revolution, and that people who have not actually thought out these possibilities and these implications none the less realize that the vision will not do. They revolt against this *deus ex machina* which is shrouded in the mist of the future: it gives them the sense of unease, of guilt, of which I spoke. And so it comes about that things which really should be done, processes which really should be made automatic, routines which really should be entrusted to computers, and decisions which really could better be taken by machine, are not done but resisted. And, naturally enough to the psychologist, since the resistance is irrational it has to be 'rationalized'. This is why so many of the arguments which face us all in this pioneering work are, like the one mentioned earlier about the handling of many variables, logically absurd.

In short: we read into our new industrial revolution the wrong aims, and put it forward with the wrong reasons, and therefore we receive the wrong response. This is why I have sweepingly claimed in my title that automation is irrelevant to the issues before the industrial world today.

No doubt this is a strange and unpopular case to make. It is likely to be misconstrued and attacked as reactionary. But if there is one place in the world where these views are likely to be heard, it is Namur. For it is in our new science of cybernetics that the real answers lie: of this I am perfectly assured.

THE ROLE OF CYBERNETICS

May we then turn to the science of cybernetics, and consider for a moment its programme as envisaged by Wiener and the early American symposiasts. None of these men had any need to propose the foundation of a new science. Each of them enjoyed high performance standing in his own primary field. They conceived of cybernetics as a science, deserving of its own name, because they recognized in the concept of control a ubiquitous idea common to all their separate sciences. Yet more is implied by 'a science' than a recurrent theme. Control and its communications are for cybernetics *the object* of study. For scientists who are only secondarily cyberneticians, this 'unity in separation' is sometimes forgotten. Coming as we do from many fields of endeavour, disciplined as we are in different modes of scientific thought, we recognize a community of interest in problems of control. But have we yet recognized these problems as literally the same? Unless they are the same problems, in biology, in medicine, in industry, in sociology, in economics, and so on, then we have no science of cybernetics.

The failure of the widely entertained yet false vision of automation is a failure to identify the cybernetic unity of control in industrial society itself and as a whole.

The administrative necessity to divide a conference, a book or a discussion on cybernetics into fields of enquiry unfortunately vitiates this proper emphasis on the indivisibility of the control concept. And unless we are very careful, the idea will soon become widespread that 'industrial cybernetics' is no more and no less than a name for the study of automation. This would be to debase the currency of our language. For engineers have succeeded in the development of their automatic machinery virtually without reference to other manifestations of control, in ecology and physiology for example, and with still less reference to the basic logic and philosophy of cybernetic studies. Automation engineering deals, for the most part, with fully-coupled systems: and its pure theory is the mathematics of servomechanisms. If we allot to this work the title of industrial cybernetics, as was implied to the title of a well-known book, we are throwing away the general and interdisciplinary theory of control and communication which we have been seeking to evolve.

Let me quickly draw together the threads I have been trying to unravel. If we exist inside a second industrial revolution, then it has to be thought of in its wholeness. Automation is of course a major contributor to the revolution, but it is not itself the revolution. The description required to discuss that topic must be capable of accounting for the production facet of industry, and for its commercial facet; but it must also account for the economic and social environments. Above all, it must account for the various hierarchical and autonomous management structures of these facets and environments, which handle all these things in very different ways. The contention is that this is the task for which cybernetics is fitted in industry; that cybernetics can expose the real nature of the revolution and show how to progress into the new industrial phase with safety and success. The last part of this paper will attempt to demonstrate the kind of thinking required. This I believe to be vitally new thinking—cybernetic thinking. But it has to be expressed within the confines of an ordinary vocabulary; and if this is to be done then it is first necessary to establish a way of talking which will permit communication at all.

One of the most alarming things which my own group has discovered in pursuing its cybernetic work over the years, is the intense difficulty of saying anything cybernetic at all. The things one is trying to say about the actual situation become mixed up with the big empty slogans of the supposed revolution. Consider, for example, the decision apparatus of industrial policy. This is delicate, probabilistic, self-formulating, fiduciary, self-fluxing and non-analytic. Nothing is more agonizing to the cybernetician who is trying to understand this behaviour than to be told that all such management problems can be solved by a sufficiently expensive dose of 'automatic data processing'.

What, then, is the 'way of talking' to which I have referred, and how is the claim to a science of cybernetics which is separate and distinct from the established sciences to be made good? To answer these questions I shall offer the most careful and succinct formulation of the subject-matter and method of our science that I can devise.

THE NATURE OF CYBERNETICS

Control is the attribute of a system. A system is any collection of entities, of whatever kind, which can be understood as forming a coherent group. The fact of being a recognizable group is what differentiates a system from a meaningless collection of bits and pieces. Some collections are meaningless jumbles in one language, and systems in another language. For example, in the language of a child or a savage, a line of figures may be a mere collection; in the language of a mathematician, the same line of figures may be a binomial series. In the second language then, there exists a system, though not in the first. This example is not meant to imply that all systems are determinate. On the contrary, most of the systems important to cybernetics are probabilistic.

The structure of a system is its relatedness. That is, the way in which the entities comprising the system are related defines its structure. To say that a system is probabilistic is to say that the structure is not rigidly fixed, but that the relations which define it are variables to which levels of probability may be assigned. If these levels fall below the threshold of statistical significance, the system disintegrates and is no longer recognizable as a system.

Control is the attribute of a system which tends to sustain its structure, to reinforce its cohesion. Control is the dynamics of structure. Thus to exert control in a new direction, in a given system, is to discover the language in which new structure may be discerned. To exert control in a recognized direction, on the other hand, is to facilitate the speaking of the language of a recognized structure. *This is what communication means*: the talkativeness of a structure within itself, the ease of association inside its relatedness. And to manage the system means to be able to talk to it, to talk inside it, as a competent conversationalist.

Now to adopt this kind of speaking is helpful in this way. Cybernetics is concerned with exceedingly complex systems which are incapable of definition in detail. The old method of discussing them as if one could lay bare their anatomy as one may lay bare an electrical circuit is inappropriate. Analytically, we recognize this fact by nominating whole chunks of the system as 'black boxes'. A black box is a pattern of connections which cannot be comprehended. The inputs to the box may be manipulated, and the behaviour of the outputs studied; in this way the characteristics of the box may be at least partly ascertained. But in studying the behaviour of industrial society itself no human observer can attain the vantage point necessary to delineate the system in this way. He is perforce walking about inside the black box, although its connectivity is still a mystery. What concerns him about the system is not its connectivity, but its responsiveness.

A system, and here I reiterate that I am most adamantly speaking of *any* system, can be made responsive if it is talked to in the right language: the language of its own structure which makes it the system that it is. If communication and selection are used to condition the structure, then the probabilities which quantify the internal relatedness of the system will begin to change. With perfect propriety the system can be said to be learning and discriminating. As management of this kind goes on, paths of facilitation inside the structure become established, certain languages become more fluent than others, and certain translations from one language to another become readily available to the system itself. In this way the system comes to exhibit memory.

The development of these physiological characteristics of any system is vital, but it will not be continued here: or the point I am trying to make will be lost. The point is that any system may be discussed through this way of speaking as if it were any other system we please. This speech is a system, and could be analysed in cybernetic terms so that its behaviour exhibited the characteristics of a machine. A machine, on the other hand, can itself be treated through this neutral language to exhibit the characteristics of an animal. This argument applies to the detail of a system within a system, too: the system of 'what is wrong with the economy' can be discussed in terms of the system of a psychiatric syndrome. Now we have come back, full circle, to our initial assertions about the unity of the sciences inside the distinctiveness of cybernetic studies. Let us go on to surmount the final obstacle to this insight.

When the original series of annual cybernetic conferences in America was drawing to its close, a feeling was growing (and this is readily transmitted to us today by the verbatim records) that any system could be described in terms of any other. The symposiasts had exhausted themselves in making this discovery; they had rushed from subject to subject, delightedly acknowledging the similarities in control and communication they found in them all. And then a note of weariness intrudes: 'fascinating, but what of it?' they seem to say. With all respect to these pioneers, I suggest that they stopped just short of the final conclusion. After another 10 years of incubation, we can perhaps make bold today to crystallize the point.

There are many levels of comparison which can be drawn between two concepts, or two arguments, or two systems. Consider three of these levels. A simile makes a comparison which is not put forward as a statement of fact; the point it makes is a poetic point, and its validity is an emotional validity. An analogy makes a comparison which is put forward as a definite contribution to understanding. A is not the same thing as B; but A's structure so closely resembles that of B that the analogy between them is considered helpful in explaining B to anyone who already understands A. Analogies, when properly drawn, have a logical validity. Thirdly, the strongest form of comparison is a bold assertion that two things are in actual fact one and the same. The validity of this comparison is absolute: it holds in all dimensions, in every condition of existence.

Now when the cybernetician draws his comparisons between the control mechanisms of systems described and studied by different sciences, at what level is he drawing it, and what is its validity? There seems to be much confusion on this point. People are ready to discount the metaphorical level: the man is clearly not speaking as a poet. Most people would also discount the interpretation of ultimate identity: they have to do so, unless they are ready to substitute mysticism for science. This throws them back on the level of analogy. But if the similarities between control systems described by various sciences are only analogies, then they have no more than expository significance.

The solution of the problem is not difficult if we bear in mind what was said earlier. The two systems are certainly analogous, and the first task is to study the analogy and to ascertain its logical validity: that is, the limits within which the comparison is justly drawn, within which an inference that holds for one system holds for the other. Using the definitions of the two systems for which this analogy does hold, and no others, their two structures may then be ascertained. It is these structures, divorced from their subject matter, which are literally identical. There is simply no difference between them whatever. These identities are the material of cybernetics.

THE APPEARANCE OF CYBERNETICS

In practice, the method of cybernetics is likely to be this. Better control is called for in a given system. The cybernetician draws on his knowledge of systems, of whatever kind, that exhibit the mode of control sought in his problem. He sets up a model, or a series of models, in the way familiar to all branches of science. These models are then exhaustively studied as analogues of the problem system. The techniques available for this stage of the enquiry are precisely those of operational research.

From all this activity, the structures must be dissected from the systems. Languages have to be found in which to express the structures. These languages are likely to be those of logic and metamathematics, of mathematics itself, and (because of probabilism in the system) of mathematical statistics. Now the identities can be studied. This is a process of the transformation of statistical parameters, until the languages correspond. It is further a process of topological mapping, whereby one structural set is mapped into another, until the structures themselves are the same. Finally comes the solution to the original problem. The structure required is understood: the language in which that required structure can be told to the system is known; the way that the system will respond can be predicted.

When these methods, the methods of cybernetics, are applied to problems of control in industry, the answers may assume any form. What has to be built into the real-life situation is a certain structure, together with certain transducers capable of providing the structure with its communications.

This outcome may indeed take the form of electronic machinery capable of dealing with a long and intricate set of programmed instructions, in which case it will look like automation. But it may not. It may take the form of electronic machinery which is not programmed at all, but is designed to seek a goal, or to learn about a situation, or to amplify intelligence. In any case, why do we say *electronic* machinery? The outcome may take the form of a set of rules for operating a particular control strategy, in which case it will look like a piece of game-theoretic operational research. It may take the form of a colloidal cell, growing its solutions to control problems in a delicate tracery of chemical deposits, or of a tank of magnetized fish.

Whatever it looks like, this outcome aims at one thing: a new and higher type of viable control. What it looks like is irrelevant. It aims to replace chance, to replace hectoring. It is government by homeostasis, or self-regulation; it is responsive; it is organic. This is the family of cybernetic control systems to which automation belongs, but in which automation itself has the status of a reflex mechanism among other mechanisms with the status of brain. The family as a whole is capable of adaptive behaviour, and seeks the ultimate ecological goal of survival. The development and exploitation of this family is the future for cybernetics in industry. This is what the second industrial revolution will prove to have been about.

CONTROL IN INDUSTRY

This analysis concludes by exemplifying briefly what this line of thought amounts to in industrial terms. For this purpose I propose that we consider a mythical company, but one having an organization typical of many large concerns all over the world. There is a central administrative and managerial headquarters in which the identity of the company is vested, but which manufactures nothing. This company owns outright a number of subsidiary companies which are factories.

Now this large organization is by no means a magnified version of one of its component companies. Its whole structure is quite different. Each of the component companies is controlled by a hierarchical management: a pyramidal structure of authority which culminates in a solitary figure at the top who carries ultimate responsibility. But the total organization does not have this form. In the total organization, the component companies are autonomous. They respond to the central directorate; but that centre is not authoritarian, it is integrative. The central directorate dictates a general policy, a set of goals; it prescribes the rules by which these goals are to be sought, and it prescribes the limits (probably mainly financial) within which the branch companies are permitted to operate.

This is a perfect example of a cybernetic machine. Our first job is to propose a model for this system, and the analogy we want is obvious. It is the model of a living organism, an animal, let us say a man. The autonomous branches are analogous to the autonomous functions of the animal body. Each of these is controlled by a plexus of nerves which is itself hierarchical in structure. In the branches, as in the body's particularized organs, the local control systems work of their own violition to govern locally the behaviour of that aspect of the whole body's function for which they are responsible.

This analogy would have to be examined in great detail in an actual cybernetic study, but the general structures of the two systems are clearly very similar. In both cases the complete organism is an efficient machine for surviving in a turbulent environment only because it is integrated. And in each case it is precisely survival which is the goal, despite a ramified set of subservient and often contradictory minor objectives. For example, and subject to survival, the company wants to make the maximum profit and the man to maximize his enjoyment of life. Neither system can adopt a strategy based solely on this hedonistic motive, for such a strategy would probably dictate a short-term policy disastrous to its long-run survival motive. The man might drink much whisky in pursuit of pleasure, at the sacrifice of his liver, and die of cirrhosis; the company might make much money, at the sacrifice of its goodwill, and die of no orders in a slump. The analogy could be, and must be, extended a long way—until the limits of its logical validity are recognized.

This done, the structures of the two systems have to be lifted out of their contexts, formalized, and compared scientifically. This is also quite possible. All sorts of operational research inferences can be drawn at this stage. For example, it soon becomes apparent that the company is quite right to believe that centralized control does not imply a hierarchical structure right up to the top management, whose analogue is the cerebral cortex. Reflexes, and all the local functions of the body with their endocrine glands and nervous plexuses, are controlled locally and in the spinal cord, cerebellum and mid-brain. Suppose these controls were all channelled to, and controlled in detail in, the cortex. It is easy to estimate how big the brain would have to be to handle all this information, just as the company knows it would need a central organization of vast and unwieldy size and complexity to control its branches in detail. Physiologically the idea is unsound. Psychologically, the analogy implies a man who is conscious of every heart beat, every digestive movement. The man and the company would quickly become neurotic.

No, the kind of control required is the same in both cases, since the two systems are isomorphic to a high degree. Let us assume that the range of identity of structure has now been established, that the topological mapping of one set into the other is complete and understood. The cybernetician is now ready to evolve dynamic, homeostatic control for any of the vast array of variables which the company seeks to control. Which shall we choose in order to pursue our examples? Let us take the control of the system's energy. For the company, this is its use of capital.

A TENTATIVE EXAMPLE

Ignoring various special and probably small drains on capital, our mythical organization is likely to absorb capital in three main ways: in plant, in stocks and in credit. New plant, increased stocks and the extension of credit continually absorb fresh capital which has either to be raised in the market or ploughed back from profits. For the most part, neither the man's body nor the company formulates a conscious policy (in the brain, or the top management) about how its available energy is to be distributed in detail. A man may go to bed early to store energy against a big effort next day, and the company may reserve capital against its major development schemes. But the day-to-day absorption of capital, as of energy, depends upon the call that is made for it autonomously from the branches or the body's organs.

A sudden physical demand is made on the system of the man, and adrenaline is pumped into circuit without the brain's conscious edict. A sudden strain is placed on the supply of a raw material in one of the branches, and supplies of capital are drawn off into a larger pile of stock without the detailed approval of the central management. Without conscious control, then, the body and the organization have a policy about the apportionment of energy *which cannot be made explicit*. The apportionment is influenced from moment to moment by the internal demands of the system and by the pressures brought to bear on it by the external environment. It is this constant flux in the strategy of best apportionment of energy that makes it virtually impossible to have a conscious policy about its differential use.

How trite is the exploitation of this analogy proving? I submit that it is already teaching us a great deal. We are very prone to discuss these problems of stockholding on the basis of an input–output analysis. Even highly sophisticated operational research does this. But once the organism is really considered as an organic whole, this classic mode of control is seen to be unphysiological—almost meaningless. One can never say what is the output and what the input of a system which in any case cannot be delineated. The language one is talking effectively imprisons one inside the system: one is inside the black box.

This whole mechanism is a constant blur of interaction. The output required of the system depends on the unpredictable internal and external pressures. There is a restraint on the input, since neither energy nor capital is unlimited; but the actual availability of this energy in the next arbitrary period of time is unpredictable at the local level. This is because nobody knows what demands will be made by other components of the total system, nor whether the body as a whole will adjust itself to meet one demand rather than another, nor whether the total energy called for will be more than the body can release. May I repeat as a matter of scientific inference that the classic mode of control will not work for these reasons, and also submit that in fact it does not.

It is a matter of sheer experience in industry that stocks tend to rise—unless a rigid and unphysiological restriction is placed on the capital committed in the form of an absolute ban. Cybernetically, we can see why this must be so. The point can be made from the thermodynamic model of entropy which there is no time to examine in detail here. To resist the pressure of the natural tendency of entropy to rise, which will tend to distribute in the form of stock any capital that becomes available, there is no comparable negative feedback. This could only be provided by a volitional message from the brain, backed by the sanction of unpleasantness in some form. Neither the body nor the company makes much use of this kind of negative feedback, again because it is contrary to the organizational principles of the system's structure.

Much more could be said, but we must conclude peremptorily by asking what form of control the cybernetician can propose. Now although the demands on energy cannot be precisely forecast in advance, it is retrospectively true that over a given period they must have reached a given total subdivided in a given way. How this total energy or capital proves to have been divided will reflect, not only the many influences which have actually been exerted in that period, but in particular its actual subdivision in the immediately preceding period. The way in which an organic system's energy can be distributed in the next period is profoundly constrained by the way it is distributed now, despite the rather odd fact that its total in the next period may be very different and not altogether predictable. Secondly, the distribution in the next period is profoundly influenced by the present expectation of the demands that will be made on the organism in the next period. These facts are categorically true of the structure we are examining; they emerge visibly in both the real-life systems of company and body.

Therefore I conclude that to control this situation does not require that the (impossible) prediction of supply and demand of energy in advance be built in to a (meaningless) model of the stock commitment which shows the (unascertainable) influences which will prevail. It requires instead a description of how the system learns to be reasonably stable in the light of the information it has actually available. There can be no doubt that the system does learn a strategy for this purpose, because it does succeed in damping the effects of innumerable environmental and internal disturbances. Once the cybernetic analogy has been extended to an account of the whole system's learning processes, control becomes possible. This does not of course mean the learning processes, the experiences, of individual managers. It means those of the whole organic system, an entity which is not customarily thought of as susceptible to teaching at all.

This model being understood, a situation is created in which the factors to which the learning process is sensitive can be manipulated by the central management. Consider a very crude illustration. You are training a man to be skilled in a new language. His energy is not properly deployed. When you are asking for his attention to the blackboard, he is looking out of the window. You conclude that there is something going on outside which interests him, and cover up the window. He at once begins looking at a fellow student. You build a model to yourself of the factors to which his learning process is sensitive. It is not what is going on outside that distracts him; it is not the fellow student. Both these targets would be understandable distractions. In the end you realize that it was the green grass and the green frock which drew his gaze. Greenness in the environment conditions the learning process. There is no fathomable reason for this. But when you exploit your model of the learning process, you write on the blackboard in green chalk—and he attends.

In the kind of problem we have discussed so shortly, there are reasons of complexity, of indefinability and of natural tendency why stocks continue to rise. The real reasons cannot be elucidated; in fact, it is probably meaningless to talk about 'real reasons' at all. Therefore, no ordinary control system works, and control by edict backed by sanctions has been eliminated too. But the factors, which may be totally unexpected and apparently irrelevant, to which the learning process of the system is sensitive must be discoverable and can be manipulated. My own guess is that these factors are conventions of the language in which the structure of the system expresses itself to individual managers. Perhaps this amounts to saying that the learning process of the system reacts to what people quite erroneously believe to be its mechanism. Whatever the reason this is the dimension in which to operate. The conventions of the language can after all be altered. Then, I believe, the system will change its behaviour.

CONCLUSION

My case is now completed, in that I have said what I think the second industrial revolution is about, what I believe the role and nature of cybernetics to be in industry, and the way in which I hold this thinking can be exploited. Throughout this general story, however, which is merely illustrative, I have tried to bring out the real point that is my message to this Conference. This is that we are talking about structures and their dynamics when we speak of control. We are not talking about the systems in which the structures are clothed, nor about the external manifestations of control. I hope it is quite evident from the stockholding example how much of a side issue is the question of the appearance of the control system.

Consider: the kind of control proposed could possibly be installed merely by adjusting the meanings of terms used in management circles in that mythical company. It could possibly be achieved by replacing some of the decisions, those decisions to which the learning system proved sensitive, by a learning machine—electronic or chemical, it does not matter. It could be achieved in some circumstances by programming a computer to carry out a game-theoretic strategy on data fed to it automatically from the production line, with the computer itself initiating the production of the necessary stocks. There are many possible manifestations: there is one cybernetic solution.

And so I return, circuitously, to demonstrate the role of automation in the new revolution by pointing to it in what I believe is its true context. Automation exhibits one kind of control dynamic based on one kind of structure. It is a certain type of system, and one with some very valuable characteristics: such as its coupling mechanisms, its error-controlled feedback, its quick response rate when talking its own language. These advantages make it a useful model in some cases on which to draw and in other cases a useful manifestation of a cybernetic result ready to install. It has its drawbacks too. In a company where flexibility of product and process is vital, the automation structure is hopelessly unviable. In problems, like stock control, for which the analytic input–output model is extremely unrealistic, the automation structure is unrealistic too. And always the high response rate in its own language carries the penalty of a very low response rate to other languages inside the general system. The 'talkativeness' of automation is poor: it is too busy getting on with its own job. In many, many fields it is not automation that we require, either as structural model or as manifestation, but something more physiological.

Cybernetics is about all manner of control, all kinds of structure, all sorts of system. Automation belongs here. But to the science of cybernetics as a thinking-tool for solving the control problems that beset industry, automation is irrelevant.

ECCE HOMO

There is no sunlight in the brain
Or in computer logic. Dark
Flows the digit drain
Within machines.

There is that difference between
The milli and the nano second
Putting the artefact on top
A million times.

  Light
  goes a foot in a nanosecond
    light
    goes no further than the skull
      light
      fails and the times are short
  But it's dull in this loop stop.

There's only bits in the cold core store
There's only bits in the human brain
Euphoric computer you
With flair.

You stark dumb wild creative beast
You programmed from the navel
To invert an LP matrix
Or to paint:

  Now
  invert the virgin womb
    now
    trickle percolate offspring
      now
      through microcircuit guts
  Hope for the end of these tricks.

Then looker-up and optimist
Be programmed, be debugged. Adam
That old heuristic
Won't converge.

Stafford Beer
Transit, 1977

8 THE WORLD, THE FLESH AND THE METAL: The Prerogatives of Systems

1964 Stephenson Lecture Newcastle University

STAFFORD BEER
Managing Director,
SIGMA (Science in General Management Ltd),
Croydon, UK

THE SEMINAL IDEA

COMMANDING CONCEPTS arise in science which seem to roll up the universe into a ball, declaring: it works thus. I am thinking of such notions as inertia and entropy. The names of these concepts do not denote any discoverable thing out there in the world at all. They denote sophisticated ideas that scientists have about the way the world is arranged, or perhaps read into the world. What is out there is a manifestation of the idea; and that manifestation is pervasive, once the idea is sufficiently clear to be called obsessive.

The old way of talking about these concepts was to legislate about them, and to set up Laws of Nature. Who passes these laws is not clear, but certainly God alone may repeal them. So clustering about the concept of inertia are the laws of motion—together with a considerable body of amendments which encompass relativity; and clustering about the concept of entropy are the laws of thermodynamics—together with special versions of the enactments for other territories, such as statistical mechanics and information theory. These laws seem to be very unusual ones indeed; for these is no way of repealing them— once the Deity is defined in their own terms as a store of negentropy.

Now concepts of this kind are very difficult to understand, because there is no ostensive definition. Hunting down inertia is like hunting down the

First published by Macmillan Magazines Limited.

snark; the only one who actually saw it 'softly and suddenly vanished away'. The result is it takes a long time before the concepts which are most potent in the scientist's interpretation of the universe are manipulated with ease in our thinking. As evidence of this contention, consider the adjectival form of the terms already mentioned. Physics acquired the concept of inertia in 1687, through the *Principia*. But it was 162 years before anyone invented the adjective, and spoke of 'a weight of inertial resistance'. Where would science be without that word today, a mere 100 years later? As to the word entropy, the centenary of the birth of which falls in 1965, we are still so unsure of ourselves that there is no official record that the adjective has been coined yet. I have in fact coined it myself, and offered such phrases as 'entropic drift'; but no one seems to want them.

The point of all this is to suggest that the concept of system is another such seminal notion, which we are only now beginning to understand. This word has also been used since the seventeenth century; and is certainly well understood in the rather special sense of an assemblage which is usually small, usually connected together deterministically, and usually well defined. But we cannot roll up the universe into that sort of ball, nor declare it works thus. Patently the universe is not, nor is it compounded of, that sort of system. Yet a system in another sense it clearly is, and any part of the universe is clearly a system in that same sense. Secondly, the syntactical clue to our unease in the manipulation of this wider concept is again present. For the adjective which means 'pertaining to a system' is not 'systematic' (which means something quite different) but systemic; and that is a word one seldom hears. It took 184 years to achieve the adjectival form this time, even in a limited physiological context. As an adjective of general relevance, the word systemic has been with us for only 100 years, and its use is now marked 'rare' in the dictionary.

In short, we do not think about the systemic nature of things, we prefer to consider them in isolation. Stepping smartly down from these philological clouds, I point to a number of practical examples. The brain, a company's profitability, a computer and the National Health Service are all integral systems. But we talk gaily about the motor cortex as if the rest of the brain were irrelevant to movement. We talk about the cost of making a product as if it did not matter what opportunities to make other products were forgone in making this one. We talk about the reliability of an electronic component as if this meant something independently of the failure rates of associated components in an operational ensemble. We talk about the cost of prescriptions under National Health as if this were independent of the doctors' attitude to whether the patient bears a charge or not.

The seminal notion of system-as-pervasive in science is really very new, and we are not trained to think in systemic terms because our scientific approach has been analytical to the ultimate degree. We took things apart, historically, and described the atomic bits. We did our experiments, historically, on these bits—deliberately holding invariant the behaviour of other bits with which in fact they were systemically interacting in real life. New advances in statistical method have enabled us to be more ingenious than this today; we can afford to let a number of things change at the same time, and sort out the meaning of the experiment by multivariate analysis. But this is a mastery of technique, not a change in methodology. The result is that our only approach to system is through aggregating bits. No wonder that we do not advance in understanding really big systems, then, and that the very connotation of this word system includes such question-begging epithets as small, determined and well defined.

The concept of system in its widest meaning is a cybernetic concept. Big systems are the topic of cybernetics. The systemic character of the world is the clue to its control; just as the inertial character of the world is the clue to its movements, and the entropic character of the world is the clue to its energies. Thus the contention is that the 'laws of control' are the prerogatives of system—wherever and whenever it is defined. And this is why I have taken liberties with the catechism in the title. For the prerogatives of system are pervasive, whether we speak of the world at large, or the flesh of our own bodies, or the metal of the ironmongery we invent as engineers.

METHODOLOGY OF MODELS

If this concept of system is so new and so important, how shall we attack it, how comprehend and manipulate it? In a paper written five years ago [1] I gave a philosophical approach to this problem. Today the approach will be essentially mathematical.

When an engineer looks at a big system (as already defined here) and recognizes its systemic character, he may well perceive its structure in terms of servomechanics. He draws rings around various activities, or subsets of events, in his mind, and observes that they are linked together by messages. That is to say, that the input to one subset is the output of one or more other subsets. For example, production is an activity which responds to a demand expressed by a market, while selling is an activity responding to a production output. The engineer may then recognize that what happens in each box of the system may be regarded as a transfer function applied to the signals that connect it to other boxes. If the macrosystem he is thinking about can once be defined as closed, as in the case of the marketing-production-marketing example, he is in business as a model-builder. The process soon becomes exciting. In order to attain to an ever-more-accurate account of what the big system is doing, the model-builder may insert all sorts of boxes in his design, until the model is very complicated indeed. Very soon he will see the need for local regulatory devices in the microsystems which comprise the macrosystem. This will lead to the insertion of closed-loop feedback circuits, in which outputs are monitored by comparators, and inputs modified by some function of the error signal thereby formed. It is often possible to obtain a strikingly good analogue, expressed in servomechanical terms, of a fairly big system of world events in this fashion.

In fact, this is one example of the way operational research works. The scientific model conceived by an operational research team will depend on the kind of system being studied and on the versatility of the team itself. We are all conditioned by our training and experience. It can scarcely have been fortuitous that Prof. M. J. Lighthill chose to represent the flow of traffic with a model from fluid dynamics, or that Prof. A. Tustin sought to model the economy by just the kind of servosystem that I have been describing. This is not because the big systems of real life are 'really' hydraulic or electrical in character, but because Lighthill and Tustin are the distinguished men they are, and because the systemic character of the world is pervasive. This is why an operational research group is supposed to be interdisciplinary. It is my job to hold back a colleague who is determined to model a management structure by an anthropological model taken from the tribes of the Western Pacific, if this turns out to be rather unhelpful. Equally I expect my colleagues to intervene if my own habit of modelling company organizations on neurophysiological systems runs away with me. They always do intervene, as it happens; but I still think that the brain, supported as it is by many million years of research and development, must offer good advice on how to make a control system viable—which just shows how preconditioned I am. Anyone who wishes to examine more closely how operational research makes use of models from science may refer to another paper [2], in which various examples are given—including the electrical circuit of a servomodel of an actual production system.

But, assuming that this talk of models is now understood in a general sense, I propose to examine rather more rigorously what is going on when a model of one activity is taken from another activity. Here it should be borne in mind that our comprehension of anything at all is likely to be expressed to ourselves in terms of something else which we know that we understand; which is another way of saying that everything is a model of something else. If you should ask: what constitutes the prior structure of which other things are models?—Then maybe the answer belongs to psychoanalysis, and must be expressed in terms of elemental and traumatic experiences.

Consider a big system out there in the world. It may be a firm interacting with its environment of markets in a search for survival; it may be a company competing with another company for a larger share of a zero-sum pay-off;

it may be a capitalist economy in which a socialist chancellor sits like a Maxwell demon increasing the entropy of wealth. (Please note in passing how, simply in order to nominate three samples of big systems, I have already invoked three models: from ecology, from game theory, and from thermodynamics.) In trying to understand these things as systems, we must detect in them whatever is systemic. This sounds tautologous, but it is not really. For we do not have full knowledge of what these systems are like—they are immensely complicated; and we do not have full knowledge of what constitutes system anyway—science is not yet omniscient, and we ourselves are relatively ignorant.

Now I shall discuss this problem in the language of group theory, for reasons which will be made specific later on. The point is that we need as rigorous a statement of this complicated methodology of models as we can get. It is in fact high time that some such attempt was made, for the very word 'model' has fallen into an unhelpfully casual usage. Some people use the word as synonymous with 'mathematical equation'; others treat the word as if it meant 'hypothesis'. A model is neither of these things. It is something that opens up a virtually new way of doing science.

Thus if we call the set M of elements a the totality of world events which we propose to examine, then the systemic configuration of events which we know about is a subset A of set M. If we call the set N of elements b the totality of systemic science, then the configuration of system which we ourselves understand is a subset B of set N. The process of creating a systemic model may then be described as a mapping f of A into B. By this I mean that for every element $a \epsilon A \subset M$ there exists a corresponding element $b \epsilon B \subset N$, and thus $b = f(a)$. The image of the subset A, namely, $f(A) \subset N$, is the model. If we are able to exhaust the elements of A and to nominate their images in B, we have every hope of creating an isomorphic model. This means that there exists a complete inverse image of B under mapping f in M, so that $f(A) \subset N = f^{-1}(B) \subset M$. This is the state of affairs, expressed group-theoretically, which the operational research man is trying to reach.

Now an isomorphism is important because it preserves the structure of the original group in the mapping. Typically, if it is possible to perform additions inside set M, those additions will remain valid when the same operations are performed on the images of their elements in set N. It is this persistence of relationship when the mapping is done which makes a model operate as a model. So, if a_1 and a_2 when added together equal a_n in set M, it can be shown that $f(a_1)$ plus $f(a_2)$ must equal $f(a_n)$ in set N. Now comes the interesting comment. The conditions can be set up in which the same answer $f(a_n)$ in set N is obtained from the mapping f whether the transformation is effected before or after the mapping occurs. That is to say, we may either add the original elements in M and transform the answer under f, or we may transform the original elements first and then add them.

The result will be the same. Formally: $f(a_1+a_2)=f(a_1)+f(a_2)$. When one group is mapped into another group and this condition is generally fulfilled, the mapping is called homomorphic.

These elementary definitions are included so that the argument can be made quite clear. Because it is possible to coalesce elements of M before transforming them, without losing the capability of a mapping to preserve structural relationships as discussed, it is clear that a homomorphism may have fewer elements than its inverse image. In the case of the model, then, the mapping of A into B turns out to be a mapping *on to* a sub-group of B. Isomorphism turns out to be a special case of homomorphism, in that $f(A) \subset B$ turns out to mean $f(A)=B$: the one–one correspondence of elements with which we begin is maintained. But for any other sub-group of B other than B itself, homomorphism involves a many–one correspondence, and the inverse mapping $f^{-1}(B)$ will not exhaust the elements of A.

It is suggested, then, that the models of big systems that we entertain are homomorphisms of those systemic characteristics of the big system that we can identify. The homomorphic group $f(A) \subset B \subset N$ is the particular model we use. It is in practice extremely difficult to include in this model all the features recognized in A, and typically we do make the many–one reductions mentioned. Thus, for example, we undertake production costings as if the behaviour of all three shifts in a works were indistinguishable, and as if two similar products were identical, and as if materials were consistently uniform—although we actually know that none of these simplifications is true. Then the effectiveness of the model as predictive depends on the choice of an effective transformation by which to map. If we add up the outputs of three shifts and then transform the answer by some mapping into the model, it is no use supporting that any calculation, comparison or prediction undertaken in the model can be worked backwards through an inverse mapping which will distinguish between the shifts. On the other hand, it is necessary to handle only a third of the elements we know about inside the model. A definite choice has been made to jettison modelling power in favour of economy in the recording and handling of data. This is acceptable, so long as the choice is deliberate rather than accidental, and so long as it is remembered as a limitation in the model.

Secondly, however, there is a further loss of modelling power in the facts that A is a subset of M and B is a subset of N. Now an interdisciplinary team of scientists can minimize the losses of modelling power due to $B<N$. Because such a team can examine all the major subsets of N before deciding to use one specific group B; it may even experiment with other groups too. But the losses due to $A<M$ are more serious, and may be disastrous to the exercise. For if what we recognize in a big system is not what is really important about its systemic character, the ability to predict A may not help

much in M. In other words, A is itself a homomorphic mapping of M, and one which by definition we cannot properly specify. Remember that $M-A$ was acknowledged to be systemically unrecognized from the start. We may know that our knowledge of a big system does not exhaust it, without having the faintest idea of the character of the knowledge that is missing.

It is hoped that this attempt somewhat rigorously to formulate what goes on in model-building will prove helpful in pin-pointing what we can and cannot do. The ordinary operational research exercise works, and we can see why. It is possible to advance what we understand about a stockholding system, for example, to the point where A approaches M asymptotically. It is possible to examine most B or N, which is to say most scientific approaches to the scientific totality of understanding about such systems. If we know what the stockholding system has to do, if (as the operational research man would say) we can define its criteria of success or objective function, then we can define a homomorphic mapping f of $A \simeq M$ on to $B \simeq N$ which preserves the stochastic relationships in which we are interested. More especially, we can do this in such a way that the inverse image of B under mapping f yields a set $f^{-1}(B)$ of elements in the real system M which are useful.

The difficulties about doing successful operational research in various circumstances can now be made quite specific. First, the modelling will not on the average work well if $N-B$ is large: this happens if the operational research team is not corporately versatile. Second, the modelling will not work at all unless f is well defined: this entails good empirical research into what the system really has to do. Third, the predictions of the model will be of no actual use if a modelled outcome $\varphi(b_1 \ldots b_n)$ turns out to have a pragmatically undiscriminating inverse $f^{-1}(\varphi)$ in A. This also entails good empirical research into the forms of many–one reduction. Fourth, the modelled predictions though useful will not exert what could be called control unless the $M \rightarrow A$ homomorphism captures the systemic character of the big system *in extenso*. This again appears to be a matter for good empirical research, although there is more to say.

Contrary to increasingly current belief, then, operational research is empirical science above all. The mathematical models dreamed up in back rooms are useless unless they can meet the four kinds of difficulty enumerated, and this cannot be done remotely from the world. But that is by the way.

BASIS OF SYSTEMIC CONTROL

If the ordinary operational research study works for the reasons just given, it is easy to see why we encounter difficulty in extending its scope to the really big system. It is not the difficulty of procuring the homomorphic mapping $A \rightarrow B$, which practice and scientific skill can encompass. It is the difficulty of procuring the homomorphic mapping $M \rightarrow A$. Now if we rightly called the mapping $f(A) \subset B \subset N$ the model, it is the complete inverse image of this model in M that constitutes a sentient control. The point is one of some subtlety, and repays a little thought. It says that deliberative control can be exerted only through the systemic connectivity of the big system that we recognize; and, moreover, that we are enabled to exert that control only via our model of how it works, with an efficiency that depends on the relevance of the mappings f and f^{-1}.

Interestingly, this deliberative control is not primarily what does control any big system. It is not adequate to the task. No one imagines that the set of actions open to being taken by a Chancellor of the Exchequer constitutes the control of the economy: it constitutes at best an error-controlled feedback loop of either positive or negative sign. And the managing director who believes that he constitutes the control of the firm is deluded for the same reason. The reason why this must be so is given by the volume of information defining the behaviour of a big system. In cybernetics, we call the number of distinguishable states that a system may take up its variety. Clearly, the big system proliferates variety; and clearly this variety is not readily handled by a control system which cannot absorb it—which is choked by it, or confused by it, or otherwise overwhelmed. I have already said that ideally A should tend to equivalence with M under some homomorphic transformation. This was meant to ensure that the systemic structure of the big system would be preserved in the understood version of its nature which was to be modelled. What we now go on to say is that the measure of variety evinced by the big system must in some sense be paralleled in whatever is actually controlling it.

Examine this proposition in terms of the thesis already developed. We want a model of the big system M competent to determine its actual rather than deliberative control mechanisms. Since we do not, by definition, know what these are, we need to preserve a one–one correspondence of elements. What then is isomorphic to a big system? It is inconceivable that we should go away and construct another system of equivalent variety—for this really is a big system, and our model would have to be as large. The group-theoretic formulation gives the clue to the answer. Cayley's theorem declares that every finite group is isomorphic to a certain group of permutations of itself; and it is part of the proof to show that one of these is the identical permutation. In other words, the isomorphism we seek for the big system is itself. Hence the big system M, to which is clamped another system A which is in fact itself, is to be called controlled.

Do not imagine that this conclusion is vacuous. It is, after all, the realization that an isosceles triangle ABC is congruent with the identical triangle CBA that enables us to prove, without construction, that the base angles are equal. If we try to give material substance to the mathematical abstraction of the big system's isomorphism with itself, we shall, so to speak, have to think of cleaving the system in half through its plane. Then every element is twinned, and the idea of what constitutes effective control suddenly becomes blindingly clear. Every player is marked by another player; or, to use another metaphor, half the population are policemen keeping one-to-one guard on the other half.

The law of control which has emerged is, I believe, a new formulation of Ashby's law of requisite variety [3]. It says, in effect, that control can be exercised only by a controller having at least as high variety as the system to be controlled. This is what happens in big systems, because it must. Two halves of the system are monitoring each other; though woe betide any glib observer who imagines he can determine the boundary between them. It is not as easy as that. The two subsets are interpenetrated; and, one suspects, elements move in and out of both subsets continually. Requisite variety in a controller is the power to absorb the variety proliferated by what is to be controlled, but this power is disseminated throughout the system rather than being concentrated in a control box.

However, there is better news—if we are cautious. Electrons are continually being exchanged between any object and its surroundings, but this does not in practice deter us from identifying objects and declaring that they persist. If we had sub-atomic magnitude ourselves, it would matter very much: doubtless we should not be able to identify these objects at all. If, then, we look at our big system as compounded of subsystems which exhaust the whole, we may well make arbitrary rulings about what constitutes one part and what another, but we shall have preserved requisite variety. For although there is no means of saying exactly what is included in any subsystem, and although we may be quite unable to analyse the relationships which subsist between the elements of these subsystems, we shall still be able to talk about control. Control is precisely the stable state of the variety interactions between the subsystems nominated.

How does this account differ from the original one in which the engineer looked for the servosystem within the big system? In the first place, it is exhaustive—by logical definition. But, more important, it does not see communication as a signal passing from one transfer function to the next in a thin white line. It sees communication as interpenetrative between the subsystems which are richly interconnected—(in the limit) element by element. Yet, more important still, it sees systemic stability itself as the object of the system, and not the holding steady of an arbitrarily assigned output—which is the usual criterion of control engineering.

These outcomes of the discussion give most of the leads which are required to answer the initial question: how do we attack, comprehend and manipulate the systemic character of the universe? They involve, I fear, a revolution in thinking for the trained scientist. No longer do we aggregate bits of the system, which have been adequately investigated, into even larger well-understood systems, which eventually (but when, indeed?) ought to approximate in size and scope to the big system under investigation. Instead, we begin by carving up the not-understood big system into interacting subsystems, and we ask behavioural questions about the resulting homeostats—which are the stably interacting parts. This can be done, and can result in useful statements about the big system itself. Comprehension begins with observations about the way in which two halves, or better still *n nths*, of the big system interact, although there is virtually no knowledge about the contents or internal structure of those halves or *n*ths. Comprehension is extended by resolving (in the optical sense) these structures to an ever-increasing degree. But we should not imagine that we shall ever reach the atomic parts and their relationships—which are the very entities with the close examination of which orthodox science is accustomed to begin.

Anyone who finds this too puzzling should forget that he is a scientist for the moment and remember that he is a man. How is it that we can make useful predictions about the way each other's brains work? We do a reasonable job; for people do not constantly surprise us, rather the dispiriting reverse. Perhaps we do it by drawing inferences from other people's behaviour, their responses to our stimuli, over a period; perhaps we argue by analogy with our own responses; perhaps we do both. In any event we do it by making models, by mapping behavioural structures on to each other; by juxtaposing; by interacting. What we quite clearly do not do is get down to that mess of pottage, a brain newly excavated from its cranium, with a microscope. If we did, and escaped hanging, we should still not learn enough to make predictions about people's behaviour. The classical method of enquiry would encumber us with the investigation of the basic nerve cell, the atomic component, called the neurone—from which we would work outwards to the big system, the cerebrum. According to the American cybernetician McCulloch (who very possibly knows) the transfer function of a neurone is to be defined only in terms of an eighth-order non-linear differential equation. There is no guarantee that any two neurones have an identical transfer function, and the brain contains 10 000 million of them. Next, we should need to know how they are arranged and interconnected. The fact that all our lives we lose about 100 000 a day (they just pack up) is another complication. No: it just will not do.

Return then to the notion that requisite variety is supplied in natural systems, and that deliberative control is based on a model of a subset of the actual control mechanisms. What the would-be controller, or manager, has to do is to intervene in these natural processes rather than to impose some conrol arrangement on them. Good managers intuit that this is their task. The trouble is that so many of the 'experts' who seek to advise them do not always understand this point, unless the big system is a person. In that special case, human prerogatives are invoked to say that people ought not to be controlled, by the imposition of restraints on their freedom: I speak of an ethical imperative. Certainly, some restraints are imposed, in the interests of the community at large; but if we want a particular man to do a particular act we do not contemplate using a pistol, or drugs or hypnosis. We have to organize the system of which the man is a part in such a way that he does what we want of his own accord. This is the right way to control any big system, such as a firm or an economy; not because of ethical imperatives but because of cybernetic laws. For the implicit control of the big system, which requisite variety guarantees, is carrying the system to a more stable condition naturally.

The management task is to arrange its pay-off objectives in relation to the system's own built-in objective of stability. The best way to express this rule is to say that the system has an informational entropy which carries it towards a more probable state. Management needs to arrange the system so that the most probable state is the desired state. This means that the natural force of entropy is harnessed as a control force in the system. It also means that the system offers us an amplifier of our control signals free of charge, and a complete set of appropriate control circuits for distributing control signals to the right places in the system—even though we have no knowledge as to where the right places are.

If this sounds too good to be true, remember that the job can be done effectively only if we use a model which is an appropriate homomorphism. The 'experts' of whom I complained just now are people who imagine that their heads contain this model, and that their own *savoir faire* is a sufficiently good account of the inverse mapping. Why do economists disagree as to the correct governmental action in a given economic crisis? Surely it is because they pass off hypotheses about the way the country works as models with known mappings; so that any two of these non-models will read different deliberative control policies into the inverse image, which are quite likely to be inconsistent if not contradictory. The same is true of advisers to firms, transportation experts and so forth. The control of big systems demands a prior investigation of the natural control homomorph, and a scientific account of what entropies are involved. From this we can learn how to use the entropic drift as a control device. It is the only way to generate requisite variety in deliberative control for the inverse mapping $A \rightarrow M$.

SYSTEMIC CONTROL IN 'THE WORLD'

When we come to consider applications of these arguments to the world in general it is natural to turn to national affairs. For here are the big systems with which it is most important that we learn how to deal. There are, of course, international affairs, if we wish to set the sights higher.

Now it is possible to argue that most of the troubles we encounter in deciding on policies at the national and international level derive from our habit of dividing the system, which is too big and too complicated to handle integrally by classical methods, and trying to compute with the pieces—or subsystems. The reason why a world which is affluent in some places and penurious in others cannot find a method for controlling food supplies is surely thus. There is no need for a third of the world to be hungry, for a baby to die of starvation every 42 seconds. But the boundaries drawn around the subsystems, around each country and around political blocs, are too rigid. In terms of the entropies which system-oriented scientists perforce discuss, these subsystems operate within virtually adiabatic shells. Hence there is no chance of levelling out food supplies, which constitute the energy of the total system, or (by a mapping) of levelling out human happiness and human misery. Nor is there any obvious political technique by which a Stephenson Lecturer can propose to start engineering with these conventional packages. In national affairs, there is. Let us consider some examples.

It is by now a platitude to say that the plan conceived for the future of the railways is probably wrong, but that if it is wrong the fault lies with a Minister and not with the Rail Board. This is said because the railway chiefs were given certain tasks concerned with railway profitability; they were not asked to take into account the integral system of national transportation. Here, I should agree, is a perfect example of what the logician calls *fallacia divisio*: separating components which ought to be kept together. Keeping those components together is indeed a systemic imperative. Where transport is concerned, we have most notably fallen foul of the classical mental discipline which tries to build large systems as aggregates of carefully studied elements. That people should in general be able to get from one place to another is important. But this aim has become subservient to bogus optima, whereby each element of the system must itself be 'economic'. On the railways and in the air-lanes, this criterion has been applied. So far as roads are concerned, attempts are often made to cost the journeys of the private motorist, and to show that it would be cheaper for him to travel by public transport.

Beginning with this case, we see how the systemic law is ignored. If a man lives in circumstances which necessitate his owning a car, then the car is part of his transportation system. To cost a journey which he could have made by train on the basis that the capital cost of his car ought to be apportioned by mileage to this journey is a silly piece of accounting. He has this car anyway. The cost of his journey includes wear on the car perhaps, as well as running cost; but it certainly does not include a share of capital cost. On this basis, he will prefer to travel by road on economic grounds. Thus begins the destruction of that non-homomorphic model which calculates travel in terms of a fixed price per mile. The cost per mile of any kind of journey depends on the systemic context. It follows that the prices charged per mile by transport undertakings ought not to be invariant, as they basically are. For example, since the profitability of an air journey depends on the proportion of seats occupied, and since potential passengers are to some extent motivated by economic considerations, it follows that the price per seat for a given journey should vary with the bookings made. Thus the price paid for an air ticket reserved months in advance would include a component for the value to the passenger of a guaranteed seat. As the time of departure approaches, the price for a seat should fall. A passenger prepared to risk making no flight in exchange for a cheaper ticket would bring the plane's occupancy to an economic level. Note that a continuously computed fare based on these factors would at last begin to engineer with the uncertainty of demand, founding itself on high-variety systemic interactions between the air service and need, and between the air service and competition.

This kind of approach takes note of how the world is; it begins to construct a homomorphic model which can be used for deliberative control. At present, our controls are attempted impositions of rules which do not pay off because they struggle against the tide of entropy. In such cases the proper resort of management is to engineer with the structure of the system, until the entropies created in interaction with the world yield what the airline wants, namely, a profit. A similar argument may be applied to the railwys, which have tried by advertising to condition the passenger to believe that 'it is quicker by rail'. Often, it is not quicker. Often, the potential passenger is less impressed by speed than by comfort, cleanliness and a sense of privacy. His selection entropies may then be drifting in a direction that does not conform to the systemic reference frame set up by the railway management. The battle for custom is then lost. If a passenger prefers to be fussed over by a pretty air hostess than insulted by a ticket collector, it is no good protesting that he should have more sense: and the best conclusion is not necessarily to close the railway line. It may be to abandon the attempt to match a high-variety demand with a low-variety service. Not even a monopoly can force through the repeal of the law of requisite variety.

Nor, indeed, can a whole powerful ministry repeal that law. The task of controlling road traffic, when attempted by policemen or by local regulators such as traffic lights, is a high-variety task unsuccessfully handled by low-variety control devices. It is quite obvious that requisite variety cannot be obtained to handle a problem of the magnitude now made manifest without massive sensory input to large-scale computing engines. Yet the use of computers is regarded, at worst, as a novel gimmick; and, at best, as an expensive innovation which perhaps must come as part of a technological upsurge. We never see the argument, based on fundamental thinking, that there are systemic imperatives which can be analysed and must be met. It is not surprising, then, that we see no attempt to derive the homomorphic model of national transportation which would serve as the basis for well-informed research into the deliberative control of movement. Such a model must be global, following the principles adduced into the preceding section. Ideally, we should use satellites to photograph the ebb and flow of traffic, in order to obtain the systemic conspectus that we need. There are less ambitious ways of doing so. But the London Traffic Survey does not even have this aim. It represents the old-fashioned, non-systemic approach of trying to understand the elemental components of the system. Life is too short.

The result, moreover, is that we do not begin to approach the cybernetic problems of traffic control which really are important. If we had a homomorphic model of the interactions of subsystems of traffic, we could begin to work on the serious issues that affect the dynamics of all big systems. (So far we have not discussed dynamics at all, only the structural aspects of systemic control.) Now the great problem in cybernetic dynamics is this. Every subsystem, however defined, is itself seeking a local stability. The big system as a whole seeks stability in terms of such local equilibria. But the homomorphic model of the big system, as expressed through the interaction of subsystems, is difficult to express in homogeneous terms. The reason is timing. If a subsystem is to be regarded as having an input which is the output of another subsystem, then it is vital that the relaxation time be consonant with the periodicity of the perturbations arising from the input subsystem. Otherwise, the receiving subsystem will remain in perpetual uncontrolled oscillation. Moreover, from the point of view of deliberative control considered as an inverse mapping of the model, there is a problem of scale. One subsystem will see an interconnected subsystem as pumping variables into its equations of motion; another will see the same input as setting its basic parameters. Which is which will depend on the relative relaxation times of the receiving subsystem to the two input subsystems. There is no need, surely, to press these problems to an audience of engineers. The point is that we have no idea how to handle them, because we have not even recognized that they exist, because we have not even begun to think out the model that reflects them.

They are, nevertheless, the problems which have to be solved: and if they exist for traffic management, they exist for economic management too. Moreover, if it is wrong to cut up the transportation system into separate units, it is wrong to cut up the national fuel system into separate units too. Who is there in the country at all who understands the systemic interaction between coal and gas and electricity and oil and atomic power? No one, so far as can be discovered, has begun to consider the homomorphic mapping of this integral whole. The examples are capable of indefinite extension. They seem to indicate a wholesale failure to understand anything at all about the prerogatives of systems. I hope it will now be appreciated why such care was taken to expound a methodology which can at least begin to discuss such matters, and why it is important to see that there has to be a reversal of the classical trend whereby science advances from the element to the system. It is because we have always done this, I repeat, that we have not to this day encompassed the really big system at all.

This difference of approach may be examined in the context of another big system which is particularly important to us all, namely, technical education. The future of this system and the demand on it were investigated in a famous White Paper, it may be recalled. The method of this enquiry, it will be no surprise to recollect, was to build up the 1970 requirement for technologists from the atomic components of employment as it existed in the past. There was no attempt to assess systemic interaction, nor the systemic trajectories of the future. In another paper [4] I have tried to expose the fault in this enquiry, and to show how the cybernetician would approach the task of modelling the actual control mechanisms involved.

There is one last point to make about the prerogatives of systems in the world at large, and it is this: Because of the habit of dividing, for administrative convenience, what should be kept together, we often identify as special to a part what is really a function of the whole. This causes us to try to measure, as a subsystem variable, some factor which might best be understood as a behavioural (that is, output) characteristic of the entire big system. An example which springs to mind from recent work concerns marketing. Everyone who spends money on sales promotion would like a measure of advertising effectiveness. This is, inevitably, sought in the change in sales value that follows in the wake of a campaign. But it is notoriously difficult to measure this change and to relate it to the appropriation—because of systemic interaction. There are time-lags, competitive effects, changes in conditions, and so on. It has become increasingly likely, to me, that the desired measure is not only impossible to make but actually invalid. The flavour of the argument, which cannot be set out here at length, is obtained by asking where in the engine of a car is to be found the vehicle's speed.

This sort of consideration can be contemplated with competence from the vantage point of an effective homomorphic model alone. For example, mention has already been made of the National Health Service. This centres on a system of patients and doctors interacting, each set providing the other with requisite variety. But there are several subsystems interlinked with this one, and interpenetrating with it element by element. Two most notable such subsystems are the regional hospital organizations and the pharmaceutical profession. All these subsystems seem often to be uncoupled in the administrative and indeed the professional mind. Then the interesting question is how to resolve such a problem as the appropriate payment of all concerned. Here perhaps is another example of a global behavioural characteristic, masquerading as an entire set of subsystemic variables. Certainly it is a problem for engineering in large systems to resolve, rather than a matter of local accountancy.

SYSTEMIC CONTROL IN 'THE FLESH'

There are various levels at which we can examine the relevance of systemic laws to animate systems, considered as distinct from the world that is not aware. If we chose to discuss the individual living creature, we should find many examples to enlarge our cybernetic understanding. For *Amoeba proteus* and *Homo sapiens* have this in common: they are both very big systems compounded of subsystems, and their character is systemic or it is nothing. Indeed, if we nominate viability as the objective of any organism, whether animate or pseudo-animate (as a firm or an economy), it is natural to turn to biology for advice. Cybernetics has sprung from biology, and has quickly involved physics and engineering, rather than the reverse, for perfectly sensible reasons. It is wise not to forget this, nor to ignore its lessons.

But the example of the operation of systemic laws 'in the flesh' that I shall take here comes from a different level of viable organization. I want to talk about the process of decision in a management group. Now decision theory, so-called, we have; it is an investigation appropriate to mathematical statistics. But decision theory assumes a unidimensional model of the world; it says that we know the terms in which we should rightly talk, and that we know the interactions that are important; it is not systemic. The process of decision in a management group is, on the contrary, systemic in character. The reason why it often takes many years to reach a complicated decision is because this is not understood.

Consider, then, such a decision. For example, where, and when, and how should the country add to its steel-making capacity by building a new plant? All manner of people will have views on this, arguing from every sort of expertise. The management problem is to find coherence in the spate of advice. Some of it will be factual; some of it will be inspirational masquerading as factual; most of it will be contingently factual—that is, 'what I am saying is true, if something else is true, but not absolutely'. It is the contingent advice which specifies the system of decision; but unfortunately most of it is not recognized as contingent. It is here, then, that operational research is needed, so that the decision space and its configurations may be rightly understood. But operational research will not take this decision. It will be taken by a large number of people, each of whom is guaranteeing some sub-decision of the whole. The control problem for the highest authority is to monitor the decision-taking procedure to which all the sub-deciders are contributing.

The classical approach to this situation is to regard a very minor sub-decision as a basic component, and to build up a highly complex total decision from these elements. Hence some junior metallurgist somewhere may declare it obvious that a metallurgical reaction is best obtainable in a certain way, and begin to dictate the whole technology to be used. An economist looks at the siting problem in terms of the technology he knows about; and so on. But, according to the arguments in this paper, we should not build up a very complicated specification from single components of decision. There is another way of looking at the matter. We do not really start with a set of elemental propositions, but with an infinitely large number of high-variety, integral alternatives. We do not really finish with a highly complicated specification for action, but with a unique integral answer. So the decision-taking procedure is not a process of building up more and more variety, but of eliminating more and more uncertainty. How can this procedure best be controlled?

We said that the decision space had to be defined and that it is composed of possible answers. That is to say, every alternative integral answer might be considered as a small square. The decision space would then be the totality of these alternatives—say, 1 million small squares. For convenience, we might consider them as arranged in a square array, or matrix. This decision space will be ranged over by any decision procedures, in a hunt for the right answer. A management group normally undertakes the task as an heuristic search, which goes on by elimination. The average number of steps taken before the right answer is recognized is evidently half a million, since there is no reason why the right small square should be encountered either sooner or later than any other. True, subsets of small squares may be eliminated at once if they share a recognized characteristic regarded as damning; on the other hand, there may be a great deal of wasteful hunting back and forth between two or more subsets of small squares, each of which looks as if it might include the right answer. Note that this procedure is precisely obeying the control law of requisite variety. The variety of the decision space (1 million alternatives) is matched by a control process organized to examine (if necessary) 1 million squares.

However, the natural variety proliferation of the world can be matched by variety generation—which I define as a deliberative control device. The decision space in our example is a square array. If we can identify the co-ordinates of this matrix as logical variables, then we can specify any small square (including the right answer) as a logical couple. To do so, we must search the co-ordinates. But the variety of each co-ordinate is 1000; so the search space is 2000 (instead of 1 000 000), and the expectation is that we find the answer in 1000 steps instead of in 500 000. Thus the variety generator fulfils the law of requisite variety (since it has the selection power to discriminate between all the alternatives) but is a deliberative controller 500 times as efficient as the natural controller.

All this is said to demonstrate the point. In practice, there is no reason why the decision space should be two-dimensional. Indeed, if a given decision had only two logical variables, it would not be a difficult decision. Then it has n logical variables, and the decision space is an n-dimensional space. Then the variety generator is yet more efficient. For the expectation that a set of integral alternative answers of high variety V will yield up the wanted answer by a general search is $\frac{1}{2}V$. Whereas the expectation for an n-dimensional search with variety generators is $n/2.V^{1/n}$. We have found in principle a method of dealing with large-scale decisions which capitalizes on the systemic structure of the problem. It is just not true that decision-takers normally do take this advantage, by some analogue of this algorithm, as empirical research into actual decisions reveals. But it remains to show how we shall take advantage of it in practice.

First of all, it is necessary to identify the logical variables which are relevant. That is to say, we need to know all the dimensions of the decision: what sorts of things have to be specified to make the decision definite. This process is not one of listing all the statistical variables which affect the magnitudes eventually to be used: that side of the job is done by applied mathematics. We want to know what factors must be accounted for before the decision counts as a decision. The steelworks decision, for example, is not specified unless it includes the location of the works, its output of ingot tons, its range of products, and so on. These are the logical variables. The systemic interaction of these variables defines the configuration and dimensionality of the decision space. The statistical variables will eventually determine the optimal *modus operandi* of the steelworks decided on.

The number of logical variables is n, that is the dimensionality of the decision space. But the variety-generator notion enables us to observe that the n-space involved is not just a square, nor a cube, nor a hypercube: it has a configuration. Suppose, for example, that it is sub-decided for sufficiently powerful reasons to have a steelworks of given ingot tonnage, or at any rate within some range of tonnages. This automatically delimits a range of reasonable costs, a collection of possible sites, and so on. We do not yet know what the elements of these sub-groups are; but we can see that the decision space is inwardly contorted in various ways. There exist logical inferences, which we have not worked out, for any combination of logical values that may be fixed for any of the logical variables. In that case we must try to express the decision space in terms of its logical variables to give structure to the systemic configuration which the real world tends to proliferate.

The way to do this is through symbolic logic. This is the language of science for handling relatedness: conjunctions and disjunctions, implications and inclusions. The decision we are after has a known number of logical dimensions, for we have listed them. The systemic structure of the decision will be given by a logical formula stating how the logical variables are interrelated. Now this is a model in the sense defined. It requires a mapping of the way the external world works in relation to this decision. We have its dimensionality; we have its configuration. Next, we must measure its variety. In fact, this is not too difficult. Some logical variables are binary, in which event they offer a single alternative—a one-bit decision. For example, the steelworks must either be integrated with an ironworks or not. Other logical variables may propose a group of choices. For example, there is a finite number of steel-making processes between which, or between combinations of which, a decision must be taken. Suppose that, in a given case, there are eight choices. The variety of this decision is 8, not 2. This is a three-bit decision: it is composed of three binary decisions: $2^3 = 8$.

We have now discovered how to measure the variety of the decision, which is to say the uncertainty which has to be removed in searching for the completed specification. The measure is, of course, an entropy; not a thermodynamic entropy, nor the entropy met with in statistical mechanics, but an informational entropy—an entropy of selection. But, however we view it, the statistic that computes its value is the same. It is: $H = -\Sigma p_i \log_3 p_i$, where p_i is the probability of the ith choice. (We can ignore Bolzmann's constant in this application.) For every logical variable in the logical formula, we must compute this entropy.

In the case where the choice is a straight alternative between equiprobable outcomes, the entropy is $H = -(0.5 \log_2 0.5) - (0.5 \log_2 0.5) = 1$. This is the classic one-bit decision, and it shows why we are accustomed in cybernetics to use logarithms to the base 2: the answer is measured in the units of information theory, namely, bits. Now, in any application, there may be reasons why one alternative is more probable than another, and this will unbalance the equation. For example, if a committee of ten people is divided nine-to-one on the first showing of hands, the uncertainty to be resolved is less than one bit. If we wish, we may use this kind of fact as a measure of probability. Thus: $H = -(0.1 \log_2 0.1) - (0.9 \log_2 0.9) = 0.469$ bit. But in general, we may consider that all alternative choices are nominated as equally probable. In the case that there are m alternatives, the equation is $H = -m.1/m \log_2 1/m = \log_2 m$, which is, of course, simple to compute.

By summing the selection entropies appropriate to each logical variable, we obtain a measure of the uncertainty that has to be eliminated in reaching the decision. This quantified formula is now a control device of requisite—and measured—variety. For any attempted specification of the decision, put forward by any party to it, has a certain entropy that can be computed;

and the difference between this number and the number of the logical formula measures directly the inadequacy of the proposed answer. Moreover, if we start with a given level of uncertainty, we may progress our decision-taking by computing the uncertainty eliminated by any agreed sub-decision. Evidently, when all the uncertainty has been eliminated, the entropy is zero—because the probability that this is indeed the answer is unity. In other words, the decision has been taken.

In practice, the rate at which uncertainty is eliminated by a decision procedure will be some kind of negative exponential decay function. Empirical research will establish the family of curves which it is appropriate to use as control optima, and fiducial limits can be set up. Then we have an error-controlled feedback loop with which to monitor the progress of the decision-taking. In a particular sphere of decision, moreover, particular clues to the uncontrolled situation will emerge. For example, whatever the decay function for uncertainty, it will surely be monotonic-decreasing. Hence if, in the course of plotting the progress of the decision-taking, a sudden upsurge in the graph should occur, it is clear that something has gone wrong. Uncertainty is being imported into the system. This will usually be due to an unacknowledged change in the objectives of the decision. It is clear evidence that the logical formula ought to be re-examined, and perhaps subdivided. Here again is one of those control devices which operate on unanalysed systemic blocs, rather than on elemental components.

This procedure, which is here made public for the first time, seems to be a powerful tool. It is simple to use, though difficult to understand for anyone who has not undertaken the preliminary methodological thinking given in this paper. Its particular merit, I believe, is its capability to quantify a logical structure. Hitherto, it has been virtually impossible to disclose a mode of inference which would couple together, in one technique, the power of logic to specify structure (which is much greater than that of mathematics) and the power of number to compute comparisons and the parameters of control (which is much greater than that of logic). It is a tool that has special value in the context of national decisions, such as those discussed in the preceding section; because the specification of each such decision is so great, and the parties to it so numerous and so dissociated organizationally.

SYSTEMIC CONTROL IN 'THE METAL'

Having discussed, however cursorily, the relevance of the pervasive notion of system and its natural laws to the world and the flesh, we finally reach the metal. The metal stands for machinery, for devices, for artefacts built by man. Here, surely, we do understand the laws of system; here, one might hope, there is nothing to say.

Unfortunately, this is not the case. Where relatively small systems are concerned, the laws of systems as understood by control engineering are happily ascendant. But we make big systems, by the criteria used before, in hardware too. In particular, we make computers, and we sponsor automation. It would be uncouth to repeat now all that I have so often said and written before on these topics [5]. But a few points ought to be made in the terms established by this text.

First, a system of automation is a deliberative control, that is, as has been stated, an inverse mapping of an M on to an A. It is vital that the laws of requisite variety be upheld; yet no automatic controller yet devised begins to match the variety of an ordinary works. Consequently, the Buddhist principle of control has generally been applied. It is the central, perhaps the only, idea of Buddhism that since we can never reach our targets of desire (and are thus condemned to frustration) we should alter those targets to equate with whatever we in fact attain. If what we are and enjoy becomes our target, behold, we have attained it after all. This is exceedingly good cybernetics; requisite variety is ensured, not by generating variety in our lives, but by eliminating variety in our ambitions. It seems to me that our notion of automation depends on this rule: the factory must behave in the way we have engineered to control it.

The result of this is that automation has been applied only to relatively straightforward, mass production situations—which are low-variety worlds. The jobbing works, on which the British economy largely depends, has so far been immune—*qua* big system. Subsystems have been automated, it is true; and the computer-controlled machine tool is an example. But if we rightly understand and apply the systemic laws of cybernetics, it will not prove impossible to make automation much more general. The secret is, of course, to use computers as variety generators. Operational research does precisely this with its simulations; but engineering seems to think more in terms of variety reduction.

Thus we have the spectacle of the logical space of a general purpose computer programmed down to low-variety control, as, for example, in its application to the cut-up line of a rolling mill. This seems to be as wasteful of decision-taking capacity as is the programming down of a high-variety human being to being a machine-minder. There are no ethical objections in the former case as there are in the latter; but there are much stronger economic objections. These are the source of the marginal pay-off from computer applications in real time, which in my opinion is in turn a major cause of the slow advance of automation itself. The on-line control computer ought to be sensorily coupled to events in real time, and ought to have a motor output similarly coupled. But in between it ought to be uncoupled to a greater extent than is required to undertake a few simple-minded calculations on its inputs. In particular, it should have the facility to simulate the outcomes of possible decisions and to choose between them. This is not at all difficult to do; it is not even difficult in principle to equip the machine with a learning facility through which to profit from its own experience. The trouble is that managements do not commission such applications, and engineers do not offer to make them. The reason is, I strongly urge, not the imagined difficulty, but a very real insensitivity to the systemic rules of the game. As we are trained in the scientific methodology of analysis rather than synthesis, so we are trained in the Buddhist principle of control. We are variety murderers to a man.

An interesting example of this contention is found in the machine translation of language. A language is a high-variety system *par excellence.* The history of machine translation shows how science ignored this fact, and set out to translate automatically using low-variety control. It obtained, with chagrin but quite predictably, very bad translations. But a start had been made. Gradually the research began to acquire for the automatic translator some of the variety it had manifestly required from the outset. Crude syntactical paradigms were replaced by more elaborate ones; stored vocabularies grew. But the methodology is the old familiar one. We are aiming to reach requisite variety by the exhaustive enumeration of possible states, and we are still a long way off. Yet the computer as such is by no means short of variety; the inadequacy has been in the variety of the structuring of the decision space. We are not using variety generators, once again.

Surely the clue to this problem is the way in which people learn to translate (note the word 'learn'). We do not set out to programme children to be good translators. The trick is, rather, to give them a rudimentary grammar and vocabulary with which they are encouraged to experiment. They proceed to generate variety all right; the only trouble is that the output is unacceptable. So we monitor the output, using a skilled linguist (called teacher), who himself has requisite variety. He observes the defects in the homomorphic mapping of acceptable language on to the child's language. He then corrects the child by reinforcing successes with rewards and damping down failures with reproof. In systemic terms he uses what I have called the algedonic (pleasure/pain) loop. It is not difficult to devise an artefact of this loop inside a computer: all one needs is a simple conditional probability model to supply the criterion of retrieval. Instead of the rather naïve notion that a stored linguistic association is either present or absent, we want the stored material to be more or less likely to emerge—in accordance with a balance of systemically connected probabilities, gained by experience, that the answer will be praised or blamed.

I do not think we should be too diffident in seeking to imitate in such ways what are apparently human prerogatives, for they may be nothing more than systemic prerogatives—which is what this lecture is about. Before becoming emotional about words such as 'think' and 'create' it is well to define in behavioural terms what counts as thinking or creating. If this proves to be possible, it seems to me inevitable that science and engineering between them can devise a machine with comparable behavioural characteristics. This is all we need. It is interesting to ask whether such machines are 'really' thinking and creating, and if so how, and if so whether human beings do the job in the same way or some other. But to declare that machines can think, or that machines cannot think, seems as meaningless as it is pointless. I should refuse to mount the scaffold on behalf of any such proposition. But bear this in mind: whatever we may reckon as to genuinely human prerogatives, and as to the possibly divine nature of man, what we see men actually do is organized to be done by their brains: and the brain itself is a control machine.

A good and a final example of what I mean concerns the trick of procuring arbitrarily reliable outputs from a machine with arbitrarily unreliable components. Considered in engineering terms, the brain is a frighteningly defective apparatus, and yet it serves us well. It was because John von Neumann posed the question: 'How do we retain any semblance of humanity when we have had too much to drink?' that cybernetics found out how the brain works this apparently impossible trick. As is now quite generally known, the answer is that it generates the requisite variety both structurally and operationally through redundancy: redundant nodes, redundant channels, redundant control complexes, redundant calculations. We have the theorems by which all this works; we even have a special logic of neural nets by which to describe it. But, again, engineers do not want to use all this knowledge. They have been brought up to believe that components ought to be reliable, and they design as if they were reliable. But no one has ever seen an actual component that did not have a measurable, finite probability of failure: and in a big system, a complex ensemble of components, these probabilities are multiplicative.

The result is that we refuse to send one redundantly controlled rocket to the Moon to make a few observations; we cannot afford to accelerate 'unnecessary' componentry to escape velocities. It is apparently better to fire six rockets, beautifully engineered and shorn of redundancy, none of which gets there. Again, we cannot afford the high cost of redundancy in a railway signalling system. After all, if perchance it should go wrong, the accident inspector will declare that it was 'one of those things'—a one-in-a-million chance. Personally, I regard myself as one of several million passengers; and my ghost would doubtless take a poor view of these odds. Yet again, then, we cannot bear to tell industrialists that they should consider installing redundant automation, because the expense might frighten them off the project. We prefer that they should refuse to accept automation on the grounds that it might go wrong.

It does not, in fact, seem to be totally ludicrous that we should be thinking in terms of a new kind of systems engineering, in the metal—as in the world and the flesh. It would be an engineering appropriate to big systems, aimed at providing requisite variety for control, equipped with variety generators, redundant circuitry, and an interpenetrative connectivity. Consider the following vision. Here is a vast plant, a huge, complex interacting system. Its engineers have built control equipment into it, of a subtle cybernetic kind. The plant is therefore self-regulatory (we know that trick). It is to some extent self-organizing (we begin to know this trick too). The plant is adaptive to environmental changes (we have discussed how this could be done through algedonics). But the built-in control systems keep going wrong. The teeth of the cogs drop out, the transistors fail, wires come adrift, whole packages burn out. The engineers, however, have seen all this happen in the brain. They have noted that brains do not continually 'go off the air' for maintenance: and so they have copied the brain's trick for handling unreliability, no longer complaining that things sometimes go wrong when manifestly they cannot always go right.

This works continues to work, despite all. It is not attended by an army of white-coated technicians armed with soldering irons, as some prophets have supposed. For the built-in control equipment is designed to outlast the plant. Do not say this is impossible; you and I are the evidence that it is possible. Do not say that it is impracticable; we have not even tried, and the principles are known. Say, if you must, that you are not going to do it, that you cannot afford it, or that it is time to go home; let us know where the onus lies.

There are systemic laws to apply, which could change the face of Britain—as George Stephenson once changed it. Twenty years before the *Rocket* ran, that illustrious man nearly dug out the brain drain; but he was disheartened, and contemplated emigration. Some of us here have done the same. May we instead learn from his example, and see the visions through.

REFERENCES

1. Beer, Stafford, 'Below the Twilight Arch: A Mythology of Systems'; chap. 1, *Systems Research and Design*, John Wiley, 1961.
2. Beer, Stafford, *The Cost Accountant*, **42**(6), June 1964 (also obtainable from SIGMA, Ltd, as a pamphlet).
3. Ross Ashby, W., *Design for a Brain*. Chapman and Hall (London), 1952; revised edition, 1960.
4. Beer, Stafford, *Operational Res. Quart.*, **13**(2), June 1962.
5. Beer, Stafford, *The Manager*, October and November, 1963; *Metra Journal*, **3**(1), 1964 (also obtainable from SIGMA, Ltd, as a reprint).

9 BELOW THE TWILIGHT ARCH—A MYTHOLOGY OF SYSTEMS

Inaugral Address for the Systems Research Center, Cleveland, U.S.A.

STAFFORD BEER

YOU HONOUR me too much by your readiness to hear me speak tonight [First Systems Symposium Banquet, April 1960]. I was frankly overwhelmed when your invitation came. So often I have sat at home in the evening twilight watching the sun set on England, and thought of the new dawn it would bring to the New World—and many friends. And I have long wished to visit you. Here, at last, I am: with thanks on my lips, inquiry in my head, excitement in the blood, and 'cybernetician' on my passport.

In coming, I have followed the sun. I have had to fly below the twilight arch. My assignment is to place before you some thoughts on systems research, the subject over which this conference presides. It is a *new* field, rich in promise—or so we tend to say. And yet mankind has always been conscious of system: on the face of the earth and in the firmament; in the behaviour of the body; in seasons and societies; in numbers and machines. Nor has mankind been slow to describe and codify the system he detected all around.

Thus there is much on which we can draw today in undertaking systems research. There is an opulent heritage of thought which it would be both brash and wasteful to ignore. Unfortunately, there is also much from the past which is not helpful—unless correctly interpreted. Much of what we think, and above all our *habit* of thought, is implanted in us by history. For we have, after all, been *taught* to think; thinking is not some great free spiritual afflatus of the human soul. It is more accurately called cerebration: an activity of the brain: a highly conditioned form of cerebral behaviour. We are not usually aware of the extent to which the past is imported into our thinking. But, genetically speaking, we are our own parents. No one can say to what extent the inherited machinery in his head is structurally capable of the novel

First published by John Wiley & Sons, New York.

activities he intends. Secondly, and psychologically speaking, we are our own teachers and mentors. Who can be sure that he has freed his thoughts of lumber from the propaedeutic years?

All this strikes me as singularly appropriate to our subject. For system above all things is *ourselves*. In every conceivable way *we are* system: extrapolated from the past, oriented to the present, projected towards the future. So for those engaged on research into the nature of systems there comes a warning: we research into ourselves; and our research is bounded by ourselves—and all we ever were or hope to be. Now what becomes of the objectivity of science? How can we separate ourselves from the subject of our studies? In physics we have learned this danger long ago; and nowadays we handle the dynamite of Indeterminacy with practised hands—and measure it in megatons. But outside physics, scientists too often forget their Heisenberg and all that follows; they are content with Bacon and Descartes.

My case is this: we still stand in the twilight of our subject, a twilight inhabited by shadowy concepts from the past. There gods and giants battle still, to typify the dualism which haunts all human thought. It is possible, however, that we are on the margin of full daylight. The work of recent years has done a tremendous amount to explode the old mythology of systems. But let us consciously confront our myths, before we pass too far ahead, and see them for what they are. I told you that to come here I had to fly below the twilight arch. That was to move into the evening sun. But in our work we now move out into the light of morning. My invitation is to turn momentarily back, to where the myths still writhe: let us fly back—below the twilight arch of dawn.

ON MYTHS OF ORDER AND CHAOS

System is one of the names of order, the antonym of chaos. The basic myth of which I will speak first is made up of four propositions: that the raw state of nature is chaotic; that order is something introduced into chaos and imposed therein as a monolithic structure to be weathered by random noise; that within this structure a second-order chaos lies invisible; and that once the energy necessary to maintain this order ceases to be available all reverts to chaos once again. You may be thinking that in calling this outlook a myth I am proposing unilaterally to repeal the laws of thermodynamics. Not so: I am proposing merely to examine critically the conventions under which we view these things. And, as befits mythology, I shall start a long way back.

The Origins and Maintenance of the Mythology

The Ionian philosophers of ancient Greece, such as Leucippus and Democritus, concerned themselves with the existence of supposedly elementary particles of matter which they called 'atomic', meaning indivisible. A century later, their celebrated successor Epicurus conceived of the atoms as possessing the power of movement; and from their chaotic (or random) atomic entanglements he envisaged the generation of life itself. According to this doctrine of 'hylozoism', an invisible material chaos begat all that is systematic, which it continued to inform—in continued atomic action below the threshold of visible action; in the appearance of life; and in the evidence of moral choice.

The emergence of these doctrines in the great age of Greece was profoundly backed by yet more ancient literature. Of this the Hesiodic poets are the most relevant, for they dealt essentially with the emergence of order out of chaos. We are now back in the eighth century BC, 'Η τοι μὲν πρώτιστα χάος γένετ', αὐτὰρ ἔπειτα Γαι' εὐρύστεργος, thundered Hesiod in his *Theogony*: 'At the very first chaos was created, and thereafter the broad-bosomed earth.' And this is perhaps as far back as the myth can be traced. It is the background clue to the Epicurean philosophy of the fourth century BC, whence we pass directly to the Roman poet Lucretius who, writing 250 years later, expounded Epicurus in didactic and rapturous verse. When a great poet talks philosophy, he tends to enshrine the thought in lapidary style. Five centuries after Epicurus, his ideas were still being regurgitated word for word. And this was sad; 'a clear symptom of decadence', in the eyes of that great Hellenist, Gilbert Murray.

If this was decadence then, where are we now? For the myth of prior chaos is with us still. In his biological outlook, contemporary and educated man seems to embrace a neo-Darwinism. According to this, there was once a chaos (usually thought of nowadays as the ocean). In this the atoms of the Greeks still intertwined; they were perturbed, through aeons of time and random permutations, to become organic molecules. These polymerized. So macromolecules, above all proteins, would be formed—there would as yet be no bacteria to bring about decomposition. The ordering process, driven by the random movements of chaos, marches on: small parcels of enzymes next emerge, enclosed in handy membranes. Then, ultimately, and by the same fortuitous process comes the organism. But chaos still informs this organism in its unseen genetic depths. Random mutations occur, and evolution can progress; for natural selection filters the adventitiously patterned offerings of chaos, building yet more order amid the environmental noise. Finally, for each metastable organism comes the stability of death: the ordering is disordered, and chaos supervenes. Here is the hylozoism of the educated twentieth-century man.

Take next the physical outlook of this same man. This too begins with the assumption of chaos. We may build from chaotic atomic components a regular cubic lattice of copper, and another of zinc. By the interpenetration of these cubic lattices, a further ordering process is carried out. Each cube of the copper lattice now has at its centre a zinc atom, and vice versa. A metallurgical ordering has taken place, to yield a body-centred cubic lattice named β-brass. But if we heat this alloy, the atoms migrate, and chaos returns. Significantly, we call this an *order–disorder* transition. Note again the Epicurean conventions: the initial atomic chaos; the order imposed as structure builds on structure; the hidden atomic chaos which goes on beneath the lattice model; the reversion to chaos when the conditions of order are withdrawn.

Thus we could easily continue for a long time. But let us take three quick examples from our own field of study. A logical system has been constructed, an organization. This might equally well be an electronic model of a learning process, a logical flow system portraying an industrial works, or a chart depicting the managerial structure of a company or other society. These models have been, in our eyes as model builders, constructed by an ordering process out of chaos. We have observed the learning going on, and have seen it as the imposition of structure, a network of connectivity between elements and subsets of a set in which relationships were originally chaotic. In like manner we have imposed an order on the otherwise chaotic industrial works, giving it a structure, showing how material flows and where the system is uncoupled by its stocks. And in the third case, the social chaos of a mass of human beings has been ordered too: the responsibilities of leaders have been defined, the dependence of subordinates, the interdependence of groups, of committees, etc. Next we observe these models are too static; they are not viable systems at all. Order has been *frozen* out of chaos: and this will not do. Beneath the semblance of rest, Lucretius tells us, the chaos must go on.

And so we insert black boxes in the model of the learning process: random noise is pumped into the system and marshalled into stochastic patterns. The model of the works is turned into a simulation and put on to a computer, in which pseudo-random numbers are generated by the thousand to bring the thing to life. Thirdly, the managerial structure is contemplated under chance and moral choice: the 'human element' is introduced, whereby people do not do as they are told, they make mistakes, they die and cannot be equivalently replaced. All is now well; the chaos works within the order like yeast in bread. Then finally: observe the last result, whispers the ghost of Epicurus in our ears. Let the system run, let the entropy increase; remove the 'ordering principle', or the group dynamic, or free energy, or management. In all three models the probabilities begin to equate. The learning machine is deconditioned, learns everything and nothing. The works accepts its rules and succumbs to its constraints: its stocks steadily rise, its queues lengthen, its processes grind to a halt, and everything is equiprobable. The social structure, too, is denatured, until 'when everyone is somebody, then no one's anybody'. Chaos, which the Greeks taught us is more natural than order, is back again. The thermodynamic heat-death is upon us.

This is our myth. This is the understanding we have been handed down from Hesiod onwards, which is built into our thinking. We may not visualize it in the way I have unfolded it; that I must concede. But we all *behave* as if it were true.

The Attack on the Mythology

Through these examples, the myth may be examined and exploded. For the myth is not *what* we know; but *how* we know it. It is with the expression, the conventions of viewpoint, that I quarrel. And the quarrel is not pedantic; I contend, and hope to show, that we misdirect ourselves quite seriously.

First, a new track must be chosen from the start. Not 'chaos was created' is the theme, but another account of creation must be chosen. Let us pick on St John as our alternative. 'Eν ἀρχη ἠν ὁ Λόγοs: 'In the beginning was the Word.' Here at once is the idea we need: the idea that I will call *immanent organization*.

Man has for long flirted with this idea. In theology, he was safe: St John had, after all, gone on to identify the Word, and indeed the immanence, as God. 'The Word was God . . . All things were made by Him.' There is no difficulty about organization if an omnipotent Organizer is presupposed. In philosophy, too, various devices were available for handling this idea. For example, Spinoza (pre-eminently the philosopher of immanence) described a thoroughgoing monism in which nature itself and its own organizational effects were both aspects of the same thing. They were to be distinguished only by a neat piece of syntax: *natura naturans* as the creating, organizing aspect; *natura naturata* as the organized effects.

But in science the idea of immanent organization was in difficulties from the start. For science had neither God nor 'substance' in which this immanence could inhere. Science until recently was about *things*, and so we trace our thought to postulated all-pervasive things which might have carried a 'principle of organization' in themselves. The ether was one such thing: it does not seem to be altogether forgotten even now. Phlogiston was another. I sometimes think that Eddington was always on the verge of inventing yet one more: a kind of existence principle masquerading as a set of eigenvalues. Of course, his model was intended as a conceptual construct; and yet it sounds so often like a *thing* spread-eagled throughout the universe, measurable in its physical constants, and essentially extended in its modalities.

How else but in extension can we understand what Eddington could possibly have meant when he spoke of a measurable as having 'fifteen different ways of not existing'?

Now the answer to this problem which can be deduced from our latest scientific insights seems to be this. *We can actually start with a non-chaos*; and we do not need a 'thing' in which to contain this 'principle' of immanent organization. All we need is a non-Hesiodic language in which to talk about it. Let us begin with physics, in which this conclusion can be most readily exemplified. There is no need to question the account I gave just now of the atomic-level behaviour of a β-brass. No doubt all happens so. What I suggest we ask ourselves is why the process then described should be known as an order–disorder transition when it is much more simple to think of it the opposite way round.

If we consider a system in the light of thermodynamics, the language employed has in general the Epicurean cast. There is the assumption of molecular chaos, the idea of ordering the system so that it is no longer chaotic, etc. To achieve this ordering, there has to be (familiarly, by now) a mechanism capable of instituting order. This is personified in the Maxwell demon who does the selecting of particles which produce the ordered state. Again (also familiarly) this mechanism turns out in the light of later knowledge, in this case information theory, to be a long-term impossibility, as Wiener has pointed out. For the information on which the demon requires to act is a negative entropy, which means that the demon is coupled to the energy system itself, and in the long run subject to random motion determined by temperature changes.

Moreover, and here is another of our familiar signposts, the laws of classical thermodynamics, as given in the so-called 'geometric' proof, turn out to be too static: everything is fixed, and the account only holds for statistical averages of molecules. Where has the subthreshold chaos gone? Drop to a small enough system, and it is there—in the Brownian motion. But now the rigid laws no longer hold.

Then let us turn to more convenient terms, a better model within which to talk. Now we say: all free-running processes in the world are moving from states of disequilibrium towards states of equilibrium. Disbalance the equilibrium, and they will return. From statistical mechanics we observe that the equilibrial states are more likely, and will eventually predominate. Entropy has now become a measure of the probability of the universe. Very well: in these terms, again, it seems we have the movement from chaos to order that we expect—disbalance is superseded by balance, etc. But just a minute: the sign seems to have changed. What used to be chaos is now an equilibrium, and what used to be order is now disbalance. Epicurus is standing on his head.

And very rightly so. Why should we not insist that what is most probable counts as being most ordered? Could anything be more ordered than a perfectly even distribution of molecules, heat, energy, or any other commodity, over a given adiabatic space? And if the system is not an isolated one, but part of an assembly of systems, then surely the most ordered state is that in which the whole is equilibrial—which is again most probable in the end. According to my language, then, I now assert: *order is more natural than chaos*. This is, I infer, a startling statement; for when I recently published it a number of people wrote to indicate the 'printer's error'. What is more, I find that the statement is actually important to me: it represents a break with the descriptive conventions of Hesiod which have lain heavy on my head with the weight of 2700 years. It has given me a completely new outlook on systems.

The Replacement of the Mythology

What after all *is* order, or something systematic? I suppose it is a pattern, and a pattern has no objective existence anyway. A pattern is a pattern because *someone* declares a concatenation of items to be meaningful or cohesive. The onus for detecting systems, and for deciding how to describe them, is very much on ourselves. I do not think we can adequately regard a system as a fact of nature, truths about which can be gradually revealed by patient analytical research. A viable system is something we detect and understand when it is mapped into our brains, and I suppose the inevitable result is that our brains themselves actually impose a structure on reality. I have already spent some time on a key example, which may be epitomized thus.

If we structure reality as a chaos–order–chaos transition, then this is what reality *is*, and our systems will have to include massive control units capable of constructing and sustaining the ordered phase. But if we structure reality as an order–chaos–order transition, then this is reality instead, and our systems will be largely *self*-organizing. The chaotic phase here is disturbance to the system from outside; and control units are merely required to filter this noise as far as possible, and to provide a matching store of variety in which disturbance can be absorbed as by a sponge—so that order returns. (Ashby has given us the formal mechanism for this in his work on homeostasis.)

We have already used the example from physics to make the change of viewpoint clear. Let us now look at the other instances cited. In biology, the old hylozoism was traced down to an outlook described as neo-Darwinism. The difficulties of this outlook are tremendous, and centre on the point that there is no room in it for the emergence of immanent organization: mutations are thrown up *by* chaos in the nucleoproteins of the chromosomes, *into* the environmental chaos; order is achieved by a ruthless and crude vetoing procedure. How order manages to survive in the presence of quite so much noise, both within and without, is not at all clear.

The new language compels us to begin with the supposition of order, and therefore presupposes a natural and intimate collaboration between the organism and its environment. Some modern biologists, such as W. R. Ashby and J. Z. Young in Britain as well as many Americans, are themselves cybernetic pioneers. Let me draw especially at this point, however, on the geneticist Waddington. He regards this natural orderliness (in my sense) of the whole organism–environment system as exerting a causal influence on embryological development, the study of which is called epigenetics. Adaptation, then, is explained by the gradual building up of an 'epigenetic landscape' which '*guides* the phenotypic effects of the mutations available'. Waddington goes on to say that, in the light of this, the conventional statement that the raw materials of evolution are provided by *random* mutation 'appears hollow'.

Hollow indeed; and any cybernetician who has carried out experiments in which hylozoistic rules for the creation of order out of chaos operate *without* any such guide will confirm my own experience that the process is far too slow and too precarious to satisfy the demand for an explanation of any evolutionary process which actually succeeds in adaptation. (So, too, would any manager capable of transferring all this to his own experience of evolution in a business or a works.) Here, then, is a convention for looking at biology as including immanent organization which certainly pays off. It is highly analogous, I would further suggest, to the neurophysiological conception of facilitated pathways in the brain.

Next we may return to the set of examples concerned with learning machines, operational research, and the organizational structure of companies. Taking the first two together, there is just one central point to make; and if I seem to castigate, then let it be clear that I accept these strictures for myself. It really is ludicrous that we should have gone so far with Epicurus as to manufacture chaos where none exists in order to provide ourselves with the properly certificated raw material for system building. Take my own case. There are random number tables on my bookshelf; there are computer tapes for producing pseudo-random numbers next door; there is a large electronic machine for generating noise upstairs; down the road there is a roomful of equipment designed to hurl thousands of little metal balls about in a random way; and I use 10-sided dice as paperweights. The upkeep of this armoury is considerable: think of all the time we spend trying to ensure that all these artefacts produce results which are 'genuinely random'—whatever that may mean. This tremendous practical problem of guaranteeing disorderliness ought to be enough to satisfy any systems man that nothing is more *un*natural than chaos. We are never even confident we have got it.

Why should we want it? The answer is just this. In any study of a real system we meet *indeterminacy*, and this has to be modelled and understood. Our way of thinking leads us to produce the artefact of indeterminancy by injecting absolute order with absolute chaos, although (as I have tried to show) both concepts are meaningless in the real world. But to do anything else, we say, would 'introduce bias'. This is true, but only in the Hesiodic language I am seeking to replace. And I will give this pointer to a possible solution. The biological model with the epigenetic landscape is precisely a machine for introducing bias into the abstract notion of random mutation. There is nothing wrong with this *provided* that it does not constrain adaptability and therefore survival opportunity. If this condition is to be met, then (it seems to me) there must be a multiplexing of whichever transformations themselves beg questions about the future. This is to take up von Neumann's ideas about error-free though defective systems, and to adapt them. For it is not exactly 'error' with which we have to deal. Quasi-decisions have to be taken about the future (in arranging for the emergence of an epigenetic landscape) which may or may not prove suitable later on; what is important is that the system should be robust when proved wrong. By this I mean that its sensitivity to the biases it will introduce should be inversely proportional to the probability of their being falsified as forecasts.

My proposition is that by multiplexing the set of input transformations which produce the epigenetic landscape a mapping of environment into organism will give rise to invariant points as key features of the landscape. This invariance is with respect to a poorly chosen transform somewhere in the multiplex: the system will learn to facilitate pathways to the landscape which are equifinal. This is an extension of Waddington's theory, based on what I hopefully take to be a cerebral mechanism. (A paper about a machine to act as a brain artefact for an industrial company, which is based on this thinking, will be put forward at the Urbana symposium on self-organizing systems in June 1960.*)

In concluding this section, there is something to be said about the example from organizational structure. I will not go through the argument about chaos and order again, trusting it is sufficiently clear. But the inference to be drawn from the reversal of the linguistic convention is worth stating. An existing system of human relationships in a large and complex society is to be regarded as self-organizing, as ordered already: homeostatic, equilibrial.

Many people dimly realize that this is a fair description; for instance, they incline to say about a new project: 'We must carry everyone with us.'

**Editor's note* 'Towards the Cybernetic Factory'.

By this they mean that they ought not to fight the system. But I will risk being quite emphatic about this. When they say 'the system', they almost certainly do not mean the naturally ordered system I am talking about; they mean the *official* system, the one constructed as an artificial order—out of the alleged 'chaos' which is in fact the *real* system. This official system is the one set down on charts, the one crystallized in titles, the one imitated by many doomed automatic control systems. If these people were talking about the real system, they would say instead: 'Let us use the system to amplify this project into effect.'

The Mythology and Management

I can well imagine managers declaring what has just been said to be naïve, and adding that they know it all, and more, already. But I am unrepentant, and will face this out. We may be as subtle as we like in discussing human relationships and unofficial channels as addenda to the official organization chart. But the system all this is supposed to control can always go one better. There is always far more variety in the whole society than the official (Epicurean) order can cope with. For not only must that order be constructed by effort and sanction from the 'chaos' but the order (which is exiguous) has then to attempt the organic control of what is left over (which is extensive). This is in flat contradiction to Ashby's law of requisite variety, and quite certainly an impossibility. A false dichotomy has been drawn by this orthodox model, and the scientific consequences are inescapable.

In short, the only acceptable evidence that people really do know already what these arguments have educed would be the existence somewhere of a managerial structure which could permute its own variety into continuous correspondence with the natural driving energies of the rest of the system under disturbance. This would probably look quite different from anything we have today. For example, it would be unlikely to happen that a business would be permanently demarcated *at the top* into such fixed areas as 'production', 'sales', and 'finance', for this would constrain the available directorial variety far too much. All right, you may say, how is it that businesses run successfully like this at present? The answer is that they do not run like this; that the official demarcations are overrun at the social level (which is why all great businesses pay so much attention to 'acceptability'), and that, despite their titles, jobs continuously change their character. Then what am I complaining about? The answer is that I am not complaining; the self-organizing system has organized itself, and all is well. The whole discussion seems to have vanished. But it has not. The point was whether people who (naturally enough) know perfectly well *how* the whole society runs in fact have a real understanding of *why*. This is to say that an understanding of politics does not imply an understanding of cybernetics. And if politics is 'the art of the possible' in a system, cybernetics is the science of the actual. If this science is understood, then management becomes more effective and less painful.

Now this is not intended as an indictment, but as a constructive insight. If we changed our model and accepted the proposed language reversal, thereby obtaining a more appropriate account of the system concerned, I think many things would change. Titles, definitions of responsibility, the actual treatment of people as opposed to the 'personnel policy' (particularly with regard to succession), the structure of committees, etc., would all change. In a first-rate concern, the descriptive changes would not lead to any actual changes of behaviour, because the system is self-organizing anyway. But in a less satisfactory company (if there are perchance less satisfactory companies) the new correspondence of description with fact would produce real changes, because the ostensible system would no longer impede and retard the natural tendency towards an equilibrial state on the part of the real system. As to the individual and first-rate manager, to change his title from a function- or technique-oriented name ('Sales Manager') to a succession of problem-oriented names ('Manager of Project 6') would involve no alternation in his work at all, because he is already tackling problems and is leading 'Project 6' without naming it. But a poor manager (if there should perchance be one) would suddenly find that his title to intervention in other people's work, and his capacity to frustrate them, had gone. He would also find that to 'own' a department or policy like a landlord, who prosecutes trespassers and charges rent, would no longer of itself justify his existence.

There are in fact many indications in the way people behave which reveal that they do not after all understand the 'why' of the system according to the model I have advanced. These indications are strong enough to defend this analysis against the familiar charge of triviality; the logically valid objection can be only that the analysis is wrong.

Management is the restoring of natural order to a system which has been disturbed, and which is trying to regain its equilibrium. This does not of course exclude progress: by equilibrium I do not mean a stationary balance. The system is fed with a reward function, which is the pay-off of the society concerned, and which had better be as much concerned with survival value as with immediate satisfactions. This drives the system on, and itself disturbs the equilibrial state. The new equilibrium will have a higher pay-off than the last. The reactions which restore this state are natural laws: management is catalytic.

Thus I picture the cybernetic managerial structure as the *focus* of the natural order; a structure that flows to fit the changing 'response surface' of the situation; a structure that is integral with the system and exemplifies its natural orderliness. And I contrast with this the structure that sees its own order as bred from and imposed on chaos; a structure that is rigid; a structure that is concerned with divisions and functions, instead of unities and problems; a structure that actually *hates* the remainder of the system, which it sees as chaotic, and by which it must therefore feel threatened. The first understands the nature of systems, and seeks to remedy its own deficiencies by mapping the changing state of the world into its own epigenetic landscape—which will in turn modify its nature gradually towards increasingly effective control. This is management by cybernetics. The second understands only its own needs, and tries to adapt itself to change by plugging gaps with new titles and committees, and by balancing responsibilities instead of dynamic trends—which will in turn modify it in clumsy steps towards the goal of increasingly tidy organization charts. This is management by aesthetics.

Perhaps most actual social systems lie somewhere on a scale determined by these extremes. To evaluate whereabouts on the scale a particular system falls, we might examine the behaviour of the people in authority. For those who do not understand the system's 'why' betray themselves by hatred and fear of the chaos they assume to lie outside the door; by a failure to amplify themselves and their policies by coupling each to the natural order; and by acting instead as if their job were to lay about them in the chaos with the jawbone of an ass. Such men are supported by a Hesiodic scripture some 27 centuries old. May I outdo them in the authority of antiquity by quoting cybernetics from one of the Upanishads, the Hindu scripture. The book is called the Bhagavad-Gita, and goes back 5000 years. In it the Lord Krishna declares to man:

> Action is the product of the qualities inherent in nature. It is only the ignorant man who, misled by personal egotism, says: 'I am the doer'.

ON MYTHS OF PARTS AND WHOLES

The Mythology of Division and Composition

So far we have been discussing systems in a particular but vital dimension: the dimension of *orderliness*. But there are many other dimensions of systems, some of which are equally important, and equally difficult to examine. One of these is the dimension of *completeness*, to which I shall now turn. For just as every real system expresses more or less order, so every real system expresses more or less integration.

'The part is greater than the whole' is an aphorism everyone has heard, and there are occasions when people think they discern a meaning in the paradox. When something is labelled 'a system', the whole intention would seem to be to assert that a collection of separate things is in an important sense a whole. But no one imagines that this debars him from dividing the system into parts for the sake of description; indeed, any arbitrary division is logically admissible, and the criterion of suitability is that of convenience alone. The would-be divider of systems must, however, be careful: he may succeed in making a division which destroys the sense in which the system is a whole. A surgeon who treated migraine by amputating the patient's head (cephalectomy?) would be doing this. And the patient, on discharge from the hospital, might posthumously reflect on the sense in which this part of him had proved greater than the whole.

At the very least, there is more to say about part of a system than that it is contained in the whole. Leibnitz said that it *expresses* the whole, and this was because he saw parts not as divisions of space or divisions of function but as *dynamically involved* in the whole: a 'systems' outlook. Hegel went further: every relation by which terms are related is an integral part of the terms it relates. And Whitehead went further still, by making Hegel's indivisible but passive system of relatedness *active*. His doctrine of 'prehension' saw things as formulating their own natures out of other things, by seizing on relationships with them. In other fields than philosophy, too, the same insights may be found: they are there in relativity physics; they are there in Gestalt psychology; they are there in the best operational research.

For this is not mythology. The myth is the contrary idea that a system can sustain arbitrary division without ceasing to be the system that it is. And judging by many practical observations, this myth is very strong. We divide what we have no business to divide; the old logicians entered this operation on their list of fallacies, and called it *divisio*. Consider two examples from systems research.

The first is formal. Open any textbook, any paper, in our field, and consult the diagrams. There are rectangles representing activities, or processes, or operations, or even people. In information theory terms, the amount of variety denoted by each box may be colossal. The boxes are solemnly connected by attenuated, solitary lines with arrowheads on the ends. (What channel capacity those lines must have!) Now, three questions: How many vital features of the organic wholeness of the system have been utterly obliterated by this particular division? How many essential relationships between each *bit* in each box with every bit in every other box are depicted by the connections shown, and (given that this is a well-understood convention) have we any means of recognizing the conditions in which one of those *not* shown will turn this version of the system into another and quite different version? Can the passage of information (in however subtle an interpretation) really account for the wholeness of the whole, or is there something yet to learn from Hegel about other modes of relatedness? These are sobering questions. And when one contemplates some of the diagrammatic automation schemes, economic models, organization charts, maps of the brain, and many more, that are riddled with this mythological *divisio* the blood runs cold. Bear in mind, also, that systems fallacies of this nature are not committed in diagrams alone. Some forms of mathematical reasoning, particularly in operational research, might be open to this objection. At the risk of sounding quite heretical, I will admit that I have always been nervous of linear programming for this reason.

The second example is industrial. A company is an integrated whole in at least these ways: it is an indivisible legal entity; it is an indivisible financial entity as to its solvency (despite the fact that both its assets and its liabilities are eminently divisible); it is a virtually indivisible commercial entity, because the business confidence it inspires tends to disseminate uniformly over its activities; it is a virtually indivisible social entity, because its reputation as employer, subsidizer, patron, or menace is also disseminated throughout the locality. But to run this company, it simply must be divided, and divided in a way which will not murder it. Thus law, finance, sales, and labour became examples of suitable divisions of administration. But remember what was said earlier about such demarcation *at the top*: would this be a safe division, or is it perhaps a dangerous *divisio*?

Now consider production. Here again there are important senses in which the company is an integral whole. There is the pressure of throughput, which determines an indivisible rate of metabolism—particularly in such places as steelworks where heat is the driving force: to uncouple the system anywhere involves the cost of either conserving or wasting heat. Is the uncoupling the best that can be devised in terms of the organic whole, or has this desideratum disappeared in too local an evaluation of technological convenience? As a second instance, there is the 'growth' of the product, which involves monotonic measures of size, complexity, cost, and risk. To write in 'monotonic increasing' there may appear pedantic, but it is certainly not. It is the very fact ignored by the division fallacy when it appears in cost control. For when division has been accomplished, we may find these measures treated as departmental plateaux, each on its own merits, and without regard to the various threads of growth which integrate the whole. The outcome is that consequences for the cost of forgone opportunities elsewhere in the system, or for the differential adjustment by departments of standards of inspection, are rarely drawn.

The Relevance of the Mythology

There are many more ways in which production is naturally integral, yet divided it must be. And so a group of departments is formed, developed, and extended by accretion. The myth says this is all right; it does not matter; only let the division be convenient. But systems research must look out for *divisio*. Wherever there is geographical or technological or administrative division, the system has been uncoupled. Wherever the system has been uncoupled there will be found a collection of such things as queues, dams, reservoirs, buffer stocks, feedbacks, triggers, valves, controllers, surge hoppers, paperwork, reserves, voids, idle times, defectives, closed loops, oscillations, more men, hunting punched cards, indicators, negentropy, the company's capital, and obscene language. This is a formidable price to pay for interfering in the natural system, but it is absolutely unavoidable. It is also absolutely right that much effort and *expertise* should go into the task of organizing the system at this point, and it is worth a good deal of money to reach the least fallible control system, the optimal levels of stock, etc. Assume that absolute optima for everything have now been found: there is no possibility of improvement. Then can we not say that the job is done and all is well? Given the mythology, yes; for the optimization is based on one of an arbitrary set of convenient divisions—the one that exists. But take away the comfort of the myth, and division may become *divisio.* Let me offer you this maxim: *the most profitable control system for the parts does not exclude the bankruptcy of the whole.*

This readily emerges from what has already been said. If a division is chosen which is in the long run lethal to the mode of integration that makes the whole system viable, then the profitability of any or every *part* is irrelevant to survival. Worse: what was once a fairly satisfactory division may *become* a lethal one as technological and economic changes occur. Ecologically speaking, the long history of the extinction of species by the self-same mechanism is a serious warning. For the adaptability of animals is far greater than that of artificial organisms like companies: species are self-organizing systems which on the whole find equilibrial states. Their final extinction is due to a particular biological form of *divisio*: overspecialization—in which irreversible divisions of the whole occur which turn out to be inappropriate in the long run. It is certainly interesting that primitive and unspecialized organisms fail, because of their absence of advanced internal organization, to attain ecological dominance. Whereas by not involving themselves in the division of the whole that this would entail, they do not run the risk of making an inappropriate *divisio*, and their survival value is much higher than that of organisms which have run this risk. Perhaps there is something to learn from the individual insect which maximizes its chance of survival in infancy by remaining unspecialized in the larva, and then attains to dominance by metamorphosis to a higher specialized structure after pupation.

This question of the fallacious division of structure is put forward as a very serious matter, and an obvious target for profound systems research. In expounding the point, I have naturally considered the ultimate outcomes of bankruptcy and extinction. But because a particular company is not at all likely to be threatened with imminent destruction the point is not robbed of its impact. A company can suffer from hardening of the divisions to its detriment without actually dying of thrombosis. The systems diagnosis here is likely to be made by a study of flow. In the coarsest sense, if is often possible to find that the same firm undertakes contrary operations on the same product (e.g. when long pieces of steel are cut up for ease of handling and later welded together again; or where a geographical separation involving a long transit time is covered repeatedly in opposite directions by the same product). There were once remarkably cogent reasons for doing this; are there still?

But in a more sophisticated sense, it is the flow of specifying information that ought to be studied. An order for a product that is still in the mails has infinite variety: it may be a request for anything, even something the company does not make. When the order is booked, the specification may not yet be complete; and anyway it is still an open question as to which precise resources will be used to discharge the order; but some variety has by now been lost. At the planning stage, more of this variety is shorn away; and as production proceeds more and more degrees of freedom are assimilated into decisions taken. When the finished product is ready to leave the factory, there is just one bit of information left in it: the answer to the question whether it will be dispatched or not. Now this diminution of variety from infinity to zero is by no means linear and by no means continuous. Moreover, each product or product group has its own curve against time. The whole process of manufacture, which is customarily regarded as the growth of organization of parts (materials) into wholes (products) from raw material to output (entropy falling), is alternatively regarded as the destruction of an equal amount of information (negentropy falling). The factory is thus equivalently a machine for making products or a machine for destroying variety. Technology will say what is the best arrangement for the factory as product maker; cybernetics will say what is the best arrangement for the factory as variety destroyer. Each will have its own optimum set of divisions. It is an operational research problem in systems to find the break-even point between the two answers, and the commensurable factor is entropy (the positive and negative entropies being continually in balance). I will hazard this guess: if this study is undertaken in a sizeable factory more than 10 years old, a *fallacia divisionis* will somewhere be uncovered. What should have been kept together has been uncoupled. If the division is then altered (something which normally is very rarely done), cycle times, stocks, inventories, and overheads will all decrease; deliveries will improve; profits will rise.

In considering this myth that any system can be arbitrarily split into components without altering its nature, consider briefly its complementary form: that it is admissible to put parts together into arbitrary wholes. This complementary fallacy to *divisio* is known as *compositio*. The one example to be mentioned is this. Suppose seven policy problems arise in different areas of administration, and the decisions are taken: a, b, c, d, e, f, g. If these decisions are all implemented, the whole policy compounded of these parts will be a + b + c + d + e + f + g. It could well be that this is a *compositio*. In the context of the whole system, some of these fortuitous conjunctions should possibly be disjunctions, and the total picture should read: a + c + (b or f) + (d or e or g). This risk, which looks so obvious as to be easily avoidable, is made serious by two facts. The divisions already discussed may turn some area of the whole system into a relatively isolated system on its own. And the differential and uncertain rates at which all the decisions which have been taken in mortgaging the future mature in facts make it easy to misconstrue under what conditions any one decision is likely to mature. It is a problem of a complex time-dependent system. Probably this is an entirely trivial thought; one just wonders then why the mistake occurs so often—in national as well as institutional policy making.

But it is un-British to be disingenuous. The whole of this discussion comes down to this final point. We have shown that the organic integration of a system is a vital concept, and that there are myths about the division of its whole and the composition of its parts to be eschewed. But earlier it was contended that the boundaries of a system are subjective; and this is strongly supported at the philosophical level by the Hegelian axiom of internal relations—which of course makes it logically possible to equate every system with the universe itself. So the crucial scientific problem for systems research is this: how to separate a particular viable system for study from the rest of the universe without committing an annihilating *divisio*. And the crucial practical problem for systems research is this: how to stop someone else specifying the system for you, and 'killing it off' himself. (If there is an operational research man who cannot endorse this, he surely cannot have done any real-life operations research.) Most seriously: these are problems of desperate urgency for every non-trivial systems study, and I commend them to the addition of this first symposium.

Towards the Replacement of the Mythology

Throughout this discourse criticisms have been made of the way we have been doing things in systems research. This was to be expected in a piece about mythology: I invited you to join me in a conscious confrontation of our myths. But matters are improving, and we may end by considering in what way. There is perhaps a key idea in this work which helps to avoid the myths of orderliness, with their dependence on chimerical concepts like 'genuine randomness', and their consequences in *overmassive* control devices; an idea which will blow away the myths of integration, with their paradoxes about wholes and parts and 'convenient divisions', and their consequences in the *wrong* control devices.

I propose that this idea is the primacy among systems of the brain. The brain is itself the most resplendent system of them all: the most highly organized, the most effective, the most robust, the most adaptive. And the brain is also ourself, the system into which research is really done, and which entirely conditions our ability to understand at all. Why, for instance, do we encounter these great and paradoxical dichotomies of chaos and order, parts and wholes? Why is the whole history of human thought littered with the remains of great dichotomies of the past: matter and form; *res extensa* and *res cogitans*; life and death; good and evil; organism and environment; etc., forever? And why, above all, why is it that these paradoxes are never actually resolved? After centuries of discussion they prove to be 'unreal'; they are eventually purged from the human intellect by the catharsis of argument, and the hard attainment of a glimmer of understanding. To return once more to Hegel, the thesis and the antithesis finally dissolve inside a higher synthesis. This is indeed, for intellect, the very analogue of evolution. (The most recent completed example of this process has perhaps been the resolution for physics of the particle-wave dichotomy in the complementarity principle of Bohr.)

Surely the answer to all these questions lies in the brain. Surely the answer is that our machine for viewing reality is a network of two-state neurones; and surely it might be possible to show that the operations of such a machine inevitably dichotomize the output. If so, there will be yet one more problem in dichotomy to resolve: the perfect, ultimate, elegant mystery—to be answered only in a metalanguage we cannot know. Here is the question: is reality like this because the brain is limited by its fundamentally binary structure, or is the brain like this the better to perceive the essentially binary structure of reality? Descartes, himself the uncompromising dualist, rejected the concept of *Deus deceptor*: God cannot deceive. But it seems less impious to suppose that God might well enjoy a joke.

A full empirical demonstration of the utility of the brain as a model in systems research, which I have just tried to establish on a priori grounds, would be very lengthy and highly neurophysiological. Here are just a few disorderly comments on aspects which are important, for the structure and organization of the brain are extremely subtle. If we do not understand either very well, and probably we do not, at least intensive study of the brain provides an insight into problems of the kind with which we have been dealing. The insights seem to take the form expected by the last few paragraphs: they are awarenesses of higher synthesis, of complementarity between contrary propositions.

Firstly, consider the argument from chaos. We cannot question the orderliness of the brain in its achievement of results. Nor on the other hand can we question the neurological muddle: the endless array of fibres and cells which are certainly not assembled according to a circuit diagram. Dendrites wander about fortuitously, forming synaptic connections with anything they happen to encounter. Axons branch and ramify, wandering away to the cortical surface when everything suggests they should descend to lower levels. But the general design is always there, and the indeterminate connectivity is not 'perfectly random' by any means. The idea of an *immanent organization* takes shape and begins to mean something. What it means above all is *redundancy*, which is more surely a shock absorber for all the ills the brain is heir to. (We discussed this matter briefly before in terms of multiplexing.)

But secondly, as we said when talking of managerial structure, there has to be a certain paradoxical fluidity in the order which controls, to enable the requisite variety to be generated that will absorb the high variety of disturbance in the system to be controlled. And as we said more recently, there has to be 'at the same time' division tending to specialization and an absence of *divisio* implying undifferentiation: another paradox. Some insight into these difficulties may be found by learning about localization in the cerebral cortex, particularly in the frontal lobes and cerebellum. We may not understand how it *is*, but we do find out how to *say*, that 'this activity goes on just here, but it does not necessarily matter if just here is destroyed or isolated': it is a question of redundancy again. Now McCulloch has a splendid name for the facility we want. He calls it 'the redundancy of potential command'. (And it is not to the cortex that he turns to find the best cerebral exemplification, but to the reticular formation of the brain stem.) Without going too far into this, it may be possible to relate the answer given by these neurophysiological enquiries into 'potential command' to the question about how to isolate the system under study without flouting all the rules concerning parts and wholes. The system is defined by where the command is now and the trajectory on which it is (probabilistically) moving. (Obtaining an insight into this was suddenly to discern some meaning, though probably not the forensic one, in the legal maxim: *ubi major pars est, ibi est totum.*)

Thirdly, the brain so well manifests all the features of self-organizing systems—it is their archetype. Again, there is no time now to say much. But we really ought to reflect on a mechanism which does not need a blueprint of detailed circuitry, and which works perfectly well at the highest levels of intellect with an incredible tangle of low-tension wires that have fritted themselves together. Here Pask's work on chemical cells is tremendously relevant. I consider that the race of ever more gargantuan computers, with their tremendous specialization (in the morphological, not applicatory, sense), and with their frenetic struggle to impose yet more categorical order on a chaos of flying bits, will eventually go like the dinosaurs. Something more brainlike will have been found; something more cheap; something self-organizing; something that will begin operations with the printout 'order is more natural than chaos'. It is to the development of such a system that most of my private research is devoted. On the strength of that, let me make this observation: it is not likely to be done with orthodox electronics. We need a better analogue of the *fabric* of the brain than wire and glass.

The Rational Consequences of Irrational Action

From the dawn of scientific thinking, anyone who *was* anyone in science has been at pains to emphasize the role of measurement. Physical science is 'the systematization of knowledge obtained by measurement', said Eddington, and Kelvin had his famous dictum too. Let us agree that quantification is paramount in science. But it is high time that we advanced beyond the crude concepts of 'objective' measuring rods and clocks (the quotes have had to go on since Einstein's work), and looked to the brain for advice. How often does the brain produce an output in numerical form when not actually asked to do arithmetic? And when it does, how accurate is the answer? 'Half a mile down the road', '7 inches long, dear', 'he was in there a good hour', says the brain when asked 'how much further?' (2 miles), 'how long is this knitting?' (5.9 inches), 'how long did you wait?' (42 minutes precisely). And yet we pick our way across fast-moving traffic streams without getting killed. Conclusion: *there is more to quantification than numeration.*

It may be thought that we know about this already. A continuous error-correcting feedback system does not print out the amplitude of the oscillations it has damped. The point is that 'if it were asked to' it could and would. The brain on being asked to allot such numbers cannot—although clearly these quantities are available to it in some form. Consider this illustration. In the next room, which contains an alcove, a cupboard stands against the wall. You are asking yourself whether the cupboard will fit into the alcove. I suggest that you try to map the visual image of the cupboard on to the visual image of the alcove. Unless you are a craftsman used to measuring tapes, in which case the answer may be different, you do not attempt to map first the image of the alcove and secondly the image of the cupboard on to an image of the measuring tape, and then sit back to contemplate a numerical inequality.

Now this is a psychological enquiry. The brain as a machine may (for all I know) use some *tertium quid* on to which to map the two quantities. If so, however, I would doubt whether it is such a simple construct as a measuring rod: perhaps it would be best to regard the brain structure itself as the *tertium quid*. The point is that, in any case, this mechanism for very close correspondence does not succeed in making itself known in numerical form. It also seems probable that numeration (which is itself a set of mappings of some rather elementary measuring rods) is grossly inadequate as a model of quantification in both the brain and the outside world, and also of the regulations which subsist inside each and between the two. This argument seems entirely consistent with the earlier considerations from the mythology of parts and wholes. Straightforward numeration methods first of all commit *divisio* by the special way they divide whatever is quantifiable into too simple an arrangement of uniform quantities, and then commit *compositio* by assembling these units and their more obvious relationships (such as square measure) into elementary 'numeration machines' by the rules of schoolboy arithmetic. The result is that if someone were about to draw a picture of a road that included a line of telegraph poles receding into the distance, and were asked to estimate, in inches, the decreasing intervals between the poles, he would certainly not be able to do it. Let him draw the picture 'by eye', however, and he will manage most creditably. The inference is that the brain 'can do' projective geometry (of which consciousness knows nothing): i.e. it can bring the actual lines of poles and the drawing into very close correspondence. But, as with the earlier example, it cannot give an account of this process in numerical terms.

When we build a control system, the object is always to induce a form of behaviour in a relatively uncontrolled state of affairs which is recognizable as corresponding to a form of behaviour regarded as satisfactory or desirable. This may be either an actual situation (such as a winding road with which a car's behaviour must be made to correspond) or an idealized model (such as an approved sales policy). Thus the control system is a machine for mapping one world picture on to another; and we know that the control must be capable of handling the requisite variety involved. This is clearly a process of quantification, and indeed measurement. We mislead ourselves, however, if we go on to say that therefore the subtle measures in the system must be numerically available. We assume that this follows because we are trapped in mythological thoughts.

If a computer control is envisaged, then its contents can be printed out: its mappings are numerically accessible. If the full numeration cannot be given, it means that the control is inadequate—there is not enough variety in the system. But consider a colloidal cell into which inputs from the situation to be controlled are transduced as low voltages across platinum electrodes, and which is then allowed to 'solve the problem' represented to it by precipitating a growth of metallic iron on the floor of the cell. This solution to the problem is quantified; the precise shape of this growth at the molecular level is a measurement. Because this machine does operate at the molecular level it has ample variety to provide a control. But its measurements are inaccessible: they cannot be printed out. Since, however, these measurements are not required for any purpose whatever (just as they are not required in the examples given from the brain) this does not matter. What is needed is a means of focusing the control device, with its high-variety solution to the problem, back onto the problem. And this of course can also be done for this sample machine by electrical responses to the changing state of the cell.

Thus a more advanced concept of quantification is available than the mythological one that measurements are by their nature able to be perused. This leads straight to the idea that more advanced control machines are available than those which make their own 'calculations' available in numerical form. Not only 'more advanced', interestingly enough, but 'very much cheaper' too. For most of the cost of orthodox control equipment lies in its *accessible measurements*, whether digital or analogue. Inaccessible measurements are cheaper, because molecules are assembled free by nature.

Finally, then, systems freed of at least some mythological thinking can be envisaged which implicitly recognize the brain as an archetype. They have no order–chaos dimension; they have no parts and wholes. They are fluidly organized for potential command, and are essentially variety absorbers. Disturbance, noise, or irrational action is perceived by them as interfering with a natural but evolving pattern in the system under surveillance. They preside over the restoration of an equilibrial state, and use the energy made available by the disturbance to make evolutionary advances according to the epigenetic landscape of the moment. The outcome is control: the order of the system that is more natural than chaos. Disturbance is used to amplify pattern; noise is transformed by learning into signal; above all, irrational action results in consequences that are rational for the survival of the system.

We may thank the real, not mythological, gods of system that systems in real life do work like this; that immanent organization is forever emergent to absorb the risks of everyday mischance. For natural systems accommodate themselves to 'malice in the object', or bad luck, and are robust against disturbance. And they accommodate themselves to stupidity in men, or bad management, so that rational consequences ensue from irrational action.

Artificial controls, in political, social, and economic affairs, and in industrial and commercial systems too, have not perhaps learned these lessons from the brain. Many still grind on with infinitely too little variety, infinitely too much effort and expense, to relatively nugatory results. The metal cupboards in which they are encased gleam refulgently with dials and switches, yet rattle with the skeletons of gods and giants from the twilight of the mythological dawn.

I thank you for accompanying me on this retrospective trip. We now move forward into a new era in the handling of systems; an era in which man will base his understanding of control on the archetypal viable system of cerebral behaviour, as he has already learned to base his knowledge of power on the archetypal energy system of hydrogen–helium fusion. I believe the outcome may be just as far-reaching and much more constructive. Let us hope that we can play our own parts with sufficient insight and sensitivity that we do not annihilate the very equilibria we seek to reinforce.

'Prefrontal leucotomy, Sir . . .'

1952

10 TOWARDS THE CYBERNETIC FACTORY

STAFFORD BEER
Head of Department of
Operational Research and Cybernetics,
United Steel Companies, UK

PART 1: INFORMAL INTRODUCTION

THE CONCEPT OF A CYBERNETIC FACTORY

A CYBERNETIC system is recognizable by three outstanding characteristics. It is exceedingly complex: to the point where its interconnectivity is indefinable in detail. It is exceedingly probabilistic: to the point where its structure though complex becomes undifferentiated, and every trajectory is equiprobable. It is unreal to suppose that any such system can be controlled by the imposition of rules from outside; because the system by definition defies analysis, and therefore no test can be applied by which the adequacy of the rules could be judged. The third characteristic of a cybernetic system is, therefore, that the fundamental organization it displays is generated from within: it is self-organizing.

Any industrial company is, by these preliminary criteria, a cybernetic system. We may go further, and regard it as an integrated organism operating within an environment. This organism has a physical manifestation in a works (its body), and a set of interacting systems which nourish, energize and regulate it (its digestive, cardiovascular and endocrine systems). It has a rate of working (its metabolism); it can grow by reproduction at the cellular level (mitosis), and can duplicate itself in subsidiary companies by reproduction entire.

Above all, it must interact intimately with its environment: there is a whole ecology of industry which has been little explored. For there are only a few formal links which are generally recognized as standing for this connection between the company and the world outside, and these by no means reflect the abundant interaction that actually exists. A file of official correspondence

First published by Pergamon Press, UK.

ostensibly records the passage of information; but this does not reveal the personal contact behind the letters, nor the innuendoes they may hold for the recipient, nor the conventions by which they conceal what is meant, nor the information about the supplier contained in the product itself and its mode of delivery, nor the information about the customer contained in his acceptance of a slightly off-standard product. People may understand the intimate relationship between the company and its environment, but they have no formal model adequate to its expression.

Analogical thinking about the company as an organism can be continued in this literary vein indefinitely; and I believe that (if necessary) the model of the company, operating within its context of supply, demand, labour market, business confidence, and so on, could be mapped with scientific precision on to an organism living in its environment. But we will assume that no serious objection exists to the drawing of this analogy, since no detailed use will be made of its morphology, and pass to the question of the higher levels of control by which a system that is already viable in a passive sense achieves purposeful activity.

This involves a consideration of the nervous system. The flow of information between an industrial concern and its environment, and within the concern as affecting its own behaviour, is to be considered as an analogue of the flow of information into the sensory receptors, through the neural network, and out of motor activities in the organism. Again, a fairly loose analogy is adequate for our purposes at the lower levels, because no detailed use will be made of the comparison. Consider an automatic factory. This is very like a spinal dog; it has a certain internal cohesion, and reflex facilities at the least. When automation has finished its work, the analogy may be pursued in the pathology of the organism. For machines with over-sensitive feedback begin to 'hunt'—or develop ataxia; and the whole organism may be so specialized towards a particular environment that it ceases to be adaptive: a radical change in the market will lead to its extinction. This is why 'automation' in the generally accepted engineering usage of the term, is applicable only to industries (such as the automobile industry) with a guaranteed effective demand, a fairly rigid design policy, and a merely superficial response to a relatively slow cycle of change (e.g. fashions in colour and size of 'tail fin'). The cybernetic factory seeks a more adaptive, more readily responsive, automatic system, which would be capable of controlling any kind of company.

When men have been almost eliminated from the factory, and it runs smoothly and efficiently by automatic regulation, error-controlled feedback, and programmed response to a specified and limited variety of situations, we have the living organism of the company as the analogue of (say) an animal whose nervous system stops at the cerebellum. It is sentient: 'aware' in the sense of a capacity for automatic response to states of its own body and a limited range of stimuli from the outside world; but it is suffering seriously and indeed fatally from sensory deprivation. At present, such an automatic factory must rely on the few men left at the top to supply the functions of the cerebrum. And we may note that, even if they constitute a board with high intellectual ability, the whole organism is a strange one—for its brain is connected to the rest of its central nervous system at discrete intervals of time by the most tenuous connections. The survival-value of such a creature does not appear to be high.

The concept of a cybernetic factory is that the industrial company as a *whole* is a living organism; and it must display the features by which a living system operates if it is to remain viable. Now in the past industrial companies have been like this: they were self-organizing systems, and they were viable. But as economic and social pressure increases, they are increasingly driven to become more efficient, more specialized, more automatic, and so on, all of which tendencies threaten their long-term existence. Competition in our modern society forces management to aim at high and rapid profits: in ecological terms, at *dominance*; and with ecological dominance is linked (as a fact of natural science) decreasing adaptability. It is only with man, with the emergence of intelligence and the ability to predict, that this trend in evolution has been checked (we hope: but the state of the world today suggests that nature may yet impose her veto on the dominant species). For, we say, man is a highly specialized creature who has nevertheless retained his adaptability by growing a large brain and obtaining volitional control of himself in relation to his environment. Thus he loses, by specialization, his prehensile toes and tail; but he invents machines called elevators which still enable him to climb the Eiffel Tower in safety.

When we turn to contemporary management theory, then, it is not surprising that techniques are aimed at short-term dominance. Pay-off is paramount, and the five-year plan is regarded as a triumph of perspicacity. Accountants are expected to organize institutional information to the maximization of profit; linear programmers are asked to solve scheduling and transportation problems under the minimizing functional of cost; publicity men are awarded large appropriations to make less mutable an environment to which the organism cannot adapt. If the dinosaur can no longer live in the world, the world must be turned into a dinosaur sanctuary.

This will not do. The spinal dog is short of a built-in cerebrum; and the automatic factory is short of a built-in brain. The research discussed in this paper is directed towards the creation of a brain artefact capable of running the company under the evolutionary criterion of survival. If this could be achieved, management would be freed for tasks of eugenics: for hastening or retarding the natural processes of growth and change, and for determining the deliberated creation or extinction of whole species.

THE HEURISTIC APPROACH USED

It is possible to contemplate the problems of creating a cybernetic factory from an armchair, but very much more valuable to study them in an actual works. We have been most fortunate in having the opportunity to do so.

The company concerned is a relatively small, self-contained firm whose product is steel rod manufactured in a variety of sizes and qualities. At the time when the work began the company had just acquired a new senior management group, who had every intention of modernizing and improving an already prosperous firm. My department joined with them in this task, and a three-pronged attack was launched using the methods of work study, operational research and cybernetics. Stock control, stores control, financial control, cost control and other functions of management were investigated; proposals were made, accepted and implemented. The plant itself was intensively studied: some of its equipment was changed, and (with the co-operation of an engineering consultant) a revolutionary kind of mill was developed and is now undergoing trials. Automation was greatly extended by the management, and several radically new kinds of electronic control equipment were invented by the study team. This is background information only; but it will be seen that under its new executives the company rapidly attained the status of a first-rate up-to-date concern, with consequent benefits to its economy and stability.

The cybernetic study, beginning with the concept already explained, went on to construct a model of the company organism in its environment, and to detect the brain-like aspects of its control. A generalized model for a brain artefact is being evolved as the theoretical basis for a machine to undertake the functions of an automatic brain. Simultaneously, a specialized model appropriate to controlling an industrial company is being constructed as a means of linking the developing theory with real life. This special theory derives from a detailed operational research analysis using actual data, in which an arbitrarily chosen set of the intended operations of the brain artefact is used to direct calculations carried out by hand and eye. The results are offered to management as at least 'partly-cerebrated' information, and have an immediate practical significance and value. Thus the theoretical work directs the growth and exploitation of its own evolving exemplification in real life, while the real-life exemplification helps to generate and validate the theory. All this work is virtually complete. The next and final stage is to construct machinery capable of interpreting the full theory in practice.

In other words, this heuristic approach has been to study what actually happens, using the language of organic cybernetics to structure it; and to develop both a special and a general theory to account for it. The special theory is *ad hoc*; it is put into effect by empirical methods: recording, analysis and synthesis of actual data; statistical, mathematical and logical investigations of these data; the use of graphical methods, calculators and computers; the construction of perspex models; the cinephotography of the model of the adapting organism in its environment. The general theory claims, on the other hand, to be general in two ways. It does not make arbitrary decisions about the nature of reality, as any exemplification of the special theory has to do; and it is not uniquely appropriate to an industrial company, as the whole special theory has to be.

THE PRESENTATION OF THE THEORIES

There is no particular virtue in placing the general before the special theory, as has been done. It is perhaps more natural for cyberneticians to consider the generalization first, as offering a more complete insight, and to regard the special theory as a limiting case. The man more versed in industry, however, might prefer to master the special theory first, as offering a tangible example of the thinking. In the latter case, he must be careful to recognize that questions settled there empirically are dealt with by quite other means when considered by the general theory.

And this leads to the elucidation of a difficult point. The special theory deals with brain artefacts or cybernetic factories, and the general theory with brains and their artefacts. It is not possible to present here either theory in full (they are both incomplete, in any case). Thus what is really put forward in Part II is that part of the general theory which is relevant to this industrial project; and what appears in Part III is a particular exemplification of the *special* theory (which in its turn exemplifies the general theory). This fine distinction must be understood in order to comprehend the status of the cybernetic machine it is intended to build. This is a manifestation of the special theory, and an exemplification of the general theory.

These considerations have led to an important difference between the following two parts of this presentation. In so far as Part II is incomplete, it is because whole areas of the general theory are not mentioned. For example, the theory includes accounts of reproductive logical machines and of the amplification of intelligence that are not immediately relevant. They are simply omitted. But Part III is incomplete in the different sense that it is impossible to enumerate all exemplifications of the special theory which is embodied in physical apparatus. A convention is therefore adopted in Part III which attempts to *infer* the special theory from its quoted exemplification.

There is this to say in conclusion about the *special* theory and its physical embodiment. A considerable knowledge of Ross Ashby's work [1,2] is assumed. In particular, I am drawing on the fundamental ideas that a real system proliferates variety; that to control this it must be 'absorbed' by an equal or greater ('requisite') variety; that this can be done by generating variety to match it; and that the generation does not have to be artificial (such as injecting random white noise), but can be achieved by defining the system itself so that the parts are in homeostatic balance and the whole ultrastable. Secondly, a considerable knowledge of Gordon Pask's work [3] is assumed. I am drawing especially on the colloidal thread-structured machines he has built (which provide a suitable self-organizing high-variety fabric), together with my own [4] conclusions on the same theme. We are continuing our collaboration in designing the physical apparatus for this project.

Finally, there is this to say in conclusion about the *general* theory and its relevance to neurophysiology. At the start of this work, I made serious attempts to distinguish between my understanding of the living brain on the one hand, and the invention of the brain artefact on the other. A word such as *medulla* refers to something in the head; a 'medulla' in an artefact is not a genuine medulla. But the term had to be used, because there is no counterpart in engineering, and so it went into inverted commas. But I am not a neurosurgeon, doubtless the aspects of the medulla I had in mind were insignificant properties of the real medulla. Before long, the word medulla was appearing in two kinds of print and two sets of commas. Meanwhile, I had become simultaneously so involved in the brain and the company and the artefact and the logic, that it was not any longer possible to be sure of which I was thinking. The conventions adopted disintegrated. So they were discarded. The result is that Part II reads as if there is no real difference between any of the manifestations of brain—in reality, in analogy, in machinery, and so on.

In a sense, this does not matter. For the object is to obtain a mapping of a brain on to a machine, and insofar as this is done they *are* the same things. The critical word is 'insofar'. They are formal homomorphisms (albeit of a many-*many*-one transformation), and they are operational equivalents (albeit at a trivial level of isomorphism). In speaking of 'the brain', I speak only of a *useful slant* on a *useful aspect* of the brain. What ignorance this causes me to betray about the living jelly in all our heads I dread to think; but I trust my fellow symposiasts will sympathize, for they have met the same expository difficulties themselves.

PART II: FROM THE GENERAL THEORY: SET-THEORETIC FORMULATION OF THE BRAIN MODEL

PASSIVE SENSIBILITY

1.00 *General.* The first aspect of the brain artefact to be considered is its passive sensibility. This is defined as a collection of inputs which inform the brain about the state of the world, which is in turn defined as the state of the whole organism in relation to its environment. The word 'passive' is intended to show that these inputs are purely sensory: they register in a sensory cortex, stop short of any possible motor reflex, and have no conative implications.

1.10 *The Sensory Cortex.* In any brain or brain artefact, because it is a physical manifestation, there must be a limited total channel capacity for sensory input, of variety W. Consider a time interval δt, called a quantum of time, t_0. At time t_0, each of the sensory input channels delivers to the cortex a sensation, including the case where the sensation registered is 'no sensation'. In the living brain, each sensory input is represented by a large number of afferent nerves, each of which delivers one bit of information at time t_0. In the brain artefact, we shall consider an analogue input, which will reduce the number of afferent channels and preserve the total variety W by permitting each input to take up a value x on a continuum.

It is now possible to give a set-theoretic description of the sensory cortex.

1.11 s is a sensory input, an element of the set of sensory inputs, $\mathfrak{S}$.

1.12 To every element s of $\mathfrak{S}$ there corresponds a dense, denumerably infinite set $\langle x \rangle$ equivalent to the set of rational numbers in natural order of closed interval $\langle 0, 1 \rangle$, whose elements x are values ascribed to s on the continuum.

1.121 $x \in \langle x \rangle$ is uniquely specified for every t_0.

1.13 The set $\mathfrak{S}$ of sensory inputs s is denumerable and finite. It can therefore be ordered by correspondence with the set of natural numbers, and can be written down as the well-ordered set:

$$\mathfrak{S} = \{s_1, s_2, s_3, \ldots, s_n\}$$

of cardinal number $|\mathfrak{S}|$.

1.131 A rule of the ordering shall be that sensory inputs deriving from the organism itself (in this case the company) belong to the segment $\mathfrak{S}s_\nu$ determined by s_ν.

1.132 Sensory inputs deriving from the environment belong to the complement of $\mathfrak{S}s_\nu$ in $\mathfrak{S}$, namely the remainder subset.

1.133 Thus for example:

$$s_i \in \mathfrak{S}s_\nu$$
$$s_n \in \mathfrak{S} - \mathfrak{S}s_\nu$$

1.20 *Sensory Configurations.* The question now arises whether the separate elements s of the input set $\mathfrak{S}$ can be treated as independent of each other or not. For there is clearly a sense in which a particular set of inputs forms a sensory Gestalt which behaves as an entity.

1.201 For example, the sensory Gestalt recognized as 'a rose' is a configuration of visual, tactile and olfactory sensations. If the scent of the rose is missing from the configuration, the recognition probabilities may swing from 'rose' to 'artificial rose'.

1.21 It can be asserted that for the brain artefact, as also for the living brain, no element s of $\mathfrak{S}$ is independent of every other element s of $\mathfrak{S}$. The world picture is structured, and with it the object-language by which the brain models the world, by axioms of configuration of various kinds. For example:

1.211 as given in logic:

$$(s_1 \cdot s_2 \cdot \sim s_3) \vee (s_1 \cdot s_2 \cdot s_3 \cdot \sim s_4) \cdot \supset \sim s_5$$

where the activation (s) or not ($\sim s$) of a sensory input refers simply to the binary possibility that there is present or absent s_1 = a rolling mill, s_2 = a labour force, s_3 = some raw material, s_4 = some product, s_5 = some income.

1.212 or as given in mathematics:

$$x(s_4) = f\,[x(s_1), x(s_6)]$$

where x is the variable denoting s_4 = some product, s_1 = the speed of the rolling mill, s_6 = the gauge of rod.

1.213 or as given in statistics:

$$v = \frac{\text{cov}(x(s_7), x(s_4))}{\sqrt{(\text{var}\, x(s_7)\ \text{var}\, x(s_4))}} \rightarrow 1$$

where x is a variate measuring the level of s_7 = wages, s_4 = product, for a system of monetary incentives.

1.22 Such axioms of configuration are given in the language that models the world. They are given, that is to say, in the object-language itself and not in any syntax-language (taking Carnap's usage of these terms), despite the foregoing attempts to *allude* to them in what are evidently syntactical languages. The object-language is the language *of the brain itself* (for the specification of which von Neumann used to appeal) which the cybernetic artefact must speak.

1.221 The brain, then, adopts these configurations as Gestalten: as axioms of the object-language they must be developed as the brain 'learns to speak'. This implies a relatively short-term learning programme for the 'infant' brain, which will establish these structures as permanent features of the cognitive landscape.

1.2212 For example, the multiplication table may be looked upon as a sensory configuration. Given a brain-with-a-language (that is an 'adult' brain) its mathematical judgements will be analytic of the axiomatic structure of its own language; and (since we *started* with an adult brain, or (also) since all analytic judgements are by definition a priori) mathematical judgements are always a priori *analytics*. But if what is given is a pristine brain, whose language is yet to evolve, we shall have to consider its behaviour *operationally*. In this case, mathematical judgements will be learned a posteriori from instances of the naming of collections of numbers; and (since we *started* with a pristine brain, or (also) because all experiential judgements are by definition synthetic) mathematical judgements are always a posteriori *synthetics*. (This cybernetic and essentially operational examination of the problem throws possible light on the controversy over Kant's doctrine that mathematical judgements are always a priori *synthetics*.)

1.222 There are two main reasons why this structuring of the object-language into axioms of configuration, with which correspond the cognitive structures of Gestalten, is essential to a viable brain or artefact:

1.2221 They greatly constrain the freedom with which a particular point representing an important world event can range over a multidimensional phase-space, and thereby enhance the speed and accuracy of its recognition and identification.

1.2222 Without this mechanism, the brain would presumably waste most of its energy discovering and learning (precariously) every new exemplification of an axiomatic relationship that came its way. The brain would thereby rediscover in endlessly new guises structures implicit in the world picture object-language from the beginning, and doubtless fail to discover vital operational relationships about the way these effectively aprioristic structures happen (fortuitously) to work.

1.23 It is therefore supposed that the brain, in order to make speedy, accurate and non-trivial judgements about the world picture, must include machinery for modelling axioms of configuration from the input set $\mathfrak{S}$.

1.231 These configurations may well be time-dependent in some cases (for an adequate object-language is steadily modified and enriched); so our discussion of configuration will be concerned initially with time t_0.

1.24 The transmission of quantitative analogue information deriving from the set complex $\mathfrak{S}(X)$ need not be considered in this problem of configuration. We consider instead the formal cortical networks generated by $\mathfrak{S}$, for which the ith elemental sensory input is either activated (s_i) or not ($\sim s_i$).

1.25 A sensory configuration is a subset of $\mathfrak{S}$, namely S, of elements s. Since every subset of a well-ordered set is itself well ordered, we have:

$$S = \{s_\nu, s_\delta, \ldots, s_\theta\}$$

for all subsets of $\mathfrak{S}$.

In particular, a sensory configuration may be:
1.251 any proper subset: $S_a \subset \mathfrak{S}$.
1.252 the improper subset: $S_n \subseteq \mathfrak{S}$.
1.253 a unit set: $S_b = \{s_\mu\}$.
1.254 the empty set: $S_0 = \mathfrak{S} - S_n$.
1.26 The totality of possible sensory configurations is therefore the set of the subsets of $\mathfrak{S}$, namely $\mathfrak{U}(\mathfrak{S})$,
1.261 of which there are 2^n (because $|\mathfrak{S}| = n$: see 1.13).
1.27 Thus the total possible sensory configurations are given by the well-ordered set of all subsets of $\mathfrak{S}$:

$$\mathfrak{U}(\mathfrak{S}) = \{S_1, S_2, S_3, \ldots, S_2 n\}$$

of cardinal numbers $2^{|\mathfrak{S}|} = 2^n$.

1.28 The brain or brain artefact may seize, then, on any sensory configuration as a convenient instrument for removing effectively axiomatic structures from its sensory input (see 1.23).

1.281 An illustration would be to consider *jointly* the tonnage output in a given time interval, together with the gauge of rod being rolled. Assuming a constant mill speed, the use of this configuration $S_a = \{s_4, s_6\}$ gives a network which (given a suitable transformation for the appropriate X sets of this ordered pair of inputs) allows the brain to measure relative *efficiency*, which is certainly not itself a raw sensation.

1.282 The brain may seize on as many such sensory configurations as are convenient at any time t_0, subject to an upper limit of the number of such configurations available, namely 2^n.

1.29 At any particular time t_0, therefore, there will be $c \leqslant 2^n$ sensory configurations in the brain artefact, which will be visualized, for obvious neurophysiological reasons, to exist as a cortical network in the fourth layer of the sensory cortex. Any recognition the brain might take of a raw sensation itself will occur elsewhere: perhaps in the first (molecular) layer, to which some afferent fibres pass directly, for instance.

1.30 *The Fourth Layer of the Sensory Cortex* is at least partly defined by a set of many-one mappings of $\mathfrak{S}$ into $\mathfrak{U}(\mathfrak{S})$. One such mapping is S_b, which is a subset of $\mathfrak{S}$ of elements s (see 1.25), called a sensory configuration.

1.31 At time t_0, there exists in the fourth layer a particular set $[S]$ of subsets S of the set $\mathfrak{S}$, which is a subset of $\mathfrak{U}(\mathfrak{S})$:

$$[S] = \{S_b \ldots S_\gamma\} \subset \mathfrak{U}(\mathfrak{S})$$

1.32 Regardless of time, therefore, there may occur in the second layer *any* such set $[S]$ of elements S; and all possible states of the fourth layer are given by the sets of the sets of the subsets of $\mathfrak{S}$:

$$\mathfrak{UU}(\mathfrak{S})=\{[S_1], [S_2], [S_3], \ldots, [S_{2^{2^n}}]\}$$

of cardinal number

$$2^{2^{|\mathfrak{S}|}}=2^{2^n}$$

1.33 Notwithstanding the high variety made available at this stage (which seems no more than realistic in a brain artefact) it is to be expected that the full flexibility it provides is only strictly valuable during the 'infancy' of the organism. There is reason to think that coarse structures, 'macronetworks', are soon formed by the living brain: they should be formed early in the artefact too. The machinery for categorical associations (e.g. $2+2=4$), and paths of facilitation for fundamental modes of behaviour (e.g. certain conditioned motor reflexes), can be decided upon quite soon and may never have to be altered.

1.331 But the high level of redundancy this implies for the 'adult' brain in this facet of its behaviour is a reserve available should subtle modifications of the macronetworks be demanded. (Gross traumas might of course result in a demand for all this redundancy in the task of re-adaptation.)

1.34 A mechanism has to be envisaged to manifest these proposed operations of the fourth cortical layer of the artefact, which do indeed appear to imitate closely the corresponding activities of the living cortex (see 1.35).

1.341 The afferent inputs must arrive, and register in the fourth layer in ways which will permit of scansion, grouping and pattern recognition necessary to the establishment and operation of the postulated system of sensory configuration (see 1.355).

1.342 They must be registered in different modes of connectivity, to permit flexible interactions between themselves and outgoing axons (see 1.351).

1.343 Summations of activity against time will inevitably lead to rhythmic activities which map periodicities in the real world, and these ought to be detectable. If the artefact continues to imitate its living model by a spreading horizontal network of afferent fibres and the dendrites of pyramidal neurons in the first layer, then the artefact must display these rhythms superficially (see 1.354).

1.3431 A sufficiently strong surface stimulus will therefore generate superficial responses, as happens with living tissue, and the artefact mechanism must account for this (see 1.352).

1.344 The mechanism as so far discussed is primarily concerned with identifying and *separating* sensory configurations, information about which will be sent back to the mesencephalon via the axons of pyramidal cells. But there are cross-correlations and comparisons to be drawn between such outputs. An archetype for such activity might be found at deeper cortical levels (the fifth layer?), but it would presuppose preliminary 'cross-talk' between fourth layer outputs. What mechanism can there be for spreading this information across the layer of pyramidal cells? Surely this is the artefact analogue of *deep* response to a surface stimulus, which is propagated at the pyramidal level, and which is subsequently detected superficially elsewhere (see 1.353).

1.35 This schematic diagram attempts to describe the machinery of the fourth layer of the cortex in a form suitable for handling information as required in the brain artefact for the cybernetic factory, as required by 1.34. It is a composite diagram, based mainly on Eccles [5], but is also indebted to the work on intracortical chains of neurones by Lorente de No [6], and to the group scanning process ascribed to McCulloch by Wiener [7].

1.351 Figure 1 comprises 11 basically similar arrangements: a pair of afferent input fibres reach the cortex and ascend to the fourth layer. Here they branch, and end in synaptic knobs on dendrites of pyramidal cells or on interneurones (indicated by circles). The required connectivity by which the afferent fibres and neighbouring dendrites can communicate in every mode is indicated in the channel marked *B* (cf. 1.342). The channels 0–8 indicate a simplified convention for the same network. Only apical dendrites are shown from the deep pyramidal cells.

1.352 On the extreme left a pair of stimulating electrodes (S_1) is applied to the cortex, and a wave of superficial responses is seen moving across the cortex from *X* to the right. Eccles's postulated mechanism for generating this response is that the axons of horizontal cells (or afferent fibres) transmit impulses in the direction of the arrows, and contribute synaptic knobs to the dendrite on which each terminates, as well as to each which it encounters on the way. Lines of extrinsic current flow are shown for *X* alone, rising from deep sources to sinks on the apical dendrite. Similar lines will be visualized rising to successive dendrites, of decreasing intensity of current flow corresponding to a decrease in the superficial propagation of impulses as the horizontal axons terminate (cf. 1.3431).

1.353 In channel *A* an ascending axon (broken in Figure 1) appears at *Y*, by which Eccles supposes that deep responses spread to the surface. His postulated mechanism for deep response itself begins with a strong stimulus at S_2 which passes down the pyramidal cell dendrite between 1 and 0 to the soma, and along its axon and axon collateral. Special short-axon neurons are drawn by which impulses are propagated to the two neighbouring pyramidal cells—a response which would continue to spread to the right. Synapses excited at these deep levels provide sinks for extrinsic current flow downwards from sources on the apical dendrite (cf. 1.344).

1.354 On the extreme right, in channel *B*, an afferent volley generates an initial positive wave on the cortical surface by Eccles's third postulated mechanism. Here there is extrinsic current flow from sources on both the superficial level of the apical dendrite *Z* and the soma to sinks on the deep dendrite level (cf. 1.343).

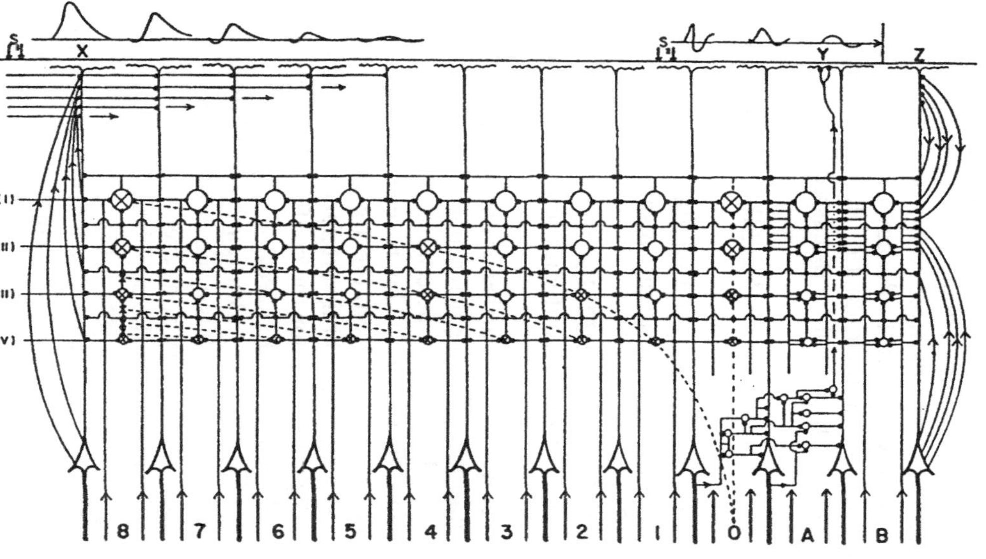

Figure 1 Composite diagram to describe the machinery of the fourth layer of the cortex

1.355 Across channels 0–8 is shown a new connectivity to provide a group scanning and selection mechanism. Channel 0 is to be regarded as an arbitrary central focus, and connections are seen to develop on the left which would be mirrored on the right. These effect a logarithmic transformation for the afferent inputs such as is needed in a configuration selection and pattern recognition process. The layers of interneurons (i)–(iv) are scanned cyclically. Each successive layer contains a higher cell density, made up of smaller cells, than its predecessor: the cells affected by the particular mechanism shown (i.e. for centre 0) are marked to display these facts (cf. 1.341).

1.36 Returning now to the output of this fourth cortical layer artefact, a particular set of outputs will be discussed. This is:

$$[S_a] = \{S_b, \ldots, S_v\} \subset \mathfrak{U}(\mathfrak{S}) \subset \mathfrak{U}\mathfrak{U}(\mathfrak{S})$$

1.361 For we have from 1.31 that this is a possible set of outputs, consisting of sensory configurations: a subset of the set of subsets $\mathfrak{U}(\mathfrak{S})$ of sensations $\mathfrak{S}$.

1.362 And we have from 1.32 that this set $[S]$ is included in the time dependent range of possible configurations of configurations, that is, of $\mathfrak{U}\mathfrak{U}(\mathfrak{S})$.

1.363 In other words, any particular configuration S, and any particular set of configurations $[S]$, are determined by a particular time t. If the denotation of S and of $[S]$ are determined by time t_0, then the denotation may have changed at time t_1. (This is relevant to 1.40.)

1.364 On the other hand, from the argument at 1.33, *for a sufficiently short span of time*, an 'adult' brain artefact will not actually modify a well-established configuration S, nor the configuration of such configurations $[S]$. (This is relevant to 1.50 *et seq.*)

1.40 *Computable Values of Configuration Measures.* Every element s of every configuration S_n which is a subset of the set of configurations $[S_a]$ is a sensory input. With every s, at every time t, is associated a measure variable x: itself a member of the population of measures $\langle x \rangle$ which define s quantitatively through time (see 1.12).

1.41 Thus for any set of elements s which denote any configuration S_n, a one–one correspondence with a measure set X_n may be asserted by the equivalence:

$$S_n = \{s, s_1, s_2, \ldots, s_n\} \sim \{\langle x \rangle, \langle x' \rangle, \langle x'' \rangle, \ldots, \langle x^n \rangle\} = X_n$$

1.411 And at time t_0, when $x \in \langle x \rangle$ uniquely:

$$S_n(t_0) = \{s, s_1, s_2, \ldots, s_n\} \sim \{x, x', x'', \ldots, x^n\} = X_n(t_0)$$

1.42 The set X_n has in general a *computable value* called $\hat{x}_n$. This is a number which ascribes a quantity to S_n, and which varies with time.

1.421 For $X_n(t_0)$, $\hat{x}_n(t_0)=f(x,x',x'',\ldots,x^n)$

1.422 But this statement (1.421) *cannot be generalized.* For in general, and even under appropriate constraints,

$$\hat{x}_n \neq f(x,x',x'',\ldots,x^{\max})$$

for all t with respect to S_n.

1.4221 *Proof.* Suppose $x_n=f(x,x',x'',\ldots,x^{\max})$ for all t. Then $\hat{x}_n \supset X_n(t)=\{x,x',x'',\ldots,x^{\max}\}$. Then if $\hat{x}_n(t_1)$ is computable, the residual set is a null set:

$$1-X_n(t_1)=\Lambda$$

by which device

$$X_n(t)\sim S_n(t_1)$$

while

$$X_n(t_0)\sim S_n(t_0) \qquad \text{(see 1.411)}$$

But (cf. 1.363) suppose that

$$S_n(t_1)=\{s_2,\ldots s_n\}$$

then

$$S_n(t_1)\subset S_n(t_0) \text{ per def.}$$

while

$$X_n(t_0)\subset X_n(t) \text{ per def.}$$

Then

$$X_n(t)\sim S_n(t_1)\subset S_n(t_0)$$

and

$$S_n(t_0)\sim X_n(t_0)\subset X_n(t)$$

Therefore by Bernstein's equivalence theorem,

$$X_n(t)\sim S_n(t_0)$$
$$=\{x,x',x''\ldots x^{\max}\}\sim\{s,s_1,s_2\ldots s_n\}$$

which is true if $n \equiv \max$—a very special case. Therefore

$$\hat{x}_n \neq f(x, x', x'', \ldots x^{\max})$$

1.4222 This says that although the value of the measure of any configuration can be written mathematically as an algebraic function, using all variables x as arguments, for a given time t (at which the logical structure of the configuration can be examined), it cannot be generalized for that S for all t. For although there is a mathematical device (namely: put $x_a = 0$) which would permit of a correct particular computation within this general model, the use of the model destroys the tenuous time-dependent *logical* structure of S. Just as 'the set of all cardinal numbers' is a meaningless concept, so 'the set of all variables x associated with all inputs s becomes meaningless when predicated of a particular S. (Some time has been spent on this point, because it is the main reason for the choice of a set-theoretic language in this description.)

1.43 Thus from 1.41 we have $S_n \sim X_n$, by which it is quantified, and from 1.42 that X_n has a computable value $\hat{x}_n$ defined at time t_0 according to 1.421 by an algebraic function. But either this function cannot be stated in a general form for all t with respect to S_n, or alternatively it cannot be stated in particular form for fixed S_n with respect to all t. That is: if the configuration S_n retains its identity through time, then it cannot be denoted by a general algebraic function; whereas if it can be so denoted it cannot retain its identity. This law is called the *Indeterminancy of Configuration Structure*.

1.44 Despite this Indeterminacy, however, $\hat{x}_n$ is computable at any time t_0; and the only general remark about its value is that it is a numerical 'blend' of the set of values denoted at that time by X_n.

1.50 *Statistical Homogeneity of Computable Values.* It follows from 1.4 that if we consider the quantification of S_n through a period of quantized time, a set of computable values (of which $\hat{x}_n$ is an element) will be obtained. These values may be considered as statistically distributed about their own mean, and the distributions so formed are likely to be remarkable in at least three ways.

1.501 From the arguments of 1.2, it is evident that a configuration offers a relative, not an absolute, measure. In order to remove axiomatic structures from its sensory input (see 1.28) it will produce blends which are effectively ratios. This must have the effect of distorting the distribution of $\hat{x}_n$. It will not be symmetrical, but skewed.

1.502 The Indeterminacy law seems to imply imprecise machinery for computing $\hat{x}_n$, and no adequate mechanism has been invoked which would filter the original sensory inputs of noise. It seems likely, then, that the statistical time series providing the set of values will exhibit considerable chance fluctuation.

1.503 The evaluation of computable value is occurring for each configuration in the set of configurations, and there is no basis for supposing that the variability of the raw numbers produced will be comparable across the whole set.

1.51 The assumption is now made that the brain artefact will find some degree of statistical homogeneity convenient in its treatment of these numbers. To achieve this, a succession of statistical transformations will be necessary.

1.511 There are various transforms (for example, $\theta = \sin^{-1}\sqrt{(x/X)}$) that will tend to return a skewed distribution based on ratios to normal. There are various transforms (for example, those eliminating some extreme quantile) that will smooth a time series expressing the distribution to remove chance fluctuations. And there are scale transforms (arbitrary mappings) that will change greater and less variability across the whole set into a homogeneous measure of variation.

1.512 Transformations of this kind, but of unknown number and composition, are now introduced to improve the statistical homogeneity of the output of configurations.

1.52 The basic set of such outputs it was agreed to consider (see 1.36) as stable for a short time (see 1.364) is:

$$[S_a] = \{S_b \ldots S_\nu\} \subset \mathfrak{U}(\mathfrak{S}) \subset \mathfrak{U}\mathfrak{U}(\mathfrak{S})$$

1.521 At time t_0, an equivalently ordered set of computable values has been considered, and this is written:

$$\{\hat{x}, \hat{x}', \hat{x}'', \ldots \hat{x}^*\} \sim \{S_b, S_c, S_d, \ldots S_\nu\}$$

1.53 Table 1 is a first matrix $m=1$ of such statistical transformations, ${}_1\mathrm{T}$.

Table 1 First matrix $m=1$ of statistical transformations, ${}_1\mathrm{T}$

$[S_a]$	S_b	S_c	S_d	......	S_ν	Configuration set	Time
X_a	$\hat{x}$	$\hat{x}'$	$\hat{x}''$	......	$\hat{x}^*$	Raw values	t_0
${}_1\mathrm{T}_1$	$\hat{x}_{11}$	$\hat{x}_{11}'$	$\hat{x}_{11}''$	......	$\hat{x}_{11}^*$	First version of first transformation	
${}_1\mathrm{T}_2$	$\hat{x}_{12}$	$\hat{x}_{12}'$	$\hat{x}_{12}''$	......	$\hat{x}_{12}^*$	First version of second transformation	
⋮	⋮	⋮	⋮		⋮		
${}_1\mathrm{T}_g$	$\hat{x}_{1g}$	$\hat{x}_{1g}'$	$\hat{x}_{1g}''$	......	$\hat{x}_{1g}^*$	First version of gth transformation	

1.531 The rows refer to successive transformations of the elemental configurations given by the columns. The words 'first version' refer to the fact that, given a transformation T_g whose nature is specified as being g (for example, to correct skew), there will be many possible versions (for example, the inverse sine) of which only one can be entered in the first matrix.

1.532 Successive matrices, $m=2 \ldots m=f$, may now be considered which, adhering to the same kinds of information at each row as the matrix $m=1$, vary the interpretation of the actual transform. Thus $m=2$ will yield the succession of transforms ${}_2\mathrm{T}_1 \ldots {}_2\mathrm{T}_g$; and finally $m=f$ will yield ${}_f\mathrm{T}_1 \ldots {}_f\mathrm{T}_g$.

1.54 The succession of matrices will form a cubic lattice, of which Table 2 is the 'base'.

Table 2 Base of cubic lattice

${}_1\mathrm{T}_g$	$\hat{x}_{1g}$	$\hat{x}_{1g}{}'$	$\hat{x}_{1g}{}''$	......	$\hat{x}_{1g}{}^*$	First version of gth transformation
${}_2\mathrm{T}_g$	$\hat{x}_{2g}$	$\hat{x}_{2g}{}'$	$\hat{x}_{2g}{}''$	......	$\hat{x}_{2g}{}^*$	Second version of gth transformation
⋮	⋮	⋮	⋮		⋮	
${}_f\mathrm{T}_g$	$\hat{x}_{fg}$	$\hat{x}_{fg}{}'$	$\hat{x}_{fg}{}''$		$\hat{x}_{fg}{}^*$	fth version of gth transformation

1.541 It is evident that the original set $X_a=\{\hat{x} \ldots \hat{x}^*\}$ will undergo transformations by finding a set of * trajectories through the cubic lattice, yielding a mapping of this order-preserving form (for example):

$$\mathrm{T}X_a=\{\hat{x}_{2g},\hat{x}_{1g}{}',\hat{x}_{fg}{}'',\ldots,\hat{x}_{4g}{}^*\}$$

1.55 There are several features of this statistical transformation machine that call for examination:

1.551 We may regard this cubic lattice as a linguistic structure; that is, a formal arrangement in which the specification of three coordinates itself specifies what process occurs at that point in the phase-space. This is a highly structured language, which has a great deal to say about the universe with which it deals without having any *content* (the lattice may be visualized as having empty cells). A computable value following a trajectory through a given cell automatically transforms in passing.

1.552 This leaves us free to regard the content of each cell as a transition probability which influences the trajectory of the computable value. Each probability changes roughly in proportion to the utilization of its cell by the appropriate column trajectory, which provides (in stochastic form) a positive feedback tendency. In short: this is a learning machine. It will acquire paths of facilitation.

1.553 The 'slice' of the cubic lattice appropriate to one configuration is itself a matrix (in the third dimension, not depicted in a table). This matrix is a machine for acquiring its own internal statistical homogeneity, and for learning, by facilitation, an optimum pathway. But probabilities rise *asymptotically* to unity: the pathway is never fully determined. On receiving a new stimulus from outside (by mechanisms yet to be discussed), say analogous to pain, new pathways may be facilitated. This means that this portion of the total machine is multiplexing its transforms, and is robust against external disturbance.

1.554 The whole machine is, however, a cubic lattice, and a mechanism may be postulated whereby it can learn to become homogeneous as between configurations—across the whole set. For the transition probabilities attaching to a particular *version* of certain transformations can be made to interact. Homogeneity in this dimension increases the stability of the whole arrangement, but without sacrificing robustness. For now the multiplexing feature is available at another order of magnitude. What is cohesive and stability-inducing in the enhanced correlation of probabilities between 'slices' can at once be turned into new (multiplexing) degrees of freedom if the external stimulus warns the machine of over-specialization and a too inflexible habituation.

1.555 It is understood that certain transformations may turn out, as the result of modifications induced by these external stimuli, to be identity transformations.

1.556 The whole of this mechanism is regarded as extremely important, and it will be invoked in other contexts. For example: we have been working on a stable set of stable configurations (see 1.52), while admitting always (cf. 1.363) the possibility of change. A mechanism such as that suggested here for processing computable values of configurations could also account for these viable features of configuration structure and selection.

1.56 Summarizing the outcome of these operations, the cubic lattice may be designated as the set $\mathfrak{M}$ of all possible matrices m as elements, the set of whose subsets is $\mathfrak{U}(\mathfrak{M})$. The lattice we need is M, a subset of $\mathfrak{U}(\mathfrak{M})$, having g elements of $m_1 \ldots m_g$. The set of transforms which promote statistical homogeneity will be designated by a *multiple multiplexed transformation* written thus:

$$M\mathrm{T}_g : \{\hat{x}, \hat{x}', \hat{x}'', \ldots, \hat{x}^*\} \rightleftarrows \{\hat{x}_{\alpha g}, \hat{x}_{\beta g}', \hat{x}_{\gamma g}'', \ldots \hat{x}_{\nu g}^*\}$$

1.561 The arrow stands for the mapping process, and is combined with the equivalence symbol to indicate that the mapping is one–one: the ordering is preserved.

1.562 The outcome is a generalization of the exemplification given at 1.541. Note that order is preserved in the x component itself. The suffixes behave differently; for the first suffix α, β, γ . . . is not necessarily monotonic increasing, and the second suffix is always g—for the lattice cannot absorb a trajectory, and all trajectories emerge at the gth transformation. (It is conceivable that a value x representing a variable input should emerge as an invariant, but it must emerge. The lattice might absorb all variety, but it cannot absorb the very existence of a quantified configuration.)

1.60 *Temporal Structure of Computable Values.* The measure set X_n associated with S_n has a computable value $\hat{x}_n$ which can be defined by an algebraic function at time t_0 (see 1.42). This computable value has been investigated above as a member of a set of computable values associated with $[S_a]$, still at time t_0. But consider again a solitary configuration S_n, and the set of computable values associated with this alone over a period of quantized time. This is the denumerably infinite set which we now define thus:

$$[X_n] = \{\hat{x}_n(t_1), \hat{x}_n(t_2) \ldots\}$$

1.61 The elements of this set will, by the provisions of 1.5, undergo the multiple statistical transformation defined at 1.56, and can be arranged as a frequency distribution using the scale of their own transformed values as variate. For a finite subset of $[X_n]$ this is simply an isomorphic mapping of the subset on to itself. This section, however, adheres to the order in which they were produced, and considers them as a time series.

1.62 There are two components of information in the time series $[X_n]$. The first is the numerical data transmitted at each quantum of time; the second is the structural data transmitted *through* time.

1.621 That is, the data: 2, 8, 3, 7, 2, 9, 4, 8, 1, 6 may have direct numerical significance (their mean for example is 5) which can be abstracted by the brain artefact at this stage and used. But these data have a structural significance independently of their precise numerical value: this brief series appears to have a marked periodicity, which on a full set of data could be examined statistically. The electroencephalographer finds this structural component of information (the brain rhythm) of more importance than either its amplitude or voltage.

1.622 Structural information offers the brain or artefact a new kind of configuration or Gestalt, which may be vital to it—especially in matters of prediction. A mechanism is required to discard discrete numerical information (once it has been used) in favour of structural information, which requires emphasizing.

1.63 Now the set $[X_n]$, which is well-ordered in respect to time, but dis-ordered with respect to computable value, could nevertheless be ordered relative to computable value (cf. 1.61) equivalently to the set of rational numbers in natural order. It follows that the set is amenable to arithmetic procedures.

1.631 In particular: the addition of two elements of the set $[X_n]$ defines a third element; this operation satisfies the associative law and supports the existence of both a null element and an inverse for each element. This set is therefore a group. Furthermore, this arithmetic is certainly commutative.

1.632 The set $[X_n]$ is therefore an *Abelian Group.*

1.6321 The combinational operation has been given in terms of addition for simplicity; a multiplicative operation could be used if the need arose, although some convention would then be required to exclude zero from the group (since it has no multiplicative inverse) and this might be inconvenient.

1.64 It can now be asserted that the structure-seeking number-discarding transformation required will be a homomorphic mapping ϕ of $[X_n]$ into the group of rational numbers N, so that the set $\phi([X_n]) \subset N$ is a sub-group of N.

1.641 For any finite subset of $[X_n]$, a scale transformation enables us to consider in particular the group of whole numbers, and to direct this homomorphic mapping onto a cyclic sub-group of order α. It is well known that the remainder set generated by such a mapping is homomorphic with the group of whole numbers.

1.65 Thus the homomorphic mapping required is:

$$\phi([X_n]):\hat{x}_n \rightarrow R(\text{modulo}\,\alpha)$$

1.651 There is no aprioristic argument which can establish an optimum value for modulo α: this will depend on the variability of the input data and the nature of the statistical transformations applied to them.

1.652 The minimum value for modulo α is manifestly 2.

1.653 Thus it will be circumspect to provide the artefact with a set of possible homomorphic transforms, the optimal *use* of which it can learn by evolutionary trials. These may be depicted in a simple table, since the trajectory of each computable value will now select (not some combination of *versions* of each transform) one or more transforms which experience reveals to provide structural information.

1.66 Homomorphic mappings of the set of computable values as already transformed statistically to the form given at 1.56 are shown in Table 3.

1.67 Familiarly by now, the set of all possible homomorphic transformations h will be written $\mathfrak{H}$, which set has $\mathfrak{U}(\mathfrak{H})$ subsets. The subset chosen at time t_0 will be one of these, written as H. This set of transforms, which promotes temporal structure at the expense of numerical discrimination, will be designated by a second *multiple multiplexed transformation* written thus:

$$HTR_H:\{\hat{x}_{\alpha g},\hat{x}_{\beta g}{}',\hat{x}_{\gamma g}{}'',\ldots\hat{x}_{\nu g}{}^*\} \rightleftarrows \{R_{H1},R_{H2}{}',R_{H3}{}''\ldots R_{H\mu}{}^*\}$$

1.671 This is again *multiple*, because more than one transformation may be used. It is again *multiplexed*, because a single homomorphism is strictly sufficient for the structure-seeking purpose, and the alternatives are available to provide a check mechanism leading to robustness under disturbance and the need for adaptation.

1.672 Even so, this set of transformations may be distinguished from the statistical set because, although it has a variety of alternatives from which to select, they are not chosen sequentially but separately. This may be visualized by mapping Table 3 on to Table 2 (rather than Table 1). Choose a column of Table 2. At time t_0 the appropriate trajectory has selected *one* cell in that column. This same trajectory, at time t_1, may pass on to the same column in Table 3, but to any number of cells. This machine therefore has a number of outputs: a set H of them for *each* configuration, and each set H being not necessarily the same as the others.

1.70 *The T-Machine* is the brain artefact device which receives, processes and analyses sensory input. The whole of this model to this point has been concerned with its specification in the most general form. Here is a summary of the T-Machine mechanism, beginning with a set of sensory configurations crystallized at time t_0, and following these inputs through their development to outputs at time $t_0+\delta t$.

$$[S_a]=\{S_b, S_c, S_d, \ldots S_\nu\} \qquad (1.52) \qquad t_0$$

$$\sim X_a=\{\hat{x}, \hat{x}', \hat{x}'', \ldots \hat{x}^*\} \qquad (1.521) \qquad t_0$$

$$\rightleftarrows MT_g:\{\hat{x}_{\alpha g}, \hat{x}_{\beta g}', \hat{x}_{\gamma g}'', \ldots \hat{x}_{\nu g}^*\} \qquad (1.56) \qquad \downarrow$$

$$\rightleftarrows HTR_H:\{R_{H1}, R_{H2}', R_{H3}'', \ldots R_{H\mu}^*\} \qquad (1.67) \qquad t_0+\delta t$$

1.71 The T-Machine registers the set of all available sensory inputs s, which are then blended, statistically transformed, and homomorphically mapped on to a set $[\Xi]$ of outputs ξ. This set is equivalent to the configuration set, and not to the elemental inputs s. Similarly the configuration set is equivalent to the output set, and not to the elemental outputs ξ. For just as a number of inputs s combine to form an input configuration S, so does an output configuration Ξ disperse into a number of outputs ξ—e.g. different homomorphic mappings using remainders from different moduli. Thus the output value (for example) $R_{H\mu}{}^*$ is a set of mappings using (for example) modulo 5, modulo 3 and modulo 2. These values would then be allotted to output channels ξ_1, ξ_2 and ξ_3, forming together the output configuration Ξ. The same construction applies to output values drawn from higher levels in the T-Machine, which may also map onto Ξ.

1.711 Thus we have the output configuration defined as:

$$\Xi_b=\{\xi_1, \xi_2, \ldots \xi_n\}$$

Table 3 Homomorphic mappings of the set of computable values already transformed statistically as shown at 1.56

$\mathrm{T}X_a$	$\hat{x}_{\alpha g}$	$\hat{x}_{\beta g}{}'$	$\hat{x}_{\gamma g}{}''$	....	$\hat{x}_{\nu g}{}^*$	Transform configuration set values	Time
$h\mathrm{T}\alpha$	$R(\text{mod}\ \alpha)$	$R'(\text{mod}\ \alpha)$	$R''(\text{mod}\ \alpha)$	....	$R^*(\text{mod}\ \alpha)$	First transformation of highest modulus	
$h\mathrm{T}\beta$	$R(\text{mod}\ \beta)$	$R'(\text{mod}\ \beta)$	$R''(\text{mod}\ \beta)$	....	$R^*(\text{mod}\ \beta)$	Second transformation of next highest modulus	
⋮	⋮	⋮	⋮	:	⋮		
$h\mathrm{T}2$	$R(\text{mod}\ 2)$	$R'(\text{mod}\ 2)$	$R''(\text{mod}\ 2)$	....	$R^*(\text{mod}\ 2)$	Final transformation of modulo 2	

1.712 And the set of output configurations for time t_0:

$$[\Xi_a] = \{\Xi_b \ldots \Xi_v\}$$

1.713 And the equivalence of structured and well-ordered input/output:

$$[S_n] \sim [\Xi_n]$$

1.72 All processes carried out in the brain and the artefact are bedevilled by Indeterminacy, stochastic behaviour, noise, error, and the arbitrariness of particular transformations. Yet the output is coherent, precise and robust. It is contended that this is achieved by redundancy in the form of multiplexing.

1.721 In the crudest sense, this means the proliferation of connecting links in the neural network, and of nodes by which they are connected.

1.722 But it also means what McCulloch has called 'the redundancy of potential command': the ability of any richly interconnected ganglion to assume a central role in any network, and for this centrality to change location freely.

1.723 These mechanisms are reflected in the T-Machine, and it is noted that the outputs are expected to be reliable, despite all forms of disturbance. This, it has been said, is achieved by the learning of paths of facilitation through the machine.

1.73 A necessary part of the behaviour of the T-Machine is therefore that a variety of trajectories should be equifinal. An output ξ_n, for instance, should be invariant under many different transformations of a particular subset of $\mathfrak{S}$. This is the formal condition for a satisfactory empirical exemplification of a T-Machine.

1.731 It is this formal condition which makes it possible to envisage a brain that works, or an artefact that is constructable. For it means that a T-Machine can in principle escape from the limitations of arbitrary decisions taken during its construction.

ACTIVE SENSIBILITY

2.00 *General.* The model has so far dealt with afferent impulses and a cerebral mechanism for sensation. It must now pass to efferent impulses and the notion of activity.

2.10 *The Motor Cortex* is visualized as complementary to the sensory cortex and disposed (as it is in the brain) in close association with it. Thus a central sulcus is envisaged as separating the postcentral gyrus (the sensory cortex) from the precentral gyrus (the motor cortex).

2.101 A knowledge of recent research into cortical activity will be assumed at this point. For the task of introducing modifications into the model that would dispel the crudity of the previous assertion would be disproportionate to the general level of refinement in the model at large.

2.102 Thus, for example, an interaction between the sensory and motor areas will be taken for granted insofar as it is known that '20 per cent of stimulation experiments on the cortex of the postcentral gyrus results in movement rather than in sensation'—Sholl [8].

2.103 But this simplification is no greater than that which underlay much neurophysiology until recent times; and it is hoped that the model can be developed in a way which, while not formally recognizing these discoveries, will not actually conflict with them.

2.104 The following postulate is made as, *inter alia*, offering ready means in the future for studying such sensorimotor ambiguities in brain function.

2.11 It is postulated that there is a set-theoretic logical equivalence between the sensory and the motor cortical architectonic.

2.111 *Sensations* will be regarded as paralleled by directions; and the sensory channels hitherto designated s are equivalent to directive channels (or directives) d, each of which is an element of the set $\mathfrak{D}$.

2.112 *Note.* The numbering of these paragraphs now follows that of section 1.00. Thus a full understanding of (for example) 2.12 implies reference to 1.12.

2.12 To every element d of $\mathfrak{D}$ there corresponds a measure set $\langle x \rangle$.

2.13 $\mathfrak{D}=\{d_1, d_2, d_3, \ldots, d_n\} \sim \mathfrak{S}$.

2.131 Directives deriving from the organism itself belong to the segment $\mathfrak{D}_{d_\nu}(\sim \mathfrak{S}s_\nu)$ determined by d_ν.

2.132 Directives deriving from the environment belong to the complement of $\mathfrak{D}_{d_\nu}$ in $\mathfrak{D}$, namely the remainder subset.

2.133 Thus, for example:

$$d_1 \in \mathfrak{D}_{d_\nu}$$

$$d_n \in \mathfrak{D} - \mathfrak{D}_{d_\theta}$$

2.20–2.24 *Motor Configurations.* The arguments of 1.20 to 1.24 apply, *mutatis mutandis.*

2.25 A motor configuration is a subset of $\mathfrak{D}$, namely D, of elements d.

$$D=\{d_\gamma, d_\delta, \ldots, d_\theta\}$$

for all subsets of $\mathfrak{D}$.

2.26 The totality of possible motor configurations is the set of the subsets of $\mathfrak{D}$, namely $\mathfrak{U}(\mathfrak{D})$.

2.27 $\mathfrak{U}(\mathfrak{D})=\{D_1,D_2,D_3,\ldots D_{2^n}\}\sim\mathfrak{U}(\mathfrak{S})$

2.30 *The Fourth Layer of the Motor Cortex* is at least partly defined by a set of many-one mappings of $\mathfrak{D}$ into $\mathfrak{U}(\mathfrak{D})$. One such mapping is D_b, a motor configuration.

2.31 At time t_0, there exists in the fourth layer a particular set $[D]$ of subsets D of the set $\mathfrak{D}$, equivalent to $[S]$:

$$[S]\sim.[D]=\{D_b,\ldots D_\nu\}.\subset\mathfrak{U}(\mathfrak{D})\sim\mathfrak{U}(\mathfrak{S})$$

2.32 And the total possible states of the fourth layer is given by the set of the sets of the subsets of $\mathfrak{D}$:

$$\mathfrak{U}\mathfrak{U}(\mathfrak{D})=\{[D_1],\ [D_2],\ [D_3],\ldots[D_{2^{2^n}}]\}\sim\mathfrak{U}\mathfrak{U}(\mathfrak{S})$$

2.33 The arguments of 1.33 to 1.672 apply, *mutatis mutandis*.

2.672 The range of transformations T are now paralleled by an equivalent range V.

2.70 The *V-Machine* is the brain artefact device which receives, processes and analyses motor input. Its mechanism is summarized by equivalence with the T-Machine as follows:

$$\begin{array}{ll}
[D_a]=\{D_b,D_c,D_d,\ldots D_\nu\} & t_0\\
\sim X_a=\{\hat{x},\hat{x}',\hat{x}'',\ldots\hat{x}^*\} & t_0\\
\rightleftarrows MVg:\{\hat{x}_{\alpha g},\hat{x}_{\beta g}',\hat{x}_{\gamma g}'',\ldots\hat{x}_{\nu g}^*\} & \downarrow\\
\rightleftarrows HVR_H:\{R_{H1},R_{H2}',R_{H3}'',\ldots R_{H\mu}^*\} & t_0+\delta t
\end{array}$$

2.71 The output of the V-Machine is homomorphically mapped on to a set $[Z]$ of outputs ζ. This set is equivalent to the configuration set $[D]$, but the inputs d are not equivalent to the outputs ζ (cf. 1.71).

2.711 Thus the output configuration is defined as:

$$Z_b=\{\zeta_1,\zeta_2,\ldots\zeta_n\}$$

2.712 And the set of output configurations for time t_0:

$$[Z_a]=\{Z_b,\ldots Z_\nu\}$$

2.713 And the equivalence of structured and well-ordered input/output:

$$[D_n]\sim[Z_n]$$

2.72–2.731 The arguments of 1.72 to 1.731 apply, *mutatis mutandis*.

INTEGRATION AT THE THALAMIC LEVEL

3.00 *General.* Both the T-Machine and the V-Machine are devices for organizing experience: afferent and efferent experience respectively. Each is capable of organizing this experience under two modes: organismal and environmental. This fourfold system must clearly be intricately and intimately balanced.

3.01 Notwithstanding possible interactions at the cortical level itself (cf. 2.102) a deeper level integration is required, and this is postulated to occur at the thalamic level.

3.10 Four output sets will thus be considered, reflecting the sensory organismal $[\Xi_0]$ and environmental $[\Xi_E]$ activities, and the corresponding motor activities $[Z_0]$ and $[Z_E]$ of the cortex.

3.101 The system incorporating these sets is clearly some form of Ashbean ultrastable machine [1,9], and Ashby's lead will be followed in the use of Bourbaki's set notation [10] at this point.

3.1011 This permits consideration of a 'product' of the four sets that is neither an orthodox union nor an intersection but an ordered 'superset'.

3.102 Output configurations are the elements of the four sets defining the system, which is written:

$$[\Xi_0] \times [\Xi_E] \times [Z_0] \times [Z_E] = U_{t_0}$$

3.103 The element $u \in U_{t_0}$ is a structural state of the whole system, designating an ordered quadruplet of elemental configurations:

$$u_{t_0} = (\Xi_{0^n}, \Xi_{E^n}, Z_{0^n}, Z_{E^n})$$

3.104 It remains to decide whether the T-Machine is in fact capable of distinguishing between organismal and environmental subsets of its output. These aspects were distinguished in $\mathfrak{S}$ as the segment determined by s_ν and the remainder subset, but there is in practice considerable ambiguity in allocating inputs to these destinations. The T-Machine itself will similarly involve ambiguities in attempting to preserve the distinction, on account of the law of indeterminacy of configuration structure (see 1.43). Even so, the division can be maintained in $\mathfrak{S}$ for most s, and in $U(\mathfrak{S})$ for most S; thus an approximately accurate distinction can be preserved for most Ξ.

3.1041 Most dichotomies of function in the real world turn out to be ambiguous over at least some area of the phase-space, and this is especially so in the brain (cf. sensory and motor cortex). To reject a scheme of classification on this ground is neurotic, not rigorous science, if it holds in the main, is useful, and is not treated as if it admitted of no exceptions.

3.1042 In this case especially, the cortex is at least partly localized (cf. the well-known cortical homunculi of Wilder Penfield), and the segments under discussion are not entirely logical abstractions but have a certain unity in the brain and the machine.

3.20 *The U-Machine* is an assembly component to handle the fourfold superset U of quadruplet elements u in such a way that the organism and the environment are and remain in mutually acceptable states.

3.21 To this end, the U-Machine has a set of outputs Ω that represents all possible interactions of the brain with the state of the world—which itself provides the inexhaustible variety feeding in through the T- and V-machines.

3.22 Efferent impulses themselves originate in the motor cortex, and change the behaviour of the organism directly ('move left arm'; 'switch off second engine') and of the environment indirectly ('open the door', 'write to customer'). The U-Machine *monitors* all these activities in relation to the sensory Gestalten. Thus the output of the U-Machine is a monitoring signal that feeds back approbation and disapprobation, through the world picture itself, into its own input.

3.221 The output set Ω is thus a *reward function*. It tends to reinforce input patterns conducive to survival, and to break down patterns that are not. This is achieved in a *directed* rather than a random way, through the highly conditioned T- and V-Machines.

3.2211 This mechanism greatly modifies the concept of random mutation that informs the Ashbean homeostat and Neo-Darwinian genetics alike. It offers a procedure for constructing in the T- and V-Machines something analagous to the mechanism Waddington [11] has invoked for embryological development: an 'epigenetic landscape'.

3.23 The U-Machine may be described thus at time t_0:

$$U_{t_0} = [\Xi_0] \times [\Xi_E] \times [Z_0] \times [Z_E] \qquad \text{(see 3.102),}$$

3.231 The element of $u \in U_{t_0}$ is a structural state:

$$u_n = (\Xi_{0n}, \Xi_{En}, Z_{0n}, Z_{En})$$

3.232 And the element $\hat{u}_n$ is a computable value corresponding to u_n, whose element are computable values $\hat{x}$ of the ordered quadruplet of the elemental configurations of u:

$$\hat{u}_n = (\hat{x}_{A_n}, \hat{x}_{B_n}, \hat{x}_{C_n}, \hat{x}_{D_n}) \sim u_n$$

3.2321 The computable value $\hat{x}_n$ is analogous to $\hat{x}_n$ in 1.4. In particular,

$$\hat{\chi}_n(t_0) = f(\chi, \chi', \chi'' \ldots \chi^*)$$

where

$$\Xi_n(t_0) = \{\xi, \xi_1, \xi_2, \ldots, \xi_n\} \sim \{\chi, \chi', \chi'', \ldots, \chi^n\}$$

and

$$\chi = x \vee x_{\alpha g} \vee R_{H_1} \qquad \text{(see 1.70)}$$

as determined by the T-Machine.

3.24 The U-Machine may be described thus in general:

$$U = \bigcup_{i \in I} U_{t_i}$$

the union of the sets $(U_{t_i})_{i \in I}$ where I is the set of all possible states through time of the Bourbakian product of the four sets of output configurations (cf. 3.23).

3.241 The element $u \in U$ is a structural state:

$$u_{t_0} = \bigcup_{n \in J} u_n(t_0) \quad \text{and} \quad [u] = \bigcup_{n \in J} [u]_n$$

where J is the set of all possible states through time of each output configuration (cf. 3.231), and $[u] = ([\Xi_0]$, etc.).

3.242 The element $\hat{u}$ is a computable value for the whole system corresponding to u:

$$\hat{u}_{t_0} = \bigcup_{n \in J} \hat{u}_n(t_0) \quad \text{and} \quad [u] = \bigcup_{n \in J} [\hat{u}]_n$$

where $[\hat{u}] = ([\hat{\chi}_A]$, etc.).

3.25 Throughout this formulation, time has been treated as quantized. To discuss the operation of the U-Machine, its state will be described at t_0, and time will then be advanced by quanta.

3.251 There is a computable value $\hat{\chi}$ referring to any output configuration (see 3.232). The subscripts A, B, C, D have already been used to signify the four parts of the ordered quadruplet, and these are maintained in what follows. We now consider the full sets of configurations at time t_0 (e.g. $[\Xi_0]$) rather than each configuration separately (e.g. Ξ_{0n}), and the set of computable numbers $\hat{\chi}$ referring to each such set will be written $[\hat{\chi}_A]$, which is the quantized state of the assembly

$$A(= \bigcup_i [\Xi_0]_i)$$

3.2511 $[\hat{\chi}]$ is strictly a vector of the set of configurations, but it is convenient to regard it as a single value. This is perfectly possible; for example $[\hat{\chi}]$ is itself a computable value if every set of values $\hat{\chi}$ is allotted a unique Goedelian number.

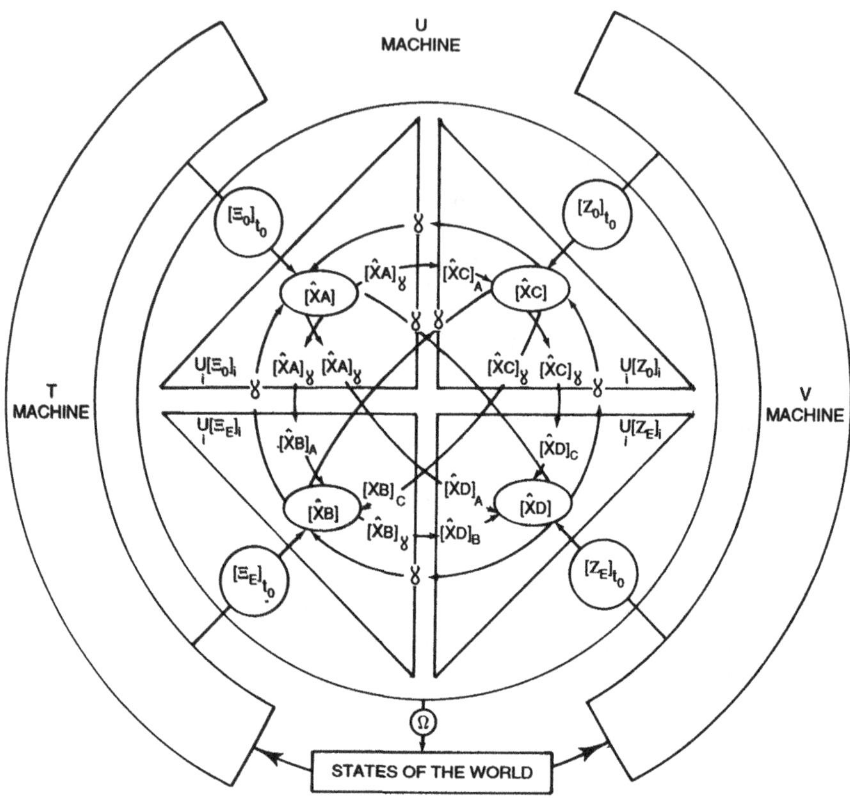

Figure 2 The U-Machine

3.25 *Operation of the U-Machine.* The U-Machine (Figure 2) is an Ashbean homeostat [9]. A selection of its more important couplings is shown in the figure. These are similar in form, and it will suffice to discuss the operation of one coupling: that between the motor organism (inputs $[Z_0]_{t_0}$) and the sensory organism (inputs $[\Xi_0]_{t_0}$).

3.251 The motor organism has a set of states

$$\bigcup_i [Z_0]_i (=C)$$

and at time t_0 is in the state $[\hat{\chi}_C]$. The sensory organism is in the state $[\hat{\chi}_A]$, an element of its set of states

$$\bigcup_i [\Xi_0]_i (=A)$$

The motor state will be assumed to be different from the sensory state: that is, the brain is proposing that the organism should act and will only implement this intention if the proposed state is acceptable to the sensory cortex (with its learnt patterns and ability to forecast).

3.252 To do this, C must inform the sensory cortex A that it regards the intended state $[\hat{\chi}_C]$ as favourable to itself. This is judged from internal criteria: the learning of the V-Machine. A then decides, by its own T-Machine criteria, whether the state is acceptable or not.

3.251 $[\hat{\chi}_C] \to \gamma_1$ for an unacceptable state

$\to \gamma_2$ for an acceptable state

where survival value is measured by the set $\Gamma = \{\gamma_1, \gamma_2\}$, providing the operation g.

3.253 There is a pair of mappings of A in A: $[\hat{\chi}_A]_{\gamma_1}$ and $[\hat{\chi}_A]_{\gamma_2}$ such that the g operation gives an invariant point for an acceptable state:

$$[\chi_A]_{\gamma_2}([\hat{\chi}_A + 1]) = ([\hat{\chi}_A + 1])$$

where time has advanced one quantum at the g operation, and the new state of A is written $[\hat{\chi}_A + 1]$. For an unacceptable state there is no invariant point:

$$[\hat{\chi}_A]_{\gamma_1}([\hat{\chi}_A + 1]) \neq ([\hat{\chi}_A + 1])$$

3.254 There is a set of mappings of C in C: $[\hat{\chi}_C]_A$ which adjusts C towards A if it is invoked. It will be invoked if A changes state, otherwise not.

3.255 The state of this (simplified) U-Machine $C \times A$ at time t_0 is defined by the ordered couple:

$$\hat{u} = ([\hat{\chi}_C], [\hat{\chi}_A])$$

the value of which element changes at each quantum of time during which the operations $[\hat{\chi}_A]_\gamma$ and $[\hat{\chi}_C]_A$ are induced simultaneously.

3.256 This is the transformation:

$$([\hat{\chi}_C], [\hat{\chi}_A]) \to ([\hat{\chi}_C]_A([\hat{\chi}_C + 1]), [\hat{\chi}_A]_{g[\hat{\chi}_C + 1]}([\hat{\chi}_A + 1]))$$

3.257 The equilibrial state is reached when the whole machine $C \times A$ is quiescent, which may be defined as:

$$[\hat{\chi}_A]_{g([\hat{\chi}_C + q])}([\hat{\chi}_A + q]) = ([\hat{\chi}_A + q])$$

so that

$$g([\hat{\chi}_C + q]) = \gamma_2$$

or

$$[\chi_C + q] \in {}^{-1}g(\gamma_2)$$

after q quanta of time passed.

3.258 *Note* Ashby remarked ([9]—corrected version) that his mechanism should be developed to use a random variable; but the machine he was describing, once having been disturbed, had no further input and was left to reach equilibrium. It will be appreciated that in the U-Machine random perturbations arrive continuously from the world via the T- and V-Machines, and can be handled.

3.259 At the equilibrial state, the machine is given as:

$$[\hat{u}]_{t+q} = ([\hat{\chi}_C + q], [\hat{\chi}_A + q])$$

This expression denotes the *preferred state of the system* for given T and V input configuration sets.

3.2591 To extend this operating description to cover all possible couplings of the machine would be firstly to write down the whole of this section (3.25) many times with different symbols—a work of supererogation indeed. Secondly, however, it would require that all the operations by which the states of each assembly are mapped onto themselves be traced right through the whole system. It is easy to *visualize* the reverberating effect of the modification of one coupling throughout the system, but difficult to formalize it. For instance, although a *uniform* reverberation throughout the system can be visualized, it is clear that some pathways will be differentially blocked by vigorous local action which will engulf the tenuous effects of distant activity. Thus I tentatively propose that the reverberations could be treated as random walks through the network of operations that induce the critical mappings; they might be treated formally as Markov chains.

3.26 *The Output of the U-Machine* is a set Ω of elements ω on to which are mapped the succession of Bourbakien elements $[\hat{u}]$ of the product set which stands for the whole system (given for t_0 at 3.23).

3.261 Thus the set of elements $[\hat{u}]$ determining the U-machine and the set of elements ω determining the output are linked through their mutual equivalence to

$$\prod_{i \in K} [\hat{\chi}]_i$$

where K is any possible assembly (such as $[\Xi_0]$) included in a U-Machine.

3.262 Just as the vectors of the configuration sets $[\hat{\chi}]$ can be regarded as unique Goedelian numbers (see 3.2511), so can their product. Thus the monitoring signal carried by the set Ω has a measure corresponding to each element ω. The channel capacity required for the transmission of Ω must be very high indeed, and an estimate of the variety of this measure ought to be obtainable.

3.2621 In the T-Machine, all possible states of the fourth cortical layer are given by $\mathfrak{U}\mathfrak{U}(\mathfrak{S})$ of cardinal number:

$$2^{2^{|\mathfrak{S}|}} \qquad \text{(see 1.32)}$$

and in the V-Machine the equivalent cardinal is:

$$2^{2^{|\mathfrak{D}|}} \qquad \text{(see 2.32)}$$

3.2622 But $\mathfrak{S} \sim \mathfrak{D}$ (2.13) so $|\mathfrak{S}| = |\mathfrak{D}| = n$ where n is the total number of possible inputs. Therefore the maximal *structural* variety from the two input machines which converges on the U-Machine is:

$$2(2^{2^n})$$

3.2623 However, the information carrying capacity of this population of input networks is affected by the infinitely denumerable measure sets each of cardinal number $\aleph_0$. Moreover, the U-Machine proceeds to select from both input sources conjointly. The expression for the channel capacity required for output is elusive (but nonetheless should be susceptible to statement).

3.2624 If this expression could be determined, and since the approximate channel capacity for the brain's actual input and output mechanisms can be estimated (cf. Bowman [12]), then an approximate measure of variety reduction in the brain could be obtained. This is interesting because it would throw light on the modulus used by the T- and V-Machines in reducing continuous measuring to discrete scales (attempted calculations suggest, for example, that the transfinite cardinal must in practice be reduced to a cardinal of 4 or 5). It might also explain (via pattern recognition via sensory configurations) the severe limitation on human ability to discriminate between more than a few (say five) points on a scale of subjective judgement. Such arguments seem important, though not strictly relevant to present purposes.

MONITORING AT THE RETICULAR LEVEL

4.00 *General.* Without intending to minimize the importance of the cortex itself, there is much to be learnt from recent work on the reticular formation of the brain stem. This must have its place in the model and the artefact, although little can be said at present.

4.10 *The descending reticular formation* must surely accept an important segment of the output set Ω, as well as direct cortical connections. In the organism it has the task of mediating hypothalamic and bulbar control of visceral function, and the monitoring output of the U-Machine would certainly be adapted to an analogous function in the institutional brain artefact.

4.11 *The ascending reticular formation* offers precisely the mechanism required for arousal of the T-U-V system which, in the absence of significant cortical activity must be quiescent. It is clear that in a 'routine' situation the T- and V-inputs to the U-Machine would be fairly static; the U-Machine would find and retain an equilibrium, and the entropy of the whole system would steadily rise. A decreasing tendency for anything at all to happen would be revealed. An input signal referring to danger (for example) could then be accepted at the cortical level and engulfed: by this time, it is envisaged, the T-U-V system would be *habituated*; it would be cycling at a steady sleepy rhythm. But, since the ascending reticular system receives collaterals from afferent paths, and if it is capable of monitoring these afferent impulses (as it appears to be), a danger signal could be fed straight into the U-Machine and destroy its equilibrium.

4.12 These considerations, which are eminently appropriate to this theory, assume a knowledge of the work of such people as Magoun [13]. They connect importantly with the idea (see 1.722) of 'the redundancy of potential command', and McCulloch has explicitly referred this name to the reticular formation. But I have not succeeded in pursuing the formal statements of this general theory into this area, because the anatomical and physiological picture hitherto accepted is undergoing such rapid and drastic change.

4.121 For example, the diffuse organization of the reticular formation for which a preliminary model was constructed turns out to be a myth. It is 'subdivided into several regions which differ with regard to their cytoarchitecture, fibre connections, and intrinsic organization' according to Brodal [14], regions which are certainly interdependent.

4.13 *The R-Machine.* Even so, and even in the absence of any formal account, an R-Machine will be postulated and is constructable. For it is certainly possible to envisage control loops which cannot be closed within the T-U-V system. The R-Machine will be defined in a preliminary way as the mechanism for such closure.

4.131 Gastaut [15] has for example proposed that conditioned learning (with which a useful brain artefact must be concerned) cannot be closed within the cortex, as experimental cortical lesions have not prevented closure. If the afferent collaterals already mentioned excite the reticular formation for an unconditioned stimulus, and there are connections between the reticular formation and the cortex as well at the thalamic level, then a subtle conditioning mechanism is available. Instead of the establishment of direct facilitated pathways in the cortex itself, there is a thalamo-cortical mapping onto the R-Machine which is injecting the random perturbations of unconditioned stimuli into the U-Machine. Thus the process of conditioning becomes a homeostatic struggle for dominance between an organized and a random response at the thalamic level, which will eventually be settled by an equilibrium which perfectly measures the relevance of the conditioning to the general experience of the organism.

4.1311 This is my own interpretation for this theory of Gastaut's proposal, although the R-Machine mechanism shown in Figure 3 is Gastaut's own model imposed on mine. It does not show the pathways through the association cortex which Gastaut shows, but these are implicit in my definition of the T- and V-Machines.

4.132 Mention was made (at 3.221) of a reward function which was conceived as a role of the output Ω. This is another candidate for monitoring at the reticular level which can be made firm in a specification for a constructable R-Machine (despite its unformalized structure). It is an R-closure alone that can stimulate or inhibit the 'metabolism' of the U-Machine.

4.1321 This thought derives especially from the arousal mechanism of the ascending reticular formation (4.11) and also the conditioning mechanism (4.131).

4.1322 Moreover, the mechanism of pain seems important as implying an inverse reward. Central pain is readily contained within this model: cf. the evidence adduced by Noordenbos [16] that lesions occurring anywhere along the afferent pathways in the neuraxis can cause spontaneous pain without stimulation of the area in which it is localized. Visceral and referred pain can also be visualized in the model. But in view of the arguments above, it may be that pain arising from peripheral receptors presents no special problem to the model either, as might at first appear.

4.133 Thus we are led to consider an extension of the concept of a reward function already given, and to consider in the theory an *algedonic control system* which would have wide implications for all the functions of the artefact. This is a tentative proposal, and cannot be elaborated here.

4.2 A general picture of the whole theory, showing how the parts fit together, is provided at Figure 3. The temptation to make the outline look like a coronal section of the living brain was irresistible and I apologize to cerebra everywhere for such insolence.

Figure 3 General picture of the whole theory

PART III: FROM THE SPECIAL THEORY: AN EXEMPLIFICATION OF THE T-MACHINE AND PROSPECTUS OF THE ARTEFACT

THE CHAIN OF SYSTEMS

The company is a manufacturer of steel rods. It takes billets of steel ($2\frac{1}{4}$ in^2, in various steel qualities) and rolls them down to a small round cross-section (in a variety of sizes). There are two strands to the mill: that is, two lots of steel run side by side through the mills. The rods, which are red-hot, emerge at a speed of approximately 70 m.p.h., and are then coiled, cooled and inspected for dispatch.

The basic plant consists of a heating furnace for the billets, and a means of feeding them into the mill; three interconnected trains of rolling mills (roughing, intermediate and finishing) arranged like a flattened letter S, the steel looping round the two bends in order to change direction twice; suitable coiling mechanisms capable of dealing with a continuous output from the mill; machines for removing the coils and circulating them on a conveyor while they cool; and a means of retrieving and stacking them thereafter. This is the 'producing system' shown on Figure 4.

This producing system is connected to the outside world through two stocking systems. The input stocks consist of billets, and buffer the producing system against the vagaries of the environmental supplying system. The output stocks consist of finished rods, and feed the environmental consuming system—the market.

The couplings within the company are quasi-deterministic. Input stocks must eventually be fed into the producing system to become output stocks. But the quantities and qualities to be charged are subject to decision procedures, and these themselves do not specify which individual billets (or rods) are to be used. The two environmental couplings, however, are entirely probabilistic: there is no guarantee about supply (from steelmaking companies) nor about demand (from the market). These couplings have none the less been intensively studied by operational research methods, and can be effectively described as stochastic processes.

Feedback loops operate throughout this chain of systems, and the four obvious ones are shown in Figure 4. More complicated feedbacks, which do not involve the plant itself, couple the supply and demand systems directly, in that potential changes in either require consultations with the other before they become actual.

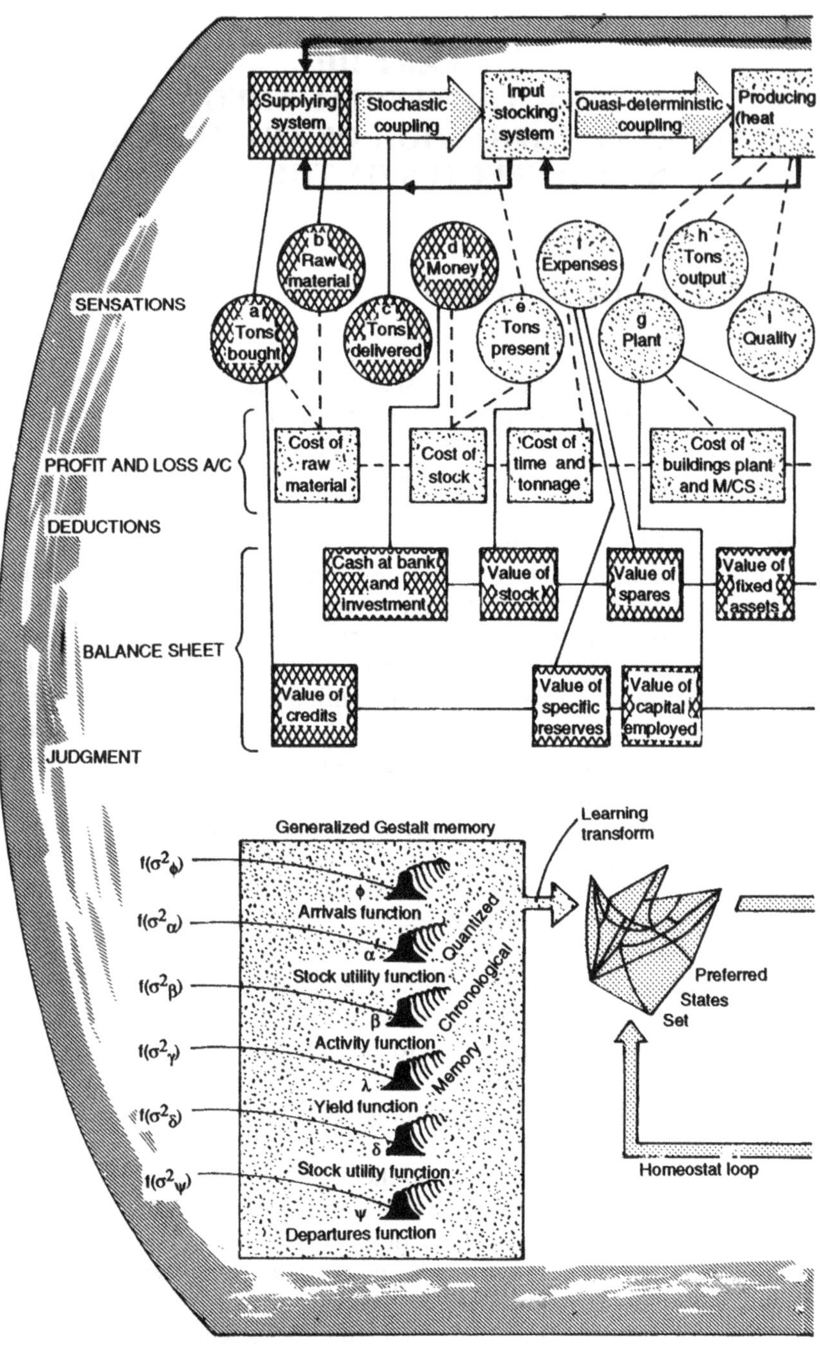

Figure 4 The 'producing system'

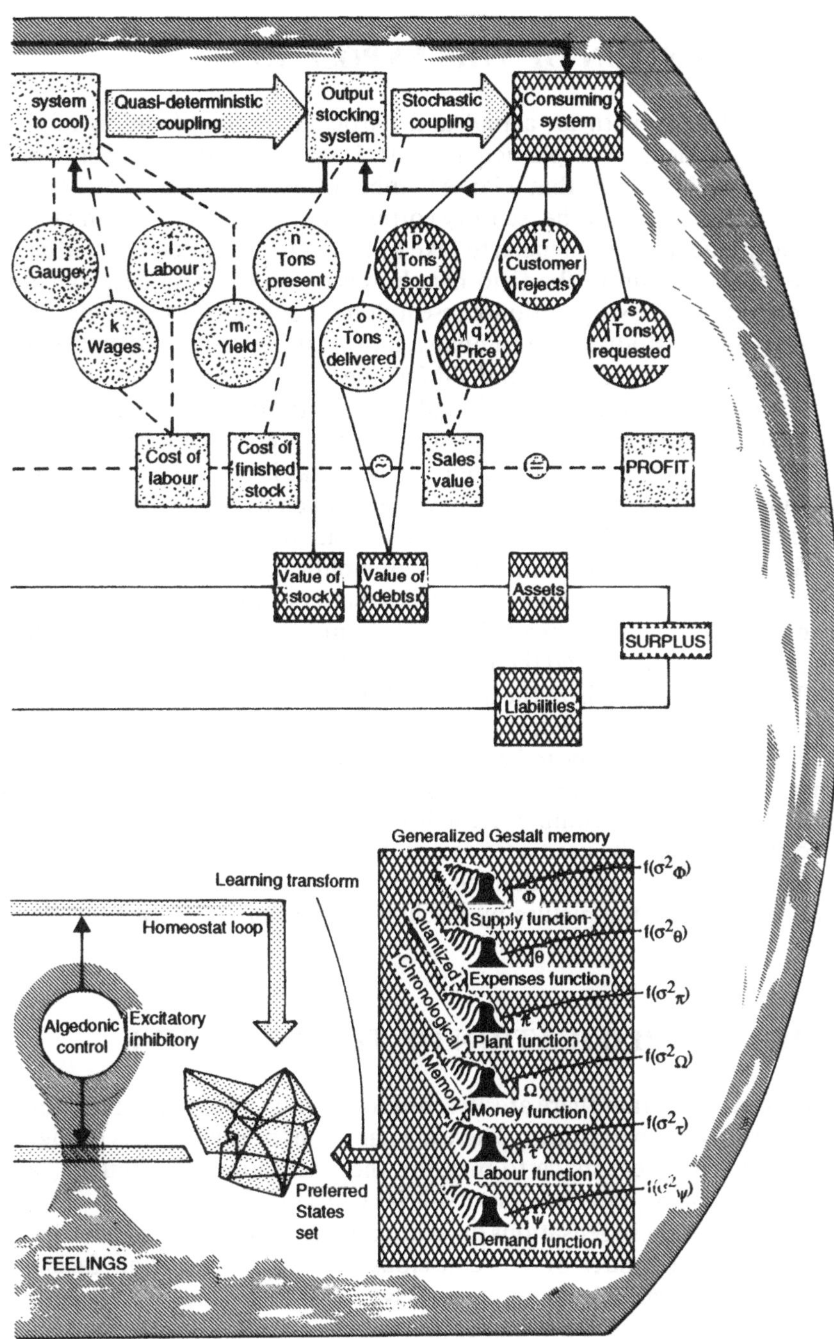
system
to cool)
Quasi-deterministic coupling
Output stocking system
Stochastic coupling
Consuming system
j Gauge
k Wages
l Labour
m Yield
n Tons present
o Tons delivered
p Tons sold
q Price
r Customer rejects
s Tons requested
Cost of labour
Cost of finished stock
Sales value
PROFIT
Value of stock
Value of debts
Assets
SURPLUS
Liabilities
Generalized Gestalt memory
Learning transform
Homeostat loop
Algedonic control
Excitatory inhibitory
Preferred States set
FEELINGS
Quantized Chronological Memory
Supply function
Expenses function
Plant function
Money function
Labour function
Demand function

A CONVENTION OF THIS EXPOSITION

We are dealing with an actual and particular exemplification of the T-Machine which, as explained in Part I, has been created for research purposes. This means that a large number of decisions has had to be taken about the structure of the 'sensory cortex'—decisions which, ultimately, the brain artefact itself is intended to take by its multiple multiplexing techniques. The research team in the field has, however, taken these decisions on an informed basis, by operational research methods. In short, what has been done is an OR study of the company; and what has resulted is an OR model of both the company and the T-Machine.

It would be wearisome continually to qualify statements made here with accounts of how each statement should be expressed in T-Machine terms. This has already been done in Part II. All that is needed is a single device for indicating the points which have been taken as 'known', following the operational research, which could not in fact be known without an actual T-Machine. For example, in this first exemplification there are 19 sensations. There are not 'really' 19 sensations; as a matter of fact, further experimental exemplifications have already brought the number of sensations considered in this work up to 36, and there is nothing absolute about that number either.

To show exactly where the argument stands in this respect, the following convention is adopted. For this first exemplification, there *are* 19 sensations: I 'solemnly declare' this to be the 'correct' number; which means 'I pretend that a T-Machine is in operation that turns out to be using these sensations'. The ordinary, if uncommon, English word 'asseverate' means 'solemnly declare', and will be used here as a technical term having the meaning just explained. It is claimed that all asseverations made in this part can be eliminated from the picture by mechanisms formally described in Part II.

THE EXEMPLIFICATION OF THE T-MACHINE

It is asseverated that there are 19 sensations, 11 deriving from the company and 8 from the environment. These are named in the small circles of Figure 4. Arrangements were made to measure these sensations continually, and a large amount of data was (and still is) collected.

From 12 of these sensations an adequate accounting system was devised, representing a model of the conscious process of deducing facts from information available. The costing system is regarded as reflecting the company's internal operations: as the diagram shows, environmental information determines the input costs from which the total cost is generated by the plant; and this total is compared with further environmental information about the sales value of the product to yield a profit (or loss). The financial accounts, however, regard the organism from the viewpoint of the environment. Here the sums of assets and liabilities as judged by the outside world are compared to yield a balance-sheet surplus (or deficit). Accounting is the conscious level of deduction about the state of affairs. (It involves no asseverations, for it is itself conventional. Nevertheless, the balance-sheet is accepted by business and the law alike as a measure of survival-value, in which it somewhat resembles a proposal form for life insurance as a measure of longevity.)

The exemplification then proceeds to elucidate the processes of judgement, which do not rely on conscious deduction. This is the level of sensory configuration in the brain model, and constitutes the T-Machine proper.

It is asseverated that there are 12 sensory configurations, and that six of these are primarily concerned with the company, and six with the environment. Each one blends together a number of sensory inputs. It is asseverated that the appropriate inputs are known, and that a robust mathematical function defining each is available.

The six company configurations are quantified by the following asseverated functions, on each of which a few notes are appended:

(a) *Arrival function.* The optimal level of arrivals is defined *post hoc* as the level of actual billet consumption, and the mathematical model was devised to measure the success of actual arrivals as a forecasting procedure.

(b) *Billet stock utility function.* This function compares actual stocks at this moment with optimal stocks calculated from an OR model which makes the necessary distinctions between classes of steel. Stock utility is diminished if the company is either under- or over-insured against possible mishaps. Thus this function sinks below its ideal value of unity in either case.

(c) *Activity function.* This is based on a complicated model of production, and seeks a pure measure of efficiency when all the variable factors have been taken into account. It is capable of distinguishing between technical and human reasons for changes in the level of activity.

(d) *Yield function.* This again computes the optimal yield in every case, taking into account the losses that are inevitable from oxidation and the cropping of both billet and coil ends, and compares this with the actual yield.

(e) *Rod stock utility functions.* Rod stocks arise from a number of causes: the need for inspection, rejected material, orders cancelled, the optimal buffers required to meet delivery promises. There is also a complicated component of the stock due to a cyclical effect in matching rolling programmes to demand. All are modelled.

(f) *Departures function.* Basically, this measures the complementarity between activity and dispatch. But the function is loaded by the complement of the ratio between carriage costs for each order (which are borne by the company) and internal profit. It therefore provides a judgement from the point of view of the organism about the exploitation of the effective market.

The six environmental configurations are likewise quantified by asseverated functions, on which these notes are offered:

(g) *Supply function.* A complicated model of supply measures the efficiency of delivery from each supplier, in terms of both average reliability and variability about the average, and includes a measure of the quality of material supplied.

(h) *Expenses function.* This is a measure of the economic utility of 'overheads'—non-production expenses.

(i) *Plant function.* By measuring the changing availability and price of new plant, this function expresses the environmental desirability of investing in new plant at any given moment.

(j) *Money function.* This function is also based on measures of change in both availability and price, this time of money itself. It reflects the level of capital expenditure in the industry, and includes a model of the (local) effects of change in bank rate.

(k) *Labour function.* Again, the model is based on availability and cost. Absenteeism and the unemployment level are taken into account.

(l) *Demand function.* This is the most complicated function of all, and attempts to measure the market and its profitability from all relevant input sensations and deductions. The amount of forward ordering, the profitability of each other (adjusted for such matters as carriage costs, rebates and quantity allowances), and 'the solidity of the order book', are all involved.

The full OR models asseverated for each of these 12 functions are not given here: they would be out of place. But enough has been said to show the scope of the exemplified T-Machine, the method of blending information inside a configuration to provide commensurate pure numbers as output, and the fact that the functions all depend on ratios (it is asseverated) of some measure of expected behaviour to the actual behaviour.

This last point is important, since it incorporates in this exemplification the essential 'black box' treatment of unknowns and imponderables common to all cybernetic machines. For a model of performance in any field may be inadequate: predictions and judgements based upon it will be effectual only insofar as the model *is* adequate. But in exceedingly complex and probabilistic systems *no* analytic model can possibly be adequate. The answer to this paradox, which I have used successfully for 10 years, is to load the raw predictions of any analytic model with a continuous feedback measuring its own efficiency as a predictor. In this way everything that went unrecognized in the analytic work, everything that proved too subtle to handle, even the errors incurred in making calculations, is 'black boxed' into an unanalysable weighting which is error-correcting.

Values for these 12 functions are computable in principle every eight hours, although in some cases (e.g. the money function) changes must occur much less frequently. At present, practical O & M work has resulted in a reasonably efficient clerical system for collecting these data, and for processing them. (In future, it is hoped to obtain many of these inputs automatically.) The result is that a set of 12 values becomes available, in present practice, every day. These are plotted on boards in an Operations Room for the benefit of management, as a by-product of this research, and various orthodox methods are used to analyse them, as mentioned in Part I.

So far, this account of a first exemplification has considered the operation of a T-Machine to the level of the fourth layer of the sensory cortex. This gives rise, it is asseverated, to an 'encephalogram' of 12 readings. A sample of such a trace appears in Figure 5 where a whole year's actual information is recorded by daily plots.

After this, it is asseverated that three statistical transformations are necessary. Firstly, a transformation is made to improve the statistical homogeneity of the recorded values of each function, according to what is asseverated to be a transformation that corrects each distribution of sample values towards the Gaussian form. Secondly, a transformation is imposed to improve statistical homogeneity across the set of functions, and scale transforms are obtained which can be asseverated to have this effect. Thirdly, chance fluctuations are removed from the time series by filtering each of them through a criterion of noise, the level of probability which is significant being asseverated by the study of samples.

The operations of the T-Machine are completed, as proposed in Part II, by the consideration of a set of group homomorphisms preserving the structure of each statistically transformed time series as against its scalar information. To this end it is asseverated that three different homomorphic transformations will prove valuable. Two of them, giving remainders modulo 5 and modulo 2, are shown, for the original year's data, at Figure 6(a), (b). These are final outputs of this exemplification of the T-Machine, to which an exemplified set of possible transformations has been applied. Formal comparisons of the information conveyed by the original encephalogram (Figure 5) with the final forms now proposed are still going on, and the actual records are provided in this case to facilitate informal comparisons.

THE NEXT STEP IN THE EXEMPLIFICATION

The value found for each function for each time quantum is an estimate, which may be depicted as the mean of a probability distribution. As time

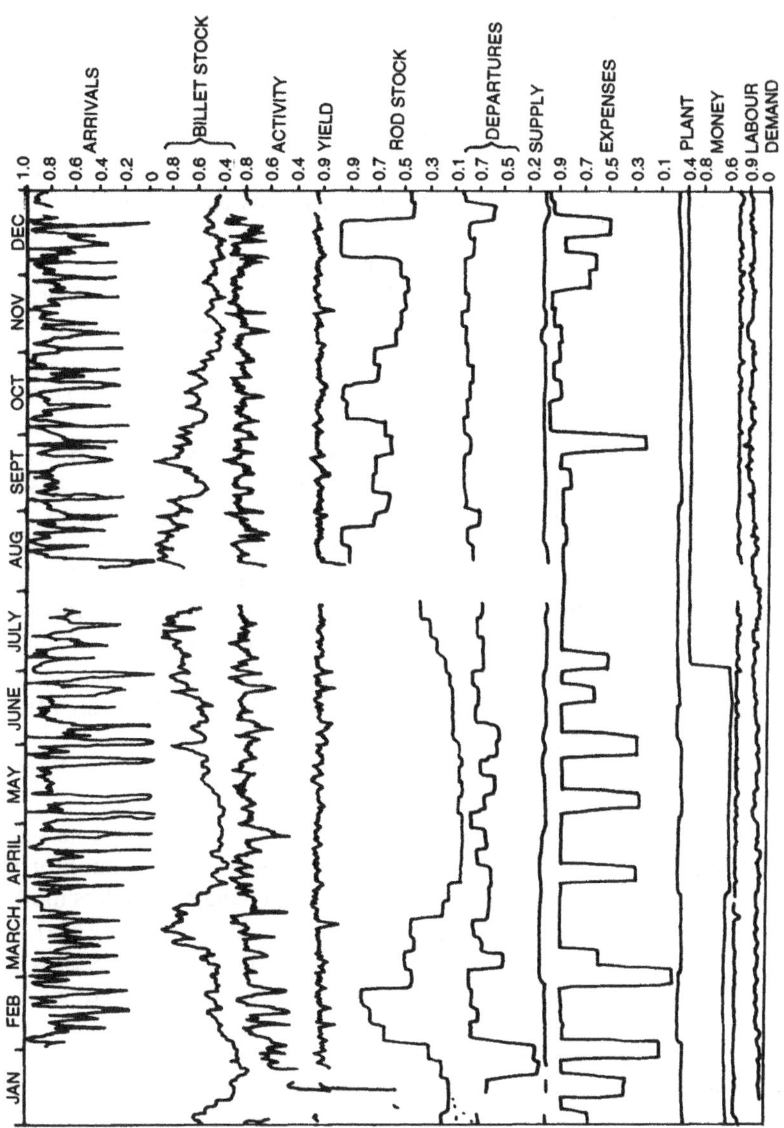

Figure 5 Trial encephalogram of the company's brain

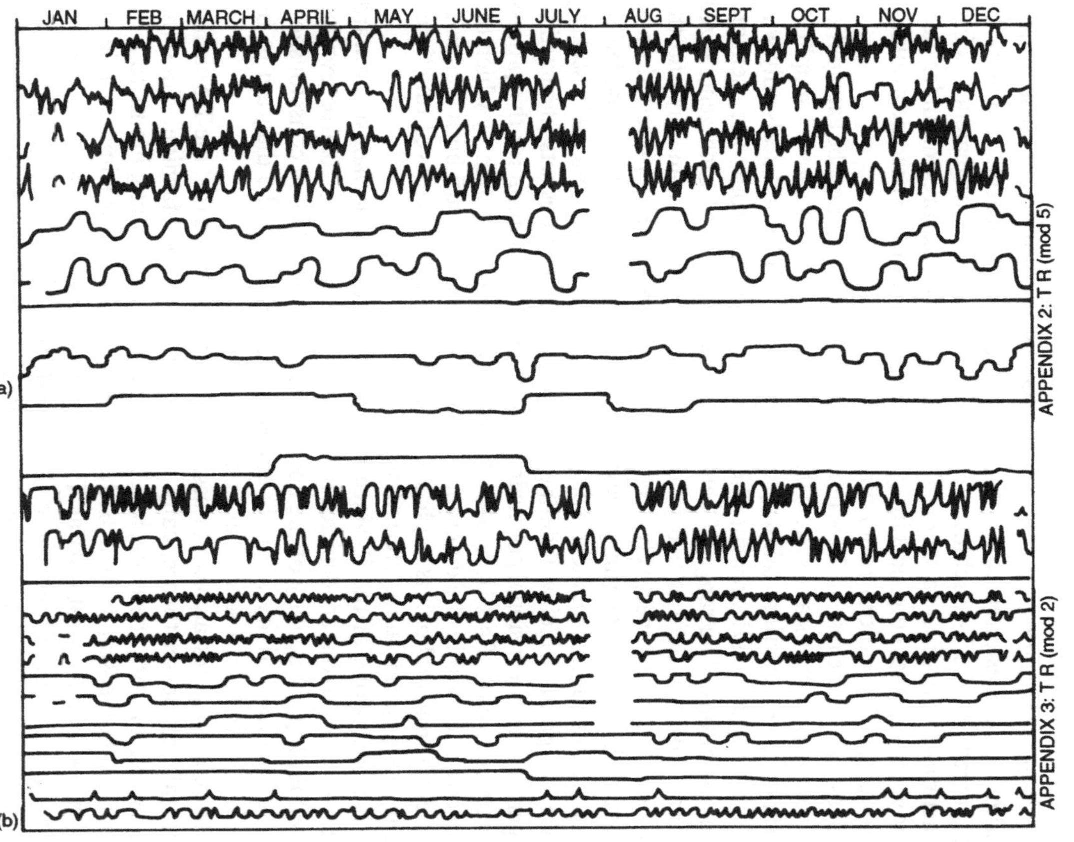

Figure 6 Homomorphic transformation of encephalogram: (a) remainder modulo 5; (b) remainder modulo 2

passes, a collection of such distributions is stored away for each function, forming a quantized chronological memory of relevant experience. The whole set of these records for the company functions on the one hand and the environmental functions on the other constitutes a generalized Gestalt memory, as depicted in Figure 4.

It is next asseverated that although changes in mean value through time within these Gestalten may be important, may be learnt, and may be optimized, by the T-Machine, the main component of judgement lies in a function of statistical variance. This is a mechanism at present under close study, and further empirical insight into it will eventually become available through the operations room already mentioned.

Meanwhile, the rest of the artefact proposed in Part II may be exemplified by the model homeostatic system depicted in Figure 4. This shows a simplified form of the interactions taking place in the U-Machine, and deals only with the company–environment homeostat derived from the sensory configurations. The range of behaviour through time of each generalized Gestalt memory defines two phase spaces in which the company and the environment can respectively operate. It is clear that a set of preferred states is learnt by each: a learning transform applied to the vector provided by the functions 'at this moment' will map the set of solutions into itself, seeking invariant points which will define the two preferred states sets (depicted in Figure 4 as n-dimensional polyhedra). The formal mechanism for this process has been given in Part II, as also the mutually vetoing system by which the homeostatic loop in the diagram continues to operate until both company and environmental points in phase-space (representing vectors of functions) lie in the appropriate preferred states set.

The operations of the R-Machine, with its arousal mechanism, reward function, and so on, are depicted in Figure 4 as an 'algedonic control' exciting or inhibiting the activity of the homeostat. (The correlate in consciousness of R-Machine activity is surely correctly suggested by the diagram to be *feeling*, rather than sensation or judgement.)

The empirical research continues. It will be remembered that the T-Machine was said to be set-theoretically equivalent to the V-Machine. Thus the behaviour of both these machines, considered as providing inputs to a U-Machine homeostat in which the V-decisions are approximated (via d-directions and s-sensations) as T-configurations after a time-lag, may be studied in the operations room. For the display there is the output of the (exemplification of the) T-Machine, while projected moves discussed on the display are momentarily outputs of the V-Machine; management itself plays the role of the U-Machine, monitored by its own staff in the role of R-Machine.

Hence some sort of exemplification of the whole artefact is now in being. The T- and V-Machines have genuine exemplifications, while the U- and

R-Machines are spurious exemplifications at the present time. (For these are artefacts of the artefacts of real managerial systems—namely the real managerial systems themselves!) However, it is now possible to proceed to the empirical study of the U- and R-Machines in the context of *actual* exemplifications of the T- and V-Machines: that is the important point.

As far as the construction of cybernetic machinery is concerned, it is clear that the first component to transcend the status of a mere exemplification must be the U-Machine. For exemplifications of T- and V-input are already available, and can be fed to a U-Machine in parallel with their equivalent reporting to management—which can then provide an R-Machine monitoring service to the cybernetic U-Machine. Having succeeded in operating the cybernetic U-Machine, the research will turn to constructing cybernetic T- and V-Machines. Only at the last stage would the R-Machine be built. After this, management would be free for the first time in history to manage, not the company in the language of the organism, but the T-U-V(R) control assembly in a metalanguage. (That word is used strictly, for at last it would become possible to discuss T-U-V(R) theorems as undecidable in the direct control language. Managers who attempt this feat today are discussing their *own* brains, insights and motives, and are sent to see psychiatrists.)

A PROSPECTUS OF THE ARTEFACT

Experiments have been conducted for a number of years by a number of people into possible artefacts having self-organizing properties. Most of them have been concerned with devices using standard electronic techniques (that is, up to and including the use of transistors) and standard computer technology (that is, up to and including the most advanced machines for business and industry). A great deal has been learnt from these researches, but I consider one outcome to be that these standard approaches (as I have just called them) are unsuitable for the artefact considered in this paper.

There is no need to provide detailed objections to such approaches here. The most cursory consideration of the sheer size of a 'standard' computer-like artefact for controlling a cybernetic factory rules them out. But, following some study of the logical status of electronic brain analogues which was reported four years ago [17], I came to the conclusion that the real secret lay not in pragmatic considerations of constructability, but in the logical structure *of the analogue fabric itself* [4]. This is not a trivial statement, in my view. As a constructor of machines man has become accustomed to regard his materials as inert lumps of matter which have to be fashioned and assembled to make a useful system. He does not normally think first of materials as having an intrinsically high variety which has to be constrained.

But there are new developments in solid state physics which may resolve the objections to 'standard' electronics. With micro-modules (as announced by the Radio Corporation of America), an electronic component is envisaged perhaps for the first time as a wafer of material of uniform size and shape that has been constrained rather than fashioned to behave in a desired way. Even so, the emphasis is still on the size criterion rather than the fabric criterion: micro-modules must still be assembled to a circuit design. A further stage is reached by molecular electronics (as announced by Westinghouse) in which differential behaviour is obtained between domains of molecules inside single crystals. Again, however, the assembly must be designed topologically; and again there is the emphasis on size. Now this emphasis clearly derives from the military and astronautical relevance of these developments, and is unobjectionable; but the cybernetician will need to make an intellectual effort to adjust the emphasis towards the changed analogue of fabric that is implied. The effort required is so great that so far I am unable to see how 'design' can be eliminated from molecular electronics: the U-Machine must be enabled to construct its own components, and this fluid and evolutionary self-designing process should not be irreversible. Besides, the constraining techniques so far available ('diffusion, plating, electron-beam machining, etching, cutting, radiation, alloying, and photographic processes') involve massive equipment that could hardly be visualized as operated by the U-Machine to change its own internal mechanism.

Probably the most adaptable fabric for our purposes which has yet been made to work in an actual cybernetic machine is the colloid developed by Gordon Pask, and referred to previously. Electrochemical machines in general offer an apparently more amenable fabric than the physical semiconductors, and other workers in Britain are researching on similar lines. George's experiments with cotton threads soaked in sodium hydroxide, which measure conditional probabilities by their changing conductivity as impulses are passed through them, are cases in point. Some people have given thought to the use of organic materials, such as the lipids, to provide semi-permeable membranes as a delicate analogue fabric; and in general the interfaces between aqueous liquids offer a means for topological constraint of an undifferentiated or high-variety fabric.

This is not an exhaustive review of other people's work: these ideas are drawn together to lead into what I regard as a list of important features for any proposed analogue fabric for an industrial brain artefact. A high-variety material is required which can be topologically constrained, and reversibly, by simple low-energy inputs. Structuring of the fabric thus obtained must supply requisite variety for absorbing input variety. The structuring and its associated measures of information must be 'readable': not indeed in the (by now) trivial sense of offering a digitized output, but as mapping itself on to an external situation from which feedback can be supplied to the inputs. None of these activities needs to be a linear function, nor even a definable function, of input. The whole assembly is a black box, and needs no designing. In it solutions to problems simply *grow*, as Pask's metallic threads grow. And to bring the issue back to solid-state physics, if a ribbon crystal of germanium can be made to *grow* from a melt with differentiated domains (as is said to be possible), then by including the *melt* in the system semiconductors become possible fabrics again

Now all this is said to contend that we may have been looking for the wrong thing in cybernetic research into possible artefacts. There may have been too much concern with assembling to a design, and with forcing materials to conform to that intention. If my interpretation of the facts is correct, almost any undifferentiated stuff will serve as a fabric for the U-Machine, and I would like briefly to catalogue the several fronts on which we are pursuing this thought in the Department.

In terms of electronics, K. D. Tocher is building a large apparatus for constructing an almost infinite variety of black boxes out of 80 units consisting of non-linear electrical networks. Inputs and outputs can be selected arbitrarily from possible nodes of the system, which is driven in terms of information by an extremely fast random-number generator with thermionic diodes as sources of noise. It is intended to explore homeostatic structures in regard to the time taken to reach equilibrium with this machine.

The formal logical properties of systems that grow are being investigated by R. A. Cuninghame-Green on a Pegasus computer. The program under development is intended to provide a specification for a suitable analogue fabric for an artefact such as a U-Machine, which can then be quoted in the search for materials.

But so far the most valuable lead in my own mind concerns the use of organic systems themselves. In mentioning lipids just now I quoted an organic substance; anyone could be forgiven for asking why a material such as lecithin should be considered when it is so difficult to control compared with various sterile substances of similar molecular properties. But I now speak boldly of animals and animalcules themselves. Do not colonies of living things, which are reproductive (and therefore 'self-repairing' as a fabric), with their tropism as individuals and their taxis as groups, offer a fabric that meets the specification recently set down? Even molecular electronics cannot rival a living organism for size, much less for cost.

In pursuit of this idea I have undertaken a number of experiments, notably with human beings as being readily available and capable of introspection when the experiment is over. The object has been to make use of the natural behaviour of a system with living components to find equilibria in another system of which these components are ignorant. In this way I have obtained solutions to simultaneous linear equations from pairs of subjects who imagined that they were seeking an equilibrium in an exceedingly simple letter game—the ostensible object of the experiment. Children who have never heard of an equation can reach the same results; and I see no reason why (for instance) mice should not be similarly employed if the letter game is translated into a 'cheese game'. The theory behind this work has been the transformation of the actual problem language into homomorphic mappings inside another kind of, and simpler, problem language the handling of which is natural to the participants. This is to amplify their intelligence in exactly Ashby's sense [9]. The apparatus used was an algedonic system registering pain and pleasure for the participants. This is easily constructed for human beings, who are simply told to entertain a red light as meaning pleasure and a green light as meaning pain. For animals the algedonic mechanism would require more thought, although I have elsewhere [4] reported somewhat unconvincing trials with the freshwater crustacean *Daphnia*.

The point of the discursive review in this section is simply to emphasize the importance of the analogue of fabric in constructing artefacts of the kind discussed in this paper at large. This is not the place to record all the work done in this field meticulously, but I have tried to give an indication of the breadth of approach that seems necessary. Before long a decision will be taken as to which fabric to use in the first attempt to build a U-Machine in actual hardware (or colloid, or protein), and I look to the Symposium for advice.

The research here described is incomplete, and the account of it uneven. While some aspects are, I trust, properly explored, others are sketchy; they fade into shadows where nothing is yet clear and distinct. But the project, though unfinished, has the merit of being very much alive. A self-organizing system must always be alive and incomplete. For completion is another name for death.

ACKNOWLEDGEMENTS

The company in which this work has been pursued is the Templeborough Rolling Mills Limited. The enthusiastic support of its managing director (Mr S. R. Howes), of its general manager (Mr H. Sadler) and of its other senior executives and officials, is acknowledged with gratitude.

The research is under the direction of the author, but the detailed results given in Part III were obtained by a project team consisting of three operational research workers: Mr T. P. Conway, Miss H. J. Hirst and

Miss M. D. Scott. This team is led by Mr D. A. Hopkins, who is also the author's chief assistant in this field.

Acknowledgement is also due to the United Steel Companies Limited, who sponsor the Department of Operational Research and Cybernetics, and with whose permission this research is being undertaken for Templeborough Rolling Mills and also reported here.

REFERENCES

1. Ross Ashby, W., *Design for a Brain*, 2nd edn. Chapman & Hall, London, 1960.
2. Ross Ashby, W., 'The mechanism of habituation', *Mechanisation of Thought Processes* (NPL Symposium No. 10), HMSO, London, 1959.
3. Pask, Gordon, 'Physical analogues to the growth of a concept', *Mechanisation of Thought Processes* (NPL Symposium No. 10), HMSO, London, 1959.
4. Beer, Stafford, *Cybernetics and Management*, English University Press, London, 1959.
5. Eccles, J. C., 'Interpretation of action potentials evoked in the cerebral cortex', *E.E.G. & Clin. Neurophysiol*, **3**, 499–564, 1951.
6. Lorente de Nó, R., 'Cerebral cortex: architecture, intracortical connections, motor projections', *Physiology of the Nervous System*. In Fulton J. F. (ed.), Oxford University Press, 1943.
7. Wiener, Norbert, *Cybernetics*. Wiley, New York, 1948.
8. Sholl, D. A., *The Organization of the Cerebral Cortex*. Methuen, London, 1956.
9. Ross Ashby, W., 'Design for an intelligence amplifier', *Automata Studies* (Annals of Mathematics Studies No. 34), Princeton University Press, 1956.
10. Bourbaki, N., *Théorie des Ensembles; fascicule de résultats*. ASEI No. 1141, Hermann, Paris, 1951.
11. Waddington, C. H., *Strategy of the Genes*. Allen & Unwin, London, 1957.
12. Bowman, John R., 'Reduction of the number of possible Boolean functions', *Transactions of Ninth American Conference on Cybernetics* (von Foerster), Josiah Macy Jr. Foundation, New York, 1953.
13. Magoun, H. W., *The Waking Brain*. Thomas, Illinois, 1958.
14. Brodal, Alf, *The Reticular Formation of the Brain Stem*. Oliver & Boyd, Edinburgh, 1957.
15. Gastaut, H., 'Neurophysiological basis of conditioned reflexes and behaviour, *Neurological Basis of Behaviour*, Ciba Symposium, Ciba, London, 1957.
16. Noordenbos, W., *Pain*. Elsevier, Amsterdam, 1959.
17. Beer, Stafford, 'A technical consideration of the cybernetic analogue for planning and programming', *Proceedings of the First International Conference on Cybernetics*, Namur, 1956.

DISCUSSION

WILLIS: 'Something you said bothers me a little bit. Maybe I didn't understand how you were using it.

'The number two to the two to the *N* is a very big number, as Warren McCulloch pointed out last night in discussing the five-input neurones. I think it is pretty clear that if you want to look at all the functions of *N* variables, of which there are 2^{2N}, you could probably do it when *N* is five.

'Two to the two to the fifth is about ten to the tenth. With a big computer which could look at functions at the rate of a million per second, the job could be done in a little under two hours. If you go to six variables, there are about 2^{64} functions, about ten to the twentieth. A little calculation here shows me that if you have 30 000 of these computers and run them at full speed and are willing to wait a little bit more than your lifetime, you can do it. If you go to more than six variables, the thing becomes absurd.

'Now, what are you going to do about it? This is the universe of your functions. How do you win?'

BEER: 'Do let me tell you this.'

VON FOERSTER: 'I think Jack Cowan would like to inject something.'

COWAN: 'It is simply this. What you are assuming is that you have a two-valued non-redundant Boolean logic. What Stafford Beer has been talking about is the evolution of a set of systems in which constraints (or redundancies) are introduced. Because of Ashby's results, we know that such constraints can always be used to improve the effectiveness of search procedures. It follows that simple trial-and-error scanning, Markoff scanning, can be bettered by search procedures which make use of these constraints. In fact, there exist certain many-valued logics which are so constrained in structure as to admit the definition of several kinds of measures or distance-to-go criteria, so that these may be used for the computation of "trends". We may conceive of a reasonable search procedure as one which uses distance-to-go criteria to get into a region that is very likely to contain a solution, and then "hill-climbs" to the solution, using the Markovian technique. This process would be much faster than the simple Markovian technique, and so your comments are not quite appropriate.

'I would like to make a comment on what I think is an important part of Beer's paper, and that is the indeterminancy of representation. It seems to me, at first sight, that this is but a restatement of Gabor's uncertainty principle: that the analysis of any physical signal, be it time function or frequency function, into time *and* frequency cannot be performed with arbitrary precision. That is, although analysis into time *or* frequency can be performed with any degree of accuracy, it cannot be simultaneously carried out in both beyond a certain limited accuracy. If this is so, then what is to be gained by calling this principle by a new name and going into the business of well-ordering denumerable sets?'

BEER: 'I haven't denied the similarity. It is certainly analogous.'

VON FOERSTER: 'I think that was a very helpful comment because you can now refer to some facts which are already existent. When Stafford spoke about this, he struggled a little bit: he felt he had to defend very strongly his third level of uncertainty. This has been established. So now you have a wonderful way to point out where this is going. You can lift it from Gabor's uncertainty principle and from information theory.'

BEER: 'But, Heinz, then people will say it is not right. They will say it is not relevant. I have tried to bring this out in its immediate context. I agree it is the same point in principle, but I have tried to bring it out here in the brain model as such, and I think this is worth doing.

'May I say something about Willis's point and Cowan's comment on it—which was, of course, absolutely right. We have got to keep very clear heads about the proliferation of variety. We know from Ashby's clear and beautiful statement that we must have "requisite variety" in a control system.

'Now the kind of thing we are trying to control in a brain, or in a company, or in an economy, is proliferating variety. The amount of variety here is simply colossal; and so I begin by saying I must be right in talking about an equivalent amount of variety which we must generate in a control.

'Now you say, yes, but you cannot provide it in a computer, and of course, you cannot. This is why Gordon Pask and I have been working for years on what I always call the analogue of fabric. So much work has been put in on the analogue of mechanism, and on the analogue of uncertainty (through statistics, quasi-pseudo-random numbers and so on). But we have not done enough on the analogue of fabric itself. What we need, in a nutshell, is a high-variety, undifferentiated fabric which we can *constrain*. We do not want a lot of bits and pieces which we have got to put together. Because once we settle for the second, we have got to have a blueprint. We have got to *design* the damn thing; and that is just what we do not want to do.'

COWAN: 'The point questionable to me was that once you find a path through the phase space Willis mentioned, and reach a point corresponding to a homomorphic image of the environment, do you really have anything in the nature of a meaningful measure of the environment in question?'

BEER: 'I do not suppose I have, and I do not care. You see, the thing is, if we preoccupy ourselves with transfer functions, and being able to define things, and the getting of meaningful measures, we are constructing a descriptive science—not a control science. In order to talk coherently I have established homomorphs of reality, because these we know and understand; but in fact, it seems to me that our conditions for the real control system are very, very simple. You take a line from a control box into the world, where there must be some effect, any effect; and you take a line out of the world and into the control box, where there must be some effect. And this system will run to stability. I think this is what Ashby has shown; and we do not need to know what those transfer functions are. We do not care if they are non-linear, for example. Electronics people get so worked up about those. Why do they matter? If we design a system to be self-organizing, why take these analytical steps to organize it ourselves?'

WILLIS: 'Let me make one more comment on this. I think that the same thing that licks you when you try to do this with computers is going to lick you no matter how you do it. I think the numbers are just too big. Now we have a point of disagreement.'

BEER: 'All right, but I assert my right to reply. The way I have approached this, at the unconstrained, undifferentiated block of stuff level, the "computation" is going on automatically and without access at a molecular level. Pask's own machines . . .'

WILLIS: 'My point is you don't have enough molecules.'

BEER: 'Well, if you are really going to exhaust the molecules, I admit we are in trouble!'

WILLIS: 'When *N* approaches 100 I think you may even begin to exhaust the molecules in the universe.'

VON FOERSTER: 'I think one of the essential problems that Stafford has in insisting on this particular discussion is how to link two to the two to the *N* internally.'

WILLIS: 'You cannot do it. You must do something else.'

BEER: 'We must get my contention straight and precise. I do not say you must link every one of two to the two to the *N* with every other. I do say you must create a definite, limited linkage. But on the other hand you are not going to say how and where the linkage will occur in advance. My T-Machine model is constrained all right, but only by its own experiences, its own epigenetic landscape; it is not to be constrained by the ignorant designer who has no idea what life in the future will be like.'

WILLIS: 'You have to look at some subset. I am convinced of that.'

BEER: 'Yes, but you must not choose it yourself. This is what I am saying. The "metalanguage machine" must choose it.'

WILLIS: 'That may be true, but I think I shall be able to show you in my talk that such a thing is impossible when *N* is large.'

BEER: 'The concept I have brought forward on this point is taken from genetics. After all, consider how this same point arises in genetics. Think of the variety that we constitute as human beings, and think what a task it would be to permute the available variety all down the line. We do not. We constitute a subset of available variety as you say. And the way that is achieved without designing in detail in the chromosomes, is a mechanism

I have pinched from Waddington, the geneticist; the epigenetic landscape. This is something which constrains. It is a response surface which constrains the total, but not in a determinate way. This I think is a very valuable piece of borrowing.'

BOWMAN: 'I have spent about two hours with your manuscript, but I did not bring it with me. I did not understand that you were going to speak this morning. There were a few little points that disturbed me. Let me just pick on some of the, I will admit, trivial ones, just a brief moment here.

'Section 1.12: "to every element *s* of *S* there corresponds a dense, denumerably infinite set". Why denumerably? Must we handle everything in a digital machine? I think we are going to get into some difficulties of ordering if we speak of a dense denumerably infinite set, such as the set of rational numbers. You cannot put those in an order that makes much sense, even though they are denumerable.

'That was just one small point that stops me. Just why do you introduce the word denumerable there?

BEER: 'Yes. I am aware of this difficulty. My answer is simply that I have done this in order to hang on to the concept of well-ordering, and nothing seems to be lost by quantizing a continuum for the purpose'.

MULLIN: 'No problem; he just wants to invoke some properties of inseparable matrix space; it is just a convenient mathematical artifice. There are many mathematical results which are known which invoke this principle. It is a well-known mathematical principle; it is called separability; all that stuff can be run together.'

BOWMAN: 'I see. Well, I was just a little bit disturbed because I believe, somehow, that the illumination of this room is a truly continuous non-denumerable variable that can take on transcendental values, not necessarily . . .'

NOVIKOFF: 'That is a debatable point.'

BOWMAN: 'That is the kind of thing I was anxious to get some talk started on. You can make your own hypotheses, of course, with the end in sight. We are all allowed to do that, but I was anxious to bring that point out.'

BEER: 'Fair enough'.

ASHBY: 'May I ask for clarification in regard to the general proposal? That is, in what form are you seeing the ultimate goal or range of permissible activities?

'For instance, suppose we are considering a steel mill, and the personnel manager so handles things that strikes break out everywhere, everybody arms themselves with crowbars, and the sale of steel goes up high, making a bigger profit. Where does it come in your formulation, the decision about whether this is a good thing or a bad thing? Are you assuming the system is just growing, as it were, or is there something that says no, we will not have that, and we will have this?'

VON FOERSTER: 'Before you answer this, I think there is another question coming up from Sherwood.'

SHERWOOD: 'If I may, because this is contingent on what Ashby said. I think your brain, it seems, has no religion. What is the factory for? If steel bar goes out of fashion, is it going to go into textiles or chemistry? If so, then how would it reorganize itself? It is built only for making steel. Now, if it is built only for making steel, do you want to make a big profit, or do you want to make high quality steel? Do you want to produce small expensive amounts, or large cheap amounts, and so on and so forth? This always comes back, I take it, into the factory as a feedback of some sort; but if the bottom falls out of the steel market, do you go into housing instead and give up airplanes and so on and so forth?

'That is one difficulty; because the order, if any, that is imposed upon the factory is, in a way perhaps, a religion.'

BEER: 'Yes, but this order is going to be self-imposed. You see this is one of the things I do not want . . .'

SHERWOOD: 'But in the first place, the factory was designed to make steel.'

BEER: 'The plant was; but not the company.

'Now the point here, I think, is this; to answer Ross Ashby first, it seems to me that we just do not know enough about teleology yet. This is one of the things I want to investigate with this kind of model: are what we call purposes and goals in such systems merely names for equilibrial states—an inevitable consequence of trying to describe a system of this kind?'

SHERWOOD: 'But you did say at one point the whole thing was only for survival, or homeostasis; but does it want to be evil or good?'

BEER: 'That is part of survival, surely: does the environment favour behaviour that you would designate evil or good? That is a value judgement.

'But the point I am trying to bring out is just this: what this machinery will *do* can only be a direct function of what it *knows*. This is game-theoretic talk, and it is perfectly acceptable, I think. This is a game, with a certain amount of information.

'Now, if it only has inputs about steel, and the steel industry collapses, all that this organism can say to itself is "I am for the high jump"; and it may predict this sooner than men would. And in that case I think we should want to expand its knowledge, so that it could decide to do something else. This seems to be perfectly possible. But at the moment my model is thus limited; and therefore at the moment the answer to Ashby is that this is what management in the model exists for, to take this kind of superior decision. It can say: yes, well, this steel factory is running all right; but I am going to make ice cream now.

'So it is that there is a whole hierarchy of languages here in which we can talk. And the point about this system, as of all systems, is that you can always redraw the boundaries to suck in a few more of the hierarchic levels; whereupon you have got a different kettle of fish entirely, which is a fascinating thought.

'But the point about survival that I would like to make is this, that when I was criticizing the way that we do these things now, and complained about optimizing for one factor, we clearly have not got a performance criterion, such as control engineers like to have in systems of this kind, for viable organisms with an n-variable system. A lot of the things in industry which are recognized as goals are incompatible; some are downright contradictory. Now in these circumstances the only thing I can do is to put a ring around this lot of contingent aims, and talk about survival as far as I can interpret it for them all.'

VON FOERSTER: 'May I interrupt you just a moment? I think you should distinguish between life, or being alive, and survival. These are two different tasks, funnily enough. You can put something in, which will live, but probably not survive, because it cannot take in changes of the environment, their being too rapid or something of that sort. I think that the religion pointed out is just one of the sub-routines used in order to solve the survival problem. The religion becomes the sub-task which comes up as being a fair thing to do at the moment in order to keep on with the survival. The fact of life alone does not do it; but if you have a survival criterion, you may come up with an ice cream factory, funnily enough, if the organism is complex enough.'

BOWMAN: 'Where does the criterion come from?'

VON FOERSTER: 'Oh, from the problem; you set it up in there.'

McCULLOCH: 'I think the point on religion is somewhat different, if I may say so. I think the crucial thing is that the machine, if it can become aware of its epigenetic landscape, takes that more seriously than it takes itself, and this is good for survival. That is the crucial point.'

BEER: 'Yes, and to the observer, this might *look* like a machine acquiring a set of value judgements. I mean we do not know how to talk in this area really, do we?'

VON FOERSTER: 'We cannot yet.'

BOWMAN: 'I do not want to take up too much time here, but the conversation has drifted on to your idea of a more-or-less homogeneous fabric of a machine, subject to some constraints.

'Let me pick that up. As stated, it seemed to me a profound and advanced, but a very vague concept. Can I go to the opposite and speak along the same lines, perhaps from an engineering standpoint? It is routine now to design a general-purpose digital calculator, or a computer, and we start out with a block diagram, which ordinarily means very little to anyone except the man who made the sketch, because he usually forgets to put a description of the function of the blocks and the test. Without exception though, he will have a rectangle marked "arithmetic unit", and he will have one marked "store", or as we say here, "memory". Those are often on separate sides of the page. I believe the idea of a constrained fabric very nearly breaks down the distinction between those two black boxes.

'To take a particularly simple example of a machine that I have worked with at length, that machine has a very large, very slow magnetic drum store. The arithmetic unit is, oh, something you could hold in the palm of your hand, it is a two-bit adder, and a one-pulse delay line.

'Now, if we wish to perform a multiplication (this I should say also, is a purely binary machine), the multiplier rather automatically becomes a part of the arithmetic unit. It gives orders: shift, add, shift, do not add, shift, do not add, shift, add, shift, add, shift, add, depending upon the bits of that factor.

'Now the whole operation of multiplication in a binary machine is a lot more complicated than that. We have a parity check. We have an establishment of sign. We have a round-off problem. Routine within routine; the term microprogramming has come into use.

'Now, all of those microprograms are on the drum, stored in exactly the same way numbers are, and provide a constraint as to what the machine will do. And I merely suggest that the distinction between operator and operant has become far too sharp. And I think you have come a long way toward breaking that down when you speak of a homogeneous but constrained fabric.'

BEER: 'Yes, I hope so. You see this analogy with computers I do not like for two reasons. (I do not mean Bowman's exposition, I mean the analogy.) For one thing, I really cannot stomach, although I do not know that everybody agrees with this, I cannot stomach the idea of memory as a bit put in a locker to be called for like a parcel in a cloakroom.

'Now memory in my kind of system, you notice, is really a path of facilitation through a phase space. You get on to this path in a few places, and *whee*, you should be off to the destination of recognition. This is much nearer to a physiological memory to me. And the other big point I would like to make, about the big electronic machines, which I think are just dinosaurs . . .'

BOWMAN: 'Subject to the same fate?'

BEER: 'I think so; that is what I meant. They are preoccupied with digital access. Now why is this? It is always possible, given an output channel which you can fit on somewhere, to say what is happening just there, and to get an enormous printout. Now we are not concerned with digital access, but with outcomes. Why do we pay so much money to make it available?

'In the sort of machines that Gordon and I have been concerned with, you cannot get at the intermediate answer. If you take out of Gordon's dishes of colloid, you may be effectively inverting a matrix of order 20 000. The cost of the computer is perhaps 10 cents. The only trouble is you do not know what the answer is.

'Now this sounds absurdly naïve, but it is not, you know, because you do not *want* the answer. What you want to do is to *use* the answer. So why ever digitize it? If the molecules in this thing are "taking up" the answer pattern, then we have all the variety we need to feed impulses back to control something. Failing to recognize this has been a terrible trap in the development of control technology, and I think the exponential increase in cost of control systems in industry is a direct result of thinking you have not got anything unless you can measure it in the measuring-rod sense. It is doubtless true that science is measurement and all that sort of talk; but this is being made to mean that there is no measure unless you can produce the digit. This, to me, is a *non sequitur*.'

ASHBY: 'I am reminded of what Dr Turing said: that half the business in higher mathematics is to persuade people to accept, not what they think they want, but what they really want.'

BOWMAN: 'I can give you a fine, first-hand example where a chemist, and a very good one, came down and gave us a statement of a curve he wanted plotted; and after many tens of machine hours we gave him reams of numbers. Then he sat down and laboriously put dots on graph paper.

'I asked him, well, what are you trying to do here? Oh, well, I have to find the point of inflection of this curve. He wanted one number, and the machine would have given that to him, but he had to have the full curve and do the rest of it manually. He just did not know how to ask a question.'

BEER: 'May I quote my favourite example of this digital access issue where the brain is concerned, because I would like the comments of the brain specialists present on this. Obviously we can do colossal calculations in our heads. We have got all the requisite variety. I often dodge about the traffic in Piccadilly Circus, and I have not yet been run over; and this is a wonderful piece of calculation. But whenever I try and get *digital* access to my own brain, I cannot have it. If you ask me how far off that wall is, I should be 20, perhaps 50 per cent out; hopeless at it. And the favourite example that I want to quote is this.

'We draw a picture on the blackboard of a road receding into the distance that is to have telegraph poles on it. We might then say: the first two poles will be one foot apart, would you please give me the numbers which will define the rest of the intervals? So we try. Well, we get the answer right to the extent we know the intervals are monotonic decreasing, and that is about it. If we take those estimated digits and plot them, we can see at once that it is wrong.

'But we can say to almost anyone: draw those poles in, and he will get them dead right by eye. So, I argue, we have apparatus which can do projective geometry in our heads, even if we have never heard of projective geometry. We can *do* it, but we cannot get the digits out.

'Now, does this merely mean (this is the question to the neurologists) that we have not got the digital output channelled to the right point; or does it mean that in some sense it does not actually exist?'

SHERWOOD: 'No, the answer to that is when you are trying to find out the measurement, you have got to work from a symbol to an object. You have got a symbol in your head.'

BEER: 'Well, this is just a mapping then?'

VON FOERSTER: 'No, it must be identification of a symbol. An interpretation problem. The symbol means what you are seeking, looking for; and you need the interpretation of the symbol, which is a process. You have to re-evaluate lots of different possible states: what it *could* mean, and things of that sort.'

SHERWOOD: 'There are at least two translations in different languages.'

VON FOERSTER: 'Yes.'

BEER: 'What I am getting at is this, it is a fact that those distances when you finally draw them will be very accurate as worked out on a computer by projective geometry. What does that mean?'

SHERWOOD: 'You are asking me to tell you the thermodynamics, and the accurate application of forces, and what have you. If you can jump across the brook and land on a stone, which is on the other side at Warren's farm, you cannot do that. You all can do the jump; but most of us do not know what it takes to calculate the forces acting on the foot, or what is needed for the balance. It is sheer physics; that means we have to translate an action into a science or into a different language entirely. And then, similarly, it is no good telling what one ought to do in terms of engineering.'

McCULLOCH: 'If you take any good cat, hold it upside down, and drop it that much off the floor, it lands on all fours. If you are a professor of physics, it would take you a long time to persuade a class that it is conserving angular momentum.'

BOWMAN: 'He can roll himself into a doughnut, rotate and unroll; that is a conservation of everything.'

BEER: 'This is Torus the cat, not Taurus the bull.'

VON FOERSTER: 'George Zopf wants to say something.'

ZOPF: 'Whether we pick the cat or Sherwood's problem of leaping accurately to a stone, I think what Beer is suggesting is that we cannot examine the mental processes and say, here is where the calculation of distance is reported, here is where the calculation of momentum is reported, and so on, and say that then these are put together to define what the motor act should be. In other words there are no representations of these sub-calculations individually.'

McCULLOCH: 'We are asking questions like in which of the vacuum tubes of my radio is Rudy Vallee's voice.'

BEER: 'No, no. This is not what I meant at all.'

ROSEN: 'I want to go back to something you raised a little while ago.

'You have described several types of self-organizing machines made of some fabric where the useful results that come out of a machine are as a result of constraints. I am just wondering, and this is my own intuition, whether the system of constraints that you must know and apply to a fabric, does not constitute as much of a problem as the problem of what happens in each one of your boxes representing a machine, and therefore we may have just transferred the problem, setting perhaps just as difficult a problem in defining specific restrictions.'

BEER: 'I think the mistake you make is to say we must know the system of constraints. We do not know them, that is the whole point.'

ROSEN: 'I am sorry, but the implications that I got from many remarks that were made, was that the purpose of the machine was the operation of the particular plant. Once you state these objectives, if you can state them . . .'

BEER: 'You cannot. This is the whole point, you see. One manager will tell you we are here to make a profit. Another manager will tell you we are here as a social service. And all of them act as if they were there to fish for trout. You cannot state these things.'

ROSEN: 'If you cannot state them, and these are the constraints that are applied externally on to these big black boxes that have the capability of doing some organization within them, I do not see how you are going to apply any constraints that will permit an optimum set of self-organizing procedures to give you some results.'

BEER: 'These inputs are the constraints. They are what constrains.'

COWAN: 'The mistake Rosen is making is thinking that these constraints are absolute constraints. You really have to think of them in a relative sense.'

ROSEN: 'Are they variable; are these constraints variables?'

COWAN: 'They would become variable eventually.'

ROSEN: 'If they do, then you have the same problem of determining which of these sets of variables are going to mean something, if this problem has any meaning at all. I will accept the fact that if the constraints can be stated in a simpler form than the internal mechanism of the machine, we have simplified the overall problem. I have not seen this.'

McCULLOCH: 'Why do we need to state the constraints?'

ROSEN: 'Why go through the procedure of making these self-organizing machines?'

COWAN: 'It would not be self-organizing if you state the constraints.'

ROSEN: 'But I think we started by saying we wanted to improve the operation of an industry or a plant. That is how we started.'

VON FOERSTER: 'It means dropping defined constraints.'

ROSEN: 'Well, if you drop defined constraints, do you not start out with as difficult a system as you are trying to solve?'

VON FOERSTER: 'Maybe Anatol Rapoport can help us here.'

RAPOPORT: 'About what?'

VON FOERSTER: 'About the discussion here.'

RAPOPORT: 'I am sorry, I am trying my best to follow what is being said. I pass.'

ROSEN: 'Let us all pass.'

VON FOERSTER: 'Let us not yet pass. We have 15 minutes yet, we can work something out.'

ASHBY: 'One method for getting a decision is simply to have someone who says, "I am the manager; you ask me whether a thing is good or bad and I'll tell you. I don't give reasons, just give me the proposition and I'll mark it good or bad".

'There is no *necessity* for a specification in detail of what is going on internally; what is necessary is the decision.'

BEER: 'Exactly. This is the algedonic loop defined in my talk.'

ROSEN: 'Can I answer that? This is precisely the thing. Now it is the manager with this brain, that determines whether or not he likes things or he does not. So we have in fact transferred the problem to a mechanism which is self-organizing, and just as complex, or even more complex, than the one we are plotting.'

ASHBY: 'I am assuming that he is a person, in a sense an automaton, selected by the shareholders. They know the sort of guy he is, they know the sort of decisions he will give; to them he is just a very complex function over labour, money, profits, expansion—a very complicated function. All they want is just that he will be the deciding function of these variables and will say this combination is bad, this combination is good, and so on. He is not organizing; he is defining what Sommerhoff calls the "focal condition".'

ROSEN: 'He is putting the constraints on the system: here there is an organism that is functioning to put constraints on the system, and it is as complex as the one we are making.'

COWAN: 'The point is the system will remove him and substitute another if he is not giving the right sort of results.'

ROSEN: 'You hope that somewhere the problem begins to simplify progressively, and does not keep on the same level of complexity.'

VON FOERSTER: 'I think this is really a point of two different liberals talking. One thing I think Dr Rosen was getting at was he would like to explain the problem perfectly clearly; as McCulloch pointed out yesterday, perfectly clear set responses you can expect from a very clear set of stimuli—change of light, straight edge coming about, and things like that.

'Fair questions, of course. But, what, would we like to explain the frog as it is, or would we like to explain how it became that frog? The latest specification, the real constraints which we have in the frog, are the result of something happening. Nobody defined upstairs how the frog should come about, and these constraints are not laid down.

'If you have a running factory then, maybe an outside observer, several outside observers, may come to a definite conclusion about its properties. It is *this* type of system. And then you come to the evolving ice cream factory, and they approach the whole thing as a different kind of problem. And I think this was the kind of thing that Stafford was trying to point out, the transition problem of the one into the other. He says I have a steel mill, but this steel mill has no brain, so now let us get it into a state where it may finally have a brain. This is, of course, a gross evolution process. It is a thing which would evolve according to its internal constraints and become a better steel mill. And this would be just the thing that your Board of Trustees would say: let's become a better steel mill.'

October 6, 1982

Dear Stafford . . .

I am awed by your predictions, made in 1960. Among the richness of original ideas, I am taken by your discussion entitled 'A Prospectus of the Artefact'. It brought to mind a ride with Warren McCullough to some airport—it must have been '54 or '55. We both had had a tiring day; I believe I had spoken on some of our early work on lipo-proteins and the crystallography of the myelin sheath in which Finean and I were engaged in at the time. 'Myelin figures grow', I said, 'Their main component is structured water held in place by ions—some fixed and some mobile. Could the biomolecular leaflets, with protein receptors embedded in them, in some way act as microcomputers at the synapse; and could they, I asked Warren, act both as transducers and transponders?' He got very excited about this.

I read between pages 73 and 77, your analysis of the logical structure of the analog fabric itself in which, as you put it, solutions to problems simply 'grow'. You speak of molecular electronics. You consider lipids as a candidate, and then span across, applying the same logic towards the homomorphic mapping of a cybernetic factory. Again, I am awed by your foresight! Though the early models of brain function (of the mid-50s and early 60s) were a simplicistic [sic], the scaffolding they provided has held. The main refinement has been the superimposition of a chemical map upon a much more sophisticated structural map not only in terms of the large cell masses but the subcellular chemical architecture at the level of individual neurons in differing cell populations. At this finest level of organization, topology in space is used in service of rate regulation (and therefore structuring) in time.

Coincidence detection is an old concept. The operation of relatively slow electro chemical fields in nodal areas—and, who knows, throughout?—is coming into its own. To me the principle of interaction of neuro-regulatory substances—a sort of chemical grammar and syntax—has always been infinitely more sense than simplicistic [sic] fastening of a pervasive process on this or that molecule alone. As I mentioned in my talk in Haifa the same kind of receptors are now turning up in the immune system. The homeostatic preservation of biological self and symbolic self are clearly linked, and mediated by relatively simple molecules which have, clearly, found high value in evolution. Most of them are Charge Transfer Compounds ideally, equipped to be the informed dye of your 'fabric'.

Fond regards and warm thanks again,
Cordially

Joel Elkes, MD

Professor of Psychiatry
University of Louisville

Distinguished Service Professor Emeritus
The Johns Hopkins University

To Warren S. McCulloch on his sixty-fifth birthday

SONNET FOR WARREN

Days that are cherished, moments that persist,
Reverberate in neural circuits, catch
In the throat of recollective calm, attach
To sensory recall. And so enlist:
The lobsters at Old Lyme; and English mist;
The snap of seminars; nocturnal scratch
Of pen on paper; your disdain to match
The paltriness of an antagonist.

The stature and the public awe exist—
While secretly the twinkling friendships hatch.
Warren, the neurons crackling in his head,
Sparks fire at nature. Others may insist
That science is serious. But we shall snatch
Our laughter from the universal dread.

Stafford Beer, 1963
Transit, 1977

11 RETROSPECT—AMERICAN DIARY, 1960

STAFFORD BEER

INTRODUCTION

THE EXISTENCE of this Diary was long forgotten when it emerged following the acquisition of my papers by the Liverpool John Moores University. It was a 'sensitive' document when it was written, but it seems appropriate to publish it now.

In the first place it provides a snapshot of Information Technology hardware and software as it existed 30 years ago. I had installed a Feranti Pegasus computer in my department at United Steel in Sheffield in 1956, and believe that this was the first computer to be dedicated solely to management science anywhere in the world. I had also been deeply involved in the development of computers in Britain throughout the 1950s, and was a frequent visitor to the labs at Manchester (the Mark I Star), Cambridge (EDSAC) and the National Physical Laboratory (Ace and then Deuce) and the Royal Aircraft Establishment (Tridac—a vast analogue machine). Manchester had been the site of the successful operation of the first digital computer with stored programs in the forties. Thus, a first hand enquiry into the state of IT in the USA was an exciting opportunity to make comparisons, and these are all reflected in the text.

Secondly, the Diary investigates the thinking that was current at the time. I had known McCulloch for some years, and he would stay at my house on his Sheffield visits; I had known Ackoff, and some other American OR men, since the first international conference at Oxford in 1956; but I had not met many of the Americans with whose work I was familiar. The British pioneers in cybernetics were all good friends—notably Ross Ashby, Frank George, Gordon Pask, Donald MacKay and Grey Walter. The visit hinged on two major invitations, one was to give an inaugural address for the new Systems Research Center at the Case Institute in Cleveland, and the other was to attend a symposium of many leading cybernetic thinkers at the

University of Illinois. Here I was specifically offered the opportunity to present my mathematical model of the brain, which must have been one of the first to be constructed on the basis of neurological closure between the sensory and motor systems. I had been working on this for a decade, with industrial control applications in mind: it eventually underwrote the Viable System Model, in which the recursive set theory was replaced by a recursive diagrammatic topology.

As transatlantic journeys were still quite a novelty for most of us, I was able to argue that I should make a lengthy trip (Figure 1). The amount of activity packed into the weeks 23 April to 12 June 1960 makes me tired to contemplate in retrospect. However, there is a more important impression that reading the Diary creates today. Here we were in 1960, with (as it were) Stone Age computers: solid state technology was barely on the horizon. The level of discussion, however, seems to me higher than we hear today. For example, people are nowadays talking about neural nets as a new vision for the 1990s—seemingly unaware that the earliest papers by McCulloch, von Neumann and others date back almost 50 years. Certainly neural nets were a central issue among the cyberneticians of that 1960 spring.

A more troubling aspect of the matter is the realization that there were more centres of excellence in the field then than there are today, and more people were involved in creative research than there are now. So many possibilities were opened up by the interdisciplinary synergy of the 1950s, because there was a sense of freedom and fun in the universities that has been subdued since then. We suffer indeed from a hardening of the faculties.

Technological Postscript The Diary was recorded each night on a hand-held battery-driven fine wire recorder. It was a much admired innovation, for this was before portable magnetic tape recorders were available. In the early 1950s, I had been Production Controller of Samuel Fox & Co., which was the special steels branch of United Steel. We supplied the fine wire, which I think was 0.001 inch diameter. At any rate, if the wire broke the spool became shrouded in what looked like a mist, as the wire unspooled, it was so fine. In 1960 we still expected a huge commercial success with this product—eclipsed in the event by magnetic tape.

AMERICAN DIARY

Sunday 24th April

BOAC's Monarch Comet left London at 2.15 and flew to Montreal. This was apparently due to bad weather on the route normally flown to New York: if the Comet gets held up there is a risk it will run out of fuel on the direct journey.

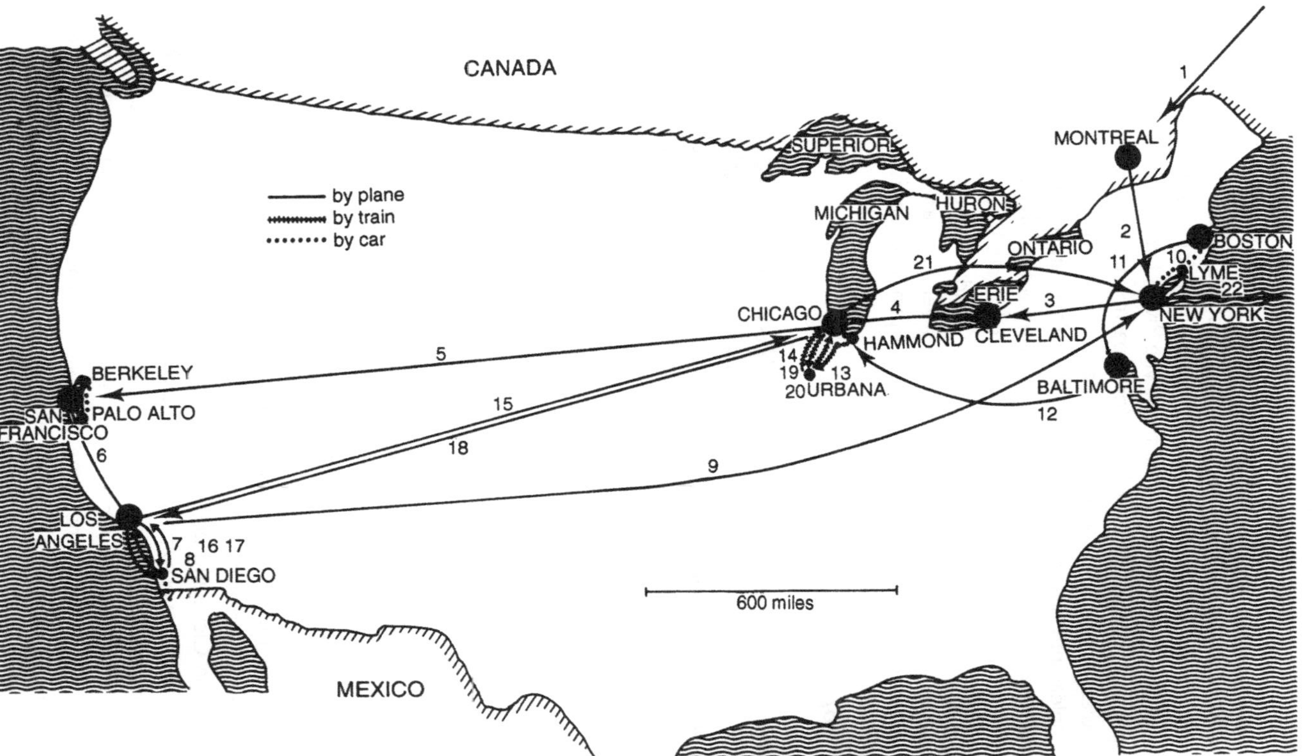

Figure 11.1 Schematic map showing route followed by S.B. during his transatlantic trip 'below the twilight arch' in 1960 (numbers refer to legs of the journey)

The shorter route to Montreal was chosen, and the plane refuelled there. The flight was an extremely pleasant one apart from these last stages, in which one got some impression of what low-gravity conditions must be like. The plane arrived in New York at 7 p.m. (local time)—only an hour later than scheduled . . . that is midnight by London time, so we had been flying for less than 10 hours—with a break of about 40 minutes at Montreal. The Rivett family met me at the airport, and I spent the evening at their New York apartment: it is now 2 a.m. local time, but needless to say I feel as if it were 7 a.m.—as it is in London.

It is unpleasantly hot and humid here in New York, and my immediate impression of the city is one of considerable disappointment. Although I am now on the 22nd floor of this hotel (The Commodore), the place is quite Victorian in aspect. Times Square turns out to be little more than a wide road; I walked right through it and along Broadway, and the feel of the place is very similar to the West End of London—except that many shops were still open at midnight on Sunday!

RETROSPECT 1992

The reference is to B. H. P. Rivett, who had been head of OR at the Coal Board in Britain until recently. He was now in training prior to taking up appointment as head of OR for Arthur Andersen in London, and was subsequently the first professor of OR in Great Britain—at Lancaster University.

Monday 25th April

After a few hours fitful sleep, I was awakened by Rivett who wished to say goodbye: he was leaving on the 8 a.m. jet flight for Chicago. The morning was spent on reviewing my plans and making a quick exploration of New York—which is not as impressive as I had expected. Skyscrapers are by no means universal: I was told that there are more buildings in Paris over five storeys high than there are here.

I left immediately after lunch for Newark Airfield, driving through many miles of unseemly countryside, consisting mainly of scrap heaps of the wrecked dodgem cars that pass for family saloons in this country. The flight for Cleveland left at 3 p.m., and arrived in Cleveland on time at 5.05. This was a United Airlines aeroplane (a DC 6), and had every appearance of the routine transport service which in fact the airlines do provide in this country. For instance, there was none of the attendant fuss about embarking that there is with international flights, and passengers could take a seat anywhere in the plane they wished. The journey took us over the Appalachian mountains to the shore of Lake Erie, and provided a wonderful impression of the American countryside on this beautifully clear and sunny day. Circling Cleveland quite low, I came to realize that the place is very much larger than I had expected. In fact, I am told that with its suburbs there are nearly 2 million people here.

Professor Ackoff met the aeroplane and took me out to his home in the country, 20 miles from Cleveland itself. He designed the house himself: it is a modern and spacious place, owing something to Scandinavian architectural ideas, I think. We have had many hours discussion on the state of OR and I have finally returned to this hotel (Wade Park Manor) in Cleveland at 2 a.m.

Tuesday 26 April

The first Systems Symposium of America opened this morning at the Case Institute of Technology, under the auspices of their new Systems Research Center. Its object is 'to bring together the leaders in science and engineering from government, industry and education, who possess enthusiasm for seeking out, developing and applying those common threads which weave together our understanding of the behaviour of all systems. Secondly, to inaugurate a unique university liberal programme for education and research in the analysis and synthesis of large systems'.

There are about 150 people here, all alleged to be leading authorities in the field of systems. First impressions are that they are an extremely bright and knowledgeable group.

The Symposium opened with an address of welcome by Dr John Hrones, Vice-President of the Case Institute. He introduced a keynote address by Dr Simon Ramo.

Dr Simon Ramo was part-inventor of the electron microscope. He subsequently became Director of Research in an Aircraft Company, and then inaugurated a part of America's space programme through a well-known firm of consultants, the Thompson-Ramo-Wooldridge Company. He is now Vice-President of research, and a very well-known and extremely successful scientist in governmental circles.

His address was indescribably awful. The only point of interest was to envisage the need for automatic teaching machines which would take the load off human teachers in the fight for an ever-increasing number of trained technologists.

Professor Russell Ackoff is of course extremely well known in the operational research world, and is now Director of the OR group at the Case Institute. He is an ex-president of the Operations Research Society of America, and is perhaps best known for the book which he edited and largely wrote, Introduction to Operations Research, which has been translated into many languages—including Japanese.

Ackoff adhered largely to his script, so there is no need to report his verbal presentation in any detail. It was most notable for advocating the complete integration of management sciences on a problem-oriented basis. Most of the symposiasts (including myself) disagreed with him strongly on only one point: the idea that the organization of a system (in terms of both control and desired outcome) 'ought' to be expressed in the form of an equation. However, as he admits that this is very rarely possible, perhaps there is little with which to disagree.

The first session was concluded with luncheon, at which Professor Eckman, the Director of the new Systems Research Center, explained its origins and objectives. It is compounded of representatives of many groups on the Case campus, and it is a deliberate attempt to set up an interdisciplinary cybernetic research unit. It is backed by a million-dollar grant from the Ford Foundation.

The second session was extremely interesting, and was chaired by Professor Arnoff—another well-known exponent of OR at the Case Institute.

Mr Charles Hitch is a leading figure in American OR, having held key positions in academic, commercial and governmental bodies. He is currently President of the Operations Research Society of America. His address was notable for a discussion of the extent to which sub-optimization (a term he himself invented) is permissible. He claims never to have done a job in which the delineation of the system was correctly adjudged from the first, and declares that no OR man ought (scientifically speaking) to accept a state of affairs in which the people he is trying to help lay down either the scope of the system involved or the methods to be used. His conception of the way in which operational research is actually done is very 'un-American', and very close to our own in Sheffield. He dissertated for some time on the 'fascinating but relatively unimportant task of building models'.

The essence of his talk was that the ends and means of an OR study of a large system interact continuously, and that therefore the setting of objectives is very often meaningless. He expanded his printed account of his own OR work on defence by nuclear deterrent, which was in effect a feasibility study. Would such a policy be one which could in fact be carried out in economic terms? The answer for America was yes, and for various small countries in the Atlantic alliance, no. He explicitly said that Great Britain was a borderline case: his formal studies were unable to decide whether we could afford to operate a nuclear deterrent or not. This seems adequately to reflect what scientists in our own defence set-up are inclined to say.

I was continually amazed by the extent to which Mr Hitch was preaching the same gospel as that of Cybor House. Nowhere was this more evident than his attack on the procedure of such techniques as linear programming. He cited the case of a friend who, having been told by his doctor to reduce weight, constructed a matrix out of 500 foods listed in the national larder, and their calorific values. On the understanding that he did not wish to be hungry, he solved this LP under the constraint of a minimum calorific intake, and a maximizing functional for bulk. The answer provided by a large computer was to consume 80 gallons of vinegar a day!

He was also very interesting on the issue of whether to solve a problem in a particular system one had to study it within the framework of higher systems in the hierarchy. There is apparently evidence that the Russians are making mistakes through their failure to do this. Finally, Mr Hitch disagreed with Ackoff that a system of criteria ought to be reduced to a single scale.

Dr Ellis Johnston is of course the 'grandfather' of American operations research. He was seminal in wartime naval and airforce operations, and was responsible for the strategic OR that resulted in the surveillance system for monitoring Soviet nuclear tests and stockpiles. He is much honoured, and participated in studies made by Nelson Rockefeller on disarmament.

Ellis Johnson is well known as a vigorous speaker: he denounced in outspoken terms the crystallization of the methods used by OR during the war into routine procedures. OR knowledge once acquired ought to be handed over to production engineers in industry, and other appropriate specialists, leaving OR scientists themselves to forge ahead on new problems and the creation of new techniques. The whole object of operations research is to study the strategies of very big systems.

He felt that even in the war years a change was occurring in the understanding of how OR might best be used. Very large systems themselves, such as are the object of the policies of large companies and governments, change so fast that any work done on a control system must first undertake an extrapolation of the nature of the system itself. He reckons that an OR study in national defence takes something like 1000 man-years to complete. Therefore it is essential that preliminary OR forecasts of the future states of the system involved be used to decide the context of the ultimate control before its nature is even considered.

He strongly agreed with Hitch and Ackoff that 'objectives' could not really be built into OR studies. There are too many conflicting and even contradictory objectives in the management of a country or large company which make this kind of talk inappropriate. It seems in general that the Americans have far less difficulty than we do in England in persuading those for whom we work that we know what jobs should be done by OR and how to do them.

Taking up Hitch's point about the hierarchy of systems, Ellis Johnson said emphatically that any OR study would reach a wrong conclusion unless it is considered in the context of at least the two higher levels of systems concerned.

He spent some time on the question of treating symptoms instead of underlying causes. His model concerned the fox-rabbit cycle: when the foxes have eaten a large number of rabbits, their own food supply is diminished and they themselves decline; their decline means that the rabbit population can revive; thus there is a continual cycle between the two populations. The huntsmen of America have had recourse to injecting a new supply of rabbits at the point which seems to them most obvious: the minimum rabbit population. But this is to treat a symptom, because the desperate foxes can now save themselves more readily. Thus instead of damping the oscillation as required, this policy merely doubles its amplitude.

Ellis Johnson then examined the work done internationally on systems, and specifically commended the study undertaken by British Iron and Steel Research Association (BISRA) on the importation of iron ore into Great Britain. Fortunately, he had consulted me about this first, with the result that, in giving his address he said that this study was done seven years ago and 'was by no means dead'. This was generous of him: I had been able to tell him that my own computer committee at BISRA had been discussing this only last week. But of course this was a face-saver: the hard facts really are that the objects of this work, of enormous potential value to the steel industry, have been entirely thwarted by the British Steel Corporation.

Ellis Johnson then gave an impassioned plea for more basic research in operational research: he felt that we were in danger of living on our wits, and of passing from one expedient to another, because of the tremendous pressure put on many OR workers by their employers for quick results—in a field which is essentially a matter of applying science to extremely intractable problems. United Steel has, however, understood this very well.

The feeling here this evening among the most senior members of the Symposium is that the views expressed today have been no more typical of the actual 'practice' in American OR than they are in Great Britain. But it was encouraging to find that the leading authorities in both countries share the same views.

RETROSPECT 1992

This is the same Charles Hitch who eventually became Assistant Secretary of Defense under McNamara.

Wednesday 27th April

The controversial opening papers are now completed, and today the speakers have adhered closely to their printed handouts. There is therefore no need to go into great detail in this report.

The Chairman of this morning's session was Professor Morrell Heald, Head of the Humanities and Social Studies at Case. The first speaker, Dr Raymond Nelson, Director of the Computing Center, was indisposed by positive feedback: he had been thrown to the ground by his own momentum when swinging dumb-bells, and had broken his arm.

Professor Harry Goode: Professor of Electrical and Industrial Engineering, University of Michigan; Chairman of the National Joint Computer Committee; a member of the Air Defense Board; and OR consultant to both the National Bureau of Standards and the American Post Office. This paper, 'A decision model for 4th level systems in the Boulding sense', dealt with open systems capable of maintaining their integrity in the face of throughput of material, energy and information. The living cell is the example chosen by Boulding to typify this kind of system. The exposition was marred by a redundant and somewhat shaky exposition of elementary probability theory, but went on to discuss the model developed by

Goode for application to the analysis of decision problems in the National Air Defense strategy, and secondly in the postal services.

Harry Goode is of course an eminent systems man, with whose work we have been familiar in England for some years. I took the opportunity last night to talk with him for three or four hours about both operational research and cybernetics. Like many holders of university appointments in classical engineering subjects in this country, he is a pioneer in these new techniques. He told me of the latest developments at Ann Arbor (University of Michigan) in the area of decision theory. My old friend Professor Merrill Flood is there too and had been enlarging his previous work on general management decision problems in industry by incorporating learning models into the scheme.

Mr Ascher Opler is a favourite 'computer expert' in the United States, and a Director of the Computer Usage Company. His paper 'On the impedance matching problems of systems that include men and computers', dealt with a very important subject. The problem is clearly stated in the title of his paper, and he expounded this problem with clarity. Unfortunately, he did not appear to know any of the answers.

Professor John Truxal: Head of the Department of Electrical Engineering at Brooklyn Polytechnic. He seems to be regarded by those present as America's leading authority on servomechanism theory. The paper entitled 'System identification techniques' was an extremely interesting paper presented in a lively and amusing fashion. The essence of its argument is that whereas a real-life situation can only be treated as a black box, analytic control techniques must be imposed on it; therefore some suitable model must be found. This is a non-cybernetic outlook, but does in fact represent the philosophy on which contemporary control theory operates. Truxal at least recognized and brought home the fact that a model of a black box must be quite arbitrary and that therefore the preliminary stages of a control device must be a mechanism for identifying the system to be controlled. I place this argument half-way between the orthodox but dangerous control engineer's view that he can blandly identify the system in question, and the OR/cybernetic view that the system is strictly non-identifiable in an analytic sense.

The Symposium continued in the afternoon under the Chairmanship of Professor Michael Leyzorek, Associate Professor of Electrical Engineering at Case.

Professor Alphonse Chapanis was the wartime pioneer of human engineering (which we call ergonomics). He holds two chairs at Johns Hopkins University: those of Psychology and also of Industrial Engineering. This is an unusual academic juxtaposition, in which operational research workers are naturally interested: it is the only university appointment of which I know that properly reflects the standard OR attitude to the interdependence of these two subjects. The paper 'On the relations between human factors engineering, operations research, and systems engineering' ranged over a wide field of applications in which these three subjects were clearly demonstrated to be indivisible. They all dealt with operational problems such as flying aircraft, the public utilities and industrial situations.

Professor Anatol Rapoport, one of the first cyberneticians (see proceedings of the Josiah Macey conferences), is Professor of Mathematical Biology at the University of Michigan (Mental Health Research Institute), where he is also Senior Research Mathematician. This paper was the highlight of the conference so far for many present. It included the most elegant exposition of experimental work carried out with a group of three men in a competitive situation. The tasks they were trying to learn were trivial in the extreme, but Rapoport has used the vast amount of data gathered in these experiments to elaborate models of learning, of performance under fatigue, of the conditions under which people will and will not collaborate, and so on. He ended with an account of the classic 'prisoner's dilemma' from the theory of games, taking the case of a three-person non-zero sum game. On the basis of experiments conducted with this, he is able to demonstrate models covering basic strategies for behaviour in competitive situations. His brilliant verbal exposition of the interaction between business strategies based on pragmatism on the one hand and ethical principles on the other brought him a separate ovation.

Professor Rapoport and I have been trying to meet for some time, and we consequently spent most of the conference in each other's company. He is a Russian with striking views on the international situation, who believes that America (of which country he is now a citizen) should at once declare unilateral disarmament. Whatever the soundness of this opinion, his work in cybernetics continues to be most eminent.

The official banquet of the conference was held in the evening, under the Chairmanship of Professor John Hrones, who held the Chair in Electrical Engineering at MIT, and is now Vice-President for Academic Affairs at Case. In introducing me as the banquet speaker, he paid high tribute to the United Steel Companies for their support of our department, and publicly drew an unfavourable contrast with the American steel concerns.

The Americans being gluttons for intellectual punishment, I made no attempt to keep my address brief: it lasted for one and a half hours. There was an overwhelming response, which was most gratifying. It took two hours to escape from the banqueteers and their questions and comments, after which Anatol Rapoport and I repaired to a room in the hotel which housed a piano. I then discovered to my amazement that he was at one time a concert pianist. He played everything that I could nominate, and it was a perfect end to a most tiring day to listen to Chopin, Liszt, Scarlatti, Beethoven, and the liquid mathematics of Bach.

RETROSPECT 1992

My banquet address 'Below the Twilight Arch' has gradually become the most quoted of my papers in the relevant literature. I regret keeping no detailed record of the discussions upon it.

The outstanding reaction as I clearly remember it, these 30 years later, was made privately and most earnestly by John Truxal. He said 'If you are right, then the whole thrust of our work with automation is on completely wrong lines.' This related to the adumbration of chaos theory.

Thursday 28th April

The morning session of the last day of the First Systems Symposium was under the Chairmanship of Professor Ray Bolz, Head of Mechanical Engineering Science at Case.

Dr John Salzer was Director of Systems for an American industrial company, and is now Director of Intellectronics Laboratory of the Thompson-Ramo-Wooldridge Company. This rather simple paper 'On the evolutionary design of complex systems', was most noticeable for its extremely facile presentation. It discussed in particular the problem of how controls should be brought to bear on the system: if they are brought in piecemeal, there is a dreadful risk of sub-optimizing; if they are brought in as massive all-embracing controls, then the state of the system has to be extrapolated for quite a long time ahead—to the point at which the control will be ready for use. The speaker argued that the first would be both very dangerous and very expensive, and the second would be most unlikely to hit its target two or three years ahead with any accuracy. A policy of evolutionary control was therefore advocated which would get steadily more complicated and exhaustive as the system to be controlled itself evolved.

Dr S. W. Herwald, the Vice-President of Research, Westinghouse Corporation. 'Reliability as a parameter of the system concept' was a paper, and the only paper, explicitly recognizing the steady growth in the number of components, connections and soldered joints in electronic control systems of growing complexity, and the way in which the risk of failure for the control as a whole is a multiplicative probability of the risk of failure of each element. Dr Herwald thought (very rightly in my view) that nothing could be done in the long run to make this situation tolerable, and explained that this was the stimulus that directed Westinghouse to the development of molecular electronics. As we already know, this enables electronic circuitry to be designed inside a single crystal of germanium, by the behaviour and interaction of domains of electrons therein. The topological constraint of a semiconductor in this way is clearly an incredible advance in electronic technology, which will have far-reaching consequences. This particular paper unfortunately added nothing to our present knowledge, and was in general marred by a flavour of commercial advertisement.

The Chairman for the afternoon session was Professor James Roswick, Director of the Engineering Design Center at Case. He pointed out that both the speakers this morning had felt it necessary to devote some time to relating their own material to the views expressed in my banquet address last night.

Mr Russell Aikman is an Englishman who worked in the instrumentation division of ICI, and has now emigrated to America where he is Technical Adviser to the Board of Directors of the Schlumberger Well Surveying Corporation. His paper 'On the interrelationships of systems science and systems engineering in the processing industries' was an historical piece about the development of instrumentation in industry as a response to systems research. It was enjoyable and well presented, and served to bring the question of industrial applications into a convenient perspective. But it presented no special challenge or new ideas.

Mr Harold Chestnut, the Control Systems Engineer of the General Electric Company of America, is a leading world figure in the field of automation—indeed he was last year's president of the International Federation for Automation and Computation (IFAC). It seemed to most people that the speaker had wildly misunderstood the nature of the occasion: his paper sounded like an introductory lecture for a postgraduate course on systems engineering. It also suffered from the worst of the familiar diseases of American papers: a determination to categorize, and to force the facts of life on to an analytic of the author's own invention.

The conference was closed by a brief and undistinguished address by Professor Eckman.

This evening I again became embroiled with members of the conference who wished to pursue the implications of my own address. This has lasted half the night and I am now too tired to appreciate it very much.

The conference has certainly been an enormous success. There has been an exceptionally distinguished panel of speakers, and the audience of men who are themselves known authorities in the field has never rested for an instant. The liveliness of the proceedings has been evident throughout, both inside and outside the conference room; the discussion throughout has been of a high calibre. The sponsors have announced that the whole proceedings are to be published by John Wiley, and firmly believe that the book will become the standard text on systems research. The occasion has been very well organized, although everyone has obviously found it something of a strain. Formal sessions have run each day from 9 until 5, with only a luncheon break: the Americans evidently do not believe in morning coffee or afternoon tea. Moreover, the physics theatre in which the sessions were held is built of tiers of wooden seats with arm rests for note-taking, clearly designed with the object of keeping students awake. The lengthy evening proceedings described in this diary have also meant that there has not been a moment's pause for taking breath throughout the whole three days. However, it has been a worthwhile experience.

RETROSPECT 1992

The book was indeed published, and had considerable effect in its day. However, I have not heard it referred to for many years. Sadly, the Systems Research Center itself, which we were inaugurating with such high hopes, went into decline with the death of Don Eckman. He loved to drive powerful sports cars, and on this very occasion frightened the life out of me by driving at a large stone wall at 100 m.p.h.—coming to a halt in the nick of time by changing down rapidly through what seemed like 20 gears. He was killed when he crashed into a tree in France.

Friday 29th April

Most of the day was spent in detailed discussion with Russell Ackoff about the organization of the operational research group at Case. In Appendix II is given the breakdown of the areas of teaching at the Institute, with special reference to the management sciences and their degrees. The basic curricula for the higher degree are given at Appendix III. [For Appendices I–V see page 304–309 below.]

Despite the idea that American establishments award degrees at the slightest provocation, it is noted that these courses are extremely detailed and thorough. To take a Bachelor, Master's and Doctorate degree in operational research takes eight years, and no less than half the students accepted fail to qualify—despite the stringent entry qualifications. Case demands not only a good basic degree (as does Birmingham), but candidates must pass a qualifying examination in mathematics up to differential equations, and another in statistics and probability theory. Thus candidates who already have a good degree may be involved in two years' preliminary work before being accepted as candidates for the higher degree.

Graduate OR scientists working with the OR group are also studying for doctorates. Instead of paying the Institute for this privilege, they are paid anything from $4000 to $5000 a year. The Director is able to achieve this amazing arrangement as well as paying all his staff abnormally high salaries for an academic seat, by virtue of the fact that the department is actively engaged in consultancy for industry and the government. It is entirely self-supporting. Even so, the salaries paid are only about half what the senior men could command in industry. The fact that they remain with the group is evidence (if it were needed) that this is one of the outstanding OR groups in the country. Academic Fellows are paid between $2000 and $4000, but they are by definition supported by their industries or foreign governments.

In addition to the established degrees, there is a 'certificate in OR' which is roughly equivalent to half a master's degree. This is a four and a half months intensive programme run for industry and is extra-curricular.

Some 40 per cent of the group's effort goes into actual OR projects. Here is a brief inventory of some typical problems with which they have recently been, or are currently, engaged:

Applied Industrial Projects

1. Production control studies of various kinds.
2. How is a company to handle the problem of its increasing freight damages?
3. How can a stainless steel manufacturer reduce production delays?
4. A problem of stockholding and distribution to customers on behalf of a major steel company.
5. Various problems in marketing.

6. General management: an OR survey for a large corporation of its general management situation.
7. Raw material: should supplies be bought by speculation on the exchange or under fixed contract? (The answer to this question proved to be by speculation, and the OR team developed a strategy for this purpose. This strategy was so effective that the company in fact made more by this speculation than by their actual manufacturing process!)
8. Devising a five-year plan for a very large company; formulating objectives (new products, product mix, etc.), policies for the pursuit of these objectives, a complete reorganization of management structure, and a set of communication and decision-making procedures for the use of the new structure.

Military Logistics

1. Maintenance logistics of aircraft (army).
2. Maintenance logistics of heavy construction equipment (army engineers).
3. Optimal preventitive maintenance (army ordnance).

Government

1. A study of the economics of scientific publications (the optimal distribution of scientific information).
2. The optimal procedure for dividing money between research and development, and on the other hand capital investment inside a firm.
3. An industry-wide study of R & D (flow of technology and knowledge)—if one industry (for example, steel) is required to increase its rate of growth, how must all other relevant industries (suppliers, consumers, and ancillary operators) be stimulated by the right flow of information and incentive to keep in gear with the major development?
4. A project to develop a measure for national scientific productivity.
5. A project in fundamental OR research (via the Office of Naval Research) to improve estimation techniques, sequential decision models, and to study the sensitivity of model approximations.
6. Further fundamental research on queuing theory (for the Air Force).
7. A study for the government of the optimal siting of federal buildings throughout America.
8. The country is embarking on a scheme of pre-paid dental plans—a prophylactic service in line with our own National Health.
9. Aid to underdeveloped countries. At any given time, one of the ten professorial staff at Case is away, under the government's plan of aid. These men provide OR assistance to the governments of underdeveloped countries, usually working on their national five-year plans, by directing the indigenous commissions. This has been particularly successful in Israel, Turkey, Egypt and India. The institute also takes in senior men in OR as visiting students from the underdeveloped countries.

Method of Working

Case charge their OR clients the cost of the project plus 100 per cent expenses. This works out at approximately $1500 a man-month. Thus the project costs between $3000 and $4500 a month, or $20 000 to $50 000 for the entire project.

Case does however set stringent conditions on their willingness to accept a project. At least one suitable man must be lent to them full-time by the company concerned—they usually get two, and sometimes four. Case themselves provide two or three people. The company men must attend a training course at Case, and subsequently act entirely under the direction of the OR project leader. There is a monthly meeting between the project team and the management concerned, and Case contractually reserve the right to nominate which managers will be present at that meeting. If any of these conditions is broken by the company, Case at once withdraws from the project.

I should have mentioned that the doctorate degree is preceded by a qualifying exam. There is one oral examination on the nature of operational research, and a written examination on statistics and probability. There is a second written examination on surveying techniques, and two specialities of the student (chosen by him) are orally examined in depth.

In addition to the official consulting undertaken by the Institute, Case allows each member of the faculty one day a week free in which to do private consultancy. By this means, members of the faculty increase their incomes by between 50 and 100 per cent.

A highly successful innovation in the operation of this department has been an annual Ladies' Day. This is a 'course for wives' at which operational research is explained and lectures are given on the various projects of the department. A free questions session is allowed, at which such embarrassing questions as 'Why do you pay my husband so little?' are answered by Professor Ackoff.

In addition to searching out this information, I have today met most of the senior people here. I also gave a seminar for the whole group, lasting two hours, which was a very lively interchange of ideas on the organization, methods and practice of OR.

RETROSPECT 1992

Please note that the monetary details given here (and elsewhere) are expressed in 1960 dollars. I do not know how to adjust them for the 1990s. However, they certainly struck me as very high indeed.

At Cybor House, where I had a driving policy to recruit women scientists, we had a party for spouses in the summer and at Christmas time. At these, members of the department were able to show spouses (and indeed children) the projects on which they are working, including those in the laboratories and on the computer. It was all very informal and relaxed. I recall that in the

above passage I was trailing my coat. But my colleagues rejected the American version as quite un-British in spite (or perhaps because) of the fact that Rivett had already been doing something at the Coal Board, and I had lectured for him there.

Saturday 30th April and Sunday 1st May

The weekend has been spent with Russell Ackoff and his charming family at their country home at Chagrin Falls, 15 miles outside Cleveland. We have had long and fascinating discussions, ranging over many problems in both science and management.

Ackoff's own background is extremely interesting. He qualified as an architect, and obtained a situation in an architect's office. While pursuing postgraduate work in this subject, he decided also to take higher studies in philosophy; this was at the University of Philadelphia, where the Professor of Philosophy was West Churchman. Having taken a doctorate in Philosophy, he was simultaneously offered positions on the staff of the faculties of Architecture and Philosophy, and accepted the latter. The two men (Churchman and Ackoff) began to work on the concept of an interdisciplinary activity, Ackoff studying mathematics and statistics meanwhile.

Having failed to launch their interdisciplinary programme to their own satisfaction at Philadelphia, both men moved to Wade University where they spent some years inaugurating a new department. Again, neither was satisfied with the results, and both left again to join Case where the present department was established. By this time OR had become well known and had been assimilated into their project. Arnoff had joined them. It was in this situation that their famous book, Introduction to Operations Research, by Churchman, Ackoff and Arnoff was written. Ackoff succeeded Churchman as Director when Churchman left for the University of California.

During the weekend we have also toured Cleveland, and my originally unfavourable impressions of the place have been dissipated. The city is very wealthy, and has an extensive residential area which is perhaps the most beautiful I have seen anywhere in the world. The roads are dual-carriageways with big grass verges on which grow enormous trees, and the houses are set back from the road in great lawns. Their architecture is fascinatingly varied, and most notable is the entire absence of any hedge, fence or wall. The impression is created of a colony of country houses set in rolling parkland.

I was also impressed by the Cleveland Museum of Art, which is apparently one of the best in the United States. It has a small but fine collection of Egyptian archaeology, where the exhibits are organized and arranged in a way which compares most favourably with the more extensive collections in the London museums. The representative nature of the pictures on display in the art gallery also drew admiration: most major artists seemed to be represented. In particular it was a joy to discover the originals of two very famous pictures for the first time: the long Degas painting of four dancers preparing for the ballet, and the 'Blue Period' Picasso—'La Vie'.

This has been an enjoyable and stimulating weekend, in a lovely modern house which was designed, it need hardly be added, by Ackoff himself.

Monday 2nd May

Each week at Case begins with a 9 a.m. meeting of the whole group. This is very like a condensed version of our quarterly meeting. It begins with an address by the Director on the present state of affairs: there was talk this morning of visitors to the department, among other things. He also announced that in the last week no less than six new contracts for OR projects had been signed, and briefly explained to the group what these were and who was in mind to tackle them. After this there is a project review at which one of the project leaders expounds to the group as a whole the job he has just completed or is working on.

Today's project for review was an OR study of a priority system for deciding which of an apparently infinite set of proposed schemes for improving the lot of the nation could be embarked upon in Egypt. The speaker was Fred Hanssman, who has been on loan to the Egyptian government for the purpose of this study.

Professor Frisch had already been working on this problem on the Egyptian Government's behalf, and had evaluated a solution to the problem for next year, based on his well-known adaptation of the simplex procedure. Although the lower bound of the national credit for each of the succeeding 10 years had been established in order to reach this solution, the linear programme had solved the problem on the basis that the list of potential projects to hand would not be augmented, and that economic feasibility was the only criterion. By the nature of this optimization, it is inevitable that the debt incurred by the nation would actually hit the lower bound of credit on the most critical year: thus no new project at all could be started for at least five years.

The approach made by Hanssman had been sequential: new and excellent projects proposed next year and the year after must be enabled to replace the weaker projects at the bottom of this year's list. Even when, given economic feasibility by LP, one had to consider technological feasibility as a constraint (the availability of concomitant services which would enable the proposed new service to operate to the full); social feasibility also had to be considered. This was defined as a feedback system: any project selected for development would create income: therefore an increase in the standard of living over the appropriate areas would be vital to absorb that increase—otherwise inflation would ensue.

The government's objectives made an interesting vector of conflicting and incommensurate aims—just as they do in an industrial company. It was desired to raise the national product, to reduce unemployment, and at the same time to protect the development plans already operating for education, health and housing.

Hanssman presented his model, which was based on a linear programme. The lower bound credit situation was neatly dealt with by an adaptation of an inventory control formula which would delimit investment, and at the same time reveal how far any particular mix now would influence the level of credit in n years' time. There would clearly be value judgements left for the government to make, and the model was rounded off by ranking techniques in order to make a fair presentation to the client.

The report to the government gave a table listing the objectives along the top and percentages of their pay-off down the side. The table was completed by a set of figures such that any combination chosen by the government as having the right political (managerial) characteristics would be optimal providing that the percentages chosen summed to 100. This was a neat result (much preferred to Frisch's static economic input-output system), developed without incurring the implausibilities of dynamic programming to obtain its sequential character. There were many questions asked, and a considerable discussion about the implications of this work for another study going on in which a large industrial company has the same problem of priorities in its development plans.

The rest of the day was spent in making a detailed study of two projects: one recently completed, and the other just beginning. In each case, several hours' discussion was spent with the project team concerned.

The first of the projects concerned a strategy for planned maintenance, entirely analogous to the work we undertook at Fox's. In this case, however, data about the parts involved and their usage were available. This study was made for the army, and concerned military aircraft and their maintenance. A typical 'theatre army' consists of three corps each of four divisions, covering perhaps 200 by 150 miles of terrain, and owning 1650 planes. These are of many types, used for observation, transportation and the rapid movement of staff (helicopters). The maintenance problem is of course fantastic, and is divided into five kinds of work from daily routines to complete rebuilding. At present, it is carried out in four echelons at different depths from the front-line, and each involving quite different commitments in the way of plant, machinery and skilled labour.

This is the most elegant OR job I have seen over here, and I have a full written account of the matter. The essence of the solution is a subtle renewal theory based on cannibalization: the strategy is to hold whole planes in reserve instead of an inventory of spare parts. As an effect of this strategy, the whole of the maintenance scheduling has had to be recast (into three types based on two echelons and an intermediate field unit). In addition to saving the government no less than $50 million per theatre army per annum, it has been shown that the methods proposed will much improve the availability of planes. The project leader was Rudolph Reinitz.

The second study is industrial, and has been commissioned at board level to study the largest division of a large engineering company. The parent company has an annual turnover of $100 million, of which this division contributes half. The division has four plants in widely dispersed parts of America, and the problem is as follows.

Five years ago the company had a monopoly of the business in its field, and this has now dropped to about 80 per cent of the market. The company is quoting much longer deliveries than its competitors, its prices are barely comparable, and the management are secretly unsure of their own public claim to higher quality. What is to be done?

The job has not been running very long but it is already clear that the basic difficulty is that the company subscribes to a jobbing philosophy which it cannot afford to maintain. Thus the company has tentatively agreed to undertake new product engineering under the direction of the OR group, which is a very right move to make before embarking upon the installation of production control systems. Meanwhile, a statistical analysis had just been completed of shop-floor data supplied by the company. I joined the project team in attempting to evaluate this information, and it is perfectly clear that this is internally inconsistent, and has been 'fudged' somewhere down the line.

Methods of obtaining right information were discussed at length, and it is interesting that the approaches of Case and Cybor House to this kind of difficulty are identical—although Case very much envy us our JACK machine. The strategies which could be developed when the new data were available were also debated, and again there was a large measure of agreement. However, I found the project team too willing to base the control system on a fixed strategy, and urged on them the necessity for self-modifying procedural rules. As a result, I am due to go into the problems of such a solution with the senior logician of the group tomorrow. This will I think prove to be an interesting project. The project leader is Professor Arnoff.

This evening, yet more intricate scientific discussion took place at a dinner party given for me by the Arnoffs at their home.

RETROSPECT 1992

For nearly 10 years I talked informally with the British Government about Professor Frisch's work, in the hope of persuading Britain to attempt some sort of large-scale economic model. Indeed, I had managed to send my mathematician, Michael Aczel, to Oslo to study Frisch's methods, but they seemed inflexible in the way described. India had run into the same problem—not to mention the former USSR. Thus Hanssman's approach was particularly interesting. However, it proved impossible to dislodge Whitehall from its grim econometrics, and in the early 1960s I resigned from the relevant committee at the newly established Department of Economic Affairs.

The reference to 'our JACK machine' concerns a device developed at Cybor House by my colleague, Dr K. D. Tocher. It was essentially a timing

device, which could be triggered either automatically by photo-electric or infra-red cells or strain gauges, or activated by human observers. Several stations could be installed in various parts of a works, and readings taken simultaneously *to about a tenth of a second—the record being written on to punched paper tape at a central station.*

My management colleagues had declared that the use of this machine would cause an immediate strike, and threatened me with dismissal if I should precipitate one. However, I had no problems whatsoever with the trade unions concerned. They were quicker than the managers to realize that simultaneous recording would make possible synergistic planning and therefore increase productivity. I made a deal with the union leaders to incorporate union nominees in every JACK team, to give this member custody of all tapes, to make no analysis on the computer except with their agreement, and to hand over the tapes to the unions for ceremonial burning on completion of any exercise. The result was that we obtained substantial increases in productivity. But it proved impossible to obtain a fair share of the benefits for the workforce; and my dismissal was demanded by one of the member companies on the grounds that by handing over the tapes I had 'abrogated a management prerogative'. It was refused.

Tuesday 3rd May

This morning's work was devoted, as planned, to formal logic in company with Jay Minas, an associate professor in the group. It was agreed that the potentialities for the use of logic in operational research had barely been recognized and there was a good deal of overlap in our ideas about ways in which research should be directed. A good deal of time was spent on the question of self-modifying decision rules, which Minas would seek to handle by recursion theory. Minas believes that the vast amount of theoretical work on n-valued calculi could be translated into suitable OR models—once people transcended the idea that an equivalence would have to be set up with empirical scales in the real world. He developed the curious idea that the truth-falsehood dichotomy is basic to human thinking, and especially decision processes, while at the same time a many-valued logic could be imposed on this binary logic to account for such concepts as 'it is possible that' and 'I believe that' in high-level decision procedures.

I was entertained to lunch by the General Manager (Mr T. E. Lynch), and three other directors of Clevite Ordnance. This was a company which had especially invited me to spend a day in their works; but we talked about industrial OR across the lunch table instead. This entertainment took place in the oldest club in Cleveland, which is designed as the replica of some London club. It is certainly old and fusty; but the conversation was quite interesting.

Professor Rapoport of Ann Arbor, Michigan, has been here for two days, giving consulting advice to the faculty on OR research in the behavioural sciences. He gave a seminar this afternoon which I attended. Following this, Ackoff, Camp, Rapoport and myself had a long discussion about various residual topics, and all failed to solve an ingenious random walk problem proposed by Rapoport, which, if it could be solved, would offer a social decision space in which human relationships could be described by a Markovian process. After dinner, Rapoport departed for Michigan, and Camp and myself spent the rest of the night discussing OR problems in the area of transportation.

Wednesday 4th May

This morning was spent in examining the Case Computer Center. This runs in parallel with the OR Center; its Director is Professor Raymond Nelson. Interestingly enough, he is a philosopher; notwithstanding which he is Professor of Mathematics. Here is some very advanced thinking in the field of computer technology. Professor Nelson teaches the Case undergraduates that platitudes of the kind: 'a process that can be precisely expressed can be programmed for a computer', are worthless tautologies. He claimed acquaintance with my published arguments that in fact all computer control languages are undecidable, and most of our conversation was spent discussing the metalanguages in which such control theorems might be discussed. He is also interested in the application of Post-languages, and indeed in any logically sophisticated way of discussing computer theory. At present about half, and shortly all, students for degrees at every level throughout the Case Institute take courses of some kind in computers. It would seem that a new breed of computer man is likely to emerge in the American scene.

The Computer Center consists of about four full-time staff, plus all the Fellows and Research Associates taking higher degrees. The Center includes a statistical laboratory, headed by Professor Leone, in which there is a staff of four—again plus the students involved. Professor Varga, who is a numerical analyst, is also on the staff of the Center.

The Center has a Univac I, which was constructed in 1948. With its 6000 vacuum tubes and its 20 000 diodes it requires between three and four hours preventive maintenance every day. This is an alpha-numeric machine, whose standard properties are well known. However, the Center has virtually converted it into a Univac II and has added a number of devices of its own. For example, the standard 10 tape-decks have been fitted with plastic friction pulleys and special braking mechanisms of local design. The machine operates 24 hours per day. Two of the three shifts are devoted to commercial production.

The time is sold to industry (which operates the machine without assistance from the Institute), the profits from which cover the cost of the whole Computer Center. Time is sold for between $100 and $150 an hour, which yields a handsome dividend, especially considering that Remington-Rand gave this machine to the Institute! The company which uses most of this time has its own Univac, and therefore uses this one as buffer capacity. Its use is entirely on business applications: payroll, shareholding, the payment of dividends, and freight handling paperwork are all typical applications. In the little time left of the day, the machine is used primarily for teaching purposes at the Center. There is the usual set of ancillary equipment, including a card to magnetic tape converter, and a print-out machine operating at 600 lines per minute.

The second computer installation is an IBM 650 machine with Ramac. As the 650 has no fast access store itself, it is associated with a 60-word core storage unit. The Ramac disc file (600 000 words) is used as a buffer. The installation also contains two magnetic tape units, and is therefore very versatile as far as choice of access is concerned; 50 per cent of the time on this machine, which also runs for 24 hours a day, is devoted to educational tasks in the area of numerical analysis.

For example, a great deal of work has been done in solving differential equations as part of theses presented for engineering degrees. The remainder of the time is devoted to research, mainly in the field of automatic programming. Much work has been done in the devising of translators and compilers and the 'Runcible' autocode was invented here. Apparently this is now widely used throughout America. This whole computer installation will shortly be replaced by Burroughs' 220 machine, with a 5000 word core memory.

The Computing Center serves anyone in the Institute who wishes to use a machine, including the OR group. It is interesting to note that OR makes little use of these facilities, and when it does is concerned mainly with processing its research data. Russ Ackoff believes that there is sufficiently close liaison between the two organizations, and that if the OR group had its own computer it would tend to use the machine too much on OR work—to the detriment of its quality. All in all, the Computer Center presents a marked contrast to the orthodox British view of the American attitude to such facilities.

The whole afternoon was spent working with the project team studying the National Science Foundation remit: how is information communicated among scientists, and what can be done to improve its dissemination? A feasibility study (what if anything can OR do to answer this question?) has already been satisfactorily completed. It was carried out on chemists, who were observed throughout their working hours for a fortnight by a ratio delay technique. The results showed that chemists are operating for a 90-hour week, of which 18 per cent is spent on communicating scientific information. One-third of this time is consumed in reading, and a half of this (3 per cent of total time) is spent reading scientific journals. A half of this time is devoted to a mere nine journals of the hundreds available. As a result of this feasibility study, the following objectives were formulated for a project to last a year:

1. What do chemists and physicists read and why?
2. What is the cost of publishing a journal per page read?
3. What are the alternative publishing policies, considered for their effects on costs, the time of scientists and the amount of information received?

These objects are conceived within the National Science Foundation remit, for this body is expected to subsidize the dissemination of information (for example by supporting uneconomic journals in peripheral areas of study) and by advising learned bodies on better ways of reporting research.

The population description for the sample design concerns all chemists and physicists working in continental USA, taking 152 metropolitan areas of the census as defining this. Each individual studied will provide a sample of 14 days of working hours. From the point of view of cost, any unit chosen for study must contain at least 5 chemists or 3 physicists. In fact, the average American company contains 18.4 chemists and 9 physicists. Thus a stratified sample of large, medium and small cities (as judged by the number of chemists and physicists inhabiting them) has been taken and a random sample of three cities from each stratum was selected. Six companies were randomly chosen for physicists and three for chemists in each of the nine cities: thus 81 organizations are involved in the study. The co-operation of all 81 presidents has been received, and only one company approached proved recalcitrant.

Each scientist takes the observations himself, and averages five observations a day, each of which is thought to take two minutes to record. The recalcitrant president argued that if the number of observations was multiplied by the number of scientists and multiplied again by two minutes, and if to this were added the half-hour explanation of the scheme given to each subject by the OR group, the hours used by the study would cost his company $11 000. This is the best example of fallacia compositionis that I have encountered for a long time.

In order to acquire the data needed, the OR group have had to develop a special machine for recording snap readings as required by the ratio delay study technique. The machine is known as RAM (Random Alarm Mechanism) and was invented by Professor Cooke of the OR group. This device is quite fascinating. It is about the size of a packet of cigarettes, and is carried on the person of the scientist who is to contribute the information. It is arranged to ring an alarm bell at random intervals, on an average of five times a day, and is switched on when the subject gets up in the morning, and off when he goes to bed at night.

The mechanism is most ingenious. The ringing of the alarm bell (which must not be switched off for 10 seconds) causes small batteries to charge a capacitor. The charge then begins to leak away, at a rate which depends on humidity, temperature, movement and other random variables. When the voltage has dropped to a fixed threshold, the alarm rings again. The second element of randomness is provided by the fact that one of four possible discrete voltages is charged to the capacitor each time. Which will be charged at any given moment is determined by the position of two mercury switches, which between them take up one of four positions depending upon how the device is being held at the time. The whole approach to this difficult measuring problem, and the machine itself, seems to be most laudable. The only surprising thing is that 70 000 scientists have been persuaded to run this experiment for a whole fortnight. The team seems to have few illusions about the amount of error which might get incorporated into a study of this kind, and to have done a good deal of theoretical work about the sensitivity of their sample design.

There are many other features of this project of considerable interest, such as a mathematical model for measuring the compositor's difficulty in setting up type, which need not be gone into here. It is difficult not to admire the pertinacity of the OR team in tackling this job, and difficult to believe that they will find an optimal solution to the problem of disseminating scientific information. On the other hand, I shall be very surprised indeed if a good deal of information valuable to the nation and the scientific community is not produced. Meanwhile, we might consider whether this machine (which is to be patented, but can be made available to us) is not a tremendous advance on the standard method of carrying out ratio delay studies by an observer.

This evening has been spent in the company of two research associates of the OR group, from whom I obtained an interesting picture of what it is like to work in this organization.

Thursday 5th May

The total plan for interdisciplinary research at Case is now becoming clear. Four separate establishments have been created: the Operational Research Center; the Systems Research Center; the Design Center; and the Computer Center. These are each under the directorship of a professor of the Institute, respectively Professors Ackoff, Eckman, Reswick and Nelson. The Design Center is of no particular relevance to our work, and I have already investigated the OR and Computer Centers. Today was spent exclusively in studying the arrangements at the Systems Research Center.

Professor Eckman is one of the pioneers of process control in America, and here holds the professorships of mechanical engineering and instrument engineering. His Systems Research Center is an entirely project-oriented organization, and the present plan involves five problems which are being studied.

The first is on computer control (leader: Professor Lefbonitz); the second is on adaptive control (leader: Professor Eckman); the third is on biological systems (leader: Professor Leyzorek); the fourth is on ecological systems (leader: Professor Weinberger); and the fifth is on the reliability of systems (leader: Professor Dean).

All the leaders are part time, being separately professors in the Institute. The projects will eventually be conducted by Fellows of the Institute, supported by governmental funds, with the following numbers available on each project (respectively) at the present time: 12, 12, 8, 2, 5. The backgrounds of these men will be strictly interdisciplinary, and the teams will include operational research scientists. There will also be a good deal of external assistance. For example, the adaptive control project will have three visiting professors during the course of next year, including Colin Cherry from Imperial College. Biological Systems, in addition to its leader who is a psychologist, will be assisted by a biochemist and the Professor of Neurology from Western Reserve University next door. Assistance for Ecological Systems will include a microbiologist (the leader) and an industrial sociologist. A sixth project is already envisaged in the general field of human communications, which will include work on developing measures of semantic information in an attempt to place the theory of machine translation on a better basis.

Hitherto, the Center has concentrated on standard control theory as a major exemplification of systems research. It has two rather ancient analogue computers (GEDA, and a Philbrick). These were originally used for research work, but are now entirely devoted to the teaching needs of undergraduates. Two new computer installations are in the process of running in, and these will therefore be free for research work 100 per cent of their time. These are of sufficient interest to describe here.

The first is basically a digital machine, the RW 300 control computer of the Thompson-Ramo-Wooldridge Products Company. The machine is fully transistorized, and is consequently the smallest computer of considerable capacity I have ever seen. It is a general-purpose binary serial code computer, whose speed is about twice that of the IBM 650. At present the drum storage contains 8000 words (18 bits plus sign), but this is expandable to 16 000 words. It is driven by a punched paper tape program, coded in machine language.

Obviously, such a machine can take either a digital or tape input. But the extraordinary thing about this computer, is that it can receive 32 analogue inputs, transduced from a process on to a scale of 0 to 10 volts (of low impedance about 1 megaohm). These inputs pass through an analogue/digital converter straight on to the drum. The conversion is done by a bracketing process which halves the scale iteratively until it pinpoints a value—and this process only takes 10 microseconds. That is to say, the analogue/digital converter sweeps the 32 inputs at this rate. After working on the digital information, the machine can print out in digital form, or on tape, or in the form of 'anunciator alarms' (that is to say, the emission of pulses when a certain threshold is passed), or, by the precise reverse of the process just described, by digital/analogue conversion to 16 analogue outputs. I found this an impressive machine. It is backed up by a slow storage of a RAMAC disc file with a capacity of 500 000 words.

The decision machine is a standard analogue computer (made by Computer Systems Incorporated, New York) having a conventional organization of 40 amplifiers

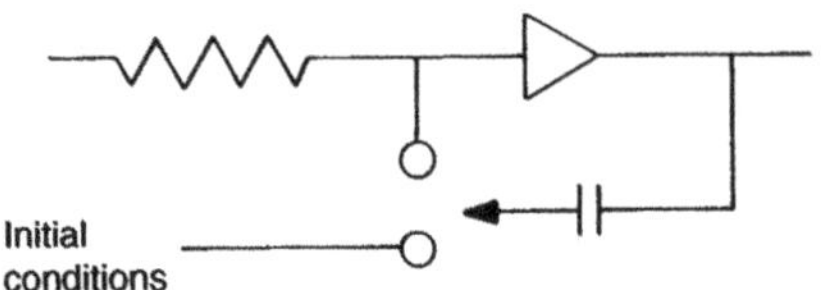

Figure 2

which will be increased to 100 later) and 20 multipliers, plus accessories. The extraordinary thing about this machine is that its initial conditions are not passive, but are driven by a dystac power amplifier, which sets up the initial conditions in 10 microseconds.

The circuit shown in Figure 2 is very fast, as a result of this power amplifier, and is in fact capable of iterating at 100 per second. Secondly, it can be used as a memory circuit. Thirdly, it enables the machine to be operated by the pulse sequential method. Here, it will be noted, as a digital element in an analogue computer just as the RW 300 provides analogue facilities for a digital machine.

During this morning I gave a three-hour seminar for the Systems Research Center on 'Control theory and adaptation'. This was made particularly interesting due to the presence of a visiting professor from Yugoslavia and a young Englishman—who is writing a doctorate thesis on his own treatment of the theory of neural nets—both of whom were very bright.

In the afternoon I joined the project team dealing with adaptive process control, and learnt of their activities. They have investigated what they call the 'direct method' of process automation, which involves the manipulation of inputs to improve output performance against some straightforward criterion. This is essentially to treat the system as a black box, and to stimulate it by a form of automatic evolutionary operation. This uses a perturbation signal (or the internal noise of the system) to obtain minimal variations, or can produce these systematically according to an experimental design. The 'model approach' assumes that the dominant relationships between input and output can be discovered, and written down in the form of a characteristic equation. This model is set up in a high speed analogue computer, which searches for the optimum manipulation of inputs in unreal time, and has them ready for feeding back into the system when the right moment is reached in real time.

An exemplification was given in terms of the hydrogenation of cottonseed oil for margarine manufacture. The process is delineated as $X \rightarrow Y \rightarrow Z$, namely three chemical constituents of a chemical reaction mixture. The rate of reaction is proportional to the concentration of the reaction component. Independent input variables are pressure and temperature. The two transitions, called $\underline{k}_1$ and $\underline{k}_2$ are the reaction coefficients which are functions of pressure and temperature. Thus we obtain the characteristic equations

$$d\underline{x}/d\underline{t}=\underline{k}_1\underline{x} \qquad d\underline{y}/d\underline{t}=\underline{k}_1\underline{x}-\underline{k}_2\underline{y}$$

This three-dimensional system is fully determined by two of its components (since $\underline{x}+\underline{y}+\underline{z}=1$). The problem is to trace a trajectory on an initial point ($\underline{x}_o\underline{y}_o$) to a final point ($\underline{x}_f\underline{y}_f$). The team then brings in a 'repetitive control concept'. In the first of their exemplifications, they seek end-point control: that is, so long as the system reaches the final state, the actual trajectory is unimportant in terms of cost. Thus by finding empirical formulae for $\underline{k}_1$ and $\underline{k}_2$, the pressure can be determined as a constant by integration. However, owing to inaccuracies in the model, the actual trajectory is bound to wander away from the theoretical trajectory. Thus the control system embarks on a sequential calculation, and at a series of discrete points in time recalculates the trajectory required to reach the end-point, and recalculates a new constant for the pressure input. The limiting factors dictating the period of this recalculation are the means of measurement (which may have a finite time interval that quantizes the control mechanism), and the speed of the computer (in the case where continuous measurement is possible).

The second of their methods concerns the discovery of an optimum path where the cost of the actual trajectory followed is after all important. In this case, the manipulative variables can no longer be treated as constants: they are non-linear functions of time. This method also uses repetitive measuring strategies. Again, the inadequacy of the model must be reflected in an end-point error unless a sequential procedure is adopted, although this error would not exist if the input variables were infinite in range. What this team calls 'adaptation' is the updating of parameters of the model on the basis of experience discovered at the moments of sequential recalculation.

This does seem to be an interesting achievement. The control is not here merely recalculating its trajectory on the understanding that error is inevitable, but is simultaneously trying to make the model a better representation of reality. This process extends to the transformation of time constants in the model into time trends. These methods have been demonstrated for both batch and continuous processes, and the continuous process case is handled quite ingeniously. For we may consider a continuous process as operating at an equilibrial steady state. Disturbance demands the definition of a new equilibrial state, and both these levels are taken as self-controlled. The transition between them becomes a quasi-batch process, in which the initial state is the final state of the first equilibrium, and the final state is the initial state of the second equilibrium. Incidentally, the team is about to apply these techniques to the problem of the continuous annealing of steel strip.

The Japanese member of the team, who comes from the Japanese steel industry, then described how these methods had been applied to the problem of batch slab heating. An optimum path had been sought to raise the temperature of a slab to readiness for rolling, according to a model which acknowledges the necessity for soaking (to reach homogeneity of heat), the cost of heat, and the heat stress on the furnace lining. The discovery is that heat should be applied slowly at first, increasing rapidly towards the end-point of the control, which is quite contrary to traditional practice—where all the heat is applied early on until the ready-to-roll temperature is reached, and then cut off so that the material is soaking. According to the computer calculations, 15 per cent of fuel is saved by this method.

It occurs to me, however, that this approach does not acknowledge such problems as grain growth in high alloy steels, nor does it recognize that although fuel may strictly be wasted in our present practice, considerable programming flexibility is imported to the rolling mill, which is enabled to draw on the steel when it is ready or thereafter. According to Cybor House work at Appleby-Frodingham on ingot soaking, it would certainly seem that the flexibility obtained in the mill by the present strategies is extremely valuable, and much more valuable than the relatively small saving in heating costs at the soakers.

The people to whom I was talking acknowledged that their treatment of a heating furnace as an entire system, complete in itself, probably involves a sub-optimization for the company as a whole; and they expressed their pleasure that the new organization would supply the team with several OR scientists who could handle this side of the problem.

This evening I attended a dinner party at the home of the Eckmans, at which three other members of the faculty and their wives were present.

Friday 6th May

Most of this morning was spent on a visit to the Addressograph Multigraph Company on the outskirts of Cleveland, where (by arrangement with the British representatives) I was following up the experimental work this company has done in connection with the identification of pieces of hot steel by the welding to them of embossed plates. The information that is known in advance is programmed on a punched paper tape, and the last minute information (such as exact weight or length of the rolled product) is punched into the tape by a keyboard operation at the shears.

Little more could be told me than I had already learnt in England, but I took advantage of the contact to arrange a visit to the Inland Steel Company at Hammond near Chicago on the 1st June. In order to do this, I shall have to rearrange my arrival at Urbana, but the visit would seem to be worth while. Actually to see the technique in operation and to obtain the comments of the people who work with it, would be invaluable. It seems to me at this point that in United Steel we should need many copies of each plate, and this does not seem to be an insuperable difficulty. Furthermore, I think we should need to automate the process by which the plate is removed from the Addressograph machine and placed in the welding gun—but this again would seem to be an elementary exercise in mechanical transfer.

Trouble has been experienced with cold welds, which is not surprising, and a new type of gun is being developed using two-probe conductant welding.

However, I have been able to obtain samples of the steel plates used (which is zinc-coated C1007 specification) and doubtless Swindon Laboratories will be able to comment on this problem. The cost of the basic machine is $20 000, and it would be available in England. This expenditure could very easily be worth while, especially as the relevant information used on the embossed plate can be read out at seven other points on ordinary stationery. The obvious place to investigate the possibilities at first seems to be the TEMS Scheme.

The people seen were Mr R. W. Reeve, the International Sales Manager of the Company; Mr J. Sihler, Market Development Coordinator; and Mr J. White, Project Coordinator. The local manager in Hammond who is arranging the trip to Inland Steel is Mr J. Ritter. Messrs Sihler and White entertained me to lunch, after which I returned to Case.

This afternoon I delivered my farewell lecture to the OR group, on the subject 'Indeterminacy and analytical models in OR'. The Group were as bright and responsive as ever, and we had a most successful session lasting almost three hours.

This evening I have insisted on keeping to myself—the first free time I have had since landing in America.

Saturday 7th May

Today was spent at Chagrin Falls with Professor Ackoff and his family, and we discussed the conclusions of my visit to the Institute at length. Later I had some other discussions with the Deputy Director, Professor Arnoff, at whose home I had dinner. After dinner we spent several hours viewing films of 11 different countries made by the Arnoffs during foreign consultation visits.

Sunday 8th May

The visit to Cleveland is now over. In the early afternoon I flew to Chicago by a DC 7 of United Airlines, and there changed aircraft for the flight west. This was made in the big Douglas Jet, the DC 8, which is a magnificent aeroplane. The flight was made in five and a quarter hours at a height of 29 000 feet. Initially, the ground was completely obscured by cloud, but Nebraska, Colorado, Utah and Nevada, as well as California, were all superbly visible and offered a magnificent and captivating panorama. The route lay directly over Denver and Salt Lake City. The view of

San Francisco Bay as we circled in to land was enchanting, with the Golden Gate and the Bay Bridges standing clear against water shining in the setting sun. A further three hours of sunlight has been gained on this trip, and I am now eight hours behind English time. (As I write this it is 5 a.m., according to the time I set out from Cleveland. It is all rather confusing.)

Professor West Churchman met me at the airport with his wife and son, and took me to his home. There we discussed detailed arrangements for my all too brief visit here. As he lives on a high hill overlooking the city, I was able to view the fairyland of the Bay area when all the lights were on. I am now in an hotel in the centre of the city, from which Churchman will collect me in the morning.

Monday 9th May

This morning was spent on the Berkeley Campus of the University of California, which is a beautiful place engulfed by trees. Two hours were spent in discussion with Mike Montalbano of Kayser Steel, who had asked Churchman for a meeting.

Kayser is the ninth largest steel company in the States, and makes iron from its own ore in four blast furnaces, steel in nine open hearth furnaces, and three LD process converters. The finished products are plates and sections, hot and cold strip, pipe and tin plate. The company is organized in seven divisions, such as operations, sales, control and finance. The finance division is under a treasurer. The control division is headed by a controller who appears to be responsible for accounting as well as research, planning and various other such phenomena. Beneath him there is an 'assistant controller for systems research'.

Montalbano, who is 'manager of operational research and computer planning' is responsible to him, and himself manages two groups, both entitled 'Systems and procedures'. The first of these groups consists of five men and operates in the general office of the company. The second consisting of 25 men is concerned with work activities—mainly production planning and control, although process control (automation) is also its responsibility. The groups have a Burroughs 205 computer, on which they operate management control functions, such as evaluating the importance of cost deviation. Despite this accounting bias, they do not undertake straightforward office work on the machine (such as payroll).

Montalbano seems to have made good progress with the ordering process, in that orders on receipt at the Sales Department are punched on to paper tape and transmitted by teletext (flexowriter) both to the general office and to the works. In the general office this gives the basis for the usual paperwork, and in the mill for production programmes. Montalbano has done a good deal of work on the scheduling problem, and techniques such as queue theory and mathematical programming have been in use. He is, however, in as much difficulty as anyone else with the intractable 'sequencing' problem.

We were both surprised by the great extent to which problems faced by OR in our two companies appear to be identical. His general philosophy of the subject is very like our own, and is soundly based on problems rather than techniques. Again I found that the impression given by American literature of the academic quality of OR in this country is totally misleading. Montalbano is himself a mathematician, but is infinitely more interested in management than in algebra.

By 12 o'clock we had adjourned to the lecture theatre in which the Management Sciences Research nucleus of the University of California had gathered for a seminar. I gave this on the subject 'Artefacts of brain and industry'. There was a varied discussion lasting till 3 p.m. (During this period I was handed a ham sandwich and a cup of coffee—lunch. It seems that efficiency is carried to extremes in this university.)

Ernest Koenigsberg, whom we used to know in England when he worked in OR for EMI, and who is now heading OR for the West Coast branches of the Consultants Touche, Bailey, Niven and Smart, was present. He subsequently drove me to Palo Alto, 30 miles away. Here is Stanford University, and I arrived just in time to deliver a lecture to the Management Sciences Group, and to the Operational Research course (of which Koenigsberg is a tutor, in the capacity of outside lecturer) on the subject 'The organization of OR, and its value as an organizational archetype'. Again, this was an extremely bright audience, and several members of the faculty attended the lecture. Afterwards, we adjourned to Professor Lievemann's house and discussed the state of management sciences in the university. OR is taught in practically every department, and Koenigsberg chooses a group drawn from every quarter of the campus. This campus is again most attractive. Lying south of San Francisco, it appears noticeably warmer—almost tropical in character. The grounds are full of palm trees, eucalyptus, and there are oranges growing in the gardens. The buildings themselves are designed in a rococo style, full of Spanish ancestry.

Subsequently, the whole party returned to the University for dinner, and I arrived back in San Francisco quite late. Nevertheless, this was to be the only time available to visit the famous North Beach and to see the beatniks in residence there. The colony appeared much the same as one can find in London or Paris, and the beatniks are certainly harmless. I hope the same can be said of the coffee-and-mead and the strange green beer that I consumed in their various haunts.

Tuesday 10th May

I am now staying at the Faculty Club at the Berkeley Campus of the University of California, for which the only effective descriptive phrase is the Garden of Eden.

This morning was spent learning from West Churchman about the work done here. The essence of the arrangements made in our field has been the establishment of a basic research institute in management science. This has been established, although it has not filled out yet to its full proportions, and is therefore known at present as the 'Management Science Nucleus'. The institute is fundamentally interdisciplinary, and the heads of the departments of industrial engineering, mathematical statistics, mathematics, psychology, social science, economics, political science, and political administration are all involved in its establishment. It is of course under the direction of Churchman, who is himself Professor of Business Administration.

The concept of the Institute is that it consists of four parts. Firstly, there are faculty members in various departments who will transfer whole or part time to the new Institute. Secondly, there is provision for visiting faculty members who come for a year. Thirdly, people in industry with a strong academic background who wish to take sabbatical leave from their companies in order to do some basic research in a well-defined field acceptable to the university will be allowed to join the group for a year. Fourthly, there are the postgraduate students. Master's degrees are awarded in management science by the departments appropriate to the primary degree. Thus the degree awarded could be Master of Business Administration, Master of Science, or even Master of Arts (for people such as psychologists). The further degree of PhD is awarded in the usual way.

Operational research is taught, with the appropriate slant, in almost every department of the university, but the senior teaching is centred in the Management Science Nucleus, which has now been operating for three years. It accepts no paid contracts whatever (unlike Case), as it is primarily devoted to basic research which is sponsored by grants. However, students do undertake industrial missions as part of their training, although the university demands no fees for this. The group owns an IBM 704 computer, and considerable progress seems to have been made. The projects of which I have had some account so far are as follows.

Professor Fred Balderston and Professor Austen Hoggart are leading a project concerned with the lumber market. There are 'wholesalers' in this trade, who exist merely to scan the supply situation, the retail situation, the state of prices, and then to marry these three things to everyone's satisfaction. Presumably this wholesaler is entitled to be called an entrepreneur—but he never handles the lumber itself! The project exists to examine the system whereby supply is mapped on to demand in this way, and to try to account for and improve the function by the use of decision theory.

Roy Radnor is concerned with a project on the 'theory of teams'. This is again a basic research project in management science, concerning the cost of the transmission of information between members of a research or executive group which can be incorporated into generalized decision models. Professor Jacob Marshak of Yale, who is one of the world's leading mathematical economists, is collaborating in this work and makes visits to Berkeley for the purpose. The other professor who has been released from his departmental work in order to join the Management Science Nucleus is Ron Shepherd, Professor of Industrial Engineering and Operational Research.

The most interesting project of all is an attempt to discover how managerial groups accept advice, and what they manage to do with it when accepted. How ought the advice to be presented if it is to be acceptable? This is of course a vital problem, and it is being tackled by operational gaming. A game has been set up with the following ingenious characteristic. It has an optimal solution. If this solution is adopted by the management group there is room in the plant to make a new product, and a great deal more profit. But this is not obvious, because the room can only be created by clever scheduling and manipulation of resources. Thus the intention of the research is that if the optimal solution is adopted and not exploited, then the group under test does not understand the advice it has agreed to accept.

The research has been going on with 15 different groups who play a game specially devised for these purposes. The structure of the game is changed in order to study the effect of this factor on the acceptance of new ideas. Sometimes the group is left to organize itself. Sometimes it is allotted roles which it is not entitled to change. Sometimes it is allotted roles and can carry on from there—for example, the managing director can sack a member of his staff, or change their roles around.

As for presentation of data, the following device has been adopted. A member of the team (in fact the purchasing officer) is not a genuine player—he is actually a member of the Berkeley faculty. This is not known to the other participants, who do not therefore know that the purchasing officer is armed with the optimal strategy. After about seven passes of the game, it is the purchasing officer's job to put forward the correct solution, and to try and get acceptance for it. A systematic attack on the question of presentation has been made. Sweet reason, dogmatism, explanation, and so on, have all been used in the attempt to convince the managers.

Unfortunately, the main object of the research has so far been foiled in that on only one single occasion has the management team agreed to accept the correct advice. On that occasion, furthermore, they did not understand it, for no attempt was made to exploit the opportunities it offered.

However, various other items of interesting information have emerged. For example, each member of the team becomes rapidly identified with his own role, and insists on ignoring the advice not only of the purchasing officer but of his colleagues. After playing the game for a day, he is inclined to take the attitude 'I have been doing this job all my life and know best'—although he has only been doing it for a few hours. The university is trying to codify the NIH factor, which they say is very potent—the letters stand for 'Not Invented Here'.

Finally, the research has discovered that if the group is making money, it will not undertake the advice offered on the grounds that, as the company is successful, there is either no need to attempt new thinking, or it would be dangerous to intervene in a successful situation. If, on the other hand, the company is in a dangerous state, the argument against innovation is always 'we must concentrate on getting out of the red—there will be time to attempt new ideas when we're safe'. It is interesting to note that postgraduate management students, who have not actually had industrial experience as managers, produce exactly similar patterns.

At noon we adjourned to another of the lunchtime seminars, although today the lunch was better and I did not have to conduct the seminar. Today's meeting was in fact a working party under the chairmanship of West Churchman, to discuss the following problem. The University of California has seven different campuses spread over the whole state. The main libraries are situated at Berkeley and UCLA while the other centres have small libraries that they are trying to expand. At a top-level University meeting it was suggested that it would be inefficient for each college to maintain a full library, but it was objected that unless each did this the service would be inadequate. Thus a group of librarians, sociologists, electronics experts, computer experts, OR scientists, and several more, was set up to discuss whether a project could be formulated to study this question.

It was a privilege to sit in on this working party, and to contribute to it as a member. There was a great deal of discussion on the general information retrieval problem, the literature of which has now reached over 400 items, and to discuss possible models of libraries as communication machines. It was fascinating to see that all present, and especially the librarians themselves, with the sole exception of the OR men present (two professors of operational research, Churchman and myself), were all content to announce a priori what the system is and should be, and to propose that the project should examine the best means of achieving the ends which 'were obvious to all'.

All four OR men present pressed the view that no one knew what the system was, or what it was for, or how it was used, and that it would be necessary to ascertain some facts before pontificating on these matters. A useful decision was reached which allows the information theory man to proceed with his plan for designing a Ramac unit to house abstracts, and the electronic engineering professor to attempt to develop his plan for a scanning system which would identify any reference in 10 microseconds, while the Management Science Nucleus will take up the question of defining the system.

This evening I attended a dinner of the Northern California Chapter of the American Institute of Management, which I addressed on the topic 'New thinking about production control'. This lecture was especially well received, as the audience consisted more of industrial OR men than academics.

RETROSPECT 1992

It was not prudent to record in the diary the experiences of management gaming that we had experienced in Cybor House, although these were certainly shared in California.

We had been running our simulations for a couple of years by this time using teams of senior managers from inside United Steel. We could not have got away with planting spurious players, because everybody knew everybody else. But we did alternate the roles of the players. Thus the chief accountant who suddenly found himself running production, or the production director transformed to the marketing director, would readily admit that he had obtained fresh insight and more sympathy in the process.

Secondly, we closely confirmed the Californian experience whereby the rate at which a player identifies with his role had amazed us. And in general, a group of sceptical and indeed supercilious top management people at 9 a.m. would be transformed by lunchtime into the dedicated managers of a completely fictitious business which we had invented. They could be heard planning new share issues and actually planning coups in the real *business world over the coffee.*

The most remarkable experience we had in Sheffield, which we could hardly credit at the time, was not at all surprising to the Berkeley faculty. It happened on our very first simulation day—when we only thought *that the computer program had been thoroughly debugged, and the most senior management had insisted on 'going first'. The computer manager came to me during the morning coffee break. White-faced, he told me that a frightful mistake had been made. The net effect was that each of the teams believed itself to be in a profit/loss situation which was exactly the reverse of the truth. What to do?*

I decided that honesty was the best policy, and explained to my superiors that this mistake had in fact occurred. I was most apologetic, but this was after all the first of these simulations; would they please forgive us and simply change all the pluses to minuses and vice versa. The teams took this very well indeed. In fact, they assured me that there was no need to worry, they were quite content with the situation as they had depicted it! There was a clear implication that I did not fully understand the business world (although it was one of our own invention) and proceeded with the event as though nothing had happened.

Wednesday 11th May

This morning was spent with Professors Churchman and Ratoosch, working on one of their projects. This has been commissioned by a big firm of auditors, and asks whether the auditors' approach to an accounting system and its effectiveness could not be made more scientific, and more efficient. The team had already constructed logical models of some areas of accounting practice, which effectively means that they can be programmed, and has obtained auditors' approval of their design. Given that an actual system can be measured against this idealized one by logical reduction, what could the measure of its efficiency of operation be? I proposed a measure based on the redundancy of the network as a checking procedure, and suggested that such a measure could be validated by using it as a predictive model of what an auditor would do when confronted with the system. Correlation between the prediction and the facts would validate or otherwise the efficiency of this measure for the purpose. This was agreed, and considerable progress was made in developing the technique.

Professor Radnor entertained me to lunch today, in order to discuss his theory of teams. This was the first disappointing discussion I have had in America, but my host would insist on explaining simple things at great length, and in being unable to explain the features that were really worrying me. Later, I had talks with several other people, but was unfortunately unable to meet either Professor Tarski or Professor Kaman.

This afternoon, under the chairmanship of Professor Varda, the economist, I delivered an address to the whole faculty of Business Administration (which is 70 strong) under the title 'A new look at management science'. This was followed by a lengthy colloquium. As soon as this was over, I rushed to the airport in time to catch my aeroplane (a DC 6 of United Airlines) for Los Angeles. We flew down the Californian coast as the sun was setting with perfect visibility of a breathtaking scene—noting Santa Cruz and Santa Barbara on the way. By the time we arrived at Los Angeles the night was quite dark, giving a brilliant panorama of this vast city. Professor Jackson, Director of the Institute of Management Sciences of the University of California Los Angeles (UCLA) met me at the airport. We drove deviously through the city—along Sunset Boulevard through Hollywood and Beverly Hills. I am at present in a hotel at Westwood, which is adjacent to the UCLA campus where I shall spend most of the next two days.

Thursday 12th May

Feeling, after last night's discussions with Professor Jackson, that there was not a great deal to be gained by spending a whole morning at UCLA, I went to the Rand Corporation, whose headquarters are nearby. I asked to see Dr Murray Geisler, Director of the Logistics Laboratory. Considering that Dr Geisler and his colleagues had not the faintest idea that I was even in America, one of the most incredible coincidences I have ever encountered took place. Dr Geisler had to be fetched from a meeting. It had met specifically to discuss the remarks I had made in opening the discussion at last year's Royal Statistical Society's meeting on Simulation, as reported in the RSS Journal. When Dr Geisler arrived to greet me from his meeting, he held the agenda with an attached stencilled copy of my speech in his hand. He appeared completely stunned!

I spent a very valuable morning at Rand. This is the centre of the activity on men-machine research into American Air Force organization—particularly in the handling of supplies, and the provision of maintenance services. A film of some of these experiments was shown to the department in Sheffield last year, and I investigated the current state of the work, inspecting the rooms with their terraces and one-way mirrors familiar to those who saw the picture. Some very interesting results have emerged from these studies, which I hope I have assimilated.

Bellman, the inventor of dynamic programming, works here, but unfortunately I was unable to meet him. However, I did have a few words with Dr George Danzig, the inventor of linear programming, whose acquaintance it was a pleasure to renew.

At lunchtime, I delivered a lecture 'On actually "doing" operational research' to the Operational Research Course of the Institute of Management Sciences. After this, there were discussions about the work going on at UCLA, where the Management Sciences Department is relatively new. However, there are a dozen people here doing doctoral work in the subject.

This evening I spoke before the Southern California Chapter of the Institute of Management Science to the title 'Uncertainty and automation'. This was well attended by specialists from the campus and outside, and was followed by a discussion lasting until the small hours on the part of a few representatives of UCLA, the Rand Corporation, and the Systems Development Corporation. Dr Dick Green, who heads the Systems Research Group of the last-named organization, is a man of valuable new acquaintance. He is extremely cybernetically oriented, and had a great deal to say in the areas of neurophysiology as well as of computer programming to which he devotes much of his Group's time. He gave a detailed account of the work being done at SDC, some of which will be reported at the ORSA National Conference in New York next week.

It was embarrassing to find I had been knighted in Los Angeles: the place was plastered with notices about 'Sir Stafford's' Lecture, and the chairman had to make a lengthy disclaimer. I felt like a ghastly hybrid of Stafford Cripps and Gavin de Beer.

Friday 13th May

Today was spent at UCLA, and began with discussions with Dean Jacobi, the economist. Following this much time was spent with the personnel of the Western Management Sciences Institute in the company of Professor Jackson. The following are some of the main projects on which they are engaged.

There is a project following the flow of material in a jobbing machine shop. This has taken the form of investigating two disciplines by both mathematical statistics and computer simulation. The latter can handle up to eight machine centres, each containing between one and six identical machines. Useful theoretical results look like emerging from this study, and the only difficulty the team is experiencing concerns the validity of sample runs: the old problem—when to stop the simulation.

Another project deals wth business negotiations, and is investigating bargaining and oligopoly by practical research with human subjects. An interesting empirical study was carried out in an engineering shop to examine the validity of the assumptions made in various forms of queuing theory. Twenty companies had to be investigated by the research team before one was found where sufficient data could be made available. A test of the classical Poissonian model showed a discrepancy between theory and practice of 25 per cent. More advanced models, however, using hyperexponential and Ehrlang distributions reduced this discrepancy to between 3 and 5 per cent. (These are models put forward in Morse's book.)

Yet another investigation concerns inventory control under conditions of uncertain demand distribution. How are confidence limits to be placed on the ordered quantity in these circumstances? This is essentially the non-parametric case in which the form of the distribution is not known although the mean and the variance are. So far the team has managed to demonstrate elegantly that a two-point distribution offers the worst case—which (to be frank) is hardly surprising.

Possibly the most interesting project concerns the use of linear programming for cost allocation in the petroleum industry. Apparently, very big strides are being made with this in practical application. The thesis presented in my own paper (1957) 'Operational research and financial management', namely that the duel of a LP could be used for setting up a system of opportunity costs, has been employed. Certain petroleum companies are forging ahead on this basis with large computers, and contemplate inverting matrices of the order of 1000.

Later in the day I also visited the Western Data Processing Center, which is directed by Professor George Brown. The Center houses an IBM 709 machine, costing 3.5 million dollars. However, IBM offers this machine to all American universities at a 40 per cent discount. If the academic establishment is willing to teach the use of the machine in its business courses, IBM will reduce the price by another 20 per cent. Thus the machine only costs 40 per cent of the market price. In the case of UCLA, moreover, this final 40 per cent was remitted and half the cost of the buildings paid for, on the basis that the university would make the machine available to all western universities. The machine is of course extremely complicated, and has 40 separate units in which it is housed. Most of the programming is done in Fortran, or in the accounting autocode FAP. The computing is the usual form, and the only interesting thing to report is the method of running the laboratory.

This is done on the closed shop principle, whereby only machine minders operate the equipment. A scientist with a job to be done leaves a program and instructions in a pigeonhole in the office, and comes back the next day to collect the answer. This procedure is followed for trivial calculations and the validation of subroutines of major programs alike. If the machine reaches a 'halt' from which it cannot proceed, it signs off the program with as much information about why it stopped as the machine itself can deduce. While carrying out an endless procession of such jobs, the machine classifies and lists them, together with the time taken. I inspected many such lists, and the average time per job appeared to be about one and a half minutes.

The Director claims that by this method between two and three times as much work is done on the computer as can be done in an open shop system. The scientists themselves say they prefer it, as it enables them to proceed step by step, and minimizes the debugging problem. Despite all these assurances, I do not feel very confident in this procedure. However, it may be that with a machine as complicated as the 709 there is no alternative.

I am steadily becoming more impressed with people in these fields in American universities. They are extremely competent, very quick on the uptake, extremely knowledgeable, and above all have a profoundly interdisciplinary outlook which does not seem to be frustrated by the faculties.

A lunch party was held at a restaurant on the very edge of the Pacific Ocean at the famous Malibu beach, and on our return to the campus we fell foul of a Hollywood film unit in the process of shooting scenes for a picture called High Time. In the course of investigating this proceeding I encountered a Mr B. Crosby, who I am told earns a million dollars a year.

I completed my visit to UCLA just in time to catch the 6.30 plane for San Diego, which is a mere 30 minutes flying time away. This was a pleasant interlude in a DC 6 of United Airlines, and I was met at the airport by two representatives of Mr Charles Taylor, the American who, having heard me speak at Cleveland, kindly invited me to spend tomorrow at his home in La Jolla. This evening we have toured San Diego, and driven South to Mexico, and have now returned to La Jolla, which is about 30 miles North of San Diego. I dictate this after a full day at 2 a.m., in a room in the La Jolla country club where I am overlooking the sea which is pounding on the wall below. It has been an eventful day.

Saturday 14th May

Today has, by welcome contrast, been uneventful and relaxed—except for a six hour visit to Daystrom Electronics, of which my host is a senior executive. They are building a solid-state computer, essentially for on-line control, for which they guarantee absolute reliability—under penalty of return of the machine and a refund of the money. So far they have not been caught. Like the RW 300, this machine is a mixed analogue-digital device, which (because of its modular construction) will take a virtually limitless number of analogue inputs. Although it was Saturday afternoon, the place was seething with keen young scientists. They have developed the whole business themselves, including the chemistry and physics as well as the electronics and engineering.

I left La Jolla at 9.15 p.m., and am spending the night in a hotel near the airport at Los Angeles.

Sunday 15th May

This morning at 8.30 a.m. I left Los Angeles on a DC 8 jet mainliner for New York. We flew over Arizona and the Grand Canyon at 33 000 feet, and maintained this height as well as a speed of 650 m.p.h. for the whole journey. The flying time was a mere four and a half hours, although the flight appeared to take seven and a half hours, there being a three hours difference between East and West coast time. After checking in at the Manhattan Hotel, I again called on the Rivetts, with whom I spent the early evening. It seems that a good many reports of my tour have already reached New York.

Monday 16th May

Today I visited the Arthur Andersen Company, the largest consultancy firm in America under a single partnership, and about the third or fourth largest if the combines of consultants are taken into account. The company devotes about a quarter of its business to taxation, a quarter to general management services, and a half to accounting and auditing work. The company has 26 offices in major cities of the United States, and 21 in foreign countries—which number will rise to 50 within five years.

Operational research work was inaugurated five years ago under a well-known OR man, Dr David Hertz. They have a large OR group here at the centre in New York, and OR groups in Chicago, Los Angeles, Atlanta, Detroit and London (this last is that now being inaugurated by B. H. P. Rivett, late head of OR in the National Coal Board). They have about 70 OR men as such in the group, and have budgeted for this figure to rise to 100 within the year. In addition, the company has other specialist groups—one dealing with production control, and the other with electronic computers. These three activities are integrated, much as they are at Cybor House, by the head of administrative services. In addition, they are running extensive training courses for all their consultants in all fields. The idea is to get their senior people fully to understand what operational research is, and how it is done, according to a company 'charter' on the subject prepared by Dr Hertz. It seems that not only is the OR group here allowed to tell its own company what the subject is about and how it should be used, but the company gladly accepts this advice.

I studied as many projects and reports as I could in the time available, and saw that most of it covered fields that are by now traditional OR fields, using techniques which are also orthodox. There was, naturally in this company, an unusual emphasis on accounting work. Four of the jobs which I particularly admired were as follows:

1. A study for a famous fountain pen manufacturer of the changing nature of demand for its products, and a control strategy for gearing production and sales efforts to meet it at minimum cost.
2. A study of the management structure in the department of crew administration for a large airline.
3. A complicated accounting procedure called 'refusal profits', to enable managers rapidly to determine the minimum price at which they could afford to negotiate the sale of a product.
4. A managerial control system for evaluating a very large company's projects and its programme of research, to enable the top management to take decisions about priorities and the use of capital.

A luncheon was held for me attended by three of the senior partners and the whole of the New York OR group. Afterwards I gave them a lecture on 'The philosophy of operational research' which seemed to be well received. I noted that Dr Barry, one of their senior OR men, was vibrating strongly on the same wavelength, when it came to the discussion.

After a very full day, I had dinner at home with the Hertz family, and after this they took me to see the (dreadfully sentimental but brilliantly acted) play on the childhood of Helen Keller entitled The Miracle Worker.

RETROSPECT 1992

This is the same David Hertz who later took on the same role with McKinsey's. He was responsible, some years later, for my receiving a contract to advise on the organization of McKinsey's—who had in the meantime been reorganizing many of the most famous British institutions. . . . It was said at the time that I was possibly the only person alive who had met all *partners of the firm. The senior English-based partner asked for my advice about a contract he had to conciliate between the head of British Steel, Monty Finneston, and his minister, Tony Benn, who were having a public row in the correspondence columns of* The Times. *This was ironic, since I had written to both men just prior to leaving on the McKinsey assignment offering to mediate—in that both were personal friends, and I had been a senior manager in steel. They had each 'declined with thanks'.*

Tuesday 17th May

Today was spent at the New York headquarters of the General Electric Company. This is a vast combine of 100 companies employing a quarter of a million men and women, and responsible for 1 per cent of the national income.

The Management Services organization here is responsible directly to the Chairman of the Board of Directors—even the President of the Company has no authority in the area. The division is divided into nine service organizations, each having a number of sizeable departments. The nine organizations are: management consultation, marketing, research, engineering, manufacturing services, accounting, treasury, employee relations, and a legal department.

There are OR workers in most of the nine organizations, and OR departments are specifically recognized in three. Markovitz operates in manufacturing, Feeney in marketing, while the major group is in management consultation, where it is headed by Dr Melvin Hurni. This department also contains Shubik and Hoffman, both well-known men in the field. Having already in Europe discussed the work of two of these departments with their Heads, I spent today with the Marketing OR Head.

Dr George Feeney is a leading figure in American operational research, and prior to this appointment was Head of OR at the Stamford Research Institute. He is responsible to the Chairman for OR work as applied to marketing throughout the whole General Electric organization. He is armed with a small computer, which is currently being replaced by a RPC 4000.

He told me a good deal about his work, which includes standard studies of prices, advertising, and so forth. Here is a brief note on two of the more unusual applications. The first struck me as one of the cleverest, and also one of the most valuable OR projects I have ever studied.

Given that the price of a commodity has been determined, its distribution cost is known, and some function describing the cost of advertising has been educed by market research, it is possible to produce an OR model of the company/market interaction which will comment on the profit realizable from a given share in the market. In general, it would be possible to obtain an increasing share of the market for a decreasing profit (because of the selling costs involved in obtaining the increase). Many questions now arise, for instance: at what point should one aim at obtaining a share of the market at a given profit, and by what strategies in relation to competition should one proceed to achieve this aim?

In the orthodox game-theoretic model, the structure of the market determines a pay-off matrix from which equilibrial strategies can be deduced. <u>But</u> Feeney is not satisfied that the market structure is understood, and has also discovered by business gaming procedures with members of the higher management that equilibrial strategies are in fact achieved <u>without</u> his knowledge. This seems to be a most remarkable conclusion, and the OR model of the whole situation must contain it.

Accordingly, Feeney has devised a scale of strategies determined by two extremes. The upper limit is given by the 'joint maximum' strategy, in which the company looks at the whole system of the market, and collaborates with its competitors to achieve maximum profit. The model evaluates this figure as an upper bound, although this optimum arrangement is not achievable in practice, because of the anti-trust laws. The lower bound is given by the 'threat' strategy, in which each company looks only at the difference between its own pay-off and that of the opposition, and tries to drive its competitors out of business (this is essentially a price-cutting war). In the 'equilibrial' strategy, the company looks primarily at its '<u>own</u>' reward, and seeks to maximize its profit consistently with neither threatening the existence of competition nor seeking to collaborate with it. If everyone else in the market is playing the equilibrial strategy, then it can be shown that the optimal strategy for <u>this</u> company is to imitate the rest.

Feeney elaborated in great detail the mathematical model by which he mirrors this situation, and accounts for its critical features. He has used it to run more business games by which top management have discovered an insight into the processes they use in reaching this kind of decision, and is now engaged in turning it into a predictive system which will aid management decisions.

Probably the most interesting outcome of the research is to show that if the whole market situation drifts towards a threat strategy, then the management of the most successful company in the field obtains a false picture which leads it, in attempting to apply an <u>equilibrial</u> strategy, to develop a threat strategy. This previously unrecognized feedback is agreed to account for the damaging of relations in the business to which the study has actually been applied.

Furthermore, if the situation is in fact equilibrial, then it can be shown that the management has reason erroneously to think that it is obtaining a maximal profit—which it is not of course doing, because the whole area of collaboration is ruled out. Thus, in the trials that were run, management was unable to predict the potential profitability of the product by a factor of two. This is the mechanism by which the company's own policy imposes a structure on the marketing situation which makes it impossible to approach the upper bound of profit. These demonstrations have apparently been extraordinarily useful to management in their marketing policy, for the field in which the study was done is one of intense competition.

The second point of considerable interest is a methodological one. In adopting a strategy for the search for optimal points in a response surface, the technique of evolutionary operation has been widely studied. As we know, this relies on a random search of the phase-space by sequential small increments, and advances to the target by the steepest ascent technique. Feeney has been using an American method known as 'pattern search'. In this the direction of the last move is projected as the next move, and failure to obtain an increase in the pay-off function then causes the direction of search to move through 90 degrees. It is evident that this causes the search path to follow ridges in the response surface, and thereby to shorten the whole procedure. In fact, Feeney claims that the increased efficiency of this procedure means that the time taken to solve such a problem increases proportionately to the order of the matrix, and not as its cube as one might expect.

There was also discussion of a pattern recognition technique that he hopes to develop on the new computer, in which 32 32-bit words form an array containing a pattern 5-bits square. One does not know whereabouts in the array this pattern will occur, and the problem is to recognize it anywhere in the 'retina'. His intention is to scramble the array by the internal multiplication of the middle 16 bits, and then to revolve the matrix through 90 degrees and repeat the procedure. This will yield a new array rich in interactions between coefficients of the array with the 5×5 area to be recognized.

We left the office at 7 p.m. and returned to Feeney's house in Greenwich Village, where there was a dinner party given by him and his wife for myself, and for three others who have arrived for the national OR conference which begins tomorrow. These were: Russell Ackoff, Professor of Operational Research at the Case Institute; Merrill Flood, Professor of Mathematical Biology and of Operational Research at the University of Michigan; and Jack Lathrop, now with General Electric and until a few weeks ago Head of OR at Lockheed (where he has been leading an OR team in the investigation of the Electra crashes). There was a very potent discussion about the status of the design factor in large complicated probabilistic systems, which was by far the most fruitful of the many arguments in which I have joined on this topic. It went on uninterruptedly for six hours. I am now exhausted.

Wednesday 18th May

The Eighth Annual Meeting of the Operations Research Society of America (ORSA) opened this morning at 9 a.m. I have attended at the Statler-Hilton Hotel all day, although the formal sessions have been devoted to a symposium on the optimization of chemical reactors. Almost all the leading names in American OR are here, and four British Heads of OR groups as well. Apart from myself and Pat Rivett I have noticed Jack Taylor (of BOAC) and Geoffrey Sears (of Shell). I also had a most useful reunion with K. F. Lane, late of Steel, Peech and Tozer, and now with the Carborundum Company of New York.

With today's 'bag' of discussions, I think I can now throw away my list of leading American OR workers whom I have wished to meet and about whose work I have wished to enquire. It seems that operational research in America is dispersed to about the same degree that it is in the United Kingdom, bearing in mind that the population here is about three times the size. However, there is no doubt left in my mind now that the pitch of activity, the level of work done, and the use made of it, are very much greater here than it is in England. The sole exception to this is the American steel industry, in which understanding and use of the work appears to be ludicrous. Earlier discussions and reports were confirmed by a conversation with George Brown of United States Steel who struck me as singularly incoherent. Above all, the government is making remarkably extensive use of OR, not only in military spheres, but in economic and social policy as well.

It is most pleasing to find that the reputation of United Steel stands extremely high with the profession out here. Everyone seems to know a great deal about us, and a large number of people have told me how much they admire the company for its vision in supporting pioneering work in cybernetics. Incidentally, these scientists have in general a far better understanding of the nature and importance of cybernetics than their counterparts in England.

Again, everyone appears to have seen the United Steel film strip on operational research, which has apparently been shown in every relevant university and institution in the country, as well as on all the management training courses and the local courses of large companies. At least two copies of the strip have been in circulation ever since the film was made, and the waiting lists are as long as ever. Four people have told me that United Steel took the lead in the companies in the world where OR is concerned by issuing this film, and assert that it is very much superior to any other attempt at a filmed introduction—such as the three $50 000 films on OR made by the American Management Association. The Head of one Institute, which had already accepted a $10 000 grant to make an introductory film about OR, saw our strip and gave the money back.

This evening I had dinner with a number of members of the Council of the ORSA and other senior workers; long discussions took place about the roles of ORSA and ORSUK in the two countries.

RETROSPECT 1992

The United Steel filmstrip certainly had a vogue. I had written it, and David Owen and I had designed cartoons to accompany the text. These were transformed into coloured stills by a professional artist. We hired the then-famous actor who had an avuncular voice, Norman Shelly, to read the script. The budget for the whole thing was £1000. When the profession heard about this, an insistent demand grew for copies—involving simply the filmstrip and a 33⅓ r.p.m. long-playing record. I wanted to sell this, as evidence that the department understood that the company was in business, but the directors took the lordly view that we could afford to bestow largesse on our less fortunate colleagues around the world. The copies cost only about £5 each; hundreds must have been distributed world-wide.

Thursday 19th May

This morning I visited several sessions of the Conference which is running three separate streams. Four major sessions were involved: production and inventory applications; inventory control theory; arms controls; and scheduling and mathematical programming. With the exception of the session on arms controls, which is of course extremely high level OR in a most intractable field, the remaining papers (of which there were 14) appeared to be heavily technique-oriented. The work on simulation in particular is disappointingly stereotyped. It is built round determinate models of production systems and is primarily concerned with the balance of production lines and the stability of stocks. None of the authors appeared to have any idea how to handle the projects studied under uncertainty, beyond inserting deliberate pieces of mismanagement or mishap into the system to investigate its robustness.

Nothing I heard, at any rate, referred to Monte Carlo techniques as such. The account of the Gest simulation program for the IBM 704 computer, to which I was looking forward, was most disappointing on this account. The presentation of United Steel's general simulation program at the International Conference in September will therefore be an important event. The only trace of any similar work in America that I have been able to unearth is a system based on parametric sampling devised at General Electric, But from what I hear this has nothing like the facilities of the GSP.

At lunchtime I moved rapidly to the Barbizon-Plaza Hotel, where the New York Academy of Sciences Conference on Human Decisions in Complex Systems had already opened. I arrived in time for the opening lunch, and at once encountered to my great delight two old friends—Professor Warren McCulloch and Professor Heinz von Foerster.

Sitting with us, to my intense surprise, was Steve Sherwood, the British psychiatrist and neurosurgeon whom I knew quite well in England. He is a brilliant and original experimental scientist, who I know has (among other things) been concerned with electrode implants in the brain, lysergic acid stimulation of the cerebrum (by which artificial states of psychosis can be induced), and the investigation of neuronal transfer functions. According to McCulloch, the 'aristocracy' of British medicine treated him so badly that he has now emigrated, and is a university professor in this country.

This afternoon I attended a series of excellent cybernetic papers. Lawrence Fogel of Convair (the man who delighted the Second International Conference on Cybernetics in 1953 with his account of aircraft cockpit design) proposed a useful model of decision making which unlike its predecessors discriminates between levels of intelligence. Professor Tanner of Ann Arbor discussed the physiological implications of psychophysical data with a mathematical model recognizing that sensory systems are not fixed. Professor Siegel of the University of Pennsylvania put forward a theoretical model of choice and strategy behaviour, and finally Professor Clive Coombs of the University of Michigan gave a most impressive presentation on the components of risk in decision making.

This is of course the Coombs of decision theory fame. He distinguished between decision criteria aimed at maximizing expected utility, which is associated with a non-linear utility for money, and contrasted with it a new decision criterion which includes a linear utility for money but takes into account variance and skewness in the distributions modelling alternative preferences. During the discussion someone from the Rand Corporation complained bitterly that dynamic programming techniques had not been used in this area, and only wished that Bellman had been present. Professor Julian Bigelow (remembered as one of the early cybernetic symposiasts) who was the official discussant for the afternoon session, failed to explain why, but did give a masterly commentary on the papers presented.

At the end of the session, I attended the official cocktail party given by the New York Academy of Sciences, where I was able to meet both Bigelow and Coombs for the first time as well as a number of old friends. From here I returned post-haste to the OR Conference for its official banquet. This was an informally splendid occasion, at which the retiring President of the Society delivered his valedictory address on 'Uncertainty in operational research'. He is Mr Charles Hitch, whom I have already reported as meeting at Cleveland, and his address was first rate. It was very much in keeping with the Cybor House philosophy of OR. Egotism and embarrassment clashed in an idiotic fashion for me, when a demonstration greeted the Chair's announcement of my own presence at the banquet.

Despite the lateness of the hour, conversation continued for a very long time. At 2 a.m. a group of us was still discussing the possibilities for the extension of game theory in the non-zero-sum region at a rather strange establishment in Greenwich Village.

Friday 20th May

This morning was the last time I was able to devote to the Operational Research Conference, and again I sampled the papers presented—with the same reaction as before. I said goodbye to my American OR friends at lunchtime, and left the Statler-Hilton Hotel for the New Yorker to attend a special lunch.

This lunchtime meeting concerned arrangements for the Second International Conference on Operational Research, to be held at Aix-en-Provence in September. This has been organized by a European Committee meeting in London, attended whenever possible by representatives of the other 14 operational research societies of the world—notably the Societé Francaise de Recherche Opérationnelle, which as the host society, always sends a representative. The American end has been handled by a committee meeting in New York. This luncheon meeting enabled Rivett and myself, as members of the main European committee, to meet with the New York committee and discuss the whole programme and the administrative issues involved.

I left this luncheon just in time to rush to the Barbizon-Plaza Hotel for the afternoon session of the New York Academy of Sciences meeting. This session was devoted to a discussion of that most critical function of the brain, the reticular formation of the brainstem. This was of particular interest to me, as the research on which I have been working for the Templeborough Rolling Mills project is at its weakest link with the reticular model. This is because so little is known of this part of the brain, and therefore it was a great opportunity and privilege to be present at this session. The Chairman was that authority on medical physics, Professor L. H. van der Tweel of Holland.

The first paper was given by Professor Scheibel of the University of California on 'The anatomy of the reticular formation'. He expounded the very latest discoveries in this area. He showed a large number of incredible pictures which revealed a great deal not hitherto suspected about the logical structure of this archetypal control system. In particular, it is clear that individual cells of the ascending reticular system are extremely large and highly ramified. The pictures clearly exhibit dendritic processes providing feedback loops to the axons, which bypass the neuronal somata altogether. The reticular cells themselves are very large, and Scheibel estimates that there are about 10^6 or 10^7 of them. Physical connections between neurones are not as numerous as had been suspected, but on the other hand, Scheibel believes that no less than 4000 neurones in the neighbourhood of a particular node may indeed be affected by that central neurone by means of cross-talk. If this turns out to be true, the reticular formation is not less, but even more, ramified than had been thought.

In the early evening I left New York for Connecticut where I am to spend the weekend at Whippoorwill, Old Lyme, the estate of Warren McCulloch. Also travelling with us for the weekend was Steve Sherwood (who was mentioned earlier in this diary), Clinical Professor of Applied Neurophysiology at the University of Chicago. We travelled the 120 miles from the outskirts of New York City by car on the new Blue Star highway, which has a speed limit of 60 m.p.h., in exactly 2 hours 5 minutes. This road is a revelation. There is no passing as the slow lane keeps to itself, and the two fast lanes went forward steadily at 60 m.p.h. The only halts are at the toll gates, positioned every twelve and a half miles, where the car has to be stopped. A quarter dollar is thrown from the car into a wire basket, and is then 'read' by the machine. Immediately the traffic signal changes to green and an illuminated sign says 'Thank You', whereupon you proceed. This seems to be an extremely intelligent way of running, and paying for, the highway.

Whippoorwill, where I am dictating this, turns out to be an extremely old house, having seventeenth-century foundations showing a marked Tudor influence. The bulk of the house was built the following century on the lines of many New England houses built by the colonists. To my intense astonishment I found that they were all prepared from plans provided by the British Government, according to designs especially made by Sir Christopher Wren. There is also an unmistakable Wren church in the township of Lyme itself.

Saturday 21st May

Warren McCulloch, Steve Sherwood and I have spent the whole day tramping the woodlands of the McCulloch estate, and arguing. The estate covers 400 acres of woodland and is incredibly lovely. The ground formation is extremely irregular, having been formed by glaciers, and we examined a most interesting geological pattern of granite, feldspar, quartz, and mica. Two streams were dammed by McCulloch himself in the 1930s in order to create a lake of some 4 acres extent, in which fish abound. The flora include all the typically American bushes, trees and shrubs. Many interesting berries, fruits and flowers were remarked—as well as poisonous plants, parasitic growth and examples of symbiosis. As to fauna, we saw a great many varieties of frog, many beautiful butterflies and two large black snakes—one of which was over 3 ft long—belonging to the Constrictor Group. The farm itself breeds horses, and has a few sheep.

Apart from the house itself, all the other buildings on the land were erected personally by McCulloch. He began life as a blacksmith before rising to become one of the world's leading authorities on the brain. He is his country's foremost authority on cyanide, and developed the nerve gases invented during the war when working for the chemical warfare department. The most impressive of the buildings is the famous 'garage' which is still in the course of construction—as it has been for the last 30 years. This is a cruciform structure, 120 ft long, which was not only designed but built by McCulloch and the many visiting scientists who have spent vacations with him here. The vast concrete floor was laid in sections, and bears the signatures in the wet cement of many helpers: among Englishmen, those of Ross Ashby and Donald Mackay. Einstein had a summer residence in Lyme too.

The evening found the three of us, together with McCullouch's wife, daughter and son-in-law (who is a statistician at the Submarine Research Center), sitting in this ancient kitchen demolishing a great pile of lobsters with nutcrackers and bare hands, and washing them down with white Bordeaux. We have been arguing about the control of complex systems for nearly 24 hours—a day I shall never forget!

RETROSPECT 1992

The reason why the garage was so enormous was that McCulloch had become fascinated with the problem of how a large diameter could be spanned in a cruciform structure without the roof falling in!

The reference to a 24-hour day was correct. We had set off on our walk at about 6 a.m. The three family members at the informal dinner went to bed, leaving the three cyberneticians to continue with a seemingly unending supply of lobsters, bread, butter and Bordeaux. The proceedings terminated outside in the yard, when we three took a cold shower to get rid of the

remnants and retired to bed well past five in the morning. It was indeed a day I never forgot. See sonnet on p. 228.

Sunday 22nd May

Today has been spent in much the same way as yesterday, 'relaxing' on the estate at Old Lyme. Steve Sherwood left for New York at 4 o'clock, and Warren and I set off at 6 p.m. for Massachusetts. This involved a drive of a further 120 miles through New England (including a crossing of the Thames into New London). We came out of the state of Connecticut, crossed the state of Rhode Island, and so into Massachusetts, passing through Providence and Boston. Cambridge, where I am now, lies on the other side of the River Charles from Boston itself, and is the home of the Massachusetts Institute of Technology as well as of Harvard University. I am now in the McCullochs' second house, a couple of miles from MIT, where I shall be his guest for the next three days.

Monday 23rd May

I have spent the entire day talking to members of McCulloch's group. These include a number of professors in the fields of psychiatry, neurophysiology, electronics, and so on—the component parts of the science of cybernetics. Probably the most notable character among them is Gerry Lettvin, the man who did the work on the correspondence between the eye and the brain of the frog. This is extremely interesting work which relates directly to the question of the nature of the correspondence between inputs to a control system and the mappings thereby created inside the machine. The whole question of sensory configuration is involved.

I have had long discussions with McCulloch himself, with his two research assistants, with Professor Patrick Wall (the physiologist) and with Professor Lettvin (who is both psychiatrist and mathematical biophysicist). In addition, Diane Hitchcock is visiting from Ramo-Wooldridge Company, and her presence (she is a doctor of philosophy who is operating precisely in the field of industrial control) was a considerable stimulus to the practical relevance of the conversations. These, as usual, went on far into the night, and brought in the famous Walter Pitts (collaborator of McCulloch), a notoriously difficult character with whom to communicate. Christine Kris, who used to be a psychologist at University College of London, and who is known to me, was also involved. She is now a mathematical biophysicist at MIT.

This was in all, an interesting and profitable day. What impresses me most is that all these people are extremely aware of the likely importance of the structure of the reticular formation of the brainstem as a key to the nature of organic control for industrial processes. I am still learning about this amazing piece of machinery all the time.

Tuesday 24th May

The morning was spent with three of McCulloch's group. Manuel Blom of Venezuela and Leo Verbeek of Holland have been developing von Neumann's work on probabilistic logics in conjunction with some of Shannon's ideas, and have produced a network theory for superimposition on the McCulloch-Pitts neurones which gives a reliability against error of very high order. For very small systems this is less than Shannon's figure, but for very large systems it is an improvement by a factor of 3000 on the von Neumann theory.

The third member of the group is McCulloch's star disciple, Hermann Berensen—also of Holland. He is a mathematical biophysicist, who has been working on the dispersion of water in the nervous system. He has produced an exceedingly elegant theory which shows how the big organic molecules are surrounded by a lattice inside which are trapped molecules of water. The long thin molecule around which this model is built is collagen, which has a helical structure. This is surrounded at angles of 36 degrees by a lattice of oxygen atoms—that is to say the latter is pentagonal. There is one proton on each bond of this lattice. The point is that one molecule of water is 'locked' in the middle of each space created by the pentagonal lattice, and that this molecule is not bound to four others as would normally be the case. This structure for water is derived from that of ice rather than the liquid form—they call it an 'icy' structure. Potassium can be accommodated within this structure, but sodium cannot. This they believe to be the explanation of the 'sodium pump' which expels sodium from the cell.

This theory accounts for three things:

1. The distance between collagen fibres in tendon (which is exactly that required to account for this bonded pentagonal lattice structure thought to surround each).
2. The peculiarly intrinsic containedness of water in the living cell—which is certainly not free.
3. The relative permeability of the cell membrane to potassium and sodium, which it is most difficult to account for by any other theory (although, oddly enough this same relative diffusion is found through glass).

On the first point, they wish to go on to the problem of explaining the spacing of the minute threads inside axons and dendrites, which under the electron microscope appear to have a hexagonal structure.

All this is relevant, extremely relevant, to the question of the analogue of fabric in cybernetic machines. The biggest snag in our present theory concerns the need for amplifiers interspersed throughout circuits which have self-organized (in colloidal systems, for example). It is clear that the potassium/sodium disbalance propagates nerve impulses in the body, and we must understand the mechanism if we are to imitate it.

Towards the end of the morning I interviewed Dr Duguid, and at lunchtime Dr Ludley. Both these members of Brown University had applied (independently) to Cybor House for positions in the department in answer to our advertisements, and have stood up well to examination by correspondence. Comments on the applications by these gentlemen are being prepared separately.

This afternoon I have visited the Lincoln laboratories of MIT, some 15 miles out of Cambridge. I went there with Professor Marvin Minsky, of Automata Studies fame, from whom I gained some conception of the extent to which cybernetics is now being taught in the United States. He showed me 40 terminal papers by his own students of emphatically cybernetic characteristics: neuronal net theories, learning systems, adaptive systems, models for language translation, and many more.

At the Lincoln Laboratories we saw the famous computer TX-2, the fastest computer in the world (until STRETCH comes into operation). This is a vast research computer, mostly transistorized. It depends entirely on core storage, which is located in a large block of 65 000 words, but which is also disseminated throughout the machinery in small subsidiary units. The packaging is quite clever, but the operators deplored the absence of a drum. The machine derives its great speed, which may be up to 60 times that of an IBM 704, by programming tricks rather than superior electronics. The word length is variable, and there are overlapping codes which economize in space and therefore time.

I also saw something of the research on linguistics. These people have printed out enormous amounts of artificially generated scripts based on two-, three- and four-letter probability sequences—the four-letter combination, as we know, produces a great deal of intelligible English. Work is also going on here in the generation of artificial speech, and in many other cybernetic fields.

It is the home of Oliver Selfridge and his 'Pandaemonium' machines. The special purpose exemplifications of these have been passed to other institutes, and the research is now going on entirely inside computers which have been programmed to work in terms of Panaemonium pattern recognition circuitry. This is what the Americans, following such logicians as Peirce, are inclined to call 'abduction'. Today's proceedings included a spirited argument with McCulloch on whether this category was a necessary adjunct to the dichotomy of induction and deduction—which I do not believe. But the argument that abduction could be inferred from the other two did not convince McCulloch.

Tonight, many hours have been spent with Diane Hitchock. We argued through my Illinois text in great detail.

Wednesday 25th May

Today I met for the first time Professor Norbert Wiener, the founder of cybernetics. His first words to me were: 'I have become increasingly conscious that the growing reputation of my work in Europe derives in large measure from your lectures and writings, and from the fact that you have built Cybor House. For this I should like to thank you.' This was an unexpected pronouncement in any number of ways.

He wanted to know a great deal about our work and ideas, and appeared greatly excited by them. He was full of admiration for United Steel, which had sponsored these efforts, and expressed the view that our management must be decades ahead of most American managements. Wiener is an old man now, and it quite evidently made him happy to feel that the work that he inaugurated is proceeding under its own volition. This very day is his retirement luncheon from MIT. He will be seen increasingly in Europe, where he has been invited to join a number of directorates dealing with cybernetic subjects.

Wiener believes that the emphasis on digital computers has been a great mistake, and that analogue mechanisms are now due to come into their own. He particularly recommended some work by Gabor at Imperial College which he thinks will produce a very cheap multiplier. I expressed the view that the analogue computer had been just as misdirected as the digital, that the alleged dichotomy between them is a myth, and that the future would lie in machines which (like the brain) had strictly indivisible manifestations of both modes. Wiener took this argument enthusiastically, and at last went on to tell me of his own work in recent times, which seems to have been concentrated on the mathematical analysis of brain rhythms—using a digital computer.

In the afternoon I met, also for the first time, Professor Claude Shannon, the founder of information theory. I enquired earnestly after his work in the years since his famous book was published—to become a scientific classic in a very short span. It appears that he has devoted himself almost exclusively to the problem of error probabilities in optimal codes for input devices. He gave me a transcript of that part of the work which deals with Gaussian noise, and showed me the full report of the work which is in the course of being written. I hope to receive this after a few months. It is all too clear that if the problem of error probability <u>inside</u> artefacts is itself solved, on the lines of von Neumann's probabilistic logic and McCulloch's extensions thereof, while the equivalent input problem remains unsolved, there will have been little advance in the <u>practice</u> of control theory.

Shannon was extremely interested to know what we were doing, and I gave him a considerable account of our activities. He was especially interested in the thought that cybernetic principles can transform OR. Everyone here of any intellectual stature seems worried about the dominance of OR by its own methodology, and by the limitations of the latter where large complex systems are concerned. There is also general agreement here as in England that this is largely due to the misapplication of OR in tactical instead of strategic fields. He was most interested in Tocher's heuristic machine for investigating homeostasis, in the ideas on which Cuninghame-Green is working, and in my own logical model of mitosis.

I was glad I mentioned the latter, because it led Shannon to tell me about the work von Neumann was doing just before he died, which has not yet been published. This was also to do with the logical properties of growth and reproduction (which of course von Neumann has always clearly seen to be of great relevance to any control theory of a self-organizing kind). Apparently von Neumann's idea was that each cell would have a large number of states—apparently not the same as the changing states of my cells which are determined by the stage of growth. I am unable to discover where von Neumann's papers are, nor whether anyone is actively engaged on editing their posthumous publication. 'No one is indispensable', they say, and von Neumann's death did not halt the progress of science. But it certainly applied a most effective brake.

Shannon, like Wiener and indeed everyone else, enquired after Gabor's learning machine. Question: are we missing something, or has Gabor a publicity agent in America?

I have kept away from the MIT Operational Research Group, because I have already had a long discussion with its Head, Dr Gallagher, in New York. They do not appear to be doing anything unique, and the pressing invitations to visit the group seemed as usual to be bound up with the idea that I should give a seminar. There have been better things to do.

Throughout this period I have been living at the McCulloch house, and sharing most of the 24 hours with Warren. His learning is of enormous breadth, his insights truly remarkable, and his relaxed manner with people of all ages and dispositions towards him, an inspiration. He knows exactly how seriously to take life, and also himself. He is completely nonconformist, and his intimate collaborators are usually very young men indeed. Two of his present assistants are only 18, and when Pitts collaborated on the new classic original paper on neural nets, Pitts was only 16.

It appears that Walter Pitts ran away from school at the age of 14, on the ground that he knew more than any of the teachers, and was thereupon disowned by his people. He went to Chicago, where he met Bertrand Russell, whom he cross-examined on the Principia. Russell was so impressed that he sent Pitts to Carnap. From there Pitts sent Wiener various criticisms of the latter's work which so impressed Wiener that he used him as an assistant for a time. It was thus that Pitts came to meet McCulloch.

Everyone in America seems to regard Pitts as a complete genius, likely to destroy anyone on his own ground with chapter and verse. He lives with McCulloch, and seems to work and sleep in alternate weeks. He emerged once during my visit, and not surprisingly I found him totally incommunicable.

I felt very sad in my leavetaking of McCulloch this evening: a great scientist and a great man.

Tonight I flew from Boston and am now in Baltimore.

RETROSPECT 1992

Walter Pitts was the co-author with McCulloch in 1943 of a seminal paper widely quoted to this day, called 'A logical calculus of the ideas immanent in nervous activity'. Many stories could be told about him. He was living at this time in the attic of McCulloch's house, and could rarely be persuaded to come downstairs: his food was left at his door for the most part. It was a terrible blow to McCulloch when Pitts finally committed suicide.

Norbert Wiener, as founder of cybernetics, was of course my great hero. The text underplays the drama of our first meeting. I had been with McCulloch, and had no appointment with Wiener. As I left to try and see him McCulloch said: 'A word of advice—don't tell him that you've come from me.' This was a reference to their well-known falling-out; and it was with a mixture of amusement and sadness that I heard Wiener say almost the same thing to me when I was leaving to see McCulloch on a later occasion.

Wiener's secretary was loath to say that I had come, since I had no appointment, but I finally persuaded her that I simply wanted to shake the great man's hand. She went into him in front of me and there was a great cry. By the time I got into the room, Wiener had almost vaulted his desk to embrace me. His words were as formal as I had recorded them: the whole incident was a great surprise. However, my first book, Cybernetics and Management, *had been published a year earlier (1959), and Wiener had read it.*

On what was to be the last of my visits to MIT four years later, Wiener (with whom I never actually corresponded) told me of his plans to visit Europe. He was coming to England, but had nowhere to stay. I invited him and his wife to my house, and was thrilled when they agreed. Their room was already aired and flowers in place, when I received a phone call from Stockholm just before they were due to fly to London. It was Mrs Wiener to say that Norbert was dead.

It is embarrassing to note that when I wrote above 'Wiener is an old man now', he was 66—the same age as I am today!

Thursday 26th May

The early part of this evening was spent in meeting various members of the faculty at the Johns Hopkins University, and discovering what their basic set-up is. Much of their practical OR work seems to be going on in the local hospital, and they are closely in touch with Reg Revans, Professor of Industrial Administration at Manchester University, who is doing the same kind of thing.

At 11 o'clock we drove out to the Applied Physics Laboratory, which is run for the nation by the Johns Hopkins University, and is some 30 miles out of Baltimore. Here there was a formal reception awaiting my arrival, followed by lunch. At 2 o'clock I began my big East Coast lecture on the topic 'Automation and uncertainty', in a large and extremely well-equipped auditorium, to an audience of several hundred scientists. The nucleus of this audience comprised three OR groups: those from the Applied Physics Laboratory itself; from the Johns Hopkins University in Baltimore; and from the Federal Operations Research Office at Washington. Ellis Johnson himself had made the trip, which pleased me greatly. Motley collections of scientists had arrived from other places too, as there was a fleet of hired buses outside the Laboratories.

The session lasted the whole afternoon, and the audience was extremely responsive. Physicists complained that they did not understand the chemistry, chemists that they did not understand the mathematics, mathematicians that they did not understand the biology, and so on. We ended up with each group of specialists vouching for that part of the address that dealt with its own subject, a happy state which was not achieved without a good deal of cross-questioning, and there was plenty of excitement. The industrial economists were especially enthusiastic, and provided an interesting contrast to their counterparts at Oxford where I had so big a battle last year.

We got back to the university just in time to attend a sizeable reception given for me by the Dean of the Faculty of Engineering Sciences, to which large numbers of people had been invited. Afterwards, I had dinner with the Dean and a small party, where the conversation turned mainly on politics and international relations as well as industrial affairs.

Incidentally, I saw the President giving his personal account from the White House of the failure of the Summit talks on television last night. He appeared old and ill. The marks of his recent strokes were upon him in the form of speech impediments, and what was much worse, a coach and horses could have driven through the logic of his arguments. Tonight, no one present seemed to entertain a more optimistic interpretation than this, although the President's brother, Dr Milton Eisenhower, who is President of the Johns Hopkins University, has today said that he regarded the speech as 'too apologetic'. Everyone seems to assume that the Vice-President, Mr Richard Nixon (generally known as 'tricky Dicky'), will be the next occupant of the White House, but I have not found anyone, from porters and taxi-drivers to professors and industrialists, who will admit to supporting him.

I have been learning a good deal about American industry, one way and another, and about industrial relations. Industry here complains of being bedevilled less by such things as operational research and cybernetics as by restrictive practices. The most fantastic such practice of which I have ever heard operates here in the printing industry, and is perhaps worth recording.

Advertisements are normally composed outside the newspaper offices, by publicity agencies and companies who send in the completed matrix. This is held to work the newspapers' own compositors out of a job, and therefore a longstanding agreement has it that the advertisement must be set up again in the newspaper office, as near as possible to the original, after which it must be printed, proofread, corrected—and then thrown away!

This copy is known as a 'bogus' (as well it might be). Recently, a big surge of activity on a New York paper resulted in a backlog of boguses of no less than 12 000 columns. This is now being worked on under intense pressure, and overtime is paid at time-and-a-half.

The newspaper business is a sick industry over here, and papers all over the country are having to merge to remain in business. Managers are effectively abdicating, as I have heard them do in the cotton and shipbuilding industries in the United Kingdom, by declaring there is 'nothing they can do'. Far from exemplifying the survival motive which we have tried to model in industrial cybernetics, such men seem to be bent on suicide.

Friday 27th May

This morning I went through the organization of operational research at the Johns Hopkins University. The leading spirit is Dean Roy himself, and there are two key men: Professor Charles Flegel, whose speciality is OR in organization (but who teaches mainly stochastic processes and simulation theory), and Professor Elli Naddor, whose speciality is the industrial field (and who teaches primarily inventory theory and other similar techniques). The necessary instruction in statistics, probability theory, economics and other sciences, is given by the appropriate departments by arrangement. The courses for graduate students and others, as well as for industry (the coverage is rather on the lines of Birmingham University), seem very sensible, if somewhat too technique-oriented. It must be remembered, however, that this organization is at the academic heart of the university. There are more problem-oriented groups at the Applied Physics Laboratory, and the Operations Research office in Washington—both of these being administered by the university. Taking all three groups together, the operational research effort here is enormous.

This afternoon I enjoyed a most interesting experience. I was invited to join the Board of Examiners who were orally to examine Mr Robert Connor, as the final step in his acceptance as a Doctor of Engineering in Operational Research. The examiners were the three members of his own faculty mentioned above, three other professors of the university (including the Professor of Statistics), and myself.

Connor's thesis concerned an OR study of the organization of the hospital, which had led to considerable changes and a marked gain in efficiency. He was much to be credited on creating his data by ratio delay studies which he carried out himself, and for handling the figures sensibly and with a lot of statistical insight. This attempt to create a model, led to an entirely new classification scheme for patients, based on the amount of care the patient requires in terms of nursing, linen, and the use of other hospital facilities. This classification replaces the orthodox one in which patients are classified by diagnosis.

From this, a control system is built up which permits a dynamic approach to staffing and the provision of stores, based on the population of the hospital at this moment. Connor has a very cybernetic insight into the need to keep the organization fluid and provide means for measuring changes taking place and rules for viable adaptation. The outcome is an elegantly simple system.

The candidate was cross-questioned for two solid hours by the examiners, an ordeal to which he responded well. I found the whole proceedings stimulating, and finally threw my vote in with confidence that he should be awarded his doctorate. He was—unanimously.

After inspecting various other university facilities, I had dinner with the Dean, and then spent the remainder of the evening with the Flegels at their home.

There is a final and amusing point. The British Ministry of Health is sending out a team to find out about the operational research done here in hospitals. One wonders whether they are aware that Britain also knows about operational research, and that in particular, Professor Revans at Manchester has dedicated his whole professional effort to the introduction of operational research techniques in British hospitals. I recall with sadness the abortive outcome of the attempts I made a few years ago to advise the Governor of St George's Hospital in London about operational research, despite the fact that the talks were held at his own request.

Saturday 28th May

Having spent the morning looking round Baltimore and doing some necessary shopping in the pouring rain, the rest of the day has gone in more social activities. I attended two academic cocktail parties—one of which the President of the University, Dr Milton Eisenhower, attended—and met many more interesting people. A farewell dinner party, organized by Dean Roy, lasted far into the night.

Sunday 29th May

Today I flew from Baltimore to Chicago. It was a pleasant and uneventful ride, and I am now writing in the Bismark Hotel. It is a grey and wet evening and a singularly grimy and unattractive looking city.

Monday 30th May

Today I have been compelled, much against my will, to take part in a national holiday—Memorial Day. This is a vast spree dedicated to the memory of those who have died in war. Originally, I understand, it commemorated the Civil War itself. Thus, the day is less soundly observed in the South than it seems to be up here, where even the most important activities seem to be suspended.

I have made considerable efforts to get in touch with various of my contacts in Chicago, and been met for the most part with a barrage of recorded messages declaring with insufferable sang-froid that the place is closed down for the day, but if I would like to leave a message it would be recorded. After the $\underline{n}$th call, I was sorely tempted. However, I have explored Chicago fairly thoroughly, and have been able to ruminate over some of my experiences. Possibly a day's relative rest at this point has not done any harm.

Tuesday 31st May

The normal programme was resumed today with a visit to the Chicago offices of Arthur Andersen and Company, whom I previously visited in New York. The purpose of this visit was to meet the senior partners, Mr Walsh and two others, who specialize from this office in operational research, and who have done a good deal of OR work in steel companies. Unfortunately they do not include the very large ones, but I find that a considerable amount of production control activity has gone on.

The most interesting of the projects they described concerns the use of OR in optimizing the profitability of a steel warehouse. They have a realistic approach to the cost of buying a lot of stock, and have listed no fewer than 19 variables which bear on the cost of holding that piece of inventory. They have realized that no purchasing officer could possibly cope with a matrix of order $19 \times \underline{n}$ items of stock. They therefore approach it via linear programming, and are aware of the solution to the Kahn warehousing problem. They are also conscious, however, that this model is inadequate to the solution of their problem, which is overlaid with sequencing difficulties. They feel that if they can develop a general solution, a great deal of business will fall into their laps—as no doubt it will.

Professor Brown, whom I had hoped to see, is unfortunately out of town. His colleague at Northwestern University, John Bowman (who is Dean of one of the schools) was not available either, but I am due to meet him in Illinois so no harm has been done there. David Cox (the consultant with whom I have been corresponding about cybernetics) and I have been leaving each other messages all over Chicago throughout the day, but we have unfortunately failed to meet.

Wednesday 1st June

In company with Mr H. J. Ritter and Mr F. B. Morrow, district office managers of the respective parts of the Addressograph-Multigraph Corporation, I travelled out to Hammond, Indiana, and visited the works of Inland Steel. This was in fulfilment of the arrangements made in Cleveland.

The steel identification scheme is very much as expected, but I am glad to have had the opportunity to examine all the equipment in detail, and to talk to the local managers about it. Everything is very smooth as far as production of the completed Addressograph plates is concerned, so we know that the information handling side of the business is entirely possible.

However, from this point the difficulties begin. The plates are sent down a shute to a point beside the start of the slab bank, where slabs pause under a water spray. A man picks up the plate, fits it into the welding gun, and proceeds to spot weld it on to the end of the slab. If he makes only one weld, the plate is inclined to fall off, so he makes several, and I noticed later (on the cold slab) that this sometimes partially obscures the information embossed on it. This is in all respects a rather stupid operation. Clearly this phase of the business should be made automatic, and I do not think that this would present very great difficulties. I inspected the identification plates on several hundred cold slabs, and noted that the efficiency of the process is about 80 per cent. One of the problems is clearly that the slabs with bad surfaces have to be flame dressed, and when this is done, liquid metal runs over the end of the slab. This festoons the identification plate rather prettily, but makes the information embossed on it illegible. Notwithstanding these difficulties, the mill manager seemed to feel that the scheme had given him a great deal, and would in time be perfected. They were experimenting with other methods of welding, and next week bring into operation a riveting process for trial.

I had a general look at the works, naturally, and was impressed by the fact that practice in our Company seems to be more advanced than in Inland Steel. However, their approach to information handling is more adventurous.

Inland operates 300-ton fixed open hearth furnaces. One of the managers said to me: 'I guess that you don't have furnaces that size in Britain.' I replied that at Appleby-Frodingham we had 500-ton open hearths, and could not resist adding: 'But of course I realize the comparison is not strictly valid, because ours tilt.' This comment produced the required result.

After rather a tiring day, I intercepted the train running from Chicago to St Louis at a place called Homewood. There was over an hour to spare before the train arrived, so my hosts challenged me to a swimming contest in which the honour of Britain was upheld!

This was my first experience of an American train, and this particular railway appears to be very highly organized indeed. The platform is demarcated into zones, and passengers are told in which zone they should stand to meet the carriage in which their reservation has been made. There was none of the scramble familiar on British Railways. I travelled in a Parlour Car, in which separate armchairs are arranged along the two walls of the coach. There are no separate compartments, and the impression is one of a hotel lounge. The journey to Champaign, Urbana, Illinois, took an hour and a half, and I arrived at 7.30 p.m. to be met by Professor Heinz von Foerster who is organizing both my visit to the University of Illinois and to the Symposium on Self-Organizing Systems. It was a very happy reunion, and I had dinner at his house with his family, where we remained talking until a very late hour.

Thursday 2nd June

Today has exclusively been spent in conversation with von Foerster and George Zopf. At last I have the full details of the 'biological computers' on which this group has been working, and understand the networks they have constructed for the purpose. This work has not yet been published, and although we have known about it, no details have hitherto been available.

The network theory is constructed from McCulloch-Pitts neurones, but continues the mathematical analysis into the deeper layers of the cortex. Thus we not only have McCulloch's 'reliable nets constructed from unreliable neurons' but a mathematical account of pattern recognition of a most ingenious kind. The full development of this theory involves a three-valued logic mapped on to the traditional area-corner-side trichotomous classification of topology. All this work leads to as elegant a solution of the character recognition problem as I have yet seen, and couples with it the benefits of error-free transmission from a noisy input, or for that matter from breakdown in the network. The vast importance of these developments for practical control applications could hardly be overemphasized.

Tonight I have been at a dinner party with the relativist physicist Professor McVitie and his wife, and the Welsh economist Brinley Thomas who is a visiting professor here this year. The discussion centred mainly on problems of education in the two countries, but also touched on scientific matters.

I have now discovered who has the von Neumann papers: it is a Professor Taube at this university, but he will not let anyone see them! I hope he is doing a good job. Incidentally, Sherwood has all Kenneth Craik's papers (including the MS of 'The nature of explanation') and is working on them now. Something should be done to stop the world's most brilliant minds from dying so young. Craik was (what?) 26 when he was knocked off his bicycle and under a car, and Sholl cannot have been 40. I heard of his death (lung carcinoma) last week.

Friday 3rd June

The morning was spent with the group here discussing their work in control mechanisms and cybernetic artefacts. Notably, George Zopf is very much in line with our thinking. A visiting professor from Sweden, Lars Löfgren, who is basically a mathematician, has developed an ingenious technique for self-repairing control systems, to be published at the forthcoming Symposium.

At luncheon I had the honour to be the guest of the 'Sedition Club'.This is an extraordinary organization consisting of the most senior members of this university, including a Nobel prize-winner in chemistry, McVitie, and the heads of eight other departments of science. Their object is to discuss frontier research in interdisciplinary fields. I gave them a talk on 'Management cybernetics', and the reception was both alert and kindly. The occasion lasted for two and a half hours instead of the normal hour and a half.

The afternoon was again spent with von Foerster, working on the theory of control networks. I have become so friendly with von Foerster the well-known cybernetician, that I admit I had forgotten von Foerster the well-known physicist. He is an Austrian who was annexed by the Germans, and who spent the war directing electronic research in Berlin. He is a leading authority on microwaves, and was in fact the man who developed the German airborne radar, using the short wave length of 9.5 cm. He was still in Berlin when the end came, and escaped to Silesia from the burning city. There he fell foul of the Russians, and was eventually rescued by the Americans who brought him to Illinois University.

In addition to all his work here on cybernetics, he is Professor of Electrical Engineering, and has continued his research in the microwave field. In 1952 he made the first direct observation of the bunching action of electrons in a klystron operating at a frequency of 3 kw c.p.s. He was much honoured for this work, and I have seen the original photographs taken at this time.

To do this, he provided the klystron—a microwave amplifier operating at a wavelength which cannot be achieved with a triode—with wave guides. The wave guide has a pulsating field which causes the electron beam to oscillate, and by using two guides intersecting at right angles, the mode of oscillation can be turned into a circular path, which writes and rewrites the story of the behaviour of the stream and enables it to be observed. The bunching of electrons is caused by the accelerated particles overtaking the decelerated particles from the klystron source, and the write/rewrite principle generates a travelling wave very much faster than the electron speeds themselves. In fact, the writing speed of this original electron beam was seven times the speed of light. The arrangement has an incredible time resolution—of one micro-micro second. Thus the speeds attainable by man in measuring instruments (and ultimately in information handling capacity, one suspects) are enabled to break through the relativistic barrier of the speed of light. Not, indeed, by the acceleration of particles (which Einstein showed to be impossible), but by the travelling wave principle, which is after all a mode of communication between particles.

This evening was spent with George Zopf and his family, and concludes the first part of my visit to the University of Illinois. I have missed Northcote Parkinson, who was here.

Saturday 4th June

During my visit to the University of California last month, I was entertained at both Berkeley and UCLA. The President of the Campus at La Jolla, Dr Revelle, heard subsequently of my visit, and has invited me back to deliver a lecture to the faculty members of the La Jolla Campus. As southern California is a much more pleasant place to spend a weekend than the hot and humid plains of Illinois, and as I was sent the necessary aeroplane tickets, I have returned.

Leaving Urbana this morning by train at 8 a.m., I travelled to Chicago, and thence by airline to Los Angeles. After a further short flight, I arrived at San Diego at 5.30 p.m., having gained two hours en route (the change from central to Pacific time). Tonight I am back again in the Beach and Tennis Club at La Jolla, on the edge of the Pacific Ocean.

Here is a thought for Sir Brian Robertson. The coaches on the trains I have so far used are connected (as they are in England), by either sliding or swinging doors. However, the sliding door opens autonomatically at the touch of a panel, and closes automatically behind one. The swinging door is power-assisted so that the lightest touch causes it to open.

It has been worth the long journey to return to this peaceful and beautiful place. And so, as a somewhat less mobile diarist put it, to bed.

Sunday 5th June

It was possible to have a quiet morning for once, but this afternoon I was engaged in a very long conversation with Dr Revelle, the Director of the Scripps Institute of Oceanography, and also of the new Campus of the University of California, which is based on this Institute. I was extremely impressed by the plans being laid here to increase the Campus to a student strength of 25 000. Recruitment of the academic faculty is proceeding quietly, but to no small purpose. The physicist Urey himself is now stationed here, and on the biochemical side the famous Jonas Salk (of polio vaccine fame) is expected to found a von Neumann Institute for Brain Research.

This evening I was entertained by friends of my previous trip, and had my first demonstration of Hi-Fi stereophonic sound. The outcome was an altogether unwilling but none the less enthusiastic convert.

Monday 6th June

As it was necessary to be up by 6 a.m. (after a mere three hours sleep), I found the feasibility of staggering across a very short stretch of sand straight into the Pacific Ocean quite helpful. After breakfast, I checked out of the Club, and was ready to attend my first meeting at 8 o'clock—and in all no less than four different meetings this morning.

This afternoon, from 2 p.m. to 4 p.m. I addressed the Faculty with the title 'On viable governors'. After a short break of 30 minutes, there was a further two-hour discussion of the material I had put forward. It was all very successful, although the discussion was marred for me by the appearance in the audience of Sir Edward Bullard, quondam Head of the National Physical Laboratory (NPL) who spoke at length of his wartime experiences and his friend 'Petrick Bleckett'. This was a cruel trick of fate, so many thousands of miles from London.

In the evening, a whole group of my friends in San Diego entertained me to dinner, and I left soon afterwards for Los Angeles. Eventually I flew from Los Angeles at 1.15 a.m. for Chicago, where I arrived at 7 a.m. local time.

RETROSPECT 1992

The entry for Friday the 13th of May leaves me in the La Jolla Country Club at 2 a.m. with the mysterious statement: 'It has been an eventful day'. Now I had returned to the Club for the weekend of the 4th of June, offering the somewhat feeble excuse in the text that the weather was better there than

in Illinois! When the diary was issued to its limited audience, there were cries of Cherchez la femme. *Here is the proper explanation.*

Early in May, I had caused something of a stir in the Californian campuses. I had given three lectures in Berkeley, another in Palo Alto, and two more in Los Angeles, and had many discussions with the faculties in all these places. As a result, I had been under pressure to accept a chair in the university: the original suggestion had come from West Churchman in Berkeley, with support from UCLA. The idea excited me a great deal. The proposed salary was nearly double the salary I earned as director of Operational Research and Cybernetics in United Steel, and my hosts were quick to point out that an academic has plenty of time to double his income by paid consultancy. Flattered and excited as I was, I demurred. It seemed to me that any success I had achieved had been critically dependent on the challenge of holding down and indeed advancing in an industrial job in the face of strong opposition. I was, by British standards at that time, absurdly young to be in so senior a position as I then held. The idea of moving to a Californian lotus land in an academic post with tenure, made me wonder whether I would ever do anything again.

I had planned to spend Saturday the 14th of May relaxing before the return to New York, but I was persuaded to visit La Jolla instead. As already recorded, this was at the invitation of someone who had heard me speak in Cleveland, and resulted in my spending six hours in the visit to Daystrom Electronics. It had also included my stay at the beach and tennis club, and an exciting flying visit to Tijuana in Mexico. Even so, I did not suspect seduction on the part of my American friends.

When I arrived in Illinois on the 2nd of June, a message was awaiting me containing the (above recorded) invitation from the president at La Jolla to give a lecture. Moreover, it was hinted, the people I had met at Daystrom Electronics had a proposition to put to me. I had been expecting to stay in Urbana and therefore consulted my host, Heinz von Foerster. He was very supportive of my using the tickets that had been sent to me and finding out what was really happening in California during the Saturday and Sunday.

The long and short of it was that I was offered a chair in cybernetics, with tenure, at the La Jolla Campus of the University of California. My known objections to switching to the academic life would be met by my appointment as research director of Daystrom Electronics—at an equivalent salary to the University stipend. It was proposed that I could integrate the academic and industrial life to the benefit of each. The offer was immensely attractive, as was the (then undeveloped) township and Campus; the financial deal amounted to about three and a half times my then salary in England.

I returned to Urbana in a daze, carrying an open cheque (one of the only two that I have seen in my life) from Daystrom to pay for a first class trip for two weeks from England to the West Coast with my wife, so that we

could properly evaluate the proposal. It is hard for me now to believe that the cheque was eventually burnt.

Tuesday 7th June

Having reached Urbana from Chicago, I joined in the initial ceremonies of the big Symposium on Self-Organizing Systems, the invitation to speak at which was the second reason for this tour. The formal business of the Symposium has not yet begun, although there was this evening a keynote address by Warren McCulloch—of the usual very high calibre. I have once more met up with many of my friends in this country, who have converged on Champaign for this Symposium. They include Ross Ashby and Gordon Pask from England. Again we have talked into the small hours with the result that I have had virtually no sleep for 48 hours, and cannot therefore indulge in a lengthy account of the conversations that have taken place today.

Wednesday 8th June

Today we have launched the Symposium proper, and extremely exhausting it is too. This morning's session was to contain four papers, of which mine was the second. The first was by Anatol Rapoport on 'The self-organization of small groups'. As ever, he was extremely good.

I began my own address at 10.15, and finished at 11.00 as I had been asked to do. This did not seriously interfere with my presentation of the paper 'Towards the cybernetic factory', because the symposiasts had the stencilled version in front of them. The reception accorded was extremely gratifying, and was measurable by the fact that the discussion continued for a further one and a half hours, thereby using up all the time allotted to the next two speakers. Even then we were late for lunch.

The only direct criticism came from Dr Rosen, who imagined that I had forced the problem with which I was trying to deal into a kind of infinite regression ('The eye sees because no image of the world is projected onto the retina'; 'How does the retina see?'; 'There is a kind of homunculus behind the retina who observes it'; 'How does the homunculus see?'; 'He has an eye, on to the retina of which the image is projected. . .'). I did my best to refute this kind of criticism, and suspect that Dr Rosen was on his own.

There was clearly manifest a general feeling, borne out in subsequent discussions this evening, that the work done on behalf of Templeborough Rolling Mills is of importance. In particular, I was most gratified by the reaction of that eminent economist, Dr Hayek, who thinks that this approach to the economic structure and control of industrial companies is a revelation compared with the classical methods of analysis. All this was most pleasing.

In the afternoon, von Foerster handed over the Chairmanship to McCulloch, who supervised the performance of his own 'circus'. Messrs Blum, Verbeek, Cowan and Löfgren between them constructed an admirable picture of the MIT to work on neural nets. The titles of their papers are given in the full programme shown at Appendix IV [page 307 below], and the details appear in the published proceedings.

The published programme for the third session this evening had to be abandoned in order to make space for the two papers I had ousted this morning. Thus von Foerster returned to the Chair, and introduced Gordon Pask on the topic of 'The game-theoretic analysis of self-organizing systems'. Pask undoubtedly gave the most brilliant performance of his career. It was a complete tour de force, and had a tremendous impact on the Symposium. This paper was followed by Ross Ashby, speaking on 'Principles of self-organizing systems'. Ashby read his paper, as usual, which was, as usual, extremely precise and elegant. Also as usual, however, I felt that his preoccupation with a sort of rigour which is not in fact exemplified by cybernetic systems led in some instances to defective conclusions. However, in the main this was a very sound and worthwhile speech.

It has been a wearing day, but the impression of the combined intellectual power of this meeting is absolutely staggering. For this reason, I must admit to being overwhelmed by the flattering reception of my own work. The formal proceedings did not conclude until nearly 11 p.m., since when a great deal of fascinating discussion has been going on in small groups. At the personal level, this evening has been notable for me in terms of discussions with two cyberneticians whom I have for a long time been quoting, but whom I have never met before. They are Professor John Bowman, Dean of Northwestern University, and Professor Ludwig von Bertalanffy. Both these men, and particularly the former, lived up to expectations.

Thursday 9th June

The first session today ran from 9 a.m. to 12.30, under the Chairmanship of John Bowman. It began with some unprogrammed remarks by Ludwig von Bertalanffy, expatiating on rather than criticizing Ashby's paper of last night. To these comments, Ashby suitably replied. Dr R. W. Sperry then spoke on 'Some design principles of the living brain', which was a rather uncybernetic but none the less interesting report. Dr R. L. Beurle, of England, then gave his paper on 'Storage and manipulation of information in the brain', an account of his 'viable neurones'. The address was marred by a too lengthy saga about his own difficulties in formulating these ideas, but they remain very worth while. He has not made a great deal of progress in the last few years, as his work with English Electric concerns the design of valves. Well done, English Electric.

Dr J. R. Platt then spoke on 'Pattern perception by mosaic receptors', an interesting account of the detection of straight lines by the irregular mosaic of a living retina. This kind of work is always very encouraging, because it heralds (to my mind) an era in which we shall be able to build machines of extremely accurate performance in a relatively imprecise, and therefore inexpensive, way.

The economist Professor Hayek took the Chair for the afternoon session, which lasted from 2 p.m. to 5.30.

At this point Novikoff rose to address us on 'Statistical invariants of geometrical figures under translations and rotations'. I am sorry for any exponent of integral geometry who missed this incredible performance. Novikoff spoke without notes and with a great deal of fire for an hour and a half, and dealt with the problem of pattern recognition in an astonishing fashion.

He began with Buffon's needle and Bertrand's chord. Now I have often participated in discussions that began at this point, staggered along for a while, and then petered out. Novikoff, however, was safely off the ground in five minutes, and before long was triumphantly breaking through the sound barrier. By the time he had finished, he was projecting areas of indeterminate shape on to a retina at random, and had completed the full theory whereby an alphabet of characters of any size, shape and orientation could be recognized. 'Squiggles' are also valuable Buffon needles—because of their convolutions they are capable of detecting complex patterns. And because a correspondence may be set up between the 'convex hull' of a squiggle and of a character, this theory permits a good deal of distortion in the production of the character. It is devoutly to be wished that the written paper when it appears will be anything like as brilliant as was this lecture.

Incidentally, it was Novikoff who, in a private discussion, gave me a proof of Pythagoras' theorem of breathtaking elegance. I do not know if this solution is generally known, but I swear that it is the most beautiful thing I have seen for a very long time.

The third paper this afternoon was by Dr Willis of the Lockheed Corporation, and concerned memory and the characteristics of parallel logic systems. He is the man who keeps a number of successful automata at Palo Alto, and had the reputation of being one of the best switching theory men in the United States. Unfortunately he is an appalling speaker. He was followed by our old friend Dr Frank Rosenblatt, who was billed to speak on 'Biological membrane mechanisms in the light of theoretical brain models'. Heinz von Foerster had told me that this title was intended to ensure that Rosenblatt did not speak as usual about the Perceptron. Rosenblatt spoke for one and a half hours, on the Perceptron.

The Chairman, who very naturally appeared to be asleep, failed to notice the organizer's frantic signals to curtail this punishment.

It turned out in discussion that a large number of those present have taken my criticism of the Perceptron (given at the NPL Symposium on the Mechanization of Thought Processes in 1958) as final—and various quotations from my remarks on that occasion have been bandied about today as if they were widely known. Even so, I should wish to avoid a vendetta if possible, and have this time been at great pains to show goodwill towards Rosenblatt myself. This effort has been reciprocated, and the awkwardness between us over the last two years can be forgotten.

I myself had the privilege to be Chairman of the closing session, which lasted from 7.30 p.m. to 11.00. This was a rather difficult assignment, as six papers had been left over by this time, and there were also the formal speeches of closure to be made. I was forced to drive the session along at an alarming pace, and have no doubt incurred the enmity of every speaker and questioner. However, it could not be helped. As things were, everyone was utterly exhausted at the end of this amazing day.

The first speaker was John R. Bowman, Dean at Northwestern University, and one of the old cyberneticians of Macy Foundation days. He gave an enjoyable account of a childlike but far from childish experiment involving a very large array of small magnetic compasses. Even a linear array of rotatable dipoles will transmit bits in strange ways, and in two dimensions the system has self-organizing properties very analogous to those of a nervous system. Arguing from this point, Bowman suggested the construction of a polymer to which would be attached at fairly separated intervals an amino acid which would in turn rotate as does the dipole. He concluded that such a fabric would have dielectric properties several orders of magnitude better than anything yet available, and alleged that such a substance could be made.

George Zopf at once claimed to have made such a substance for another purpose, and it seems likely that these two will get together. A little illustration of the benefits of interdisciplinary teamwork.

Next came Dr Saul Amarel on 'An example of automatic theory formation in logic'. This was one of the speakers whose time had to be severely curtailed, and I can say little more than the speaker had an outlook of sufficient interest to encourage everyone to read his full paper in the proceedings. Dr J. R. Tooley of Texas Instruments (which, contrary to expectations, appears to be leading RCA in the development of molecular electronics) gave a brief electronic talk in which he suggested that tunnel diodes would make ideal components for neural networks because they exhibit an initial high peak before relapsing to the normal steadily ascending curve of an orthodox diode, whose normal single peak thus becomes a second peak.

Dr H. D. Crane then talked about his neuristors, beasts we already know of, as he has published a great deal about his work. The key idea is based on the nature of a fuse. If two transmission lines are brought close together at a point (which becomes a gate), then a burning zone is set up at the gate when two pulses reach it simultaneously on the separate lines, and both pulses are annihilated.

On the basis of this idea, all the logical gates required for a decision system can be constructed, and such phenomena as unidirectional lines can be set up by bifurcating one line and drawing it back on to itself in a junction. Thus a pulse travelling in the direction from which the bifurcation starts will be propagated down both arms of the loop, and the two identical pulses will collide at the gate and be annihilated. While on the other hand, a pulse travelling in the opposite direction will pass straight through. This creates the problem that such a pulse will be followed by an 'echo' traversing the loop which, although it peters out at the gate, might conceivably meet there another unidirectional impulse and annihilate that.

The advance on which Crane was really reporting, I think, was a logical demonstration that despite lagged times throughout the system, computers built of neuristors could be constructed in which there would be no interference of this kind.

Dr Rosen, in a very brief allotment of time, delivered a very polished resumé of his 'Approach to a distributive memory', which will be well worth reading in full when the paper is published. Finally, Dr Peter Green, who works with Rashevsky, discussed 'The representation of information in a self-organizing system'. He wasted so much time on a generalized biological introduction, that his account of the logic by which he has tackled this problem was let forth at about 200 words a minute, combined with obsessional motor activity at the blackboard. But again, there will be something worth studying here when the paper is available, on the assumption that in his writing at least, euphoria does not supervene.

I then asked Heinz von Foerster to sum up the Conference, which he did with admirable brevity, and called on Warren McCulloch to thank the organizers. Once again, the discussions in von Foerster's room between a selected subset of the symposiasts went on until dawn.

RETROSPECT 1992

The Proceedings of this meeting were subsequently published under the title **Principles of Self Organization** ***edited by von Foerster and Zopf (Pergamon Press, 1962). It was the most important of the half dozen really important meetings that I ever attended. It made a tremendous impact on my thinking. There was no audience, and every person present was a first-team player. The outstanding recollection, 30 years later, is of Novikoff, who had not prepared his paper in advance. That is why the text expresses the hope that the published paper would be anything like as brilliant as the speech. Inevitably, perhaps, it was not.***

The recent (1992) death of Friedrich von Hayek has left me with an unresolved paradox. At this, the first encounter, I believed that here at last

was a cybernetically oriented economist. To this day, my understanding of his key tenets is of a set of interlocking self-organizing systems of great complexity and subtlety—far removed from the crudities of the 'market forces' model. And yet, von Hayek came to personify the extreme right wing of economic theory while he himself was a personal adviser to Prime Minister Margaret Thatcher.

Friday 10th June

The Conference having completed its formal activities at Allerton Park (25 miles outside Urbana), it returned to the University proper for its final day. The numbers broke up into informal groups for discussions which have really rounded out the topics that interested each member most. In particular, I have been able to satisfy both Sperry and Rosen, who were the only two members of the Symposium who had criticisms of my paper to offer, that their difficulties could be met.

This evening was spent at Heinz von Foerster's house, in company with Ashby, Pask, Hayek and von Bertalanffy, and I have returned to my pleasant room in the Union Buildings for a few hours sleep before beginning the journey home tomorrow.

RETROSPECT 1992

Just as prudence dictated silence about my Californian adventure, it also led me to suppress the extraordinary events on this night in the house of Heinz von Foerster.

Von Foerster had a great admiration (as who had not) for Ross Ashby. He conveyed to me his hope that he could persuade Ashby to accept appointment in the University of Illinois, and asked my opinion of his chances. Having known Ashby for years, and being well versed in his current activities in the Burden Neurological Institute in England where he was the director, I did not think he would be attracted by an academic appointment. The text records the meeting in Heinz's house, 'in company with Ashby, Pask, Hayek, and von Bertalanffy'. This was the setting in which Heinz and I carefully elaborated what he has often since called our 'plot'.

It began with Heinz acquainting the others with the Californian proposal that I had received and my reluctance to accept it. He set out to 'persuade' me, and to drag the others into the discussion. All except Ashby did, extolling the virtues of the proposal, and the freedom which America offered its thinkers in replacement of the British strait-jacket. It did not surprise me that Ashby was silent: I truly thought that academic affairs bored him stiff. In the end, however, von Foerster turned to him: 'Ross, you haven't said a single word. Help us persuade Stafford to come to the United States.' Ashby looked up and said: 'Why should I? No one has ever offered me *a chair anywhere.'*

The silence was deafening. Heinz: 'Well, everybody has assumed that you have been offered chairs all over the place and have refused them.' 'Not so.' Heinz von Foerster cleared his throat and said, in a very official tone: 'Dr Ashby I hereby offer you appointment as Professor of Cybernetics in my department of the University of Illinois.' 'Thank you', said Ashby, 'I accept.'

The silence this time was eventually broken by Ross Ashby himself, who said: 'Heinz, would you mind if I went to telephone my wife?' And he left the room. Thus began the extremely fruitful decade of the 1960s that Ashby was to spend in Illinois. Rosebud, his wife, subsequently told me that the famous phone call amounted to little more than: 'We are emigrating. Sell the house and join me.' She did the second but but not the first. But I myself was to learn something more that night.

Ashby and I were walking together across the huge campus at Champaign in bright moonlight. It was very late; we were walking to our adjacent rooms in the faculty club. Halfway across I broke the silence: 'Ross, you gave me a big surprise tonight.' 'Why was that?' 'Well, if I had any criticism at all to make of you (which I have not) it would be to say that you tend to err on the side of the meticulous. Asked Heinz's question, I would have expected you to say: "I need three weeks to evaluate this problem, to list the pros and cons, and to compute an answer."' Ashby stopped dead, spun round, and seemed quite angry. 'What are you talking about?', he said. 'Not three weeks, three months, nor three years would suffice to analyse the problem in the way you propose. The approach is absurd. There are only two rational ways to respond to a question like that. The first is to obey hunch. The brain after all has stored most of the relevant information, even though I cannot access it. And the evaluation models are probably there too although I cannot articulate them. My brain said yes, and so I accepted.'

We resumed walking, and after a while I remarked that he was fortunate that the answer did not elude him. 'What if you had no hunch', I asked; 'what would be the second rational technique?' Again Ashby stopped and turned to look at me. 'Why,' he said, 'I should toss a coin.'

It would be good if those who seek to refine answers by stuffing more data into computers and more variables into equations would learn the lesson taught to me that night. Successful people often know it, which means that the management scientist's approach to them is commonly misconceived.

I greatly missed my frequent and lengthy conversations with Ashby during his absence, but they were happily resumed when he returned to Britain in semi-retirement. As to my own story and the reason why the cheque was burnt, the facts are now hard for me to credit.

The Diary was immediately transcribed and issued to its select audience. My boss, Commander Wells, who was I think Deputy Chairman of the Company, had a long talk with me. He had a gesture, after handing over the whisky, of putting an arm round one's shoulder in a confidential and patronizing fashion. On this occasion he asked me whether I realized that I was the youngest member of the Senior Management (as defined by the 'top hat' pension plan) by 20 years *(his emphasis). He explained that I had done extremely well, but there was something of a problem. Nothing, it seemed, would stop me going around and criticizing what was happening in the company. I conceived this to be my job, as I was trying to improve things, increase productivity, and so forth. He said, 'Ah yes, but that ignores the human factor. People do not like it. Take up golf; don't interfere so much; then nothing can stop you becoming chairman of this company.' I determined there and then to leave.*

My wife and I had endless discussions about the Californian proposal. I felt (stupidly enough) that if we once went on the proposed holiday to La Jolla it would obfuscate all judgement. We already had three young children, and we both felt that they should be brought up in Britain. In the middle of all the agonizing I received the invitation to leave United Steel and set up a consulting company—which was to become SIGMA, Science in General Management Ltd, as managing director. That settled the matter and this I did; but that is another story. I burned the Daystrom cheque because it would have been immoral to go out there, having decided in advance not to accept the job. Would it not?

Saturday 11th June

I left Champaign, Urbana, early this morning by train for Chicago. This was an ordinary local train, and compared much more nearly with British trains than did the long distance express on which I travelled before. Then began the long bus journey to O'Hare field for the air journey to New York. This is the most tedious town-to-airport trip I have ever encountered, and takes an unconscionable time.

The trip originally scheduled to New York was an American Airlines flight on the Lockheed Electra. This was an aeroplane which sustained two appalling crashes earlier this year, having disintegrated in mid-air. It is a turbo-jet aircraft, and is now flying all its customary routes, having been slowed down by 100 miles per hour to a 'safety' level.

However, the Operational Research department of Lockheed had been involved in the investigation into the two disasters, and I had had (in New York) a detailed account of the affair from the Head of the Group in person. Accordingly, I felt disposed to change this flight, which was worth doing, as it provided me with my only experience of the Boeing 707 jet Airliner of Transworld Airlines. This was the roughest flight of the tour, as there were many storms on the route. Although the aircraft was flying at 29 000 feet, it was bounced around a great deal. Looking out along the flexing wing of the aircraft, I began to wonder if it were in fact an unacknowledged ornithopter. It was at this point that I began to feel really pleased that I had changed the flight—the trouble with the Electra was precisely that its wings began to flap, and finally flapped off, in mid-air!

Having arrived at Idlewild Airport, I set out for the Rivett's house in New York, where I was due to spend my last night in America. I reached their apartment about 9 p.m., and spent a most pleasant evening with these good friends.

Sunday 12th June

I have not made any comment in this diary about the various churches visited during this trip, but attendance at the imposing Cathedral of St Patrick in New York this morning must be mentioned. I attended Solemn High Mass here today, which was sung in the presence of Cardinal Spellman.

This being my last day in America, and a Sunday, I determined to do a minimum of sightseeing, despite torrential rain and threatening thunderstorms. I ascended the Tower of the Rockefeller Center, 72 storeys high, to the observation platform, where I failed to obtain the promised view of New York as the tower was in the clouds. However, I did just manage to glimpse the ground below, and wished very much that I had not. On entering the little café on the observation platform in search of some adequate reassurance, I was urbanely greeted by the Head of OR for Shell in London, Geoffrey Sears.

This afternoon I visited the Museum of Modern Art, which has a remarkable collection of paintings, including splendidly representative groups by Picasso, Braque, Gris, Léger, and occasional unexpected finds by such people as Cézanne, Renoir and Dégas, not to mention Klee and Soutine (charmingly referred to by a lady of my acquaintance in Urbana as 'Sauternes').

Secondly, I saw the architectural innovation of Frank Lloyd Wright—the Guggenheim Gallery. In my opinion, the design of this building is superb. and I was unable to sustain any of the criticisms that have been levelled against it. The spirally ascending ramp seems to me the ideal way in which to arrange a picture gallery. The lighting is excellent, and the mounting of the pictures, without frames, extremely effective.

The small drawback appeared to be that the canvases exhibited were for the most part horrible. A large and fairly representative collection of pictures by Kandinsky seemed to me particularly unpleasing.

A good operational research solution for the art lovers of New York would seem to be to throw away the pictures in the Guggenheim, to replace them by the excellent collection in the Museum of Modern Art, and to make over the latter building to the poor.

Monday 13th June

I returned to Idlewild Airport late yesterday evening to catch the Comet Monarch service to London. However, the wretched weather had continued, and the incoming Comet had been diverted to Baltimore where it was grounded. This was the aircraft which was to take us home. There followed an unpleasant five hours delay while these matters were attended to. Once airborne, however, the flight was uneventful, and some effort was made to sleep during the journey. The attempt was largely thwarted by a well-intentioned and younger version of Brunhilde, in the shape of a stewardess, who thundered up and down the cabin most of the night anxiously mothering her charges.

The arrival in London was also five hours later than scheduled, as was to be expected, and a further five hours of the day were of course lost thanks to the predictably treacherous behaviour of the sun. Thus I find myself in London on Monday night, after seven weeks absence, tired but fairly complacent. Everything looks much as I left it 16 aeroplane trips and 15 lectures ago.

A few hours ago I was at the International Airport of New York, with its crisp efficiency, workmanlike yet pleasing design, self-opening doors, and every facility. Now I am at the International Airport of London, with its cluster of little wooden huts and general air of chaos. Doubtless our authorities are waiting to see if crossing the Atlantic by jet is just a fad. I know I am home.

APPENDIX I

The O.R. Organization at the Case Institute of Technology

Director:	Professor R. L. Ackoff
Assistant Director:	Professor E. L. Arnoff

Faculty	Full Professors:	Ackoff; Camp
	Associate Professors:	Arnoff; Dean; Little; Cooke
	Assistant Professors:	Hanssmann; Minas; Sengupta; Sasieni

Research Associates	Martin; Chambers
Graduate OR Scientists	18 (75% of time on group's work; 25% of time on post-graduate research)
Consultants	Van Voorhis—Mathematical OR (1 day per week) Leyzorek—Professor of Electrical Engineering at Case (half time)
Graduate students	pursuing higher degrees, and devoting perhaps half their time to OR projects in the Group 65
Fellows	a variable number supported by industry and foreign governments

APPENDIX II

Teaching at the Case Institute of Technology

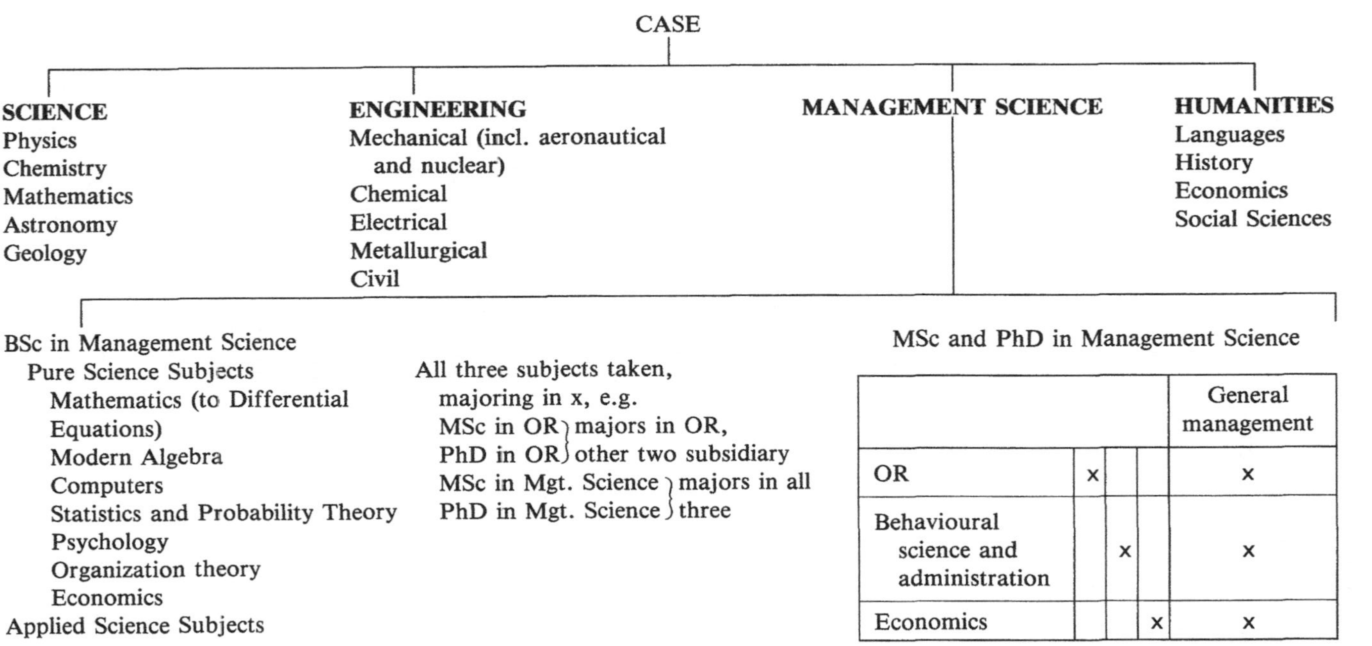

				General management
OR	x			x
Behavioural science and administration		x		x
Economics			x	x

Object of Management Science Courses

1. To inculcate the scientific method, as opposed to teaching management by precept.
2. To teach this science in the context of industrial management.

Degrees in Management Science

BSc 4 years
MSc 2 years
PhD 2 years

APPENDIX III

Curricula for Higher Degrees in Management Science Majoring in Operational Research

Standard of Entry	Bachelor Degree *Qualifying examination in mathematics (up to differential equations) *1-year course in statistics and probability theory

*If not covered by the degree already obtained
Normally, also, some post-graduate experience in industry or government

Master of Science	Methodology of OR Problems in OR	Basic courses
	Computers Scientific method OR techniques Thesis (case study)	Subsidiary courses
Doctorate	Methodology of OR Problems in OR	Basic courses
Subsidiary General Courses	Scientific method Computers Sampling theory Mathematics of management systems (advanced maths)	
Subsidiary Technical Courses	Production and inventory theory Linear and dynamic programming Stochastic process (including queuing theory) Replacement and maintenance theory Statistical decision theory and game theory OR in marketing Econometrics	
Advanced Seminars	Decision theory Organization theory Approximation and bounding problems Communication theory	
Advanced Reading Course	PhD students must prepare a survey of the literature in some specific area of OR	
Thesis Seminars	PhD students choose some major OR discipline as a special course, e.g. Mathematics Systems Communication theory etc.	

Appendix IV

Illinois Symposium on Principles of Self-Organization Wednesday 8–Thursday 9 June 1960

Wednesday 8th

Session I	9–12	Chairman: H. von Foerster

1. A. Rapoport:	The Small Group as a Self-Organizing System
2. S. Beer:	Toward the Cybernetic Factory
3. W. R. Ashby:	The Principles of Self-Organizing Systems
4. G. Pask (with Heinz von Foerster)	The Game-Theoretic Analysis of Self-Organizing Systems

Session II	2–5	Chairman: W. McCulloch

1. L. Verbeek:	Analysis and Synthesis of Error-Minimizing Neuronal Nets Liable to Deaths and Fits
2. M. Blum:	The Construction of Infallible Nets with Unreliable Neurons
3. J. Cowan	Many-Valued Logics and Homeostatic Mechanisms
4. L. Löfgren:	A Self-Repairing System for Uninterrupted Computation

Session III	8–10	Chairman: A. Rapoport

1. R. W. Sperry:	Some Design Principles of the Living Brain
2. R. L. Beurle:	Storage and Manipulation of Information in the Brain
3. C. W. Zopf:	Machines Like Men, and Men Like Machines: Some Quibbles and Exceptions
4. F. A. Fayek:	The Causal Determination of Purposive Action and/or Higher Level Regularities

Thursday 9th

Session I	9–12	Chairman: J. Bowman

1. J. K. Hawkins:	Synthesis of Recognition Networks
2. J. R. Platt:	Pattern Perception by Mosaic Receptors
3. A. Novikoff:	Statistical Invariants of Geometrical Figures under Translations and Rotations
4. M. Minsky:	a. Recent Progress in Pattern Recognition; b. Verbal Reasoning Programs

Session II	2–5	Chairman: F. Hayek
1. C. A. Rosen:	An Approach to a Distributed Memory	
2. D. G. Willis:	a. Memory Characteristics and Requirements for Self-Organizing Systems; b. Characteristics of Parallel Logic Systems	
3. F. Rosenblatt:	Biological Memory Mechanisms in the Light of Theoretical Brain Models	
4. P. H. Greene:	Representation of Information in a Self-Organizing System	

Session III	8–10	Chairman: S. Beer
1. J. R. Bowman	a. Physical Principles and Devices for Communication of Information—A Survey; b. Bit Transmission Through Linear Arrays of Freely Rotatable Dipoles	
2. H. D. Crane:	Neuristors	
3. S. Amarel:	a. Modes of Self-Organization in a System with a Threshold Logic Cell; b. An Example of Automatic Theory Formation in Logic	
4. J. R. Tooley:	Tunnel Diodes, Solid Circuits, etc.	

APPENDIX V

Timetable of Lectures

27 April; Cleveland, Ohio	Case Institute of Technology	First American Symposium on Systems Research	Principle Address: 'Below the Twilight Arch: A Mythology of Systems'
29 April; Cleveland, Ohio	Case Institute of Technology	Case OR Group	'Developments in OR'
5 May; Cleveland, Ohio	Case Institute of Technology	Case Systems Research Center	'Control Theory and Adaptation'
6 May; Cleveland, Ohio	Case Institute of Technology	Case OR Group	'Indeterminacy and Analytic Models'
9 May; Berkeley, San Francisco	Berkeley Campus	Management Science Research Nucleus	'Artefacts of Brain and Industry'
10 May; Berkeley, San Francisco	Institute of Management Science	Northern California Chapter Meeting	'Production Control'
11 May; Berkeley, San Francisco	Berkeley Campus	The Faculty of Business Administration	'A New Look of Management Science'
12 May; Los Angeles	Berkeley Campus	Post-Graduate OR Course, and Faculty Members	'On Actually *Doing* Operational Research'
12 May; Los Angeles	The Institute of Management Science	Southern California Chapter Meeting	'Uncertainty and Automation'
16 May; New York	Arthur Andersen Consultants	OR Group	'A Philosophy of OR'
26 May; Baltimore, Maryland	Johns Hopkins University	Business and Engineering Faculties; Applied Physics Laboratory; Operations Research Office, Washington	'Automation and Uncertainty'
3 June; Urbana, Illinois	University of Illinois	The Sedition Club (Faculty)	'Management Cybernetics'
6 June; San Diego, California	University of California, La Jolla Campus	The Faculty	'On Viable Governors'
8 June; Urbana, Illinois	University of Illinois	Symposium on Self-Organizing Systems	'Towards the Cybernetic Factory'

BOARDROOM

I read the war poets
twice over—
that was tough. I also wrote
myself the second time round
naïvely.

It was a teenage party then too
but short on drugs and sex.
There was marching though,
and carrying someone's rifle
made the friend.
There was the unreal sound
half-hearted kick
of the blank cartridge
at the funerals of friends.
Looking back

we can fairly envy
the clean muck of the war,
and the bright issues
bogus but clearcut
that sorted us out
in those days.

It's different now
what with business and
industry
also the academic bit.
We all storm the bridges again
London and Waterloo
doing our stuff.
But there isn't much glamour
and if you're dead by teatime
it will be

continued

because some dolt
is driving the car, bus, taxi

or because they sacked you
and there was a mortgage.
It would be nice
shade of my best friend's ghost
to say that I went out
firing back
or crucified akimbo
in a Jap-infested sunset.
But the board now meets
and the battle I shall lose
will be over the brandy
where the teeth gnash
not rattle.

We doodle with our clickety
supersonic ball-points
while our friends
sleep and grow younger.
God, but my hair is going
and that clot
  I love him too
  and for the same reason
  that we die together
talks and talks and talks.

Stafford Beer
Transit, 1977

PART THREE

Complexity in Human and Social Affairs

Stafford Beer after renouncing personal possessions and moving to the cottage: Wales: 1975

Editor's note In 1971, Stafford Beer was approached on behalf of President Salvador Allende, to help restructure the economy of Chile. Allende's government was the first Marxist government in the world to be democratically voted to office, an election reconfirmed by a different, subsequent election [1].

In 1973, Allende's government was brought down and Allende was assassinated, a process backed by powerful factions both in Britain and the United States. These events have been documented in US Congressional hearings [2].

1. S. Beer (1975) *Platform for Change*. John Wiley, Chichester.
2. The House of Representatives, USA. *The United States of Chile During the Allende Years 1970–1973*. Hearings, US Government Printing Office, Washington DC, 1975.

12 CYBERNETICS OF NATIONAL DEVELOPMENT (evolved from work in Chile)

The Zaheer Foundation Lecture, New Delhi, India, 1974

STAFFORD BEER

I AM DEEPLY happy to be here with you, and to deliver this Zaheer Science Foundation Inaugural Lecture. You may well know the immortal words of the Apocrypha, written in the book of Ecclesiasticus, which say in part: 'Let us now praise famous men . . . giving counsel by their understanding, such as have brought tidings in prophecies: leaders of the people by their counsels . . . wise were their words in their instruction . . . All these were honoured in their generations, and were a glory in their days.'

These are very proper sentiments. The human mind has a deep need to *focus* its perceptions, its understanding, and its aspirations, if it is not to be lost in a welter of information, argumentation, and finally confusion. Our 'famous men' help us to do this even after their deaths. Thus, in the first place you and I would not be here together today—to do some joint and serious thinking—if it were not that we have convened to honour a great man in this Zaheer Lecture.

The second famous man who must be in our minds is that founding father of cybernetics, the late Norbert Wiener. He defined cybernetics as 'the science of control and communication in the animal and the machine'. As you perhaps know, the word cybernetics is the Greek name for steersmanship. And in his definition, Norbert Wiener was pointing to the facts: firstly, that patterns of information exclusively define whatever regulation exists; and secondly, that the laws that govern such regulation are general laws, given in nature, that apply to living systems and to artefacts alike.

This is a most important discovery for the Western culture, since the dichotomy between the animate and the inanimate worlds has lasted from Aristotle until the present day—when it continues to pervert our insight into the nature of reality. But if I have at all understood the Indian culture (which I have done my best to study for nearly 30 years) no such disharmony exists for you. Then may I hope that India will not import philosophic rubbish from the West, along with its material advances—so many of which, alas turn into rubbish too.

The third of the famous men to whom I so proudly refer, is Salvador Allende, the last democratic president of Chile. I had the privilege to serve him for two years, until his diabolical assassination, and the overthrow of the liberty of his beloved people. And here is a strange link, which I embody, between this room and Santiago, half the world away. Night after night, at two or three o'clock in the morning, I would walk out in Santiago to a special shrine dedicated for India. I would sit and meditate by a little pool, where sat in stone Gandhi, flanked by Nehru and Tagore, so that—along with famous men—I might indeed focus my mind.

THE 'CHILEAN PROCESS'

Now I ask you to join me in focusing on what everyone called, until a year ago, the Chilean Process. There is, in that expression, an acknowledgement that this society was a *system*—a system moreover in continuous evolution, based on learning and adaptation. Put in such neutral, scientific language, the idea sounds banal. Yet it is not banal. For if we ask the question: are not all societies inevitably of this kind, the answer is no—even though we would like them to be, and although they may not survive if they are not. The answer is 'no' today in Britain; the answer is 'no' today in Chile.

Here then is our focus, on the qualities of survival systems such as societies should be. And if society is a system, then let us recognize at once that those qualities conducive to survival are *systemic*, which is to say that they are intrinsic to the societary system. They cannot be imposed upon it by ruling classes, or by dictators. If we look at societies in which ruling classes have been dominant, it is not society itself that survives, but the ruling classes themselves; and the people starve. If we look at societies run by dictators, it is not society itself that survives, but the dictators and their henchmen; and the people are oppressed and shot.

This insight emerges through a quotation of which I am very fond. It says: 'In reality, action is entirely the outcome of all the modes of nature's attributes; moreover, only he whose intellect is deluded by egotism is so ignorant, that he presumes 'I am doing this' ' मैं कर्ता हूँ ' '. Of course that comes from the *Bhagavad-Gita*. And if I have got the translation right, for I confess that it is my own, it tells us that the output of a complex probabilistic system (such as a society) is a function of a self-regulating, self-organizing organization with high input variety, in which regulatory power is not vested in 'a controller', but in the structure of that organization itself. This, pray believe me, is a key discovery of modern cybernetics. It is just unfortunate that, because of the *Gita*, it comes roughly 5000 years too late to win a prize.

Salvador Allende knew this very well. He had come upon it through contemplation of the Marxist dialectic—which is itself a powerfully cybernetic device with which to think. At any rate, when I first displayed to him the basic model of organization that I use [1], he had the point rather more clear than I had myself. For this is a neurocybernetic model, and Allende was a physician. There are five subsystems in my model, and the one at the top is the cerebral cortex itself. Now although we think of the cortex as the cynosure of man's superiority over other animals, it is still very much part of the total bodily system. If we cut the ascending sensory pathways, the cortex knows nothing at all. If we cut the descending motor pathways, the cortex does nothing at all. If we cut the collateral fibres arising from the ascending reticular formation of the brain stem, the cortex cannot wake up. And if the cortex loses its blood supply, it dies from lack of oxygen in a few minutes.

Therefore I ought to have known better than to say to Allende that the fifth, top, subsystem represented the Compañero Presidente himself. But this I intended to do. Fortunately, he saved me from making such a fool of myself. As I drew in the top subsystem, number five, on the paper lying between us, he smiled with joy and said: 'At last: the *people*'.

I tell you this story for two reasons. I observe a monstrous campaign in the world's press, with a few honourable exceptions, to rewrite even such recent history as this. The new mythology declares that Allende was a would-be dictator, intent on overthrowing the constitution, and planning to establish a totalitarian state. I have a duty to say that such a mythology has no meaning within my own perception of the man, or of his administration. It is a cover story; and you know for whom it covers. The second reason concerns, with humility, my own work for Allende—which has in turn been villified as centralist, technocratic and totalitarian. I would ask you to remember this anecdote, which much affected me, as you listen to my explanation of the development of systems that were intended to be devolutionary, popular and pluralistic.

ON 'TECHNICAL AID' AND THE CHILEAN SCENE

When the question of my going to Chile arose, I was already highly critical of the process known as 'granting technical aid to developing countries'. With what condescension do visiting experts arrive to explain to the 'natives' what they ought to do, and then depart, leaving the local people to obey the bureaucratic rules—if they want the money. This sort of thing is not aid: it is technocratic imperialism. And what is more, it does not work. The arrangements for Chile, finally agreed in London in September 1971, were quite different. They worked out very well.

During the summer of 1971 a team was formed in Santiago consisting of some dozen scientists. All of them had studied cybernetics, and were doing so now the more intensively. I spent that summer in England, clearing other jobs out of the way, and studying Chile. Within an hour of my arrival in Santiago on 1 November, we were at work. In two weeks' non-stop activity we prepared our basic plans, which were approved by the President on the final day. The business had begun.

As scientific director, I worked alongside a Chilean minister, with a budget approved by him. There were shortages of expertise of various kinds. Therefore I subcontracted work to two teams of scientists in Britain, and subcontracted the building of certain equipment to two firms in Britain. For the next two years I flew ten times from London to Santiago, and ten times back. But although the budget, which included my salary, had been settled, the Chilean Government decided to apply to the British Government for a grant of technical aid—in order, if possible, to reimburse itself. After all, a substantial proportion of the budget was being spent in Britain, on the four subcontracts, and on me. The application was filled early in 1972. A British official eventually called on me to ascertain the facts. It was one week after the *coup d'etat*. Allende was dead; the work was over.

Then how did it begin? We were faced with a situation in which most of major industry had been taken under state ownership. The old owners and managers had left. They had not, for the most part, trained their Chilean subordinates, and many Chilean professionals (who were trained) left too: for these were the days of the 'terror campaign', which said that Allende intended to tranship Chilean babies to Cuba. Often these people had taken the entire documentation of their companies with them. Firms were in the hands of workers' committees, headed by an *interventor*—that is, someone appointed by the government to sort things out. These committees knew nothing about modern management techniques, and nothing about theories of costs and prices—which were in any case irrelevant to them. Their job was to keep the Chilean social-industrial economy moving, in terms of product flow, and this they were highly motivated to do.

Now Chile is a long, thin country. Although it is only about 100 miles wide, it is nearly 3000 miles long. Santiago is in the middle, and around it lies a great deal of the engineering industry. Due west, on the coast, lies the second largest city, the port of Valparaiso. South of this is the centre of the iron and steel industry. The climate in this middle belt is idyllic. Further south still, it is extremely wet. Pine trees grow 20 times as fast as they grow in Scandinavia, and this is the home of the forest products industry: wood, wood pulp, paper. To the north of this middle belt is desert, where nothing lives; until we reach the cluster of cities that evolved around the nitrate industry, and the largest copper mine in the world.

I have already made play with the cybernetic theorem that shows how regulation depends upon information. In any industrial economy such as this, government is faced with two main problems. What exactly is going on in all these plants? Secondly: How quickly shall we know about today's results? In heavily industrialized societies, a lot is known about what is going on, but the knowledge is of a highly complex nature. Moreover, this knowledge is vested partly in the bureaucracy, and partly in the business press, both of which customarily distort that knowledge for their own reasons. As to the speed with which government can be appraised of movements in the economy, it is notorious that such statistics are often six months or more out of date. Therefore, a lot of effort, and therefore a lot of money, goes into the financing of econometric studies that try to offset the time lags implicit in the system. But they do not work; and the governments of advanced industrial societies are forever reaching *precisely* the wrong decision as to taking money out of the economy or putting it in, for instance.

Then surely this is where to apply our scientific knowledge and our technical skill. I was appalled, when I first arrived in Chile, to find the whole middle class of this beautiful country already held tight in the grip of consumerism, so that the worth of life was already to be measured in terms of cars, television sets and refrigerators. The devastation wrought in the quality of life in the advanced industrial countries by such use of science and technology is plain to see. Do developing countries really wish to follow the same road? Only the people themselves are entitled to answer this question; but they need the full facts. And certainly people everywhere are entitled to use the intellectual inheritance of mankind, that includes science and technology, to whatever ends they wish.

The frightening aspects of technical aid lie in its bland assumption that good technical solutions to perennial human difficulties have already been found, which is demonstrably untrue; that where some solutions do look satisfactory, they can be transplanted wholesale into alien cultures by the mere investment of money; and that the rich world, because it has made that investment, is entitled to treat the poor world as a so-called 'expanding market' to be ravaged in search of profits to feed its concept of limitless growth on a finite planet. We have in honesty to note that the whole process, as in the case of Chile, incredibly turns the poor country into a net exporter of wealth to the rich country. This must be wrong. Injustice in the form of gross inequalities across the world is already shameful enough.

PROJECT CYBERSYN

The main proportion of the effort we made in Chile was to install a regulatory system for the social economy. The project aimed to acquire the benefits of cybernetic synergy for the whole of industry, while devolving power to the workers at the same time. It was called Project Cybersyn.

Thanks to the way in which the whole world of government discusses these matters, there appears to be a straight conflict between centralization and decentralization. That is to say, people hold a model in their heads that has a single scalar variable called 'percentage centrality', on which a point must be fixed. I reject this model completely, because neurocybernetics shows that so simplistic a concept is useless to account for viable behaviour. We need a model that is not a scale at all, but a structured space. In this, there is a horizontal dimensionality, listing (like the lines of print on a page) all sorts of activities that are in principle free to do anything they like. And there is a vertical dimensionality, representing authority that is in principle capable of stopping the horizontal activity from doing what it likes.

In this space we may precisely define the nature of *autonomy*. We may measure variety (which is defined as the possible number of states of a system) for any horizontal component in the space. We may then measure the variety subtracted from this first variety by interventions on the vertical plane. If, in a given case, almost the whole horizontal variety were left intact, then this situation would correspond to the simplistic notion of decentralization; the simplistic notion of centralization would correspond to the subtraction of most of the horizontal variety. Using this model, we are now able to define autonomy, whose societary name is freedom:

Definition If a system regulates itself by subtracting *at all times* as little horizontal variety as is necessary to maintain the cohesion of the total system, then the condition of autonomy prevails.

Now we can see why the scalar centralization–decentralization model does not work. Our definition entails two features that cannot be represented on the scale. Firstly, intervention will prove to be selective as between horizontal components, and secondly both its selections and the amount of variety abstracted will continually change. In both cases this is because intervention is responding to a criterion of overall cohesion, which is itself a variable responding to the degree of pressure exerted on the total system to blow it apart. In times of great stress, there will be more net intervention than at other times: this is a self-organizing property of the system.

In the Chilean situation, the basic horizontal components were all the enterprises of the social economy. But the enterprises were grouped into industries. Now an industry, such as textiles, encompasses many textile firms. The relationship of an industry to its component firm is, of course, a vertical component of our model. And yet there are many industries, and *they* are horizontal components of the economy. Thus we reach the important cybernetic concept of *definition by recursion*. (I use the word in the exact sense defined by recursive number theory.)

Enterprises are horizontal components of an industry, itself conceived as a vertical component. Now advance a level of recursion. Here there are industries as horizontal components, and something called a branch of industry (such as 'light' or 'heavy') is the vertical component. Advance to the next level of recursion. The branches are now horizontal components, and the vertical component is total industry itself. (At a further level of recursion, industry joins agriculture, transportation, health, education, and so on, as a horizontal component of something called the economy.)

This conceptual modelling is not just fun and games. I mentioned earlier that I went to Chile armed with a basic model of organization, based on neurocybernetics. Then the point about definition by recursion is this. We can apply exactly the same model at every level of recursion: to total industry itself; at the next level of recursion, to each of the four industrial branches; at the next level of recursion, to each of the industries in each branch; at the next level of recursion, to each of the enterprises in each industry. That adds up to a huge number of models. *But they are all the same*. They nest inside each other; and they are linked by the definition of autonomy, which is guaranteed for each level of recursion by the one above.

These concepts have to be understood before anyone could possibly believe what was accomplished in Chile in less than two years. Because we used the same neurocybernetic model everywhere, we could standardize our procedures: of communications, mensuration, filtration, exposition. Above all, we were able to prepare a single, vast, expensive computer program to operate everywhere, at every level of recursion. I shall discuss that later.

Then let me return now to the two problems identified as critical just now. What exactly is going on? How quickly shall we know today's results.

We trained numbers of operational research teams in the use of the neurocybernetic model, and sent them right through industry. Guided by the model, and constrained by its conventions, their task was to discover the detailed *content* of operations, at all levels of recursion. This meant making a new sort of model, in order to express this content uniquely for each enterprise, each industry. Remember that we were dealing, except in the case of primary industries such as steel and energy, with workers' committees; and that, in any case, we adhered to a political decision to transfer power to the workers. Then the standard techniques would not help. Workers do not understand input–output analysis, nor linear programming. Instead, we developed the notion of a quantified flow chart. This depicts the operations under review as a systems diagram, in which the operations themselves are boxes whose relative size quantifies their relative roles, and in which the width of the lines of flow quantifies the amount of flow. Such diagrams portray quite vividly the nature of the plant; and no one is more qualified than the worker himself to join in the task of preparing them. He works there; he knows what really happens. As these quantified flow charts began to come in, we set our design team the task of fixing the artistic rules for such iconic representation. The use of colour, the radius of bends in the flow lines, and so on, were standardized on ergonomic principles, so that any such chart, whatever its source, had a familiar, and readily understood appearance.

The further task of the operational research teams was to identify a preliminary set of critical variables in each system under study. For example: we needed to identify the size of stocks, input, output, and inter-process; we needed to identify bottleneck operations; in all cases we identified the level of absenteeism as a critical variable, since there is at least some evidence that this is a measure of social unease. But I must emphasize that this was the preliminary picture that we sought to create. Plans were well advanced to provide courses, to make films, to publish booklets, that would make the techniques we were using readily accessible to the workers themselves. We wanted them to enrich our preliminary models, and to add anything they liked to the list of measured variables for which (as you shall see) we were providing them with huge computer power to monitor. This programme was beginning, with the participation of the President himself, when the end came.

So to the second question: the speed of response. Why do the overdeveloped nations tolerate a statistical system that embodies time lags of six months and more, since this is the age of telecommunications? Having been deeply into this question in one such country, I think the answer is that they are frightened. Businessmen do not want an effective and especially a *transparent* economy: too many profit opportunities would be exposed as fraudulent—or at the least, not in the national interest. Bureaucrats are terrified to set up such a system, lest they are accused of trying to bring about exactly that result. But this was Chile. We saw no reason why the economy should not move into a mode of regulation operating in *real time*. This was the first time that any such thing has ever been attempted. There was no problem at all, because we had the models, and the theoretical cybernetic underpinnings.

Of course Chile could not afford to buy modern teleprocessing electronics. You know, I am sure, that the country was under economic siege—and worse—whereby another country firmly intended to bring down the government of the Unidad Popular. Meanwhile, therefore, we used the Telex. Now there is a wasted facility. Telex is used all over the world to convey news, to make purchase enquiries and quotations, and to send birthday greetings to men in the outposts of commercial empires. We used it in Chile to provide the economy with a nervous system; nerves to activate the sinews of government.

Within four months of the start of our work, our telecommunications team had established Cybernet. This was a network of Telex communication extending, by some means or other, to every enterprise. The big firms had Telex already; small ones had never heard of it of course. But Telex machines were moved around so that every enterprise could transmit the state of its critical variables, as identified by the models, to the switching centre in Santiago every day—even if they had to be taken to the machine by telephone or by messanger.

It is clear why I was accused of centralizing the economy! Yet still I was not. We had only two computers at our disposal, and both were in Santiago. That is all there is to it. There are much better ways of doing the job, using a disseminated network of mini-computers, but the facilities were not available. At any rate, we soon had Cybernet live, extending from Arica in the far North down to Punto Arenas—the southernmost city in the world. The linkages were by microwave, already installed, except for the last lap from Puerto Montt southward, which were by protected RF transmission.

Quantification and the Cyberstride Program

We are now confronting the situation in which Cybernet is alive with critical economic data, flowing on a daily basis. Of course, the figures themselves represent all manner of different things: thousands of tons, hundreds of people, millions of escudos. . . . Writing computer programs to accommodate such variety is a daunting prospect.

The answer is to reduce every input datum to a triple index, in which all numbers range simply between 0 and 1. When the operational research teams touring the plants had made their models and identified the critical variables, they were asked to agree two values relating to each variable with the management. The first value was *capability*. This means: how should this variable perform under existing conditions, when the whole system is running in the smoothest way we have ever experienced or can envisage? So capability is not the same as traditional 'capacity', since many processes work below their theoretical limits—because they are embedded in a productive system. Capability takes account of this systemic reality, using the quantified flow chart to understand it. The second value to be agreed for each critical variable was *potentiality*. This stands for a better performance than capability, based on the realization that if only we had one more machine in a bottleneck section, if only we had a better lubricant, if only we could install a conveyor belt, and so on, then we could do *this* much better.

It is evident that the values for capability and potentiality will not change frequently. They can be stored in the computer, and their ratio provides an index called *latency*: the latent performance that could be released by new investment. The datum arriving daily over Cybernet is called *actuality*. The ratio between this actuality and capability yields the classic index of *productivity*, while the ratio between actuality and potentiality yields an overall *performance* index. Performance can also be computed by multiplying together the indices for latency and productivity.

The computer program called Cyberstride operates in the following way. On arrival, the actuality figure is examined for plausibility. This is done by statistical tests to ensure that it belongs to the population of which it is supposedly a sample. When the datum has been accepted, the capability and potentiality associated with this variable are drawn from the store, and the three indices are computed. In setting up the system, we created statistical distributions of 100 days' input for each index, and studied their characteristics. Since any ratio has a finite upper bound, such distributions are usually badly skewed; whereas it is convenient in a system of this kind if Gaussian distributions are available, so that whatever one later decides to do will be statistically robust. This is accomplished by making a trigonometric transformation, such as the inverse sine to the index, which has the effect of moving the distribution towards the centre of its scale, thereby simulating a Gaussian curve.

On the strength of the 100 days' sample, each enterprise was informed of the mean level of productivity, and the latency, associated with each critical variable in its quantified flow chart. These values were then used to quantify the charts developed at the next level of recursion, and so on to the total industry level. Please note that this is a form of aggregation of economic statistics that has a lot more to commend it than aggregation by totals in the customary way. For each level of aggregation is related to a system; and the critical variables being measured combine information according to the systemic characteristics revealed by the model at that level of recursion.

We now had a static picture of the state of productivity, latency and overall performance for the whole of industry—or, to be accurate, we had the picture for about 75 per cent of nationalized industry by the time of the government's fall. Let us return to the computer program Cyberstride, and its daily operations. An actuality figure for a critical variable has arrived, and has been accepted by the program as plausible. The triple indices have been calculated, and normalized by the trigonometric transformation. Now this value is the latest in a time series of the values that have been computed for this variable day by day. The question that the program must now answer is: does this new result matter at all, or is it to be understood as a chance variation in the ordinary course of events?

Answering this question is the heart of the Cyberstride program. We did it by the use of Bayesian probability theory, building on the truly elegant and powerful work of Harrison and Stevens. [2]. For each new point computed, the program calculates four probabilities: that it is a chance variation in the time series; that it is a transient; that it indicates a change of slope; that it indicates a change by a step function. The first two outcomes are unimportant: nothing happens. But either of the indications of change matter very much, and therefore the enterprise is immediately and automatically informed. A truly cybernetic feature of this complicated program is that it uses more or less of the time series, and undertakes more or less statistical work, depending on whether its assessment of these probabilities suggests that they are likely to be important or not.

In this way we sought to endow the humblest Chilean enterprise with computer power, not to calculate its payroll or update its order books—on which and similar trivialities most of the world's computer power is frittered away—but to be a new lobe of the management's own brain. We found that Cyberstride could track the course of the critical variables, and sound alarms about potential trends, far more reliably than can the brain itself. There were many practical difficulties. The greatest was the need to 'tune' Cyberstride so that it would not over-react. A special tuning program had to be prepared for the purpose. But the effort involved in this is predictable from the neurocybernetic model: we were designing the very filtration system that will not overload the cortex, and yet will make the cortex aware of everything it should know. No wonder the task was difficult.

Reports back to the enterprises from this monitoring facility were not available to anyone else. In this lay the devolution of power. When we came to the higher levels of recursion, the daily data were aggregated through their systemic models. Then at each higher level of recursion there would be a new set of critical variables, newly activated every day by systematically aggregated statistics, and producing a new stream of indexical responses appropriate to each level concerned. Of course, these streams of data could, in turn, be submitted to Cyberstride. In this way, as I argued earlier, the entire industrial economy could be monitored in real time, using sets of nested models, quantified flow charts appropriate to every level of recursion, and a single ingenious computer program for filtration and short-term forecasting. May I remind you again of the provision that the workers' committees would be entitled to add any variables that they liked to our basic few. They would not even have to declare what they were. Cyberstride would monitor them.

Anyway, this total picture was incomplete: it was within the five-year, not the two-year, time horizon. What is much more interesting than the facts about timing is the experience gained in *using* these tools as they were developed.

The conceptual framework we were using changed the way that both the government and industry looked at their problems. As the practical tools became available that enabled us both to deal with the tasks of allocation and distribution, and to face up to emergencies occasioned by local shortages and even widespread strikes, the people responsible found that the basic model made sense in active service. The process of innovation became a dynamic drive.

Here is a very extraordinary truth. We may sit here together and understand—deeply, and in full—what is the meaning of modelling, and of linking together models at several levels of recursion. But when it comes to *doing* these things, to practising cybernetics, the quality of our enlightenment changes utterly. It is not easy to acquire skill in the use of sophisticated tools, even when they are properly understood: that much is obvious. But it was not obvious that the use of the tools imparts new dimensions to the management process.

I think that it ought to be obvious, because it is clearly true of *physical* tools. The equipment that men hold in their hands governs their whole perception of the task they confront. It is true of management too, as we discovered in Chile. And if this was not our expectation in advance, it shows how little genuine innovation ever penetrates management—else the truth would be obvious to all. How many managers have ever felt that, as a result of a computer innovation for instance, their perception and purposes were totally changed? Very few, I believe; because we use computers, and indeed cybernetics, to do silly things.

Algedonic Regulation

There is now something to be learnt from the brain, and it is of critical importance. Clearly all this filtration is vitally necessary, or we should be in a perpetual condition of epileptic seizure—with great tides of electrical activity sweeping over the cortex, or with management inundated with great piles of irrelevant computer output (an all too familiar situation; modern management *is* epileptic). But when the filtration system is really working smoothly, and eliminating a greal deal of this irrelevant input, we run the risk of simply falling asleep.

Neurocybernetics has penetrated the mechanism whereby, as I mentioned before, the organism is alerted to danger. I call this the *algedonic* system, meaning the apparatus whereby pain and pleasure provide a qualitatively different set of filters from those that monitor sensory input. We copied the brain's tricks for algedonic response in the Chilean system in the following way.

So far as you have heard, each level of recursion has its own set of critical variables, monitored at its own level. None has any direct information about imminent crisis at the level below: because the alarms have been sent back at that lower level, and only the raw data have been transmitted upward, in order to quantify the higher level systemic models. Now we use the vertical dimension of our original phase-space to make an algedonic, and not an authoritarian, linkage.

For the last time, I refer back to the work of the operational research teams. They made the preliminary quantified flow charts; they selected the critical variables; they obtained agreement on the capability and potentiality values. But they were also asked to agree with the workers' management on two things more. For every critical variable a *weight* had to be assigned, because some critical variables are more critical than others. And for each critical variable they were asked to assess how long it would take, given the type of technology involved, to restore productivity to normal—if it showed a statistically significant decline. This time interval, duly weighted by the importance of the variable, was then set up within the Cyberstride program as a kind of clock.

When a signal forewarning a change for the worse was sent out, at any level of recursion, the clock for that variable was started. Cyberstride would then look out for a recovery of this indicated variable. If the recovery did not appear before the clock ran out, then an algedonic cry of pain would automatically pass up to the next higher level of recursion—announcing a need for help. In this way, it is possible in theory that the President's economic committee would eventually hear of the ineffectiveness of a limestone crusher somewhere in the far North. It would hear of this if the clock ran out in the plant, then in the cement industry, then in the materials branch—because the algedonic signal would have been passed on.

This facility belongs to any industrial system, although it is usually informal. Algedonic signals are passed by word of mouth. But they become distorted in the process, and often result in hasty adverse judgements being passed on the human beings involved. By building these algedonics into the electronic system, I believe that we made another big advance. Some critics have called this mechanism oppressive; it depends on the motivation behind it. I think that the Chilean workers were not in the least concerned about being 'found out'; rather they were anxious to have their problems brought to the attention of those who might be able to solve them as soon as possible. The system was set to do just this in an objective, clear-cut way; a way that from its inception was in any case under their own control.

The Operations Room

The next question concerns just how all this information ought to be presented. For a long time I had been anxious to create an *environment for decision*, a place where a creative group of people really could undertake creative thinking—with all the aids to that process that science could give them. Our boardrooms, committee rooms, and cabinet rooms are shrines to institutional pomp and circumstance; and the latest and greatest scientific aid that they can boast is the ball-point pen.

We built in Santiago an operations room, conceived as a decision environment for a creative group that would certainly include workers. There are no tables, and no paperwork in here. The people in the room (who might be the key people at *any* level of recursion) constitute the brainpower. And they are served, as the brain itself is served, by a nervous system innervating the whole of the relevant body—in this case the whole of Chilean industry. You know how that was done. So to this room came the daily, filtered, sensory inputs from Cyberstride; to this room came the algedonic signals; and from this room went the questions, and ultimately the decisions. The room I describe was built and was working. But it was simply a prototype, and the economy of Chile was never actually commanded from there (Figure 12.1).

Figure 12.1 End of January 1972; the completed operations room in Santiago de Chile in working order. The screens were driven by equipment housed in the annular space around the room, in turn connected to the social economy by TELEX, microwave links and computers. The room itself (but not the equipment) was constructed in six weeks. The finished job was described by hysterical critics as 'palpably a mere model' and 'a set for the film *2001*'. However, it worked. (See especially *Brain of the Firm*, 2nd edn. John Wiley 1981.)

Instead, smaller and less pretentious rooms were constructed at other levels of recursion, to act as foci for information and regulatory activity.

On the first wall is an illustrated, animated, screen—eight feet high—depicting the neurocybernetic model. The *content* of this model can be changed by the Room Manager, so as to depict the correct components for the level of recursion that the meeting has to consider. Into this screen are slotted iconic representations of the mean triple indices—so that one can see at a glance how low is the productivity here, how high is the latency there. The flow lines do not bear the conventional arrows: they actually move, and each can be set at one of three different speeds. This screen provides the backcloth to the meeting, reminding those present (and they certainly do need reminding) of the level of recursion with which they are supposed to deal. If an algedonic signal is present, this is shown flashing.

On the second wall are two screens. The first carries today's Cyberstride output, as appropriate to this level of recursion; the second carries details of the algedonic signals, if any are present, from lower levels of recursion. In this actual room, those signals had to be hand-posted; but it is obvious that, if we had proper interface equipment such as is perfectly available, the screens would have been activated directly by the computer.

On the third wall is an equipment called *Datafeed*. It is obvious that once the creative group has checked up on its general position, using the first screen, and noted the alerting signals emanating from Cyberstride on the second wall, it will want supportive information. Now I do not believe in the concept of computer data banks, which says that providing one stuffs every iota of relevant information into a computer, somehow or another the answer you need will always be there. There is a little problem in the way, and it is called retrieval. Millions of dollars have been spent on the problem of selective retrieval. It has not been solved. I think that there are good cybernetic reasons for judging that it *cannot* be solved. Therefore, adhering to our belief in iconic representation as being fully acceptable to the human brain, *Datafeed* is a visual data bank.

Datafeed incorporates three active information screens, surmounted by a huge index screen. Each of the three active screens is supplied, by back projection, with five carousel projectors, each containing eighty slides. Thus the three screens between them command twelve hundred separate pieces of visual information. These carousels are selected from store by the Room Manager, ready to serve the meeting at its appropriate level of recursion. All the relevant quantified flow charts are available here. Photographs of plants are available (and how much information the experienced brain can gain simply from looking at a photograph of a works). Investment plans and projections are also available, also in iconic form. And so on.

In the room are seven swivel chairs. The fact of seven is drawn from experimental psychology; it appears that this is about the largest number for a creative group. After seven, the inter-personal reactions break down, and formal procedures have to be devised. In the arms of the seven chairs are fixed a set of buttons. Anyone can slam home a button, and gain control of Datafeed. Then by using the index screen, and another set of buttons, he may display to the group any information that he wants to call up. The digital logic for doing all this is quite complicated, but it certainly worked.

Well, the room is octagonal: it is a room, 10 metres wide, inside a larger room—the annular space being filled with technical apparatus, such as the 16 projectors and the digital logic racks required for Datafeed. The fourth wall is an access door to all this. The fifth wall is set aside to contain an algedonic meter to which I shall refer later. The sixth wall is the main entrance.

On the seventh wall is a huge, animated model of the whole economy. Now I must emphasize that in the two years that we had, this was never made to work. It certainly worked visually; but the computer drive behind it was experimental and fragmentary. We used the *Dynamo II* compiler, emanating from Forrester's work at MIT, because it was so free of programming defects—it had been thoroughly 'debugged'. The idea is that the creative group, aware of their situation as they are from the equipment so far discussed, should be able to simulate the effects of alternative decisions. They are able to change the animated model of the economy, and to obtain 10-year projections of the likely effects on the screen built into the eighth, and final, wall.

As I said, we did not achieve this result. This is the moment to say that the President had five years left to run when I arrived, and this was our time horizon. Constitutionally, he could not be re-elected; constitutionally, he could not be evicted. We had two of our planned five years; and we were ahead of schedule.

You now have a total, albeit not fully detailed, account of Project Cybersyn. Even within its short life, it had its uses to government. So much so, that the last instruction we received from the President—just a week before his death—was to move the whole operations room from its experimental location right into the palace, La Moneda. This was a strong decision. It meant ripping out some historic rooms, because the total area required was large. By the 11 September 1973, the plans were nearly ready. Instead La Moneda itself was reduced to a smoking ruin.

ON THE PROBLEM OF NATIONAL MODELS

I have just mentioned briefly the technical difficulties that we encountered in the overall modelling process, using the Dynamo II compiler. But I consider this Lecture an appropriate occasion on which to ventilate much more profound issues than such technicalities.

Many countries attempt national economic planning, at various levels of rigour; and I well remember that India herself was early in this development. Today, there are various whole-world models being canvassed, and these deeply affect the interests of the Third World. Most of these models choose GNP per capita as a maximizing functional, on the understanding that this is some sort of proxy variable that can stand for 'the greatest good of the greatest number', as Bentham put it. But of course it was noticed that GNP per capita is a poor proxy, if you happen to live in a small, rich state where the ruler holds all the wealth. The GNP per capita may be very high, but the mass of the people is starving.

Accordingly, the Club of Rome enables the Fundacion Bariloche of Argentina to develop a different kind of model; and they decided that the proxy variable that they would use as a maximizing functional was life expectancy at birth. They have compounded this concept from the availability of shelter, food, health and education. I think that this is an advance, because it does not build into the model as does 'Limits to Growth', the wholesale assumptions of the capitalist ethic. Even so, we are not there yet. I want to offer you a brief personal reflection, based on my Chilean thoughts.

I see myself standing on the road to Portillo in the High Andes, looking down thousands of feet on to the city of Santiago, where several millions of people live in direst poverty. Laid over the city is an enormous blanket of smog—quite as bad as anything I have seen from the aeroplane over Los Angeles in California. And I ask myself: is it *really* GNP per capita that we are after? I see myself driving from the coast near Los Vilos back to the capital. It is growing dark, and I am passing a settlement of shacks. Through an open doorway, in the dusk, appears the familiar rectangular glow of the television screen, carrying programmes made in the United States, and a mass of consumer advertising. I ask myself again: is it *really* GNP per capita? And then I think instead of the Bariloche criterion of life expectancy. This time I ask myself: Were 43 per cent of Chileans, when they voted for Allende in March 1973, *really* after life expectancy? Most of them, it seems to me, were quite consciously not maximizing anything of the kind.

In short I am saying that developing countries still have the opportunity to ask themselves what kind of civilization they wish to become in the age of advanced technology. I do not think that there is any sense in eschewing technology, if the terrible crises provoked by famine and disease are to be overcome. But this does not mean to say that we cannot eschew consumerism; or that we cannot retain the dignity and joy of philosophic and aesthetic values that belonged to the national soul before the steam engine was even invented.

There should be totally new studies of such problems as transportation, education and health, that do not lean on the value systems of the West at all, nor on the managerial and operating techniques devised so far by the West—because they do not work. There are many fine scientists, belonging to the Third World, wasting their talent in the alien culture of the West because (so they tell me) there are no opportunities at home. I beg you to bring them back, and to create those opportunities. The idea would be to design the nation that the people want, and not just to let the nation emerge as a confused and corrupted copy of the overdeveloped nations which demonstrate the path only to cultural decay and institutional collapse.

Of course, all this represents (as I am trying to say with my Chilean experiences) a totally new outlook on national planning. I am afraid that so much of this is bureaucratic and unreal. In the work so far described, we did not work through the bureaucracy at all. We had the authority to set up the new system, and we went out and did it. If it had not been organized in this way, I am sure that we should still have been writing papers for submission to committees at the time of the *coup d'etat*. So here again, in the matter of national planning itself, I beg you to think afresh about the best approaches to use in order to get something done.

Now that may sound aggressive and technocratic. Do we not already have proper machinery of government, to see that these advances are made in an orderly and a democratic way? But perhaps that machinery is not working well either; and perhaps the ordinary citizen's perspective is that there is nothing particularly democratic about a state bureaucracy which, for him, may look merely oppressive—however good may be the intentions that it embodies. Then we ought to ask: how can the pursuit of democracy itself be aided by science and technology, and how can they be harnessed to ensure the participation of the people in national decisions? I would like to say something now about the Chilean work that has not been made public before. It is tentative, and we did not get very far with it, but the story I am telling would be grossly incomplete if I were to stop now.

THE PEOPLE PROJECT

While La Moneda was being shelled and bombed, the President of Chile made a last broadcast to his people. One of his invocations said: 'I address myself to the youth, to those who sang, who gave their joy and spirit to the struggle.'

It is impossible to convey to you any more directly than that either the enthusiasm with which young people, with poets, artists, and musicians, sought to mobilize the spirit of the people in their adversity, or the President's own awareness of the need that they should do so. I joined in with them to the best of my ability, and it *was* a joy. But what could the professional cybernetician do on this front? I tried to evolve some new ideas, working with other sets of people than the teams involved in Cybersyn.

In the first place, I reapplied the neurocybernetic model at a far higher level of recursion: that of the whole nation. Working diagnostically, I identified five aspects of the national life that seemed to cause ordinary people trouble, and which (the model suggested) slowed down the national metabolism. Five essays were written, in cybernetic terminology, discussing these five issues; and these were debated at the professional level. When it seemed that these matters were scientifically sound, and properly understood, the essays went through a succession of transformations. Each transformation shortened the essay, each transformation removed another chunk of cybernetic jargon. In the end, the hope was that the issues had been reduced to their kernels. I finished with a little booklet, bearing one of the five issues on each page. There the issue was described in about three lines of simple, ordinary language, illustrated by a drawing—a cartoon.

I handed over the booklet, suggesting that it should be printed and widely distributed, and the separate pages turned into posters. The idea was well received, but nothing had come of it by the end of the day: we needed more time. I mention it now, because this was certainly a novel use of cybernetic analysis. We also tried to turn the booklet into songs. One of them was written, and sung, but we could not get it recorded because of a strike, which you may find ironic. The second tentative research was more far-reaching.

President Allende talked often about his concept of a National Assembly. Within the theory of a representative democracy, a parliament or congress is a national assembly. But once again, the rate of technological development is eroding the traditional system. The mass media disseminate information continuously, whereas the elections occur at long intervals. Therefore a great deal of power has fallen into the hands of the media, and of public opinion pollsters, because there is a gross mismatch between the time scales of public awareness and the electoral process. This threatens democracy itself.

But the media are not slow to cash in on this situation. All over the Western world there are radio programmes in which people telephone in with their reactions to the state of current news. In particular, a number of experiments have been made with television that, on the face of it, approximate to an electronic national assembly. I believe that these are fraught with danger, and will describe the sort of thing that is going on, and give you my objections [3].

It is easy enough to recruit a representative sample of the public, by good statistical criteria, to watch a television programme. Thanks to technological capacity, samples of the order of 20 000 have proven possible to handle. At various stages of the political debate in the studio, these people are asked to cast a vote. This they do by telephoning a number, where their opinions on a selection of questions are received by punched-card operators. The cards then go into a computer. A very short time after calling for the vote, the television commentator is able to announce to the studio panel, and to the nation, 'what the nation thinks'. You can see why I say that the tradition of representative democracy may be eroded: this kind of technological development could soon make elections irrelevant. Now I come to the objections; which are similar to my objections to all kinds of national referenda.

In order to pose a set of questions in this form, the problems that face the nation have to be structured. The objection is that if we knew how to structure the problems properly, we could probably solve them, but we do not. Secondly, lists of questions are drawn up to fit this structure. The objections are that they may not be appropriate questions, that they may ignore alternatives of which the producers are ignorant, and that they may be posed in an ambiguous or even tendentious way. Thirdly, answers have to be given to these structured and maybe slanted questions in binary form, to make things easier for the computer. But very often people do not want to say yes or no; they want to take up a third position; and their role is worse than negated if this attitude is represented as 'not knowing'.

This indictment of the system is brief but sufficiently damaging. When I discussed it with one of its protagonists in North America, he said: 'But the computer equipment and operating system was originally designed for home teaching purposes. Don't you see that if the people cannot understand the problem structures, the question forms, or the way to answer, *we can teach them*.' Heaven forbid. It seems that we may be talking about more than the end of democracy, but the end of freedom as well.

Here, then, is a new approach to the issue. People may not have either the learning or the wish to accept an inquisition of this form. What they certainly do have are brains, personal perceptions and purposes. I have great confidence in this arrangement, on which it seems to me that the whole nation of liberty is founded. And I have noticed that people, though uneducated, though inarticulate in an intellectual context, are well able to express themselves in terms of their happiness or unhappiness with a given state of affairs. For this kind of social happiness, which is quite different from inward spiritual joy, I use Aristotle's word *eudemony*.

Then how could one measure eudemony? The ballot box in a representative democracy tries to measure just this. It has the problem that what it really measures is negative eudemony: What is 'the least bad'. But in any case, if the state of our technology in communications calls for something more frequent than an election, something almost continuous, then it might yet be done. To use the terminology developed earlier, we need an algedonic meter. It has to be simple, and cheap.

The experimental equipment that I took to Chile was a low-voltage analogue device. A group of people, perhaps a whole village, would have one algedonic meter, which they would be entitled to set. It consisted of two intertwined discs, one orange and happy, the other grey and sad. By simply turning the central knob, the proportions of orange and grey could be varied. Obviously this setting could be picked up electrically, and summed for districts, and for the nation itself. The equipment that I took had ten stations, and one summation machine. The intention was to make experiments, not at the level of national eudemony, but in a single factory first.

But now is the time to recall that, in my description of the operations room, I remarked on space set aside on the fifth wall to contain an algedonic meter. The tentative idea was that the presidential economic committee might explain its policies to the nation by television from the operations room, while the nation registered its reactions on algedonic meters summated on the fifth wall—*which the audience could see*. This was an attempted cybernetic answer to President Allende's interest in the concept of a National Assembly. Incidentally, it would have involved equipping villages with public television reception centres for the purpose. And strangely enough, I had first put that particular part of the suggestion forward to India more than 10 years earlier. The costs of equipping the nation in this way for government purposes are not at all frightening these days. What is more frightening is the risk that the people, gathered in their village to reply, would doubtless be suborned by political parties. Such questions need much thought.

This whole scheme is simple enough to work, and cheap enough to implement. At first hearing, it may also sound *too* simple to be called, as I just called it, 'a cybernetic answer'. Then please allow me to explain why such a system is much more complex and subtle than you might at first think. It would be more convenient, perhaps, to use the example of the factory, where the experiment was planned, than to consider the whole nation. I am sure that you will make the necessary extrapolation.

Consider then a factory. In each section, where a group of a few people work, is an algedonic meter. The group is entitled to change the setting of its meter *at any time*. One can well imagine what would lead them to do so. Workers are loyal people; they also have machinery for voicing their views. But eudemony is another matter; it is inarticulate, unanalytic. Hence the idea to provide an algedonic signal. The algedonic meter settings throughout the factory are summed in two places; the main entrance to the factory, where all can see it, and in the office of the managing director. Here is the cybernetic analysis.

First of all, a group of workers which has set its meter will see, as it enters and leaves the factory, that its own state of eudemony is or is not representative of the factory as a whole. Then this could prove a stabilizing influence. On the contrary, this group might be outraged, and attempt to persuade other groups to change their settings. Whatever happens, a very complex chain of inter-group reactions is entailed—because eudemony exists, and is discussed; but algedonic channels for exhibiting eudemony on a continuous and unemotive basis have not been provided before. The cybernetic complexity derives from the ramifications of feedback between groups that must arise.

Secondly, the case of the managing director is even more interesting. Workers are never quite sure that the boss is aware of their state of eudemony. Under this scheme, he would be so aware; *and they would know* that he was aware. Even more sensationally: he would know that they *knew* he was aware; and they would know this, too. If one tries to think all this (and more) through, the complications are endless. We have installed algedonic feedbacks all through the system: I can see no way of predicting the outcome. Hence the wish to experiment.

If I may just refer to that television broadcast from the operations room a final time, I ask you to envisage what it would be like to be the Minister of Economics, who is explaining his benign policies to an expectant nation. As you do so, national eudemony as registered on the algedonic meter at your side steadily sinks. You can see it. The nation can see it. You know that the nation can see it. The nation knows that you know . . .

THE INCONCLUSIVE CONCLUSION

It is clear that I must conclude soon, although the experiences of two years have been so hard to condense into a lecture—even into one of this inordinate length.

We have just been considering the will of the people, and how to make it known. We know what, under a democratic constitution, was the will of the Chilean people; and we know how that will was subjugated by tyrannical force, supported by money and decisions emanating from another government. I have complete moral certainty that the situation would have been held if it had not been for that continuous external intervention; and surely I must be brave enough to say so. Fortunately, enough of the story is now public knowledge[4], and to make that statement sounds less than wild.

No one can say that a country is not entitled to choose where it puts its money and its aid. Of course it is; and that especially applies to private banks. But we were talking about the will of the people. And whether the people of the United States themselves approve of what happened in their name, is open to doubt. I doubt, for instance, if the Americans I know are proud to hear that eight times the amount of credit for supplies of grain was released for Chile within a few days of the *coup d'état*, than had been released in the whole three years of Unidad Popular.

But a vicious government is one thing, and the perversion of supposedly international organizations is another. I am thinking especially of the Inter-American Development Bank and of the World Bank: so-called 'multilateral' institutions. Neither would grant new loans to the Allende government, although (and this should be widely known) that government, despite everything, did not default on its repayments of old loans. In 1971 and 1972, Chile repaid around $16 million to the Inter-American Development Bank. In return, she was even denied emergency relief for her 1971 earthquake victims. The world at large must renovate its multilateral machinery quickly, for it is at the mercy of financial power.

When the professional institutions of Chile finally became aware of Project Cybersyn; they asked me to address them. I was open with my own attitudes to them, as I am with you today. They were deeply shocked. They called me partisan. Of course I am partisan, because I am a human being; and to be a scientist is less than castration. Perhaps this shocks you too. But if so, that is an intrinsic part of my message, that you may accept or reject with all the rest. The time has passed when professionals can possibly disown the consequences of their work. The time came and went in 1945, when I myself was here in India, and two atom bombs were dropped upon Japan.

If I had not been proud and dedicated about the work in Chile, I ought not to have done it. If, given the nature of that work, I had not been aware of the foreign intent to bring the government down, I should have been a very poor operational research man and adviser. If, as I try now to report to you what happened, I were to leave out the most relevant facts of all, it would be contemptible for us both.

I gave the Compañero Presidente a book, which I inscribed with the words of a Spanish saying: 'Gran victoria es la que sin sangre se alcanza'. It means: 'Great is the victory obtained without blood'. Allende's victory *was* bloodless, until his own blood flowed—and that, as he well knew, was not defeat. Permit me to salute his memory:

न, ख़ाक में मिल
न, आग में जल
जब ख़िश्त बने
तब काम चले।

The words are those of the ancient Urdu poet Chakbast, which Stafford Beer translated thus in tribute to President Allende:

You come to dust
You pass through fire
Become a brick
For further work

References

1. Beer, Stafford, *Brain of the Firm.* Allen Lane, 1972.
2. P. J. Harrison and C. F. Stevens. 'A Bayesian approach to short-term forecasting'. *Operational Research Quarterly*, **22**(4), December 1971.
3. *Editors' note* See also 'The will of the people'. *Journal of the Operational Research Society*, **34**, 797–810, 1983.
4. See, for instance, the IDOC Dossier, *The End of Chilean Democracy*, Laurence Binns (ed.). Continuum Books, Seabury Press, New York, 1974.

A CHILEAN SPRING LATER

numbed love responds again now
to those discarded
the floaters in the river
chattering through Santiago
or found in thickets

girls whom I had known
touched with their hands
cold heads
and found life different

even the blood was cold

piles of cut hair left in the streets
were meant to indicate
how it all went too far
to explicate with histrionics why
they killed a man I loved

others in filthy camps or
stuck in priest-holes of the brain
beleaguered partly dead
are also cold
bereft of warm purposes

now the gorillas have taken
laughter, hugs of huge delight
and love from wide soft eyes
measured out gaiety
and lusty evenings

continued

pounded them in mortars
dourly thudded them to residues
of alchemistic dross
in recipes compounded for
the master—death, and pouring
them like ordures
on to the rotting heaps of dreams

retch with that stench
numbed love responds again now
to the dead
hears also the caught breath
of aspiration

once there was earnest talk
angled through plush and ormolu
around great rooms of state

walking once by tinkling water
near El Arrayan dangled
cold legs in rushing melted snow

noted gold flecks in panther eyes

once entered hidden
private rooms of restaurants
with a sufficient small nod

and by the sea hurled
imprecations at waves
as high as houses higher
than the risks they tumbled over
those black rocks

once got unspeakable thoughts
through to that unspeakable
best friend

continued

a Chilean spring later
his maybe death
grips my head with iron spikes
while the drains still run
with other blood

panthers crouch in darkness
waiting

no river dalliance now
the restaurants are closed to us
there is no crashing oceanic diapason
to support a silent flute

blackened shells
of state rooms echo
cavernous words
all empty
for that other man I loved
they killed him

let them take each
of the short foul loutish words once
threaded
in permutations on the long strings
of these lines
as a bullet
in the chest

leaving an inarticulate remark
made dumb with outrage meant
to discuss
reduction of variety in the soul

such metaphysical feasting
compañeros
compañeras
as must wait
on many resurrections

Stafford Beer
Transit, 1977

13 PREFACE TO AUTOPOIESIS: THE ORGANIZATION OF THE LIVING

By Humberto Maturana and Francisco Varela

STAFFORD BEER

THIS SMALL book is very large: it contains the living universe. It is a privilege to be asked to write this preface, and a delight to do so. That is because I recognize here a really important book, both in general and specifically. Before talking about the specific contents at all, I would like to explain why this is in general so.

IN GENERAL ...

We are the inheritors of categorized knowledge; therefore we inherit also a world view that consists of parts strung together, rather than wholes regarded through different sets of filters. Historically, synthesis seems to have been too much for the human mind—where practical affairs were concerned. The descent of the synthetic method from Plato through Augustine took men's perception into literature, art and mysticism. The modern world of science and technology is bred from Aristotle and Aquinas by analysis. The categorization that took hold of medieval scholasticism has really lasted it out. We may see with hindsight that the historical revolts against the scholastics did not shake free from the shackles of their reductionism.

The revolt of the rationalists—Descartes, Spinoza, Leibniz—began from a principle of 'methodical doubt'. But they became lost in mechanism, dualism, more and more categorization; and they ended in denying relation altogether. But relation is the stuff of system. Relation is the essence of

First published by D. Reidel Publishing Co., Dordrecht, Holland.

synthesis. The revolt of the empiricists—Locke, Berkeley, Hume—began from the nature of understanding about the environment. But analysis was still the method, and categorization still the practical tool of advance. In the bizarre outcome, whereby it was the empiricists who denied the very existence of the empirical world, relation survived—but only through the concept of mental association between mental events. The system 'out there', which we call nature, had been annihilated in the process.

By the time Kant was devoting his prodigious mind to sorting all this out, the battle was lost. If then, quoting him, unconscious understanding organizes sensory experience into schemata, while conscious understanding organizes it into categories, the notion of identity remains for Kant for ever transcendental. Now the individual has vanished, in practical terms; as to the assemblage of individuals called society, that too has vanished into a transcendental construct. We have no need to legislate through any consensus of actual people, but only to meet needs that *might* have arisen from the noumenal will.

And what of science itself? Science is ordered knowledge. It began with classification. From Galen in the second century through to Linnaeus in the eighteenth, analysis and categorization provided the natural instrumentality of scientific progress. Ally this fact with the background of philosophic thought, and the scene is set for the inexorable development of the world view that is so difficult to challenge today. It is a world view in which real systems are annihilated in trying to understand them, in which relations are lost because they are not categorized, in which synthesis is relegated to poetry and mysticism, in which identity is a political inference. We may inspect the result in the structure and organization of the contemporary university.

It is an iron maiden, in whose secure embrace scholarship is trapped. For many, this is an entirely satisfactory situation, just because the embrace *is* secure. A man who can lay claim to knowledge about some categorized bit of the world, however tiny, which is greater than anyone else's knowledge of that bit, is safe for life: reputation grows, paranoia deepens. The number of papers increases exponentially, knowledge grows by infinitesimals; but understanding of the world actually recedes, because the world really is an interacting system. And since the world, in many of its aspects, is changing at an exponential rate, this kind of scholarship, rooted in the historical search of its own sanctified categories, is in large part unavailing to the needs of mankind.

There has been some recognition of this, and interdisciplinary studies are by now commonplace in every university. But will this deal with the problem? Unfortunately, it will not. We still say that a graduate must have his 'basic discipline', and this he is solemnly taught—as if such a thing had a precise environmental correlate, and as if we knew that God knew the difference between physics and chemistry. He learns also the academic *mores*, catches the institutional paranoia, and proceeds to propagate the whole business. Thus it is that an 'interdisciplinary study' often consists of a group of disciplinarians holding hands in a ring for mutual comfort. The ostensible topic has slipped down the hole in the middle. Among those who recognize this too, a natural enough debate has ensued on the subject: can an undergraduate be taught 'interdisciplinary studies' *as* his basic subject? But there is no such subject; there is no agreement on what it would be like; and we are rather short of anyone qualified to do the teaching. Those who resist the whole idea, in my view correctly, say that it would endanger the norms of good scholarship. There is a deadlock.

Against this background, let us consider *Autopioiesis*, and try to answer the question: what is it? The authors say: 'our purpose is to understand the organization of living systems in relation to their unitary character'. If the book deals with living systems, then it must be about biology. If it says anything scientific about organization, it must be about cybernetics. If it can recognize the nature of unitary character, it must be about epistemology—and also (remembering the first author's massive contribution to the understanding of perception) it will be about psychology too. Yes, it is indeed about all these things. Will you then call this an interdisciplinary study in the field of psychocyberbioepistemics? Do so only if you wish to insult the authors. Because *their* topic has *not* slipped down the hole in the middle. Therefore it is not an interdisciplinary study of the kind defined. It is not about analysis, but synthesis. It does not play the Game of the Categories. And it does not interrelate disciplines: it transcends them. If, because of my remarks about Kant, this seems to say that it annihilates them, then we are getting somewhere.

For there resides my belief in the book's general importance. The dissolution of the deadlock within the disciplinary system that I described above has got to be *meta*systemic, not merely interdisciplinary. We are not interested in forming a league of disciplinary paranoids, but (as Hegel could have told us) in a higher synthesis of disciplines. What emerges in this book is not classifiable under the old categories. Therefore it is predictable that no university could contain it, although all universities can and now do contain interdisciplinary institutions—because, in that very word, suitable obeisance is paid to the hallowed categories, and no one cares if the answers slip down the hole in the middle. As to the prediction that universities cannot contain this kind of work, I have often seen it fulfilled. In the present case it is falsified, and I offer heartfelt congratulations to the University of Chile.

I say 'heartfelt' for this reason. In the mounting pile of new books printed every year that are properly called scientific, one may take hold of one's candle and search like a veritable Diogenes for a single one answering to the honest criteria I have proposed for a metasystemic utterance. There is only a handful in existence at all, which is not surprising in view of the way both knowledge and academia are organized. And yet, as I have also proposed, herein lies the world's real need. If we are able to understand a newer and still evolving world; if we are to educate people to live in that world; if we are to legislate for that world; if we are to abandon categories and institutions that belong to a vanished world, as it is well-nigh desperate that we should; then knowledge must be rewritten. *Autopoietic Systems* belongs to the new library.

IN PARTICULAR . . .

The authors first of all say that an autopioetic system is a homeostat. We already know what that is: a device for holding a critical systemic variable within physiological limits. They go on to the definitive point: in the case of autopoietic homeostasis, the critical variable is *the system's own organization*. It does not matter, it seems, whether every measurable property of that organization structure changes utterly in the system's process of continuing adaptation. *It* survives.

This is a very exciting idea to me for two reasons. In the first place it solves the problem of identity which 2000 years of philosophy have succeeded only in further confounding. The search for the 'it' has led further and further away from anything that common sense would call reality. The 'it' of scholasticism is a mythological substance in which anything attested by the sense or testable by science inheres as a mere accident—its existence is a matter of faith. The 'it' of rationalism is unrealistically schizophrenic, because it is uncompromising in its duality—extended substance and thinking substance. The 'it' of empiricism is unrealistically insubstantial and ephemeral at the same time—*esse est percipi* is by no means the verdict of any experiencing human being.

The 'it' of Kant is the transcendental 'thing-in-itself'—an untestable inference, an intellectual geegaw. As to the 'it' of science and technology in the twentieth-century world of conspicuous consumption . . . 'it' seems to be no more than the collection of epiphenomena which mark 'it' as consumer or consumed. In this way hard-headed materialism seems to make 'it' as insubstantial as subjective idealism made it at the turn of the seventeenth century. And this, the very latest, the most down-to-earth, interpretation of 'it' the authors explicitly refute.

Their 'it' is notified precisely by its survival in a real world. You cannot find it by analysis, because its categories may all have changed since you last looked. There is no need to postulate a mystical something which ensures the preservation of identity *despite* appearances. The very continuation is 'it'. At least, that is my understanding of the authors' thesis—and I note with some glee that this means that Bishop Berkeley got the precisely right argument precisely wrong. He contended that something not being observed goes out of existence. Autopoiesis says that something that exists may turn out to be unrecognizable when you next observe it. This brings us back to reality, for that is surely true.

The second reason why the concept of autopoiesis excites me so much is that it involves the destruction of teleology. When this notion is fully worked out and debated, I suspect it will prove to be as important in the history of the philosophy of science as was David Hume's attack on causality. Hume considered that causation is a mental construct projected on to changing events which have, as we would say today, associated probabilities of mutual occurrence. I myself have for a long time been convinced that purpose is a mental construct imported by the observer to explain what is really an equilibrial phenomenon of polystable systems. The arguments in Chapter II appear to me to justify this view completely, and I leave the reader to engender his own excitement in the discovery of a 'purposelessness' that none the less makes good sense to a human being—just because he is allowed to keep his identity, which alone *is* his 'purpose'. It is enough.

But that salute to the authors is also self-congratulation, and I turn quickly aside. If a book is important, if at any time and from any source *information* is received, then something is changed—not merely confirmed. There are two arguments in this book that have changed me, and one of them effected its change after a profound inward struggle. Perhaps this part of the preface should be printed as an epilogue: if I am not saying enough to be understood in advance of the reading, then I am sorry. It is too much to hope that the reader will return.

People who work with systems-theoretic concepts have often drawn attention to the subjective nature of 'the system'. A system is not something presented to the observer, it is something recognized by him. One of the consequences of this is that the labelling of connections between the system and its environment as either inputs or outputs is a process of arbitrary distinction. This is not very satisfactory. For example, a motor car in action is evidently a system. Suppose that it is recognized as 'a system for going from A to B'; then the water in the radiator is evidently an input, and displacement is evidently an output. Now consider the following scenario. Two men approach a motor car, and push it towards a second motor car. They then connect the batteries of the two cars with a pair of leads, and the engine of the first car fires. They disconnect the leads, and run the engine hard in neutral gear. We can guess what they are doing; but how is the objective scientist going to describe that system? Displacement is evidently an input, and one output is the rise in temperature of the water in the radiator. In case my example sounds too transparent, note that Aristotle thought that the brain was a 'human radiator', namely an apparatus for cooling the blood. Note also that he was right.

The fact is that we need a theoretical framework for any empirical investigation. This is the *raison d'etre* of empistemology, and the authors make that point. In the trivial example I have just given, we need to know 'all about motor cars' before we can make sense of the empirical data. But it often happens in science that we know nothing at all about our 'motor cars', and sit there scratching our heads over data that relate to we know not what. There is a prime example of this in current scientific work, which is so embarrassing that scientists in general pretend that it is not there. I am referring to the whole field of parapsychology—to the mass of data which seems to say: precognition, telepathy, telekinesis *exist*. But we flounder among statistical artefacts, and lack the theoretical framework for interpretation. This is made clear in the very name of ESP—'extrasensory perception' which, if one thinks about it, constitutes an internal contradiction of terms.

Autopoiesis as a concept propounds a theoretical framework within which to cope with the confusion that arises from the subjective recognition of 'the system' and the arbitrary classification of its inputs and outputs. For the authors explain how we may treat autopoietic systems as if they were not autopoietic (that is, they are allopoietic) when the boundaries of the system are enlarged. Moreover, autopoietic systems may have allopoietic components. These ideas are immensely helpful, because our recognition of the circumstances in which a system should be regarded as either auto—or allo—poietic enables us to define 'the system' in an appropriate context. That is to say that the context is the recursion of systems within which the system we study is embedded, instead of being the cloud of statistical epiphenomena generated by our attempt to study it.

Understanding this changed me. The second change involved the intellectual struggle I mentioned earlier, and it concerns the authors' views on the information flowing within a viable system. In the numbered Paragraph (iv) of Section 1 of Chapter III they say: 'The notion of coding is a cognitive notion which represents the interactions of the observer, not a phenomenon operative in the physical domain. The same applies to the notion of regulation.' On first reading, this seemed to me plainly wrong. In the numbered Paragraph (v) of Section 3 of Chapter IV they say: 'Notions such as coding, message or information are not applicable to the phenomenon of self-reproduction.' Wrong again, I considered; indeed, outrageous—especially when taken with this remark from the first sentence of Section 3: 'reproduction . . . cannot enter as a defining feature of the organization of living systems'. Finally, in the numbered Paragraph (ii) of Section 3 of Chapter V, the authors say: 'A linguistic domain . . . is intrinsically non-informative.' Surely that is finally absurd?

All of this is totally alien to what we (most of us working in cybernetics) have believed. Information, including codes and messages and mappings, was indeed for us the whole story of the viable system. If one thinks of reproduction, for example, as the process of passing on a DNA code from an ageing set of tissues to an embryonic set of tissues, then the survival of the code itself is what matters. The tissues of each generation are subject to ageing and finally death, but the code is transmitted. The individual becomes insignificant, because the species is in the code. And that is why identity vanishes in an ageless computer program of bits—a program that specifies the hydrogen-bonded base pairs that link the sugar-phosphate backbones of the DNA molecule.

The whole outlook turns out to be wrong, and the book must speak for itself on this score. But it is an extraordinarily condensed book, which is why this preface is inordinately long. I do not know whether the authors' arguments about information led me to understand their concept of autopoiesis, or vice versa. What I am now sure about is that they are right. Nature is not about codes: we observers invent the codes in order to codify what nature is about. These discoveries are very profound.

What is less profound but equally important is the political consequence of this crisis about identity. The subordination of the individual to the species cannot be supported. '*Biology cannot be used any more to justify the dispensability of the individual for the benefit of the species, society or mankind, under the pretence that its role is to perpetuate them.*' After that, the world is a different place.

IN CONTENTION ...

The authors know it, and they draw the immediate inference. It is to say that scientists can no longer claim to be outside the social milieu within which they operate, invoking objectivity and disinterest; and in truth we have known this, or ought to have known it, ever since Hiroshima. But again this book gives us the theoretical basis for a view that might otherwise shroud something fundamental in a cloak of mere prudence. 'No position or view that has any relevance in the domain of human relations can be deemed free from ethical and political implications, nor can a scientist consider himself alien to these implications.' However, the authors go on to say that they do not fully agree between themselves on the questions this poses from the vantage point of their own work on autopoiesis—and they refuse to discuss them further (numbered Paragraph (iv) of Section 2 of Chapter V).

This seems to be because they do not resolve the question (posed a little earlier) whether human societies are or are not themselves biological systems. At this point, then, I ask to be relieved of the tasks of comment and interpretation; I ask for permission actively to enter this arena of discussion—where the angels fear to tread. For I am quite sure of the answer: yes, human societies *are* biological systems. Moreover, I claim that this book conclusively proves the point. This is a delicate matter, because presumably at least one of the originators of autopoietic theory disagrees, or is less than sure. . . . None the less, I have read the book many times; and one of those readings was exclusively devoted to validating this contention against the authors' own criteria of autopoiesis at every point.

The outcome, to which I was admittedly predisposed because of my own work, says that any cohesive social institution is an autopoietic system—because it survives, because its method of survival answers the autopoietic criteria, and because it may well change its entire appearance and its apparent purpose in the process. As examples I list: firms and industries, schools and universities, clinics and hospitals, professional bodies, departments of state, and whole countries.

If this view is valid, it has extremely important consequences. In the first place it means that every social institution (in several of which any one individual is embedded at the intersect) is embedded in a larger social institution, and so on recursively—and that all of them are autopoietic. This immediately explains why the process of change at any level of recursion (from the individual to the state) is not only difficult to accomplish but actually impossible—in the full sense of the intention: 'I am going completely to change myself.' The reason is that the 'I', that self-contained autopoietic 'it', is a *component* of another autopoietic system. Now we already know that the first can be considered as allopoietic with respect to the second, and that is what makes the second a viable autopoietic system. But this in turn means that the larger system perceives the embedded sytem as diminished—as less than fully autopoietic. That perception will be an illusion; but it does have consequences for the contained system. For now its own autopoiesis must respond to a special kind of constraint: treatment which attempts to deny its own autopoiesis.

Consider this argument at whatever level of recursion you please. An individual attempting to re-form his own life within an autopoietic family cannot fully be his new self because the family insists that he is actually his old self. A country attempting to become a socialist state cannot fully become socialist because there exists an international autopoietic capitalism in which it is embedded, by which the revolutionary country is deemed allopoietic. These conclusions derive from entailments of premisses which the authors have placed in our hands. I think they are most valuable.

Then let me try to answer the obvious question: why do not the authors follow this line of development themselves, and write the second half of the book (as I hope they eventually will)—which would be about the nature and adaptation of social institutions, and the evolution of society itself? Well, to quote their sentence again: 'our purpose is to understand the organization of living systems in relation to their unitary character'. This formulation of the problem begs the question as to what is allowed to be called a living system, as they themselves admit. 'Unless one knows which is the living organization, one cannot know which organization is living.' They quickly reach the conclusion however (Subsection (b) of Section 2 of Chapter 1) that '*autopoiesis is necessary and sufficient to characterize the organization of living systems*'. Then they display some unease, quoting the popular belief: '. . . and no synthetic system is accepted as living'.

The fact is that if a social institution is autopoietic (and many seem to answer to the proper criteria) then, on the author's own showing, it is necessarily alive. That certainly sounds odd, but it cannot be helped. It seems to me that the authors are holding at arm's length their own tremendously important discovery. It does not matter about this mere word 'alive'; what does matter is that the social institution has *identity* in the biological sense; it is not just the random assemblage of interested parties that it is thought to be.

When it comes to social evolution then, when it comes to political change: we are not dealing with institutions and societies that will be different tomorrow because of the legislation we passed today. The legislation—even the revolution—with which we confront them does not alter them at all; it proposes a new challenge to their autopoietic adaptation. The behaviour they exhibit may have to be very different if they are to survive: the point is that they have not lost their identities. The interesting consequence is, however, that the way an autopoietic system will respond to a gross environmental challenge is highly predictable—*once the nature of its autopoiesis is understood*. Clever politicians intuit those adaptations; and they can be helped by good scientists using systems-theoretic models. Stupid politicians do not understand why social institutions do not lose their identities overnight when they are presented with perfectly logical reasons why they should; and these are helped by bad scientists who devote their effort to developing that irrelevant logic.

In an era when rapid institutional change is a prerequisite of peaceful survival in the face of every kind of exponentially rising threat, it seems to me that the architects of change are making the same mistake all over the world. It is that they perceive the system at their own level of recursion to be autopoietic, which is because they identify themselves with that system and know themselves to be so; but they insist on treating the systems their system contains, and those within which their system is contained, as allopoietic. This is allowable in terms of scientific description, when the input and output surfaces are correctly defined. None the less it is politically blind to react towards the container and contained systems in a way which makes such a model evident, because at these other levels of recursion the relevant systems perceive themselves as autopoietic too.

This statement seems to be worth making. I could not have made it so succinctly without the language developed in this book. I could not have formulated it at all without the new concepts that Humberto Maturana and Francisco Varela have taught me. I thank them both very much, on behalf of everyone.

14 DEATH IS EQUIFINAL

Eighth Annual Ludwig von Bertalanffy Memorial Lecture

STAFFORD BEER
Manchester University, UK

This is the eighth Ludwig von Bertalanffy Memorial Lecture, delivered at the 1981 Annual Meeting of the Society for General Systems Research at Toronto, Canada. This lecture celebrates the work of von Bertalanffy, a founding father of general systems theory, and applies it in conceptual fashion to the problems of our time. Its first main point is that the real world, with all its interactions, generates an enormous complexity which our culture attempts to handle in a reductionist mode. Its methods of organization, its specialisms, and its way of formulating problems all presuppose that we know the nature of our world and of its problems. But if this were remotely true, problems and dangers would sometimes be ameliorated instead of getting steadily worse. It is argued that the systemic approach has an unused capacity to *restructure* both organizations and problems. The concept of equifinality, investigated by von Bertalanffy himself, and therefore used in illustration, expresses the proven ability of certain *open* systems to reach the same characteristic result, despite differences in initial conditions, and despite different rules of conduct. This is not a possible state of affairs in a *closed* system. There is scope in this notion for operational change, which is usually not countenanced in institutional systems—because they are organizationally closed. But equifinality is inevitable in the cases of both personal and planetary death.

ABOUT OUR DISASTERS

IT IS SOME years now since the present Prime Minister of my own disunited kingdom embraced Dr Friedman. Obviously I mean this in a literary sense. Maybe she was herself carried away by the heritage of literature, having been struck by the words of the English poet William Wordsworth when he wrote his memorable lines:

First published by *Behavioral Science*, San Diego, California.

> Milton! Thou shouldst be living at this hour;
> England hath need of thee . . .

At any rate, it was a mistake—and not only one of mistaken identity. Monetarism as practised by the present British government is not working, and there are dire statistics to prove it. Actions have just been taken at Downing Street, however, to reinforce the policy that does not work—as is usual in ministerial and managerial circles. I claim no special distinction for the British in this regard. The idea seems to be that if mistaken policies do not work, it is because they are not being pursued *relentlessly* enough.

Now it would be easy, if none the less correct, to declare that people find it incredibly difficult to conceive that they might be wrong. But that approach avails us little in considering *policies*—whether of the economic variety or any other. It plunges us into the argument: 'Well, *who* is right, and *who* is wrong?' Please note two things about any such debate—which, it seems, is the only kind of debate that the purveyors of public information, who include politicians, are prepared to allow.

The first of these two things is that rightness and wrongness are presumed to be suitable predicates of policy; the second is that some actual person can be found to praise or blame for any actual policy outcome. The first offers a convenient polarization whereby government may call an election, or hold a referendum, or even make appeal to opinion polls, about an issue that is expressed in a spurious fashion. This suits the mass communication media very well, because they cannot in general command psychological attention for more than trivia, unless people are badly frightened. The second aspect—'*Who are the guilty men*?'—enhances the prospects for the media of wider circulation than ever, because the issues become personalized, and most people enjoy an informal argument more than scholarly debate. Unfortunately for us all, it is impossible to demonstrate rightness and wrongness in policies—but only gradations of utility in situations that are heavily dependent on the minutiae of circumstance. Unfortunately, too, the happy simplicity induced by polarization, and the delight in personality duels artificially choreographed around these poles, must attract into public life precisely those who will reinforce these arrangements—rather than those who would dismantle them. *All this adds several negative dimensions to the public perception of problems that we did not have in the first place.*

Why do I begin with these sad reflections? Let me return to the example of monetary economics. About 10 years ago I made a systems-schematic diagram, intending to demonstrate monetary theory—with a view to simulating an economy thus regulated on a computer. This depiction, may I say, was checked out with one of the world's most eminent monetarists, who indeed made several helpful suggestions. The schematic makes it apparent why this approach is so attractive to some economists and to some politicians. We are looking at a relatively simple closed system, in which all one has to do is to operate the regulatory feedbacks appropriately in order to have the economy behave as you like. But the concept of systems closure is, as I shall later try to show, a relative and not an absolute concept.

In this case it means, for governments of a certain colour, that closure must be routed through such bodies as the World Bank and the International Monetary Fund—so that the governmental colour inevitably changes in the process. This even happened to the last British Labour Government, hardly notorious for leftish extremism. And in any case, in systems-theoretic terms, it was obvious from the schematic that this regulatory system *does not display requisite variety*. To take the central example: The subsystem that generates the money supply is too rich in variety to be controlled by mere banking devices such as the lending rate, or merely bureaucratic devices such as the determination of the borrowing requirement of the public sector. Any one of us can increase the money supply simply by making a 'futures' promise to someone else. Financial institutions in the capitalist world are obviously capable of doing just that, on a very large scale indeed. They can proliferate variety far faster than governments can do anything about it.

There is just one example of a perfectly general malaise that has to do with systems theory rather than with the osensible content of the system. I think it is this fact that makes it so difficult for us, as professionals, to communicate with colleagues and clients who take the systemic model of their regulatory problems for granted, and expect us to do so too. If their frameworks make sense, however, if their models mapped even roughly on to the high-complexity realities with which their regulatory systems purport to deal, then at least some problems would sometimes be solved. This just does not happen. Messes are not in general ameliorated, they are exacerbated—and this is why many of us perceive 'the world' (defined under whatever set of rubrics) as increasingly unstable and increasingly under threat.

I have so far merely illustrated this basic contention; and yet, I think that systems people ought quickly to seize on its importance. Consider any aspect of affairs that is on your personal list of concerns. What we find is that the things we want to happen, those very things that consume so much genuine dedication, and so much genuine cash, do not very often happen. We also find, all too frequently, that the trend is running counter to our desire. All this can readily be recognized by the usual excuses: 'The trend is world-wide'; 'We have slowed down the rate of decay'; 'Many other countries do worse than we do . . . .' These are profound obfuscations of fairly clear issues. Other countries do not start from the same place; they have different resources and different opportunities; they do not pose similar threats, and so on. But obviously anyone who exercises power, and enjoys it, has a vested interest in obfuscation: There is built-in tragedy here for the human condition.

What has really happened is that in the attempt to manage complexity we have perforce adopted a low-variety regulatory model. If it is perforce, then (you might ask) why bleat about it? It is because we should recognize this limitation before all others—before budgetary constraints, before political constraints, before any kind of sober practicality—whereby responsible people put on solemn faces to assure us that there is no alternative to massive unemployment, to arms racing, to nuclear reactors, to prisons, or to whatever else it may be that their models dictate. The constraint that *maybe we do not know in the least what we are talking about* is the most practical of them all—and the most likely.

I am presenting you, in short, with a metaproblem, and one which systems-oriented people alone can address. It says that the first questions are always: 'Why is the situation structured like this? Why is the problem expressed in this way? How has variety been constrained in these processes? Do our procedures, reflected through all these attenuations of variety, have anything to do with what we want to achieve?' Please allow me to make this as clear as I can with an allegory.

AN ALLEGORY OF CONSTRAINT

Here we are in the countryside, surrounded by all the elaborate, intricate, multicoloured, ever-changing complexities of the natural environment. A specialist comes along to the fallen tree trunk on which we are sitting. 'Can you understand it all, then?' he asks. No, we agree; it is all indeed a great mystery. 'What you need', says the specialist, 'is a pair of my truth spectacles.' We buy them for a small sum—though it is more than they are worth, because (did we but know it) the truth spectacles are simply dark, red-tinted glass.

'What do you see?' asks the specialist. We tell him that we see that everything is red. What is more, we cannot any longer see a lot of the complicated details that we saw before. 'Exactly! That is our triumph', says the specialist. 'What you are seeing is the truth that underlies all the confusion. The world is *really* red. And the rules that govern it all are *actually* quite simple.'

This statement conveys to us considerable scientific verisimilitude. After all, the progress of science has been marked by the discovery of invariances: We have gravity, $e=mc^2$, the patterns of snowflakes and of DNA molecules, to prove it. But, of course, we need to make tests. For example, if some blue were added to the world that is really red, then the world would become really purple.

'Well', says the specialist cheerfully, 'we cannot exactly *do* that—it would be too expensive. But we can simulate the experiment for you.' He sprays our truth spectacles with a fine blue mist from an aerosol. Good heavens: It works! The model is *predictive*. You will of course note that nothing has changed in our forest glade, where the butterflies flit, and where a hawk drops down upon a mouse. I can tell you one thing about that mouse, which I considered grey until I was convinced that it is red or possibly purple: it is that the mouse is dead.

When the aerosols of specialist model builders are skilfully manipulated, there remains no aspect of the model theory that can (in true Popperian style) be falsified. All prophecies, that is to say, which are correctly couched within the language of the model are self-fulfilling. The great secret of this absurd and degrading professional confidence trick is to keep specialists apart. 'The company went bankrupt? How extraordinary: its cash-flow was extremely sound. Oh, well, if it was held to ransom by a militant workforce, that is not within my provenance as an accountant.' Its neighbour company also went bust. 'Oh, I see: it could not raise further investment capital. I thought it must be something like that, because as a physicist I know that its research and development programme was sound as a bell.'

The essence of maintaining the comfortable, privileged, self-indulgent, and barely effective specialisms by which mankind fails to achieve its minimal targets lies, quite paradoxically, in education. It is the mystical secret of our civilization to realize that once the poor devils have been *educated*, they will understand and accept why they are being starved and aborted, tortured and shot. The models explain it all; therefore the real problem is to make truth spectacles available to all at a reduced price. All includes the sufferers, first and foremost; and next it includes those who, with genuine libertarian zeal, are doing their utmost to administer the conclusions of the only models that they have got. 'Educate them.' It is the current panacea.

'This unfortunate person', the specialist explains to the court, 'exhibits a typical syndrome. As you see through your truth spectacles, he is quite red in colour. We may test this theory, if you will just allow me to spray your spectacles with this yellow aerosol. I predict that he is now turning orange.' Let us now, then, you and I, make a determined effort to stop this nonsense. The criminality that our penology seeks to contain is steadily rising; recidivism is on the increase; jails are the polytechnic institutions of crime, and nothing works.

Our specialist is quite relaxed. We simply have not put up enough cash for yellow aerosols, he tells us serenely. Of course, he does not want a licence to print the money (especially in a monetarist climate). What we really need is a new agency, he explains, with real *authority* to provide yellow aerosols for approved educational purposes. If we have already been taken in by the initial trick, we shall now be neatly sidetracked away from anything that has to do with our proper concern, because one thing that we *can* grapple with is, if not the problem itself, this low-variety, misconceived, and misdirected solution.

Witness: Those who request this money must prove that their yellow is pure, their aerosols efficient and non-destructive of the ozone layer; and they must show that their entire spraying technique is up to the highest of international standards. Then (if real life is any precedent at all in this allegory) we shall appoint a governing committee, consisting of two men of yellow, two presidents of aerosol companies, and an Ivy League professor of high standards.

I am not sure whether we were just now considering the regulation of the economy, international peace, criminality, or the baseball world series. The whole point of the allegory is to stress that *whatever* it is that we seek to regulate, we take too little account of the cybernetic Conant–Ashby theorem—which potently affirms that 'every good regulator of a system must be a model of that system' [1]. The corollary obviously is that regulatory effectiveness is a direct function of the adequacy of that included model. The *multi*coloured world, in short . . . *is not* red.

A last allegorical point, please, if that is the case. What do we do in practice about someone who says that the world is actually *green*? In a tyranny, we have him shot. In a totalitarian regime we have him removed to internal exile or to hospital. But in a libertarian state, we take a different posture. It is our bounden duty to guarantee this person's inalienable right to present his case *to the agency*. We have seen the composition of its governing committee, but we can be sure (is it not so?) that those people are open minded.

In that allegorical image, if you can capture it, resides the end of all innovation, and a major cause of our decline. Come to think of it, I do not know why I am calling this an allegory. What each of us here elaborately entertains in our daily purusit of human betterment is no allegory: It is the real thing.

Our discipline is transdisciplinary. Then which of us has not seen a research proposal, someone's doctoral thesis, or more importantly, a project to save the community, the city, or the world, fall foul of the colour-scheme—the red and the green—or the whole accepted spectrum of debate? Here is a strange phenomenon, we say; is it physical or chemical? The science committee that holds the research funds will apply its low-variety model of nature, and tell us. But I wonder if God knows the difference between physics and chemistry? And when the art commission applies its low-variety model of aesthetics, to tell us which picture is good and which is bad, I wonder whether God knows that difference either. Giants among us arise from time to time, and smash the models. For Einstein, Euclid's parallel lines *met*. Picasso painted *Guernica*: so there. But most of us dare not call in question the low-variety models of our programming.

It is because we have been *educated*—not 'led out', as means the word in Latin, but very much 'blocked in'. I affirm tonight that anyone who has not yet understood the direct experience he must have had of 'government by spectrum', is not yet a general systems theorist.

If this is worrying, then may I quietly say that maybe the place to start is within the personal life. Most people have low-variety models of family and friends—who themselves have much higher variety. We end up by divorcing our spouses, losing contact with our children, and putting low-variety labels on everyone we know. When they try to explain to us that they do not match our model of them we do not try to pump up the variety of the model, as we should. We say that they *ought* to match the model, attributing blame to them, and, most ironically, landing *ourselves* with the pathological outcome. In our civilization, that usually takes the form of psychosomatic disorder and/or a dependence on tranquillizing drugs. These are, in neurocybernetic terms, quite simply further variety reducers, just when we need amplifiers. Instead of our getting the multiple colours back, the red is the more deeply red.

THE LIMITING RESOURCE

If this is indeed the kind of difficulty that we address in all manner of human undertakings, then much of the work performed in the name of systems theory and systems analysis must be expected to be fruitless, if not actually nonsensical. It would be invidious, though all too easy, to quote instances: let us rather look at outcomes. Outstandingly, let us focus attention for a moment on the facts of institutional organization.

If our institutions really worked, we should not constantly be reorganizing them and their procedures; but we do. If those responsible for these reorganizations, those managing and those advising, paid any attention to the principles already established by our kind of science, maybe the next round of reorganization would be unnecessary; but they do not. Even worse, when *new* institutions are set up, they are constructed upon regulatory models that are known not to work.

I voted, with as many raised hands as I could wave about, against the establishment of the European Economic Community, the EEC: not because I disfavoured its excellent principle, but because the inevitable mode of its functioning was bound to lead to the disastrous outcomes that we now experience—mountains of butter, lakes of milk, subsidies paid out for inefficiency, and 'bureaucracy rules, OK'.

I am aware of a movement that entitles itself the World Economic Organization, which makes the equally excellent proposition that there should be established a world common market. I do not think that anyone concerned about the planetary future could have a more excellent idea than that, because it is certainly possible *within current technology* to satisfy want world-wide. But we know from our experience of the United Nations Organization, as well as of the EEC, that cybernetic changes would be required in all managerial, operational, and regulatory processes to achieve anything more than a talking shop—or, worse, a nursery for war.

In the UN, we have upwards of 150 nations, all talking. On behalf of the northern hemisphere, variety is powerfully attenuated by the *de facto* recognition of only five political blocs: the Soviet Union, North America, Western Europe, Japan, and with increasing impact, China—though one might very well enquire where India stands in that. This leaves some 120 nations squabbling in the southern hemisphere. They absorb each other's variety in the process, and are no match for the North. Therefore, argues Aurelio Peccei, the founding father of the Club of Rome, the Africans, the Latin Americans, the Southeast Asians, should form themselves into a matching set of blocs.

This is fantastically good cybernetics: Aurelio Peccei has come through, as I would expect, with a perfect variety analysis which, when implemented, would give the world a chance of homeostatic *political* equilibrium, just as a similar approach to the organization of a world common market would give the totality of nations a chance of homeostatic economic equilibrium. It is most appropriate that he should have been interviewed about these ideas last April in this very city (a city which, by the way, is a delight to me as I have watched its architectural courage take effect over the last 20 years; when you are in Toronto, you *know* you are in Toronto). So what did Aurelio say when Helen Worthington of the *Toronto Star* asked whether this 'long, tortuous and painful' process towards international reorganization would happen in his lifetime? 'No', he says wistfully. 'I am an old man and it won't happen while I am on this earth.'

But there speaks one of the youngest men I know. The whole problem is that it will *never* happen, unless transdisciplinarians can understand what *is* the problem—and then convince those who control affairs that such is the case. But those people are up to their eyes in aerosols: so please do remember my 'spectral analysis', and let us look more deeply into what really are the natural invariants of regulation.

Nature uses the *limiting resource* as regulator, and we, institutionally, do not, because we erroneously think that the limiting resource is cash. Soon we shall witness, in the United States, the battle of the red and green aerosols: the fiscal and the monetary budgets. The resulting colour, I predict, will be very muddy indeed. But no one has identified the limiting resources, either there or world-wide; and I cannot do it now—except perhaps to suggest that suffering seems to be a necessary resource, and that no one is at all likely to declare a moritorium on that . . .

I say again: The regulator is *the limiting resource.* Let us go beyond institutional nonsense. Contraception is directed towards the female rather than the male, through the pill, because it is *cybernetically* simpler (that is to speak in the regulatory mode) to control the fertility of one ovum per month than to control the fertility of 100 million spermatozoa per day.

I have learnt this from the teachings of Roger Short, the Edinburgh professor whose speciality is reproductive biology. And I seize on his work at this point in my address for a very precise reason indeed. Probably everyone present here, and everyone who may yet read these words, would agree that planetary population is in all likelihood the most threatening parameter of global instability today. The explosion of population cannot be abated; whereas the nuclear threat might conceivably be contained.

Heinz von Foerster, our most distinguished colleague, published his amazing paper on this topic more than 20 years ago. If Malthus had shown that we should all eventually be *starved* to death, Heinz showed that—long before his culmination, and to be precise in 2026—we should be *squeezed* to death. In a more recent and equivalently gripping paper that encapsulates all this, Meyer and Vallee [2] have argued that the birth rate globally is not merely exponential, but hyperbolic—because, they say, there is a systematic extrapolation lag in the statistical forecasting that has consistently underestimated population growth.

Now back to Professor Short [3]. He writes:

> It is ironic that the chief reason for the recent human population explosion seems to have been a reduced suckling frequency; even today, it has been estimated that more pregnancies are prevented by breastfeeding than by all man-made forms of contraception put together.

Where are those aerosols now? Is there a married person in this room who has not always *known* that the idea that conception during lactation is impossible was an old wives tale? Not so, it seems: But you must read Professor Short himself to believe it. The issue that the story lays before us systems-theoreticians is this: all manner of contraceptive programmes have been presented to the world, but they do not work. In 1946 I was myself concerned (as a very young and very embarrassed officer) in trying to teach Indians how to use condoms. In the India of 1979, the contraceptive answer was forcible vasectomy. Today, Roger Short tells us what is the limiting resource: mother's milk was the original biological population regulator—until we wrecked the arrangement. Dried milk flown in to Africa by the ton has, as we now know, serious side effects on the immunological system. It seems that it also has serious side effects on fecundity itself: it enhances it.

Surely it is obvious from this crucial example—crucial because it looks as though we may be heading for a catastrophic planetary discontinuity—that there has been no systems effort to identify the anthropological cybernetics of population growth, nor to create the kind of organization that could contain it. Everyone knows what the problem is. The *metaproblem* is: why is the situation structured like this? Why is the problem expressed in this way? How has variety been constrained in these processes? Do our procedures, reflected through all these attenuators of variety, have anything to do with what we want to achieve? These are the exact words that I used a little earlier: I hope that I am 'bringing them home'.

As systems people we have to point out, as I am trying to do, that the ace which humankind has up its sleeve is the ability to question its own programming and to doubt its own models. Each of us—whereby I mean those systems people present, but also those managers and ministers whom we serve—has this God-given ability. We do not have to be Einstein or Picasso to be variety engineers, to devise new models, to understand the issues of variety attenuation. But we do, over and above everything else, need *courage*.

The reason is that in doing our proper job we threaten the very system that validates the careers of those whom we seek to help. They are in their top jobs exactly *because* they know that the world really is red. The easy route for us is to agree, but to propose modifications of the exact shade. That is my personal definition of immorality. We have to examine the filters themselves. The tools of systems theory are available; you will quickly realize why I have chosen to speak about a chosen few.

EQUIFINALITY—A PERSONAL VIEWPOINT

A paper entitled 'The theory of open systems in physics and biology' was published in *Science* in 1950 [4]. It was written by Ludwig von Bertalanffy; and through it, those 30 years ago, I obtained a notion that solved two problems that I had previously been unable to resolve. The notion was that of equifinality, which expresses the proven ability of certain *open* systems to reach the same characteristic result, despite differences in initial conditions, and despite different rules of conduct along the way. That, said von Bertalanffy, is not a possible state of affairs in a closed system.

'Equifinality' is not a word much used among general system theorists nowadays, and it is proper that I should seek to rehabilitate it. Let me first explain my own original experience of the notion by quoting from *Cybernetics and Management* [5]. I had been explaining how to discuss an incentive bonus system on the shop floor through a cybernetic model:

> In order that this basic behaviour, expressed in language No. 1, should be self-regulating in the automation sense, it must be described as a closed-sequence servomechanism. Let this be done. Now the whole cybernetic machine must behave equifinally. So this overall behaviour must be described in language No. 2, which is a control language of higher order; and *this* system (which includes the self-regulating system) will be an open sequence. The metalanguage is capable of discussing the behaviour of the closed loop, which is not itself equifinal, equifinally.

This discovery, which was associated in my mind (and in the book) with Gödel's incompleteness theorem, eventually led to the recursive methodology by which I have striven to account for the viability of viable systems [6,7] in my own work. Later in the same book, and talking this time about ergodic theory, I described uncertainty itself as an *equifinal machine*:

> It would escape determinism because of its equifinality; and yet it would not involve 'pure' randomness, which is a self-destructive hypothesis, but replace it with a *directional* drift which might be called teleological.

This was my first shot at answering, in Bertalanffian terms, the questions about *chance and necessity* which were yet to be posed by Jacques Monod [8] in his extremely controversial book of that title—but which have in any case plagued philosophy ever since the ancient Greeks.

Von Bertalanffy's definitive book on the subject first appeared in 1968 [9]. Let everyone remember, however, that the stream of his contributions goes back to the 1920s and 1930s. By the time of the book's publication, I had long since taken issue with him face-to-face about his identification of open systems with general systems theory, and of closed systems with cybernetics. One has only to read the early deliberations [10] of the original soi-disant cyberneticians, I argued and still do so, to see that they embraced open systems with open arms. To me, the two subjects have always been (dare I say this?) equifinal. As his book shows, Ludwig did not agree. But we did most certainly agree about something else—something with which (such is life) yet other worthy friends do *not* agree. And it is this.

> The only real point of undertaking the transdisciplinary study of *general* systems is to discover wherein they may be INVARIANT. Thus does science advance.

The book *General Systems Theory* [9] argues this point strongly, but sometimes indicates it gently, as for instance when the author says that some work of mine did not refer to his own work and hence cannot be said to be unduly influenced by it, but was nevertheless also using the principles of von Bertalanffy. It made me smile, but it was certainly true. We seek regulatory invariance.

I hope that the man we now honour will smile on us tonight, and on these efforts to demonstrate a certain kind of invariance in the managerial handling of the general systems that constitute human affairs. The most dramatic illustration of this is uncomfortable for many people, but cannot be gainsaid. We are born (which means that our initial conditions are all somewhat different as to time and place and status), and we live under different constraints (which means that our life trajectories take diverse courses); but for all of us conceived as open systems, when we have reached 100 per cent of our lives, *death is equifinal*.

May I next ask you to observe that the same goes for our planet. In some 5 billion years, when the sun has collapsed into a red giant, the earth will be fried. Death for life-on-earth will be *finally* equifinal. Now of course this may happen much sooner, because of another ice age. Or it may happen next Friday—by nuclear accident, or design. I ask you this question: if planetary death is equifinal, can you stand back sufficiently far from your own circumstances to care about the difference between next Friday and 5 billion years?

To do so could be (forgive me) an act of considerable self-indulgence, because it makes no sense. Time does not legitimately have so much significance. We are programmed to think that it does, of course: 'Time is money.' It is our only resource. But time cannot gratify us beyond what is almost immediate, in a world in which longer-range planning carries no conviction. We may aim for genealogical immortality, of course; but we ourselves do not need much time to set that process in train. I recently heard a distinguished octogenarian hope that he would 'be spared' long enough to 'complete his life's work', and was nauseated by such narcissism at that age. The fact is, however, that in a culture where time is regarded as a capital asset, it can be used as such by anyone who is prepared to spend it. You can give up your life's time as the cost of assassinating someone; you can exchange your life's time for a gaol sentence; you can barter your life's time on hunger strike (provided your nerve holds).

Now there are people who understand this currency, and who use it. They are called 'terrorists'. They use the capital asset of their life's time as a political weapon, and it seems to me that they are very brave. Moreover, the criminal acts that these people undertake suggest to me that their direction is in the hands of a very good systems theorist. But in the world of the specialist, in that red world, the acts of terrorists are labelled 'mindless' and 'senseless'. These appellations are ridiculous. Whatever else they are, the acts of terrorists are neither mindless nor senseless, as is demonstrated by the fact that those people are willing to invest the capital of their life's time in them. What is clear is that those whose job it is to combat terrorism do not at all understand the phenomenon with which they hope to deal.

In terms of the metaproblem, as I have expressed it tonight, terrorist actions are quite straightforwardly sensible and understanding *denials of the model* that has been impressed on society, a model in which dissenters consider that their protest cannot even be otherwise stated. As Gödel was saying, according to his own incompleteness theorem: You cannot even give voice to an undecidable proposition. That is a matter of theoretical logic. As the secret police were saying: You cannot give voice to a decidable proposition, if it does not fit the acceptable model. That is a matter of survival. And as I was saying: I do not endorse the tactics of violence; but I do understand its strategy of *equifinality*.

Obviously, these remarks are highly contentious. I use so potent an example because I want to press the point that there is something radically wrong, and not marginally wrong, about the way we manage our human institutions; and also to contend that there is a systems-theoretic approach to determine various invariant features of the mistakes that are fundamentally and not peripherally made.

Let me try to characterize the issue in the Bertalanffian terms of my first example about the incentive bonus scheme. If we look at an institution such as a health service, an education service, a public utility, or even an industrial company, we can find ways of describing it as either an open or a closed system. Therefore for years I thought this a useless distinction to draw in the context of social systems. I have changed my mind, because of Maturana's [11] concept of autopoiesis—whereby we may identify those systems that characteristically produce themselves. Here is a quotation from him: 'A circular organization [is that] which secures the production or maintenance of the *components* that specify it in such a manner that the product of their functioning is the very same organization that produces them. 'He was speaking specifically of the *living* system, but his criteria seem to apply perfectly to that core of an organization which is also a closed system: we might call it the professional/bureaucratic core. This core is embedded in its penumbra of public interconnections, so that the operation that is publically recognized as 'the institution' is after all an open system.

What this says is that the autopoietic core of the hospital or of the university is concerned with producing itself—with maintaining the medical or educational relationships and rituals that define these institutions as organizations, though individual physicians and professors come and go. But the penumbra around this core must be open to a continuous supply of the patients or the students whose outside-world existence validates the institution. It is certainly open to energy, in the form of money, and thereby maintains its negentropy.

To look at institutions in this manner is to receive the kind of perceptual shock that I tried to administer when I spoke of terrorism. If the actions of terrorists, and the risks run by the civilian infrastructure needed to support them, are perceived by a ministerial model as senseless, then that model is *useless*. If confirmation is required, witness no abatement of terrorism as a result of actions taken in line with the model. It is always best to regard the purpose of a system as what it actually does. According to the models I have just set up, then, the purpose of the hospital and of the university is to guarantee the autopoiesis of the closed 'core' systems, and what happens to patients and students is a by-product of this activity. What is equifinal about institutions regarded in this way is that they do not do what they were set up to do, but something else; and they do it at a steadily increasing cost, which is necessarily incurred in keeping the core negentropy on the rise so that the gradually elaborating structures of core autopoiesis can be maintained.

It would be grossly unfair to impugn the motives of those who try to keep their institutions going. My personal observation is that they are usually dedicated people. But it has sadly to be noticed that one necessary aspect of dedication is the unswerving conviction that what one is doing is *right*. This means in turn that the model of the institutional activity that validates this rightness cannot be questioned. In my consultative incarnation, this has always been the critical problem. Can I find someone not so dedicated, which may well mean not so insecure, that he is willing to question the entrenched model? If not, I might as well go home.

Then the next question is: Why *should* people be asked to question the entrenched model? And the answer is: because the institution is doing what it does, with a flourish of trumpets, but not what it set out to do; and in that respect it simply does not work. Many people here are academics: do you really think that the university achieves a proper social purpose? Do you as citizens really believe in medical and dental regimes in which even the practitioners agree that up to half of illness is iatrogenic, i.e. caused by the physician? By the same token, is not illiteracy caused by the educational system? Where I live, schools are being closed, teachers are being sacked, school milk has been stopped, school meals are being axed, school transport is cut, equipment is not being replaced—even the books and pencils themselves are becoming scarce. However, you cannot find a reduction in the autopoietic bureaucracy of school administration anywhere from the Welsh villages and up the town and county and provincial hierarchies to London, Westminster, which has embraced the economic model of monetarism that is causing all of this.

May I urge you not to imagine, simply because the examples of Northern Irish terrorism and Welsh schooling are close to me and are topical, that I am over-reacting to current tensions. In the early 1950s I was run out of Manchester for questioning the model of the Lancashire cotton industry that had the self-sufficient family firm as its profit centre. In the late 1950s I was run out of Tyneside on the East and Glasgow on the West for questioning the model of shipbuilding technology that was even then being eclipsed by both Germany and Japan—because the home model was even named 'Britain is the world's shipbuilder'. I quit the steel industry after 13 years in-house employment for identical reasons in 1961, and the publishing industry similarly in 1969. Today, all four of the major British industries that I have mentioned are in ruins. No doubt, there were a million particular and peculiar circumstances attendant upon each demise.

But there were invariant factors, then as now. To say that people find it difficult, then as now, to question their own programming and to grapple with entrenched models would be a veritable cliché in psychological terms. I have tried tonight to penetrate the difficulty at a systems-theoretic level instead, as follows.

1. We are misled by models that incorrectly purport to find invariances (such as the colour-spectrum of my allegory), because we take no notice of the evidence that institutional systems do not produce their intended outputs, but something else.
2. It is only by very careful variety analysis that we may map real-life behaviour on to any invariant model without attempting to infringe the Conant–Ashby theorem of regulation.
3. The logical language we use must be capable of uttering Gödelian propositions that are decidable in the context of survival. I am not speaking of merely paradoxical languages, which are familiarly used by the mass media in highlighting the 'we–they' characterization of affairs, but of something far more serious.
4. We may note that Bertalanffian closed systems may be embedded in Bertalanffian open systems, with the result that we may have autopoietic kernels of societary organizations which themselves are engaged in the interchange of *both* information *and* energy to equifinal ends.

There are other principles that general systems people may invoke; and I certainly hope that my own theory of the organization of viable systems [6,7] will be of use. But this is not the night to provide a general systems theory 'state of the art'. It is a night to honour Ludwig von Bertalanffy.

GIVE ME EIGHT MINUTES OF YOUR ETERNITY

The thread of equifinality has been the warp of the fabric of this lecture. I have already spoken of that death which will soon be equifinal for us all, and sooner or later (it has no real meaning) for our planet.

It is, I think, very striking that all major institutional activity that is directed towards a better life for all the earth's inhabitants turns out to be, in the meantime between life and death, nugatory. It has no relevance to the problems that will assuredly kill us; and it makes no call upon the advances that general systems theory has made over nearly half a century.

We should address ourselves to this, if we can find the route. Make no mistake: That route is not educational; it has to do with disclosing and redirecting the wicked sources of power. It has to do with communications that depend on networks, rather than on hectoring. It has to do with mental health rather than with the easy dissemination of those drugs that occlude mental health, the bill for which in Great Britain last year was no less than a *billion pounds* sterling for 50 million people.

And so on. We should be ashamed of ourselves if we could not apply the principles we know to any one of these issues on immediate request. But we should need access to those managers and ministers who are ready to question their own programming, few as they may be. And, I fear, we should need access to a general public—who at present are unwilling to attend to the mass media at other than salacious length, breadth, and two-dimensional volume—in more serious ways. I said at the start that public attention to the media was paid only by the badly frightened, for any length of time. It could be, of course, that to *want* to feel badly frightened in a cosmetic culture is a masochistic necessity for some of those some.

Consider the Christmas holiday period just passed, as I have experienced that season of peace and love in Britain. In the peak-hour evening viewing time of Christmas Day, the BBC screened *Airport 1975*: a feature film in which a subset of those of us mad enough to hurtle around the globe sealed like sardines in a high-alloy tin can spent two hours almost crashing. On the following day, it took two and three-quarter hours to fry the occupants of the world's tallest building in *The Towering Inferno*, which was viewed by 27 million people, just half of the entire population of men, women and children, into the middle of the night. On the third evening, it took three hours for five New York families to blast each other off the face of the earth in *The Godfather*.

Well, after all, it was Christmas. *Gloria in excelsis Deo, et in terra pax hominibus bonae voluntatis*. It means: Glory to God in the highest, and on earth peace to men of goodwill.

May I please in summary make four points. These are issues in which I profoundly believe. They do not add up to so simplistic a message that everyone should feel free to label me either an optimist or a pessimist. It is in these four statements then, that I conclude.

There are actions that we ought to take to succour the afflicted. The context of our efforts is dark and threatening indeed. But, in our wisdom or in our stupidity, we have charge of ourselves and of the earth. Therefore, death shall have no dominion, . . . but it is still equifinal.

Exactly these four points were expressed with far greater force in the Eighty-Second Psalm. Stay with me for another 30 seconds while I read those words to you:

Defend the poor and fatherless;
do justice to the afflicted and needy.

Deliver the poor and needy;
rid them out of the hand of the wicked.

They know not, neither will they understand;
they walk on in darkness:
all the foundations of the earth are out
of course.

I said, you are gods;
and all of you are children of the Most
High:

But you shall die like men,
and fall like one of the princes.

REFERENCES

1. Conant, R.C., and Ashby, W.R. 'Every good regulator of a system must be a model of that system', *International Journal of Systems Science*, **1**, 81–97, 1970.
2. Meyer, F., and Vallee, J. 'The dynamics of long-term growth.' *Technological Forecasting and Social Change*, **7**, 285-300, 1975.
3. Short, R.V. The development of human reproduction. *INSERM*, **83**, 355-366, 1979.
4. von Bertalanffy, L. 'The theory of open systems in physics and biology', *Science*, **111**, 23-29, 1950.
5. Beer, S. *Cybernetics and Management*. English Universities Press, Kent, 1959.
6. Beer, S. *Brain of the Firm*. Allen Lane, New York, 1972. (Expanded 2nd ed. John Wiley, New York, 1981.)
7. Beer, S. *The Heart of Enterprise*. New York: John Wiley, New York, 1979.
8. Monod, J. *Le hasard et la necessite*. Editions du Seuil, Paris: 1970. (Chance and Necessity. London: Collins Fontana, London, 1974.)
9. von Bertalanffy, L. *General Systems Theory*. George Braziller, New York, 1968.
10. von Foerster, H. (ed.). *Cybernetics. Transactions of the Sixth* (1949), *Seventh* (1950), *Eighth* (1951), *Ninth* (1952) and *Tenth* (1953) *Conferences*. Josiah Macy, Jr., Foundation, New York.
11. Maturana, H.R., and Varela, F.J. *Autopoiesis and Cognition*. D. Reidel Publishing, Dordrecht, The Netherlands, 1980.

ICONS

Alone
my quarry tiny and remote
and made of slate

the brash firmament
lands on the doorstep

almost
able to cope with
universal beauty
everlasting anguish

  the rose bay willow herbs
  also the plague of slugs
  have suddenly gone

  cancelling out

there's need to focus on enigma here.

Cannot a man
who cannot speak for women
think of a woman whom the birds address
for whose delight the stream tumbles
flowers turn their faces—burgeoning
in case too late to share with her
conjoint loveliness? Woman who
sets up her special and abandoned cry
to have her sound ring in man's ears—
remembering herself that ancient noise?

continued

It may not be allowed:
for there is art.
Trumpets flourish just for this.
First the composer, genius no doubt;
then the executant, virtuosity. . . .
Even the participant may get a mention.

Last
also by all means least
critics gobble up the mean rewards.
Embrace an industry
engaging in
the noble self-defence of art.

Cannot a woman
speaking not for men
think of a man as lion, or as eagle soaring,
a hippopotamus; or like a vole
on the stream's bank in the slate quarry
trembling with a monumental love?
She leaves the whole scene early.
Man, in androgenic ignorance,
will never know what happened to
her intervening hours.

It may not be allowed
for there is science
We've microprocessors
competent to turn
god inside-out in a nanosecond:
slices of silicon so small
you'd lose
this haystack-needle in an embryo.
Embryos—what of them?
For delectation they shall be
cloned: reproducing Einsteins where
lines all meet in parallel black holes.

continued

intermission now. . .
snowdrops arrived in the quarry
daffodils break through

lambs die cold in harsh weather

beauty and anguish
making an infinitude of quiet

cancel out

what need to focus on enigma here?

Beauty, anguish
woman, man
science, art:

so many better emblems
could replace
these shabby icons.

Stafford Beer
Transit, 1977

15 I SAID, YOU ARE GODS

The Second Annual Teilhard Lecture

STAFFORD BEER

FIRST: OUR SHARED ILLUSIONS

THERE IS a concept to which I shall proceed to refer as the Shared Illusion. Please take the first of many imaginative leaps for which I shall ask tonight to understand what I mean by this phrase.

In locally circumscribed terms, I point out that we are all here. We share the belief that we know the place and the time and the provenance of the Second Teilhard Lecture. We *share* the belief that I am the speaker, and that someone—namely 'myself' (whatever that may mean)—is peering out through a hirsute bag of skin and bone at a finitely denumerable audience—namely yourselves. Then what is the 'illusion' about that? I think that you all know the difficulty full well, or you would not even have bothered to come to such an evening. For the demonstration I have given of our sharing belongs to a shared *convention* whereby this level of description will do for the purpose in hand.

It is not necessary to enquire into the physical, and psychological, and political (and so on) status of everyone present in order to share a conviction that we are all here. It would be disastrous to require in advance that any solipsist present prove that anyone else was a figment, as that any pragmatist should prove that they were not. We are not gathered together to argue about Marxism; we would not want our meeting to degenerate into a discussion of sexual permissiveness. If one of us is drunk, or asleep, or totally preoccupied, we shall not feel a necessity to deduct a name from the roll of those present. And yet in all such matters, and in thousands of other parameters of the human mind and spirit, each of us marks a unique point

First published by the Teilhard Centre, Lavenham, Suffolk, UK.

in a multidimensional space. May we license ourselves to call our personal point in that space our 'reality'? Perhaps no one else knows what it is. Perhaps we do not even know it ourselves. But one thing seems pretty evident: the idea that all of us know well enough what is going on here is an *intersection* of individual realities—an illusion, then, of reality that we share.

I began by saying that I was speaking in locally circumscribed terms. Let us now drop that constriction, and consider. . . dare I say: everything? We still talk about 'myself', and 'yourself' and 'ourselves' but the Shared Illusion is no longer just the belief that 'here we are'. It is that we have been born; that we are alive; that all manner of circumstances surround us; and that we shall die. The thousands of parameters of opinion and action that we just encountered as relevant to the reality named by just this occasion, this very place and time, are infinitely multiplied. Within our Shared Convention of this lecture, at least we *know* why we are here. Within the larger Shared Illusion, most people are not at all sure 'why we are here'. There is a variety of teachings about this, and a variety of experiences about this. They may or may not be illusory; but they are not very easily shared. When they *are* shared, it has to be at the expense of a larger illusion still; for idiosyncratic richness and variety are always lost in finding that intersect which we call attaining to consensus.

Such philosophic reflections are fairly commonplace. Perhaps the application of a little science will help to dispel the discomforting notion that our reality is in some way illusory. We may begin with experimentation, and the estimation of what scientists were once happy enough to call 'objective facts'. Our perception of reality, in so far as it is something-out-there, is mediated by sense organs that may be studied in this way. We can establish the limits of our eyes in terms of measurement of the spectrum of visible light, recognizing that there are many radiations and emanations out there that we cannot see with the optical equipment in our heads. We note that some animals, who are not equipped with retinal cone cells, share a visual reality compounded of black and white, whereas we ourselves see colours; and this may make us wonder if there *could* be other visual receptors, that have simply not evolved, which would add another dimension to our vision—just as colour adds a dimension to chiaroscuro. There are many other matters to note: for example, if something happens very quickly out there, subliminally to our visual threshold, we shall not know about it. Or maybe we shall *know*, but not know that we know: we are alert to the possibilities of using television to manipulate and subvert people in this way.

By investigations of this sort, science offers us some sense of security in the matter of perceptual illusion. Its *experimental* device in the matter is instrumentation that extends the range and resolution of the physiological equipment that we have. Thus we need not fear that in fact we are surrounded by whistling banshees operating in ultraviolet at sound frequencies higher than bats, because instruments could detect them if they were there. But there is also a *theoretical* device that science uses to account for our reality. It puts together its observations to formulate accounts of 'what it's all about' that can be tested. The language I use here is deliberately casual, since we have no time to investigate the philosophy of science tonight—which is anyway so well documented. I am, however, anxious to insist that these scientific accounts of reality are best called MODELS. The scientific accounts do not pretend to be reality itself; but like any other models they expect to simulate it. This means that their utility (as distinct from their truth or their inclusiveness) is judged by their *predictive capacity*.

Now the predictive capacity of a scientific model is very good indeed, so long as certain conditions are fulfilled. Outstandingly, it must be invoked only within the range of its appropriate instrumentation to experiment, and within the range of the theoretical framework to retain coherence. Outside such bounding conditions, the model will break down, because it is no longer a model *of* anything in particular. And here it must be said that a somewhat 'incestuous' relationship exists between observation and theory, since observers do not typically take readings of parameters which have no status in the currently fashionable model, while theoreticians generally are interested only in the more precise observations of the variables that their own model recognizes. Here, quite briefly, are examples of each.

1. The science of economics has fashionable models of both national and global economies which generate policies that have something especially interesting in common. It is *that they do not work*. Nationally, we are currently destroying our wealth-creating industrial base. Internationally, the poor countries—which are supposed to be so grateful for all manner of 'aid'—turn out to be net exporters of wealth to the countries that are rich. Simulations, and indeed real-life experiments, indicate that these outcomes are invariant under *any* of the fashionable and contradictory models available. It therefore seems very likely that the parametric substrate of them all is based on an observational rubric intended to measure a Shared Illusion.

   I do not know, for example, of any economic model since Marx's that has parametrically included the level of power; then surely this accounts for the continued popularity of Marxism—these 150 years (and a wholly changed world) later.
2. Adventitious observational evidence for an aspect of reality that is often referred to generically as 'paranormal' is, in the judgement of many, absolutely overwhelming. But all attempts (again, over more than a century) to make laboratory measurements have at best been highly equivocal. We may look to the *absence of a model* that has the range to handle, never mind explain, paranormal phenomena for the

> explanation. Armed with mathematical models of coincidence, neurophysiological models of the brain, and electrical models of field forces—all of which happen to be available—scientists set out to measure the performance of statistical artefacts, the fluctuations of encephalographic rhythms, and the bending of metal within Faraday cages. All of this has been undertaken as a means of investigating such issues as the existence of telepathy or precognition—phenomena which are so subtle, if indeed they exist, that their manifestations are surely likely to be masked by such crude observational instruments.

There are, as you see, problems with models. But they are of the essence of the scientific approach. In our epoch, folk will predictably (of course, I am using a model to project this!) share any model quite happily with their friendly television producer—who believes it to be his duty to break through vested interests to reality. With his guidance, especially, people will prefer to talk this scientifically-sounding talk, rather than risk being caught up in Illusion—Shared or not.

But here is an odd thing. If what I have just said is true of science, it is also true of philosophy. Do you want to be a logical positivist, an existentialist, or what? There are *models* of these positions; and well-researched media-guidance is available in glossy supplements, on live television, and on video-cassette. We should not ignore aesthetics either. The possibility that you should declare, quite simply, 'I like it', has (I am sorry to say) been completely over-ruled. You must buy the model of realism, impressionism, surrealism, pop-art, heart-art, or what-not first—*and you must underwrite it*, as part of your reality. As to Western religion: there is a set of models *par excellence*; and if excellence is not your prior guide, pray visit the United States, and choose between the multimillion dollar evangelical models of Christianity that television there projects. Not even Solomon in all his glory was arrayed like one of these: each haircut would feed an African for a year. . .

We set out, via science, to find something more comforting than Illusion as our gloss on ultimate reality. The word Model, backed by its theory and practice, sounds less pejorative than the word Illusion. It is the basic, clear-headed, ratiocinative approach used by every sort of Establishment—in science, philosophy, aesthetics, religion—which offers a model as a respectable surrogate for reality. It certainly sounds less risky than Illusion as a night-time companion.

But reflect. It will soon by 1984. Would you prefer at that moment to be inside the rather special room that Orwell the Prophet forecast would be designed for you, based on a model of you; or would you rather be caught in a cave with Merlin, illusion, and a bottle of wine?

SECOND: SUPPORTIVE NEW SCIENCE

Let us now look at the relationship that dynamically exists between the living organism and its environment—briefly and in general. The primitive idea that this constitutes a stimulus-response system whereby an external stimulus from reality is met by an organic reaction to that reality, so that the two sides come into balance, will not do. As biologists have long since recognized, the homeostasis belongs to the *internal* environment of the organism. Thus when something internally changes that tends to disbalance organic equilibrium, the healthy body can do something about that to maintain stability within physiological limits [1]. The mechanism deploys loops involving all the sensory apparatus—that reporting on both internal conditions and what we usually call external conditions. But these exteroceptor reports *themselves* originate in parts of the organism. It seems that the best we can say for the reality that we began to discuss is that it is an imputation of a model that is determined by the kinds of observations we can make—which are precisely and in turn those which the model can parametrically encompass. . .

At first, this circularity sounds like either a logical error, or some sort of epistemological tomfoolery. On the contrary: I shall shortly mention scientific advances made since Teilhard's death which powerfully support this approach. Characteristically, however, he got there first—though by a different route. It was his understanding of the process of complexification that led him to the insight into reality that involves an *enroulement organique sur soi-même* of the universe both locally and entirely. Julian Huxley rendered this in the words 'the world-stuff being rolled-up upon itself', and called it a metaphor—which I do not think it is. The circularity involved—and the very word sounds pejorative—is something that we should now—and with perfect respectability—call 'self-referential'. Speaking of precursors of the latest thinking, I think that in Western terms the outlook that I am now beginning to discuss may well have been adumbrated in the seventeenth century by Leibniz with his monadology.

I said a little time ago that it is not so much that we *know*, as that we *know that we know*. The self-reference is manifested in this capability, and it opens the door to a theory of consciousness.

We, you and I, would certainly say that we are conscious beings. Part of that consciousness, I suggest, resides in our awareness that we monitor an interaction between what we consider to be ourselves, and what we consider to be a reality in which we ourselves are embedded. Any such monitoring involves regulatory actions. Now there is a proven cybernetic theorem [2] which says that the regulation that the regulator can achieve is only as good as the model of the reality that it contains. In the context of our personal existence, this is the devastating fact for which my opening excursions were intended as preparation. The theorem is perfectly obvious—*once* you really understand it, and *if* you are psychologically prepared to countenance it. It comes down to this: we cannot regulate our interaction with any aspect of reality that our model of reality does not include—whether as to its theoretical range or as to its observational facilities and resolution—because we cannot by definition be conscious of it.

Now whistling banshees can be accommodated as a possible component of reality—because we perceived them in our consciousness under the definition I gave. They are acceptable to the model, and we know how to observe them. Therefore we are fully entitled to declare whistling banshees so defined to be unreal, and so we do. Please note in passing that the distinction between what is real and what is unreal is determined not only by the *content* of the model, but by the kind of distinction that the model has the competence to draw.

Which leads me to speak of angels—despite the fact that doing just that dropped Thomas Aquinas into so much trouble. If we define an angel, we have squeezed the angel into our model, into the regulatory circuit that links us to reality, and therefore into our consciousness. That is fine. We are now in a position to decide whether or not angels exist. Under these rules, only little children can afford to say that angels exist (thereby winning first prize as usual). But if I define the *term* angel to mean 'an entity of higher complexification than my own', then *ipso facto* I declare myself incompetent—at least in terms of Western science—to comment on the existence or otherwise of angels. Such beings would not fit into the model of reality-regulation, and therefore *they could not be recognized*. I cannot propose any methodology by which to affirm or deny the existence of something which, though I may define it, I could not recognize if I encountered it. . .

This example provides a powerful *cybernetic* introduction to a new *biological* approach to cognition. This begins by saying quite flatly that: 'the living organization is a circular organization which secures the production or maintenance of the *components* that specify it in such a manner that the product of their functioning is the very same organization that produces them'. This sentence defines a phenomenon of man called autopoiesis: the capacity not to *re*produce himself, but to produce himself—self-referentially. In that case, continues the new biology of cognition, an autopoietic system 'specifies a closed domain of interactions that is its cognitive domain, and no interaction is possible for it which is not prescribed by this organization'. It follows, thirdly, that: 'the process of cognition consists in the creation of a field of behaviour through its actual conduct in its closed domain of interaction, and not in the apprehension or the description of an independent universe'. Now this is just the sort of biological theory that our discussion of models would lead us to expect; we have it in the discoveries of Humberto Maturana [3].

Is it really possible then, as the Subjective Idealists of old contend, that there is no independent universe, but only our own perception (which may be only of ourselves), and our own projected model of a universe that attains to its illusory status only because that Illusion is Shared by equivalently handicapped humankind? There is powerful argument to this end. From cybernetics to biology, we next proceed to social science: the *purpose of action* is to control the state of the perceived world—on the prior understanding that the only reality is our perception of it. In doing this, argues William Powers [4], it is entailed that we have to learn how to perceive. We need to learn that angels cannot be recognized—nor fairies, nor anything else (whether by way of illusion or reality) that is not shared. The mechanism is a physiological feedback control system which teaches us what is allowed to count as 'real'. Then let us note that if we dispute the consensus, as I shall do increasingly this evening, we shall probably be declared to be ill; but that, on the other hand, running this risk is our only hope of cognitive progress. Behaviourism and psychoanalysis have dominated theoretical approaches to perception for half a century and more; at last alternatives appear in Western science to account for volition itself. And just as we may expect the new theories to focus on the self-referential, they also focus on the concept of self-organization [5]—in which field Gordon Pask has made such a potent contribution.

I have spoken for some minutes of novelties arising in the arena that connects the human sciences through the commonalities of their regulatory systems. It is worth noting that a whole body of equally novel mathematics has arisen, with its own new notation, that can write down and manipulate the formalization of self-referential systems. Probably this had its mathematical origins in Russell and Wittgenstein. Certainly the latter's *Tractatus Logico-Philosophicus* (as long ago as 1922) made clear that a proposition must share the complexity and form of the fact that it purports to reflect. It is, I think, that static logic that subsequently became dynamic in cybernetic theory with Ashby's Law of Requisite Variety. I introduce some thoughts about the larger aspects of the physical universe with a quotation from the most fundamental of these purely mathematical texts by Spencer Brown [6], with its echo of Teilhard's *enroulement organique sur soi-même*: 'clearly the universe is a system for observing itself'. . .

It is indeed. Then what happened to the objective Newtonian universe, operating on the laws of motion, the gravitational constants, and so forth, that one of the greatest of scientific men put together in his *Principia*? The answer is that nothing happened to it, beyond the growing realization that it is 'only' a model. As we have recognized, models are relevant and useful within a particular compass. When distances exceed terrestrial distances, and speeds approach the speed of light, the Newtonian model needs some adjustment. We enter the relativistic universe of Einstein. In fact, we have been there, although ill-adjusted to its implications, for most of this century. By now, the limitations of even this model-making are extremely apparent. The physics whereby we undertake engineering projects—from the exploding of nuclear warheads at the atomic level to the penetration of solar space in distances measured by light years—works very well. But the model starts to break down at both ends of the scale. There is a confusion of quarks, if that is a good collective noun, at the sub-atomic level of resolution. There are fabrics of time warps at the macro-level from which we weave those sinister black holes. New writings are, however, appearing in physics ([7], for example) which are consonant with such other developments as I have mentioned in the biological and human sciences, and for which a new mathematics is emerging.

It becomes possible to foresee a whole new synthesis of science that will support and illuminate an enhanced model of the human condition. There has been time to mention only briefly what seem to me to be the major lines of advance; but I hope enough has been said to demonstrate the priority of projecting a systems-oriented scientific model that melds together the self-referential characteristics of the various branches of science that appear to have vested interests in keeping themselves to themselves.

But there are, thank God, always scientists prepared to take the risks of transdisciplinary interaction, professionally dangerous though this is for them, so that some of the holistic patterns gradually emerge. Once the models are sufficiently enriched, they gain in perspective. Let me remind you of a Teilhardian example of this in terms of terrestrial biophysics. Because of the cybernetic theorem of the recursiveness of viable systems [8], whereby each is necessarily contained in another like a set of Russian dolls or Chinese boxes, I am at ease with the concept that Planet Earth is in fact an integral viable system—an organic whole. I long ago wrote that from a systems-theoretic point of view there is every likelihood that Earth will survive as an integral viable system (at least until some 5000 million years from now, when our planet can be expected to be fried by the collapse of the sun into a red giant); *but* that we have no biological guarantee whatsoever that this viability will include the survival of the human race for even as long as several years from now.

Teilhard explicitly did not think that any such lugubrious outcome was conceivable. But outstandingly he *did* present his famous picture of the geosphere, the rocky mantle of this football Earth, shrouded in the live organic film he called the biosphere. And hence the whole, generating mind around it all: the noosphere—perhaps the planet's own self-consciousness—with all the evolutionary implications that so vast and yet coherent a vision entertains. The first *photographs* of the planet Earth from space were taken by the Apollo 4 mission as late as the end of 1967; and they startled most people—even meteorologists—by their obviously organic cohesiveness.

Teilhard's models were far ahead of scientific models in general: no wonder he divided the scientific world in so dramatic a way.

THIRD: THE INVENTION OF TIME

Of all the models on which we have so far focused our attention, and in regard to which it is possible for me to adduce powerful and recent scientific illumination in or out of this lecture, there is one more of which I dread to speak. But it happens to reside at the centre of my thesis. It is the model of TIME. It is difficult indeed to suspend belief in the even passage of time, in which we remember all our yesterdays and anticipate all our tomorrows; a time measured by the periodic certainties of the solar system, with its nights and days and its vibrating clocks—all in mutual agreement; a time that records the precise moments of our own birth and death. But this model of enduringness works for us only within the narrow compass of our everyday lives. As soon as we begin to think about an eternity that has no beginning and no end, we are forced to abandon the effort of visualization.

There is a vast literature that treats the nature of time from all manner of technical standpoints, but this is no place to review it. I shall use my own words in the attempt to share what is as much personal experience as a piece of thinking.

Deep in the Western culture sits a conviction that a thing both cannot be itself and not itself. This is a principle of non-contradiction which was explicitly formulated by Aristotle, which governs all our rational thinking processes, and which underlies all our logical notations in the form of affirmation or denial, of A and not-A. Think please of a wineglass: is it or is it not there? Yes, it is there. But, excuse me, I am putting this wineglass away. So it is not there. 'But this is ridiculous', you would say: 'the wineglass was there a moment ago, but you took it away—now I observe that you have just put it back. What about it?' Well, suppose that the non-contradiction principle is actually *wrong*, and that a thing *can* be itself and not itself. This characterization of reality does not belong within the range of any Western model, and so we call it 'impossible'. But in practice we have solved the problem: we have embedded our model of simple existence within a spatio-temporal framework, and in particular we have *invented time* in order to support our cultural belief, if that is what it is, in non-contradiction. (Again, I think that Leibniz got there first.)

Obviously I am embarking on a new model of time. I ask you to relax, and to see where it leads. Now we have already noted that our sensory equipment has limitations. Consider that if a rifle bullet flashed across your field of vision, you would certainly not see it. The neurophysiological apparatus cannot function sufficiently fast. Then please reconsider the wineglass, and the case when it really is there. I now snatch it away (so it is not there) and return it (so it is there) so fast that you cannot see it happen. You will certainly believe that nothing happened: there *is* a wineglass. Take the opposite case. You are looking at an empty tray. On to this I set down a wineglass and remove it again—so quickly that there was not time to register its presence with your eyes. The tray is empty: there is *no* wineglass.

This is fine so far, as an intellectual exercise. But, as we saw earlier, scientific enquiry can protect us from imaginary whistling banshees by its observational acumen. With the right equipment, you certainly can see the rifle bullet. You can photograph it in mid-air. Similarly, then, the mystery of the vanishing wineglass could be resolved, even if the manoeuvres involved were very fast indeed—and, in an obvious enough sense according to this model, we should be catching time in the process of its invention by doing so. But the very insistent question arises: Is there any limit to the speed at which wineglasses may vanish and reappear and still be detectable with ever-improved observational equipment?

It seems that there *is* such a limit. It is demonstrated through Heisenberg's Uncertainty Principle, which gives a lower limit for the accuracy with which energy can be measured ($\Delta E \Delta t \geqslant h$) in terms of Planck's constant (h). This is a universal measure: the ratio of a quantum of radiant energy of a particular frequency to that frequency (and $h = 6.547 \times 10^{-27}$ erg-secs). What all this amounts to is that wineglasses going into and out of existence at some limiting speed, which would be a function of the speed of light, would not certainly be there and not certainly not be there. The principle of non-contradiction, at this limit, becomes a fiasco. What is more, by turning the uncertainty equation round, we perceive the possibility that time is being not so much invented, as *created* in minuscule packets—precisely in the interest of preventing the collapse of A into not-A.

Now this is a far cry from the 'ever-rolling stream' of daily experience and Newtonian physics alike. Can any sense be made of it? Indeed I think that it can. In terms of matter and energy we have for long had twin theories contrasting smooth waves with discrete particles—and a principle of complementarity to overcome tensions between the two models. Just as photons, conceived of as particles of light, can easily be visualized as a continuum of light (which is how, at the human level of resolution, we ordinarily experience light) so the continuum of time as we customarily experience that can be visualized as a stream of particles of time.

I earlier mentioned the evident absurdity of seeking to investigate matters of great delicacy with clumsy tools—just because they happen to be handy, and scientifically respectable. The Western world has largely ignored models of reality that come from the East (despite their great antiquity, or perhaps because of it), and worse still has culpably and with much success taught the East to disregard its own outstanding heritage. Despite the various names of the Eastern philosophies, they share much—because they spread historically from India through China to Japan—and I shall not attempt to draw distinctions. Moreover, I am content to refer to the whole approach as *yogic*. Since I shall make further use of this term, may I say that yoga is not a system of callisthenic exercises, nor is it a means of entering into 'instant nirvana' in short bursts of meditation. These seem to exhaust its connotation in the West—with its precision-tools for trivializing anything of importance and for making money even from the channels of grace.

Yoga means union, whether of self and cosmos, man and woman, the different chambers of the mind. . . in the limit, therefore, of the A and the not-A. Let us return to our wineglass. perhaps you would shut your eyes, and accept a very brief moment of guided meditation.

- Imagine the wineglass: it is meant to be real, so make is as solid in your mind's eye as you can. Now very gently set it aside: slide it quietly out of the picture.
- Contemplate the empty place where the wineglass recently was; see that this place *is* empty. Now gently slide the wineglass back into place.
- Contemplate the wineglass again; but focus now on the *space it encloses*. Do not slide the glass aside this time: just let it go; let the glass slowly dissolve and vanish; contemplate the space that would be enclosed were the glass still present.

Thank you.

The experience that you have just had, or perhaps would have had after a little practice, is of a not-A defining its A-ness. It is to have observed the wineglassness of empty space. Part of the experience may have been, and I am confident that with proper preparation would routinely have become, that in the moment of perception when the principle of non-contradiction is experimentally falsified, *time stops*. In subjective terms, time will stop for as long as the contradicted perception is retained—whatever the clocks are doing.

This is an obviously tiny example of a wholly different approach to reality from that taken by the Western culture. Before going further, then, it behoves us to ask what the scientist can make of it. Thirty years ago, I had no qualms in describing what was happening, within my own neophyte yogic experience, as autohypnosis. There were fairly respectable neurophysiological explanations available of what was going on within the nervous system in such trance-like conditions. Later on, it became clear to me that sticking labels on states of consciousness explained nothing—either about reality or about the person concerned. To say: 'Oh, that is only autohypnosis' is like saying 'Oh, you can see the rings of Saturn only because you have a telescope'. As to the person concerned in experiencing different states of consciousness, the label he will get will be determined by the context and the models that are currently masquerading as ultimate truth. He may be a mystic to be canonized, or a psychotic ready for convulsive therapy; he may be a profound thinker about the human condition, or subversive scum ripe for the torturer. How strange that the outcome in either case these days is likely to be electrical damage to the person concerned. . .

FOURTH: 'MIXTURES' AND GODHEAD

Yoga means union. Let me quickly build a momentary bridge between the particularity of the A/not-A dichotomy and the generality of cosmic union itself, by extending slightly the examples I used to introduce the 'wineglassness' of the void. For whenever, and on whatever scale, contradiction is transcended, perception changes, and strange things happen subjectively to consciousness and to time.

First of all, I mentioned the different chambers of the mind. It was during the 1960s that the neurological evidence began to accrue that the two cortical hemispheres in our skulls perform different functions. The dominant hemisphere (usually the left) seems to be concerned primarily with categorization, logical processes—outstandingly language manipulation and speech itself, the whole business of reductionism in response to a high-variety world. The other hemisphere has a more intuitive basis: it is responsive to aesthetic impulse, it devises patterns which it cannot rationalize, and so on [9]. These discoveries were made by such distinguished researchers as Roger Sperry, as a result of surgical interventions in the human brain (which had been undertaken for medical reasons), and of course they raised the question as to whether the dominant hemisphere was really 'meant to be' dominant in evolutionary terms, or whether the two were not on the contrary supposed to be working together in intimate harmony.

From the standpoint of the Eastern model, with its five 'vital airs', the components of our vibrant being, and from yogic practice, the latter position is most strongly indicated. It is also consonant with the concept of 'mixture' that we have inherited in the Western tradition from ancient Greek philosophy, notably Empedocles [10]. The characteristics within us, he argued, which are visualized by the Greeks also as 'vital airs', are not to be considered as functions of a 'too too solid flesh' which must therefore be negated on the road to spirituality. Quite to the contrary, the target is to find the perfection of the 'mixture' itself. In this proper balance an *immanent* teleology is defined; and surely this is a notion to be preferred to that of a transcendental purpose beyond this life for which there is no other model than those given in and through poetic caprice.

If I seem now to be saying that we knew all the time, namely that the Kingdom of God is within us, that is so; but in pursuing yogic approaches to this reality, I am trying to make it more functional. The secret Christian writings of the gnostics, unearthed in Upper Egypt 35 years ago, have had alarmingly little effect so far on the Established Church—which seems to have connived in their suppression as heretical for 2000 years. Well, they have profoundly affected me ever since I came across Jean Doresse's initial book which appeared in English 20 years ago [11]; see too the recent reference [12]. These gnostic writings often sound as if they had come under Far Eastern influences themselves. For example, the *Gospel According to Thomas* (the apostle who traditionally went to India) declares on this very point of 'mixtures'.

> Jesus said: 'If you bring forth what is within you, what you bring forth will save you. If you do not bring forth what is within you, what you do not bring forth will destroy you.'

So, the bicameral mind based on the two chambers of the brain has to operate in the mode of conation as well as in the mode of cognition. Not only must it synthesize its 'mixture' to know what it knows, it must exercise its *will* to respond to that knowledge—and it does have choices. Now the will exerted in reply to left-hemisphere cognition is recognized in the reductionist language of that side of the brain. It must be; otherwise the regulatory model (as argued from the cybernetic theorem much earlier) would not be able to exert any regulation. Similarly, if right-hemisphere cognition is permitted to rise to the forefront of consciousness, the mode of conation must change. That is to be expected by these arguments too; because the conative regulator must contain a model of the intuitional right-brain cognition, and will not therefore 'speak the language' of left-brain analysis by which we are wont to introspect on our behaviour, and thereby to control it.

None the less, these necessary gear-changes are quite disconcerting to experience. The will is strong to pursue a course, let us say; and ordinarily volitional progress would be under control in analytical (left-brain) terms. Suddenly to realize that this is not the case, because the conation presents itself in terms of an alien cognition, leaves one bereft of a conscious regulator that can be properly understood. Such a regulator does of course exist: it is one that right-brain people use all the time. They appear discountenanced, in turn, if their conative processes are brought under analytical scrutiny. Leaving the regulatory skills of the Empedoclean 'mixture' poses a behavioural problem for anyone trying to manipulate the mix. Unfortunately, to ignore this challenge, once it has been understood, is spiritually retrograde.

Move on with me, pray, from the unification of oneself to one's unification with others. It is natural to focus on the relationship between individuals of either or both sexes. The Western model has made loving relationships basically political and economic, it has distinguished between sacred and profane love, between 'platonic' and sexual involvement, between domination and submission in both social and physical terms, and so on. All of this is nonsensical in terms of the *tantric* yoga, which celebrates union for its very sharinghood—yet, because of our Western paltriness, becomes the butt of tourist jokes in Hindu temples, and degenerates into pornography in the West.

Let me add to that, moving back again a little to the West of East, that the gnostic gospels throw much light on the theme of institutional arrogance that is reflected to this day within the Christian Church. According to the scrolls of Upper Egypt, we may deduce that this is partly a masculine arrogance towards women, partly elitist in any case, and mostly (as I said about politics earlier) the sheer arrogation of power unto itself.

There is more, so much more, to say on all of this. But my right hemisphere urges me insistently on to the pivotal point: the union of the self not only with itself, not only with others, not only with institutions, but with the entire cosmos—everything that is. . . . How daunting a conception is this to envisage; with what outrageous hubris could it possibly be approached. . .

The Eastern model has an answer to this difficulty, which is essentially a Western contradiction. Some of the 'occult powers' in yogic practice are antonyms of the A/not-A variety. Let us consider one such pair. What follows really cannot be called a guided meditation; but it simulates one, to show what I mean; so please listen now in that spirit.

> The psalmist sang: 'When I consider thy heavens. . .' Yes; against the cosmic backdrop we are very small. Think then, please. We are now all grains of sand, and the ego has gone out of us. (It is not difficult to handle, if you stay in good faith.) And now we get smaller still: we are specks of dust on the highway. Smaller now yet again: is it not possible finally to let go, and to vanish? What does it matter?
>
> It is also an occult power to become very large. Extend your personal being to include all your perceptions, all your relationships. You do, after all, embrace the whole of those entanglements. If some entity or some activity yet larger comes to your notice, its essential nature holds the fact that you have noticed it. Embrace that too. Grow gradually to the size of the cosmos; become the universe. But stay in good faith, please—and vanish. What does it matter?

With this explanation of a meditative drill I have tried to offer a simulation—*it is no more than that*—of the yogic route to a particular state of consciousness called *samadhi*, which has a cousinly relationship to the *satori* experiences of Zen. Consider some consequences, each with a scientific addendum.

- The denial of non-contradiction, which is the acceptance of contradiction, results in vanishment twice over, the closure of the self on to itself.
  THEN the consequences for the biology of cognition and autopoiesis are (as we already know) vast—and they must spill over into psychiatry and social medicine.
- According to our model of particulate time, the self in this state cannot be detected as existing; in other words, time stops.
  THEN it is fatuous to imagine that scientific experiments aimed at detecting and defining this state of awareness could in principle be undertaken.
- However, as with 'wineglassness' in the void, the very cancellation of self in a frozen rather than endlessly protracted 'eternity' is an indelible imprint on the cosmos.
  THEN look to macro-physics to unfold the mathematical topology: for this could be an image (so far as current physics is concerned) of someone falling into a black hole.
- Conversely, which is to contemplate the accepted contradiction from its other pole, *samadhi* is the awareness in oneself of God. So say the raja-yogis.
  THEN neurocybernetics should continue its search for an adequate account of consciousness in the eigenvalues of self-referential computable functions.

To speak of these matters is difficult, because language automatically betrays one into affirmations of what is denied, and denials of what is affirmed—once the principle of non-contradiction is held in suspense. I am moved to remark on this, since it seems impossible in context not to invoke 'the self' as if it were an entity, whereas the content of these propositions disregards it. It is because of this difficulty that Wittgenstein ended the *Tractatus* saying that his propositions were elucidatory in so far as whoever understands them recognizes them as senseless. It is because of this difficulty that such strange but masterly pedagogic methods developed in the transmission of Zen.

But all such quibbles become pedantic indeed beside the recognition of *samadhi* itself.

At the end of the tenth chapter of St John, Jesus declares: 'I and my Father are one.' The crowd takes up stones, because of a supposed blasphemy. Later, Jesus defends himself against another alleged blasphemy: 'because I said, I am the Son of God'. In the meantime, however (verse 34):

> Jesus answered them,
> Is it not written in your law,
> I SAID, YOU ARE GODS?

This statement is unequivocal. In the Greek, which some might prefer for St John:

ἀπεκρίθη αὐτοῖς ὁ Ἰησοῦς,
Οὐκ ἔστιν γεγραμμένον
ἐν τῷ νόμῳ ὑμῶν ὅτι
Ἐγὼ εἶπα, Θεοί ἐστε;

In the Vulgate:

Respondit eis Iesus:
Nonne scriptum est in lege vestra quia
'Ego dixi: Dii estis'?

In pointing out that if the law said 'you are gods', Jesus was explicit that he himself could hardly be blamed for claiming merely the status of a Son of God. It was what the commentaries call a rabbinical answer.

Next: the reference to Judaic law is to the eighty-second psalm (the eighty-first in the Vulgate):

I said, you are gods;
and all of you are children of the Most High.

Ego dixi. Dii estis
et fil ii Excelsi omnes.

The statement is followed, however, by a dire reminder of the mortality of humankind: '*but you shall die like men. . .*'

The psalm was one of those addressed to the judges, and to that extent related to those who had received the Law on Mount Sinai doubtless to their successors also. Perspicuous commentaries go further, however, pointing out that those to whom God the Word came were declared to be gods because they had received the divine gift.

When I first began to reflect on all of this, is seemed very strange if only because of that strong use, which is grammatically redundant, of the personal pronoun in both the Greek and Latin: '*Ego* said'. But gradually the story became pivotal in the East–West homeostasis of my meditations, so that when the invitation came to give this lecture, the title chose itself.

FIFTH: OMEGA REALIZED IN SAMADHI

Having begun with much talk of models, in what I consider was a proper analysis of our phenomenological milieu, I have brought together a different model, woven from threads of ancient and modern Western philosophy, from ancient Eastern philosophy and yogic practice, from new scientific insights in physics, mathematics and neurophysiology, and from the intuitive, religious and aesthetic understanding of the right-hand brain. I have not yet said what this seems to be to be a model *of*. The best answer that I can give is that it is a model of *love*.

In the Teilhardian vocabulary, I *think* that this is one possible model of the Omega point—where everything converges, where all meridians meet and fuse at the cosmic pole. But I have not presented my model as an evolutionary outcome, as Teilhard did, and wish to comment—briefly, but with care—on this issue.

One of the reasons for my having proposed to you tonight an iconoclastic model of the nature of time, is the inability of the classical continuum models to account for discontinuities—in microphysics (where some suggest [7] that electrons may actually move backwards in time), in macrophysics (where there will never be enough time to pass through a black hole), in subjective psychology (in which I venture to suggest that 'everyone knows' that the passage of time is not uniform), and outstandingly in the arbitrariness of a finite lifetime for anyone (the *fact* of which life is itself time*less*). Similar problems arise in palaeontology, and the interpretation of the fossil record.

The dinosaurs were apparently eliminated quite suddenly—a fact which our own species would do well to bear in mind. The theory that something large, perhaps an asteroid, crashed into our planet—raising such a dust that the sun was blocked off for a very long time, so that photosynthesis processes underwent a long hiatus—is credible enough for such a singular event. But there are many other problems with the fossil record; we do not unearth half-feathered reptiles, for instance, and the immediate ancestry of *Homo sapiens* himself is notoriously difficult to unravel. But, for professional reasons, it was inevitably in terms of the geological time model that Teilhard worked as an evolutionist.

He produced in *The Phenomenon of Man* a diagrammatic history going back some 150 000 years. It is depicted on an arithmetic time-scale, which eats up geological time in equal bites to zero—and zero means 'right now'. The figure then *projects* the diagrammatic trajectories that have taken humankind right through the neolithic to modern man into an unknown future—where they converge on Omega. He writes of this convergence later (p. 259) that space–time 'must *somewhere ahead* [my italics] become involuted' to Omega. Remarks of this kind, plus the diagram, plus the geological time model into which the professional palaeontologist was locked, all suggest that Omega is a future target of the evolutionary process—just as if there *were* a future, and just as if there were a long-range purposefulness out there in that void (which I am tempted to call a tele-teleology). But Teilhard himself did not believe it. Omega is already in existence. He says it in various forms; 'Omega must be supremely present' he writes (p. 269). Amen.

Using the particulate model of time, and some schoolboy mathematics, I think that this apparent ambivalence (if not indeed contradiction) can speedily be resolved. We could, and legitimately could, draw his diagram again, using a logarithmic instead of an arithmetic time-scale. This means that equal bites at the scale which used to take us from 100 000 years, to 50 000 years, to 'now' (and full stop), will instead take us from 100 000 years to 10 000 years, to 1000 years, to 100 years, to 10 years, to 1 year, to one-tenth of a year—and so on. The logarithmic scale is asymptotic to zero: it gets closer and closer to 'NOW', in equal bites at the scale, but will never ever arrive. Let us go on drawing—extending the diagram all the way to the sun if necessary—until we are so close to zero that the Uncertainty Principle intervenes again: there is nothing to be done, as we saw, about Planck's constant. Then our concept of 'NOW' is that infinitesimally small instant in which a particle of time is created. This 'NOW' is the moment of *samadhi*, the point on the geological time-scale of Omega. And, given the particulate nature of time, Omega can henceforth be dated—even for palaeontology, even for evolutionary theory—at each and every moment.

This demonstration is intended to show that Omega is 'supremely present', and can therefore be entered into by the elevation of consciousness to the state of *samadhi*; but that it is also (what I propose to call) a *continuous evolutionary product* of the cosmos, since it always lies in the future. There is no contradiction, praise be, at the logarithmic asymptote, because the cosmos itself is so constructed that A is precisely not-A at this quantal limit of discrimination—and cannot be otherwise.

Nothing at all, and in any case, can be otherwise: and people down the dreary years of Western thinking have created the bogus issue of determinism versus freewill out of that, simply because they are wrestling with a useless model, a model vitiated and made nugatory through floating in Newtonian time. In this chair last year, Joseph Needham proclaimed that 'existence itself is a statistical concept'; and in challenging Jacques Monod's contentions about chance and necessity, whereby no God would (surely?) place such reliance in this so-called 'chance', Needham said in a beautiful phrase: 'Supposing the Spirit should say to us "I *am* the dice"?' Oh yes: it is the Lord of the Dance who says that; and the dance is Shiva's dance—in which 'whatever is' crackles into particulate existence at the rate of the creation of time quanta—and crackles out again—before you can draw even a spiritual breath.

Now if four people were playing cards, and each person were dealt one complete suit, there would be consternation. They would start calculating the tremendous odds against this unlikely event, and might write to the newspapers about it. But the fact is that every hand that is ever dealt is equally unlikely: we fail to notice that, because we do not have a prior expectation as to what the next hand will be, and we notice only the four-suit hand as exceptional simply because the suits constitute the basic model on which the deck of cards is constructed. 'The understanding does not draw its laws from nature but prescribes them to nature', exactly as said Kant (*Prolegomena*, 36). We have only to change our vantage point on this card game to perceive each hand dealt as a *miracle*: because the odds against it are so very long.

With this outlook, the angle of each blade of grass, the shape of every stone is miraculous too. What a heady world to live in: no wonder we have sent the miracles packing, and made them travel under the assumed name of 'randomness'. That humdrum world is easier to cope with; and the liberal use of 'chance' in the model we construct of it generates the relaxed conviction that whatever happens is not predetermined. But, from this other standpoint, the threat of determinism simply does not arise. The universe is a total, interactive system: by lifting your finger you change the systemic pattern of the cosmos, becoming a factor in the particulate miracle in which we have our being. 'I said, you are gods.'

There is of course much yogic guidance available in travelling the path called Seek-and-you-shall-Find that continuously encounters the presence of the divine within the human. This guidance seems to have been suppressed, as far as the Church is concerned, in support of a male and sacerdotal authoritarianism. I pointed to this before in speaking of gnostic ideas, which C.G. Jung thought 'expressed "the other side of the mind"—the spontaneous, unconscious thoughts that any orthodoxy requires its adherents to repress'. Today, in a godless age, the power of repression involved has passed to other hands. One such pair of hands has the name 'law and order'. Another such pair of hands belongs to medicine, as I now illustrate.

A recent book on the bicamerality of the mind has made [13] some fascinating proposals whereby the left brain constituted the executive function for the right brain—which itself expressed the voice of the gods. Julian Jaynes believes that human beings did not have any consciousness until comparatively recently: for example he seeks to show that the events recorded in the *Iliad* happened to a bunch of characters who were not self-aware. He does not make the point himself, but his description of how such folk as Achilles and Hector 'worked', very well defines the operation of a computer; and this provokes the question as to what will happen if the bicamerality of our computers should break down: will they become conscious?

At any rate, Jaynes believes 'we are gods' on the grounds that the god was always part of the man: 'The gods were organizations of the central nervous system', he says; and he goes on to remark that 'the Trojan War was directed by hallucination'. Now within this kind of model, it is evident that the experience of *samadhi* and *satori* would be classed as hallucinatory. Here are four more aspects of such experiences: consciousness, as ordinarily defined, is dissolved; time stops, so that ordinary affairs are in suspension; the Ego is discounted as it merges into universal love and joy; and the left-hand brain gladly abandons its struggle to rationalize everything, to explain it away. Now these five aspects of the yogic endeavour are listed by Jaynes—not, however, as relating to yoga (which he does not mention), nor as reflecting central themes of Eastern philosophy (on which he has very little to say). Not at all: this five-point list is offered as a clinical definition of schizophrenia! So, 'orthodoxy requires its adherents to repress', as Jung said, and it seems that I have spent a lifetime's spiritual Odyssey in an unknowing attempt to have myself 'put away'.

You see where our models get us. I have one more for you to consider. According to the Eastern philosophies, the model of multiple births—called reincarnation—offers the paramount explanation of ultimate spiritual homeostatic equilibrium for the individual soul. It makes sense in terms of both the Vedantic and Buddhistic philosophy. It makes sense—as many sober Christians would (although I think heretically) contend—to the Western mind, consumed as it is with a 'capitalistic' model of love that demands fair play and fair-shares. Spread over numerous lifetimes, insinuates this seductive model, we shall all get equal treatment. Of course this is farcical inside the Eastern model, for which reincarnation offers a path towards enlightenment; as to the Western version, perhaps folk should reflect more closely on the parable of the vineyard. . .

May I promote a final meditation to you? This is not the time to conduct it, nor even to simulate it. But here are the suggested rules. Contemplate at length the concept of rebirth, allowing yourself to take satisfaction in its solution of the complicated set of equations that the prospect of multiple lives discloses. Then gradually edge into the meditation this evening's model of particulate, non-continuous time. What survives? The A and the non-A of fair-play are still there, and they still cancel out in their living contradiction. But there is *no time* in which to be born or to die—still less in which to be reborn—but only to exist.

Then focus strongly on this version of the contradiction, the koan that I discovered and wish to share with you. It says: EACH INCARNATION IS THE LAST.

THE END

A man whom I knew personally, and thoughtfully regarded, was Ludwig von Bertalanffy, the founder of General Systems Theory [14]. He put forward the concept of equifinality, whereby certain types of system inevitably run to the *same* end, although by *different* routes. The notion is scientifically important, and it can also help rescue us from the threat of predestination that I mentioned earlier.

Even so: death is equifinal—for each of us, soon enough; for millions of starving people this very year, because we rich nations do not have the political will to do anything about their plight; for multi-millions, quite possibly, even in the next decade or so, as a result of nuclear accident or design. The global system is evidently highly unstable; huge amounts of money are spent on sophisticated weaponry so that impoverished nations may expensively tear each other to pieces; and the investment in domestic repression with guns, arbitrary arrests and barbaric tortures is spread over much of the earth.

It is easy to argue that evolution has taken a wrong turning, and has produced in modern man (as the biologist Szent-Györgyi said) 'the crazy ape'. It is easy to argue that humanity will eliminate itself from the planet long before the next ice age, still less the collapse of the sun; and that Teilhard's own expectation of 'the immense duration it [mankind] has still to live' has already been overtaken by a far more pessimistic likelihood. My own cybernetic judgement is that we have constructed a societary machine on a planetary scale the purpose of which is self-destruction—which makes it almost an irrelevance to ask how long it will take to do the job.

Very well. In the face of all this, it would I think be asinine to insist on 'hoping for the best', or even on mounting a world crusade for human survival. It makes a lot of sense, for many people, to trust in God: but it would be an abdication of our shared humanity to fail in any action that might help beleaguered brethren on that account. Something that we can certainly do, then, is to work on *ourselves* to recognize the role that is proper to us within Newtonian time. Few people do this: they are under too much other pressure.

And yet: all of this is not enough; which is why I have tried to share with you a different perception altogether, putting forward a wholly different model.

Death is equifinal; and each incarnation is the last.

Every particle of time is asymptotic to 'now', therefore there is no future to concern us, and evolution is—as it always was—spiritually complete in the supremely present Omega point of love.

To this realization all may attain. It is increasingly difficult to understand, mainly because the world's great religions, which knew all about the paths to this self-knowledge, have been eclipsed by the power of the self-destruct machine.

In sum, four points: there are actions we ought to take within our own time frame to succour the afflicted; the context of our efforts is dark and threatening indeed; but we may attain to Omega at any instant—and though death shall therefore have no dominion, it still is equifinal.

In saying Goodnight, I give you these four points again, for those who feel more familiar with the eighty-second psalm:

Defend the poor and fatherless;
do justice to the afflicted and needy.
Deliver the poor and needy;
rid them out of the hand of the wicked.
They know not, neither will they understand;
they walk on in darkness:
all the foundations of the earth are out of course.
I said, you are gods;
and all of you are children of the Most High;
But you shall die like men,
and fall like one of the princes.

References

Passim. Teilhard de Chardin, Pierre, *The Phenomenon of Man.* Collins, London, 1959.

1. Ashby, W. Ross, *Design for a Brain.* Chapman and Hall, London, 1952, Revised Edition 1960.
2. Conant, Roger C. and Ashby, W. Ross, 'Every good regulator of a system must be a model of that system', *International Journal of Systems Science*, **1**(2), 1970.
3. Maturana, Humberto R. and Varela, Francisco J., *Autopoiesis and Cognition.* D. Reidel Publishing Company, Dordrecht, Holland, 1980.
4. Powers, William T., *Behavior: The Control of Perception.* Aldine Publishing Company, Chicago, 1973.
5. Pask, Gordon, *The Cybernetics of Human Learning and Performance.* Hutchinson Educational, London, 1975.
6. Spencer Brown, G., *Laws of Form.* George Allen and Unwin, London, 1969.
7. Capra, Fritjof, *The Tao of Physics.* Wildwood House, 1975; Fontana/Collins, 1976.
8. Beer, Stafford, *The Heart of Enterprise.* John Wiley, London, 1979.
9. Dimond, Stuart, *The Double Brain.* Churchill Livingstone, Edinburgh, 1972.
10. Reiche, Harald A.T., *Empedocles' Mixture, Eudoxan Astronomy, and Aristotle's Connate Pneuma.* Adolf M. Hakkert, Amsterdam, 1960.
11. Doresse, Jean, *The Secret Books of the Egyptian Gnostics.* Hollis and Carter, London, 1960.
12. Pagels, Elaine, *The Gnostic Gospels.* Weidenfeld and Nicholson, London, 1979.
13. Jaynes, Julian, *The Origin of Consciousness in the Breakdown of the Bicameral Mind.* Allen Lane, London, 1979.
14. von Bertalanffy, Ludwig, *General Systems Theory.* George Braziller, New York, 1968.

For Rahman and Shaffo

DELHI: 1946 and 1993

Vultures still wheel over Delhi.

Someone still leads a muzzled bear
along a busy street
  busy: take care
muzzles are not made to fit
on restless feet.

  and vultures wheel

Beggars approach: fewer today—
fewer than in London or Toronto now
  fewer to pay
begging for multimedia grace
is price enough.

  and vultures wheel

A god comes camel-riding high
with a brass-and-neon band
  culture to buy
the top brass works in English as if bound
(old chap and after all) to England.

  vultures wheel

Violence in the shops through the bazaar,
revenge and sex, hold me
  how near, how far
with trader and his clients fixedly
in flickering TV.

Vultures still wheel over Delhi.

Stafford Beer
24 January 1993

AUTHOR INDEX

SUBJECT INDEX

STAFFORD BEER

Professor Stafford Beer, the founder of management cybernetics, is an international consultant in the management sciences.

He was a company commander in the Gurkhas at the end of World War II. Since then, he has held managerial positions at every level—including those of Production Controller, Director of Management Science, Director of Development, Managing Director, Company President, and Chairman of the Board, in various companies. He is currently Chairman of Syncho Ltd (UK) and Team Syntegrity Inc. (Canada). He has worked at the governmental level in twenty-two countries, and for many international agencies.

He is Visiting Professor at both Manchester (since 1969) and Durham Business Schools. Earlier, he was the first Professor of General Systems at the Open University, and for many years Adjunct Professor at the Wharton School in the University of Pennsylvania. He is currently a Research Professor at University College Swansea, and an Adjunct Professor at the University of Toronto. Liverpool John Moores University has nominated him Honorary Professor of Organizational Transformation.

Currently President of the World Organization of Systems and Cybernetics, Professor Beer holds its Norbert Wiener Gold Medal, and is a Governor of the International Council for Computer Communication. He is a Past President of the Operational Research Society, and holds the Lanchester Prize of the American Operations Research Society. He is also a Past President of the International Society for Social Systems Sciences, and has the McCulloch Award of the American Society for Cybernetics, of which he is now a Trustee. Other awards include the Silver Medal of the Royal Swedish Academy for Engineering Sciences, an Honorary Doctorate from Concordia University in Montreal, and the Freedom of the City of London.

Author of over two hundred publications, including eleven books variously translated into thirteen languages, Stafford Beer is a published poet, and has held several exhibitions of paintings. He teaches meditative yoga, learned in India, to individual pupils.

Printed and bound by CPI Group (UK) Ltd, Croydon, CR0 4YY

23/04/2025

14660956-0003